INDONESIA
ASSESSMENT

**Population and
Human Resources**

The **Institute of Southeast Asian Studies (ISEAS)** was established as an autonomous organisation in 1968. It is a regional research centre for scholars and other specialists concerned with modern Southeast Asia, particularly the many-faceted problems of stability and security, economic development, and political and social change.

The Institute's research programmes are the Regional Economic Studies Programme (RES, including ASEAN and APEC), Regional Strategic and Political Studies Programme (RSPS), Regional Social and Cultural Studies Programme (RSCS), and the Indochina Programme (ICP).

The Institute is governed by a twenty-two-member Board of Trustees comprising nominees from the Singapore Government, the National University of Singapore, the various Chambers of Commerce, and professional and civic organisations. A ten-man Executive Committee oversees day-to-day operations; it is chaired by the Director, the Institute's chief academic and administrative officer.

The **Research School of Pacific and Asian Studies (RSPAS)** at the Australian National University is home to the Indonesia Project, the organiser of the annual *Indonesia Update* conference. The *Update* offers an overview of recent economic and political developments, and also devotes attention to a theme of particular importance in Indonesia's development. Financial support for the conference series is provided by the Australian Agency for International Development (AusAID). The *Indonesia Assessment* series contains papers presented at these conferences, and also sometimes includes other specially commissioned pieces.

The **Indonesia Project** is a major international centre of research and graduate training on the economy of Indonesia. Established in 1965, it is well known and respected in Indonesia and in other places where Indonesia attracts serious scholarly and official interest. The Project obtains its core funding from the Australian National University; in addition, the Australian Department of Foreign Affairs and Trade has provided an annual grant since 1980. A major activity is producing and distributing three times a year an internationally recognised journal on the Indonesian economy, the *Bulletin of Indonesian Economic Studies*, each issue of which contains a Survey of Recent Economic Developments.

The **Department of Political and Social Change** in the Research School of Pacific and Asian Studies focuses on research in domestic politics, social processes and state-society relations in Asia and the Pacific. It has a long established interest in Indonesian affairs. Each year staff members of the department work with the Indonesia Project to plan and organise the Indonesian Update Conference.

INDONESIA ASSESSMENT

Population and Human Resources

Edited by
Gavin W. Jones *and*
Terence H. Hull

Research School of Pacific and Asian Studies
AUSTRALIAN NATIONAL UNIVERSITY, Canberra

INSTITUTE OF SOUTHEAST ASIAN STUDIES, Singapore

Cover design: Alison Commar
Cover photographs: Gavin W. Jones & Terence H. Hull

Published jointly by

Institute of Southeast Asian Studies
Heng Mui Keng Terrace
Pasir Panjang Road
Singapore 119596

Research School of Pacific and Asian Studies
Australian National University
Canberra ACT 9299
Australia

Internet e-mail: publish@iseas.ac.sg
World Wide Web: http://www.iseas.ac.sg/pub.html

*The responsibility for facts and opinions expressed in this publication rests exclusively
with the authors and their interpretations do not necessarily reflect the views or the
policy of ISEAS or the RSPAS.*

Cataloguing in Publication Data

Indonesia assessment : population and human resources / edited by Gavin W.
  Jones and Terence H. Hull.
  1. Indonesia--Population.
  2. Manpower policy--Indonesia.
  3. Birth control--Indonesia.
  4. Migration, Internal--Indonesia.
  5. Urbanization--Indonesia.
  I. Jones, Gavin W.
  II. Hull, Terence H.
DS644.4   I41 1997   1997   sls97-27687

ISBN 981-3055-61-8 (soft cover)
ISBN 981-3055-74-X (hard cover)

Printed and bound in Singapore by Chong Moh Offset Printing Pte. Ltd.

Contents

Population Mobility and Urbanisation

Aspects of Human Resource Development

Public Health, Mortality, Fertility and Family Planning

Looking to the Future

LIST OF TABLES, FIGURES, MAPS
AND APPENDICES

Tables

Figures

Maps

Appendices

CONTRIBUTORS

Dr. Anggito Abimanyu is a Lecturer in the Faculty of Economics, Gadjah Mada University, Yogyakarta, and Program Director of the Inter-University Center, a research centre for economic studies. He graduated from the University of Pennsylvania with a PhD in economics, and is a specialist in energy and environmental economics.

Dr. Sri Moertiningsih Adioetomo graduated with a PhD in demography from the Australian National University. She is now with the Demographic Institute, Faculty of Economics, University of Indonesia, and is managing a large technical assistance project on reproductive health for the Asian Development Bank.

Professor Aris Ananta graduated from Duke University with a PhD in economics. He is now Associate Director of the Demographic Institute, Faculty of Economics, University of Indonesia. He is active in a wide range of innovative demographic research, with a focus on issues of social importance.

Evi Nurvidya Anwar, Msi, graduated from Magister Program of Population and Labour, University of Indonesia. She is a researcher at the Demographic Institute, Faculty of Economics, University of Indonesia. She has worked on major programs of research into population projections and fertility analysis.

Professor John C. Caldwell is director of the Health Transition Centre and Associate Director of the National Centre for Epidemiology and Population Health of the Australian National University. He was formerly head of the ANU's Department of Demography, and is currently President of the International Union for the Scientific Study of Population.

Dr. Gouranga Lal Dasvarma is director of population studies in the School of Social Sciences, Flinders University, Adelaide. After graduating from the Australian National University with a PhD in demography, he worked in Indonesia for ten years, at the Demographic Institute of the University of Indonesia and the Ministry of Population and Environment.

Dr. Agus Dwiyanto is director of the Population Studies Center, Gadjah Mada University, Yogyakarta. He graduated from the University of Southern California with a PhD in Public Policy and Administration. His main research areas are on population and development policy, and quality of care, family planning and family welfare.

Dr. Greg Fealy is completing a doctoral dissertation on the political history of Indonesia's largest Islamic organisation, the Nahdatul Ulama, in the History Department, Monash University. He was co-editor of a recent book on the Nahdatul Ulama.

Dr. Tommy Firman graduated from the University of Hawaii with a PhD in urban and regional planning. He is now on the staff of the Department of Regional and City Planning, Institute of Technology, Bandung (ITB). He has published widely on issues of urbanisation and urban planning, and has undertaken many consultancies on these topics.

Dr. Peter Gardiner worked with the US Bureau of the Census and was a consultant to the Indonesian Central Bureau of Statistics before graduating from the Australian National University with a PhD in demography. He currently works in Jakarta with a research and consulting firm, Insan Harapan Sejahtera.

Professor Graeme Hugo heads the Department of Geography at the University of Adelaide. He graduated from the Australian National University with a PhD in demography. He is well known for his research on migration - both internal and international - and urbanisation. In recent years, he has conducted a number of consultancies for the Indonesian Department of Manpower.

Dr. Terence H. Hull is a Fellow in the Demography Program, Research School of Social Sciences, Australian National University, and Convenor of the Graduate Program in Demography. From 1993 to 1996 he was attached to the University of Indonesia, working with the Center for Health Research and the Demographic Institute. His research in recent years has focused on political and cultural dimensions of population studies.

Dr. Meiwita B. Iskandar is Population Council country representative in Indonesia. Long a staff member of the Faculty of Public Health at the University of Indonesia, she graduated from the medical school of Atma Jaya University in Jakarta and gained a PhD in health services research from the University of California in Los Angeles. Her research has ranged from issues of immunisation to the social dimensions and policy demands of the HIV epidemic.

Professor Gavin W. Jones is Head of the Division of Demography and Sociology, Research School of Social Sciences, Australian National University, and directs the Eastern Indonesia Population and Development Research Project, a collaborative project with the Indonesian Institute of Sciences (LIPI). He has held long-term assignments with the Demographic Institute, Faculty of Economics, University of Indonesia and the Ministry of Population and Environment.

Dr. Firman Lubis is Director of the Yayasan Kusuma Buana, an Institute devoted to health research and action programs in Indonesia. He was educated in the Faculty of Medicine, University of Indonesia, and has carried out research in the USA and the Netherlands.

Professor Geoffrey McNicoll is with the Demography Program, Research School of Social Sciences, Australian National University and has a part-time appointment with the Population Council, New York. His involvement with Indonesia dates back to 1965, when he was attached to the Central Bureau of Statistics under the Australian Volunteer Graduates program. He has co-authored well-known reviews of the demographic situation in Indonesia.

Dr. Mayling Oey-Gardiner, who has a PhD in Demography from the Australian National University, is director of a research and consulting firm, Insan Harapan Sejahtera. She formerly held appointments with the Faculty of Economics, University of Indonesia and the Centre for Policy and Implementation Studies. Her recent research has been especially in the area of educational planning.

Dr. Yulfita Raharjo is Director of the Center for Population and Manpower Studies, Indonesian Institute of Sciences (LIPI). She graduated from the Australian National University with a PhD in anthropology. She is widely involved in research and advisory work on health and gender issues in Indonesia.

Diah Suzenti is a research assistant in the Population Information Division, Demographic Institute, Faculty of Economics, University of Indonesia.

ABBREVIATIONS AND ACRONYMS

ABRI	Angkatan Bersenjata Republik Indonesia [Indonesian Armed Forces]
APBN	Anggaran Pendapatan dan Belanja Negara [national development budget]
ARI	acute respiratory infection
ASEAN	Association of South East Asian Nations
BAPEDAL	National Pollution Control Agency
Bangga Suka Desa	Pembangunan Keluarga dengan Suasana Perkotaan di Pedesaan [Family Development with Urban Context in the Rural Area]
BAPPENAS	National Development Planning Agency
BI	Bank of Indonesia
BKKBN	National Family Planning Coordinating Board
BKPM	Coordinating Agency for Investments
Botabek	Bogor-Tangerang-Bekasi region
BPS	Biro Pusat Statistik [Central Bureau of Statistics: CBS]
CBZ	*Centrale Burgerlijke Ziekenhuis* [Central Civilian Hospital - see also RSUP]
CDR	crude death rate
CEDAW	Convention on the Elimination of All Forms of Discrimination against Women
CPR	contraceptive prevalence rate
DPK	Departemen Pendidikan dan Kebudayaan [Ministry of Education and Culture, MOEC]
DPR	Dewan Perwakilan Rakiat [National Parliament]
EPTE	Entreport Produksi Tujuan Ekspor [export processing zone]
ESCAP	Economic and Social Commission for Asia and the Pacific
FP	family planning

GBHN	Garis Besar Haluan Negara [Guidelines of Basic State Policies]
GDP	gross domestic product
GNP	gross national product
GOI	Government of Indonesia
Golkar	Golongan Karya [the state party]
HHS	Household Health Survey
HRD	Human resource development
ICD	International Classification of Diseases (WHO)
ICMI	Ikatan Cendekiawan Muslimin se-Indonesia [Association of Indonesian Muslim Intellectuals]
ICPD	International Conference on Population and Development (1994)
IDHS	Indonesian Demographic and Health Survey
IDT	Inpres Desa Tertinggal [Presidential Instruction for Assistance to Backward Villages]
IFLS	Indonesia Family Life Survey
IDI	Ikatan Dokter Indonesia [Indonesian Medical Doctors Association]
IKIP	teacher training institutes
ILO	International Labor Office
IMF	International Monetary Fund
IMR	infant mortality rate
IPD	infectious parasitic disease
IUD	intra-uterine device
Jabotabek	National capital region comprising DKI Jakarta, Bogor, Tangerang, and Bekasi
JMDPR	Jabotabek Metropolitan Development Plan Review
JPKM	Jaminan Pemeliharaan Kesehatan Masyarakat
KAMI	Indonesian Students Action Front
KB	Kawasan Berikat [bonded export processing zone]
KBPN	Kantor Badan Pertanahan Nasional [National Land Administration Office]

KIPP	Komite Independen Pemantau Pemilu [Independent Election Monitoring Committee]
Kopassus	Red Berets [military]
Kostrad	Green Berets [military]
KTP	Kartu Tanda Penduduk [Residency Card]
LD	Lembaga Demografi [Demographic Institute, Faculty of Economics, University of Indonesia]
LEB	Life expectancy at birth
MARI	Majelis Rakyat Indonesia [Indonesian People's Council]
Masyumi Baru	Majelis Syarikat Umat Muslimin Indonesia — a new quasi-party
MCH	Maternal and Child Health [program]
MOEC	Ministry of Education and Culture (see DPK)
MOH	Ministry of Health
MORA	Ministry of Religious Affairs
MMR	maternal mortality rate
MPR	Majelis Perwakilan Rakyat [People's Consultative Assembly]
NGO	non-government organisation
NHU	non-gonococcal urethritis
NRR	net reproduction rate [population]
NU	Nahdlatul Ulama [Muslim scholars' organisation]
OTB	organisasi tanpa bentuk ['formless organisations']
Parkindo	Partisipasi Kristen Indonesia — a new quasi-party
PCPP	Persatuan Cendekiawan Pembangunan Pancasila [Association of Pancasila Development Intellectuals]
PDI	Partai Demokrasi Indonesia [Indonesian Democratic Party]
Pepabri	[Association of Former Armed Forces Officers]
PHC	primary health care

PJP	Pembangunan Jangka Panjang [Long-Term Development Plan or Phase]
PKI	Partai Komunis Indonesia [Indonesian Communist Party]
PLKB	[family planning field workers]
PMA	Penanaman Modal Asing [foreign investments]
PMDN	Penanaman Modal Dalam Negeri [domestic investments]
PNI or PNI Baru	Persatuan Nasional Indonesia — a new quasi-party
PPM	Pemenuhan Permintaan Masyarakat
ppp	purchasing power parity
PPP	[United Development Party]
PRD	Partai Rakyat Demokratik [The People's Democratic Party]
PROPER	Program for Pollution Control, Evaluation and Rating
PTN	higher education public institutions
PUDI	Partai Uni Demokrasi Indonesia [Indonesian Democratic Union Party)
Repelita	Rencana Pembangunan Lima Tahun [Five-Year Development Plan]
RSCM	Cipto Mangunkusumo Hospital
RSUP	Rumah Sakit Umum Pusat
SBSI	[unofficial trade union]
SD Inpres	primary school special program
STDs	sexually transmitted diseases
Susenas	Survai Sosial Ekonomi Nasional [National Social and Economic Survey]
SUPAS	Survai Penduduk Antar Census [Intercensal Population Survey]
SVRP	Sample Vital Registration Project
TBAs	traditional birth attendants
TKBK/TMK	[mobile family planning teams]
TFR	total fertility rate
U5MR	Under-5 mortality rate

UNICEF	United Nations Children's Fund [orig. United Nations International Children's Emergency Fund]
UNFPA	United Nations Population Fund [orig. United Nations Fund for Population Activities
WHO	World Health Organisation
WTO	World Trade Organization
YKPK	Yayasan Kerukunan Persaudaraan Kebangsaan [National Brotherhood Reconciliation Foundation]

GLOSSARY

abangan	nominal Muslim
aliran	school of thought or beliefs
ani ani	small blade (used in harvest)
asas tunggal	sole ideological basis [refers to *Pancasila*]
Bandung Raya	Metropolitan Bandung
bidan desa	midwife
Bupati	head of a *kabupaten*
calo	recruiter
Camat	head of subdistrict or *kecameaan*
desa	village
dosen	teaching staff of university
dua anak cukup	'two children are enough'
Gerbankertasusila	Metropolitan Surabaya
golput	*golongan putih* [lit. 'blank group'-see Chap. 8]
Indonesia Bagian Barat	Western Indonesia
Indonesia Bagian Timur	Eastern Indonesia
KB Mandiri	self-reliant family planning
kabupaten	administrative regions
kelompok pelangi	'rainbow' organisations
keluarga sejahtera	family welfare
kelurahaan	lowest administrative unit
kesempatan kerja	[lit.] 'employment opportunity'
kotadesasi	process whereby geographical areas have mix of urban and rural activities (after McGee 1991)
kotamadya	municipality

kuningisasi	[lit.] 'yellowisation'(painting objects yellow, the colour of Golkar)
makar	anti-government unrest
mandor	foreman
Mebidang	Medan-Binjai-Deli-Serdang [Metropolitan Medan]
organisasi tanpa bentuk (OTB)	'formless organisations'
Nomor Induk Penduduk	national population registration number
Pancasila	State ideology based on five national guiding principles
pesantren	Islamic boarding school
posyandu	health posts
puskesmas	community health centre
puskesmas pembantu	health sub-centres
ramah dan manusiawi	to be treated friendly and humane
santri	devout Muslim
setan gundul	[lit.] 'bald devils'
skripsi	thesis
swarkasa	self-sponsored [migration]
swarkasa	spontaneous
taikong	agents
tidak mau tahu	'don't want to know'
warung	trade store

ACKNOWLEDGEMENTS

As in past years, many people and institutions have contributed in various ways to the success of the *Indonesia Update* conference and to the subsequent *Indonesia Assessment* volumes. Financial support was provided by the Australian Agency for International Development (AusAID), which has made a special grant to support the *Update conference series*; the Department of Foreign Affairs and Trade (through its annual grant to the Indonesia Project); and the Research School of Pacific and Asian Studies (RSPAS) at the ANU. Special mention this year should also be made of the Research School of Social Sciences, ANU, which supported our collegial involvement in organising this conference for RSPAS.

We greatly appreciate the willingness, indeed enthusiasm, of the Indonesian Ambassador to Australia, Mr Wiryono, to give the opening address at the conference; his speech is presented here as a foreword. We also thank the Director of the Research School of Pacific and Asian Studies, Professor Merle Ricklefs, and Professor Ross Garnaut, Convenor of the Economics Division, for their personal support for the conference. This year more papers were presented by Indonesians, we believe, than at any previous *Update*, and we are grateful to these colleagues for making the journeys from Jakarta, Yogyakarta and Bandung to brave the cold of the Canberra winter. We would also like to thank them, as well as other authors, for their prompt attention to our queries at the revision stage. This enabled the volume to be published in a timely fashion.

Many colleagues deserve thanks for their contributions in organising the conference and preparing the manuscript for publication. Bev Fraser and Alison Ley from the Department of Political and Social Change and Donna Reed, the Indonesia Project administrator, played major roles in ensuring that the conference ran smoothly. Wendy Cosford, Donna Reed, Beth Thomson and Lulu Turner each played an important and distinctive role in the editing and formatting work, thus ensuring the early publication of this volume. Other Project members, Liz Drysdale and Lynn Moir, were also very supportive, and several graduate students gave up some of their precious time to help with running the conference.

We are grateful for the contributions of the Head of the Indonesia Project, Dr Hal Hill, and Dr Harold Crouch of the Department of Political and Social Change, who were always ready with advice and guidance, yet gave us considerable freedom to organise the conference and prepare this volume. Dr Ross McLeod and Dr Colin Barlow, who convened the 1994 and 1995 *Updates* respectively, provided us with helpful assessments of their own experience in running very successful *Updates* and issuing timely publications.

From its humble beginnings in 1988, the *Indonesia Assessment* volume is now well established as a major annual publication. Since 1994, it has been published jointly by the Department of Political and Social Change, ANU, and by the Institute of Southeast Asian Studies in Singapore, enabling it to reach a wider audience—especially in the Southeast Asian region —than when it was published in-house at the ANU. Our thanks go to the Institute, and particularly the Managing Editor, Triena Ong, for their co-operation in bringing out this volume quickly and in handsome format.

Opening Address

His Excellency Mr S. Wiryono
Ambassador of Indonesia to Australia

Professor Hal Hill, Fellow Speakers, Ladies and Gentlemen,

Before anything else I would like to thank Professor Hal Hill for inviting me to address this 13th annual ANU Indonesia Update, a forum which traditionally assesses various aspects of life in Indonesia, including political, economic, security and other specific developments of the previous year. May I also take this opportunity to congratulate the Australian National University on its 50th Anniversary. As you know, it was only last week that Indonesia celebrated its 51st Anniversary—which means that the Australian National University and Indonesia have grown up together and it is therefore altogether appropriate that they should take a great interest in each other.

Over the years, the ANU Update has provided insightful and valuable contributions to the study of Indonesia. It has promoted better understanding in Australia of its neighbour to the near north, which seems to be always an enigma. As former Prime Minister, Paul Keating has said, '… Australians fail to understand Indonesia in all its complexity'. That might have been stated in terms that are too absolute, but I feel there is some degree of truth in it.

As the theme for this year's Update is 'Population and Human Resources', I would like to share with you some background on this topic as well as a few thoughts on Australian-Indonesian relations.

Among the many things that have been achieved in the course of Indonesia's national development, none have been considered more important than improvements in the quality of life, education and employment opportunities of its citizens. Certainly none has been more dramatic than the drop in the percentage of the population living below the poverty line, from 70 per cent two and a half decades ago to a little over 13.5 per cent today.

From the early days of the republic, Indonesia's leadership realised that a steadily broadening education base and sound health practices were necessary foundations for modern nationhood. While nation-building was the primary focus of the nation's leadership's efforts at that time, before the advent of the New Order, during the past 25 years the government endeavoured to strengthen the economic and social foundations of Indonesian society in order to maintain and strengthen national cohesiveness. It has been our experience, however, that whenever a problem is resolved, new challenges arise in its place. There will always be those second-guessing the government's system of priorities. Whatever policy the government adopts, there will always be those who gain more and those who will be less fortunate.

Naturally, those who are left behind have a tendency to complain and even become impatient. Not only are these processes of nation-building, economic development and democratisation replete with pitfalls, they also exact a social and political cost that many developing nations cannot afford, but sometimes cannot avoid. Indonesia is fortunate that by following a policy of maintaining political stability, promoting economic growth as well as equity, it has so far been able to surmount these challenges, albeit not without the occasional hiccough.

The Indonesian government is constantly identifying areas that have to be addressed in order to ensure steady social and economic development. Always of high priority are measures towards the eventual eradication of poverty among the so-called 'left-behind communities', both in the cities and in the villages. For this purpose, the Indonesian government has mustered massive resources to provide quality health care as well as expanded educational opportunities and training to improve the quality of the country's human resources which is absolutely necessary for further development. This creates a new pressure on the government; for those who have acquired an education now clamour for an appropriate place in the economic development process and this is not always possible. What needs to be done is to not only improve the quality of human resources, but also match these human resources with the requirements of economic development. This is one aspect of population planning that the government is now giving more attention to.

All our endeavours at development have been guided by a basic philosophy which is often enunciated by President Soeharto, the 'Trilogy of Development'. The three elements in this trilogy are stability, economic growth, and equitable sharing of the fruits and responsibility for economic growth. There has to be stability for economic growth to be possible; there has to be economic growth so that there will be fruits of development available for sharing out; and the sharing of the fruits of development as well as the responsibility for it has to be equitable—so that the people's common sense of social justice is satisfied and thus stability is maintained. The trilogy works like a spiral and its three mutually reinforcing elements are regarded with equal importance.

When we in Indonesia speak of stability, therefore, we do not mean imposed or enforced stability, but one that is based on the strength, resilience and creativity of the nation. To maintain that kind of stability, we must see to it that more and more Indonesians share in the responsibility for and the fruits of development. This means wider and more intensive participation in the decision-making processes which affect their lives and their future so that they acquire and maintain a sense of control over their own destiny. In a word, democratisation.

This we are determined to achieve, not at a pace that is dictated by external influences, nor as demanded by a vocal minority in the country, but one that is comfortable to a majority of our people. I am confident that it will be achieved—for the experience of many nations has been that as people attain prosperity, as the middle class grows and the people no longer have to worry about their day-to-day basic needs, they tend to grow more politically active. We just have to make sure, however, that political activism is neither a mask nor an excuse for anarchy and gross irresponsibility.

Meanwhile, through a national policy that has dedicated every means available both to increase national wealth and to ensure its equitable distribution, poverty is being systematically eradicated in Indonesia. World Bank statistics indicate that Indonesia has demonstrated the highest annual reduction in the incidence of poverty over the past two decades. Some 25 years ago, the population of Indonesia was 145 million, 70 per cent of whom lived under the poverty line. Today the population of Indonesia has increased to 195 million but the percentage of the population living below the poverty line has dropped sharply to 13.5 per cent. This is no less than a two-thirds reduction of the incidence of poverty—but what makes it particularly impressive is that a large part of Indonesia's poor started at levels close to the subsistence level. As people rise above the poverty line, they are on their way to joining the middle class. This means that we are now developing a broader, stronger middle class. The American economist Edwin Mills once observed that Indonesia's middle class '... is stronger than that in many countries in its stage of development, but fairly typical of South East Asian societies. The benefits of such rapid growth are not shared equally in any society, but all major groups have benefited greatly [in Indonesia]'.

In relation to health services, the government continues to upgrade hospitals and other public health facilities all over the country and to establish new ones where needed. Through these medical and health facilities, most Indonesians now have access to basic medical care, immunisation and vaccination, treatment of common diseases and nutritional guidance. During the past decade, the number of medical professionals in Indonesia has more or less doubled.

In the field of education, Indonesia's highest priorities today include the expansion of the educational system, particularly at the junior and senior elementary levels, and the upgrading of its teaching staffs, keeping in mind the requirements of economic growth and the realities of the job market. As a result of the government's determined endeavours in education, the national literacy rate has greatly increased during the past two decades. University enrolments have also grown rapidly, and the government predicts that by the year 2000, each year, some 3.9 million students will be earning college degrees.

In the early 1990s a key concern among government planners and private business people has been how the country could train a sufficient number of skilled workers to meet the growing requirements of the rapidly growing economy. They knew that if the country could not provide the employee skills at a quantity and quality that matched demand, there would be a tremendous loss in terms of economic opportunities and competitiveness in the international market on which much of Indonesia's prosperity depends.

In response to this challenge, Indonesia's policy-makers have begun to redefine the role of government in education: no longer would it serve as the sole provider of education but would now also assume the role of catalyst for training programs initiated and maintained by the private sector. So we now have a situation where an array of increasingly sophisticated skills-training programs are being developed by the private sector and more imaginative and focused programs are being developed by the government. Once these advanced and refined social infrastructures are firmly in place, Indonesia should be well on its way to acquiring a work force that is more capable of meeting the challenge of global competition.

New jobs created for some 15 million workers during the past decade have been the result of policies of sound economic management, leading to robust economic growth. Such growth indeed has been especially marked by rapid job creation in the manufacturing and service industries. Also emblematic is the increasing importance of private enterprise—as distinguished from government or state-owned enterprises. The private sector has now truly become the engine of economic growth and as such the chief provider of new jobs. Over the past two decades, we have seen a greater number of women enter the work force, rises in the level of the minimum wage and a general improvement in labour conditions. The labour laws of Indonesia are now being codified in conformity with ILO standards in order to ensure that the rights of labourers are exercised and respected.

Although the achievements of Indonesia in economic development have sometimes been described as 'miraculous', we have no illusions that we have solved all our problems. We know, for instance, that some 25 million Indonesians still live below the poverty line, that we have to watch our current accounts deficit and our external debt level carefully. We know only too well that Indonesia has indefatigable detractors waging a relentless propaganda campaign against the country in international circles. It is therefore vital to Indonesia that it is perceived for what it actually is, rather than as it is variously and simplistically imagined by both detractors and friends.

Indonesian society is complex enough to start with: we are 195 million people living in an archipelago of 17,000 islands, with more than 300 ethnic groupings speaking more than 200 different languages. Apart from that, we are also trying to achieve two objectives which, at least at the beginning, could and often do contradict each other: economic development and democratisation. Indeed these twin objectives have been the subject of continuing debate which will, I suppose, go on for a long time. One view, propounded by former Prime Minister and now Senior Minister Lee Kuan Yew of Singapore, is that democratisation should not be a priority in a developing country, as discipline rather than democracy is what is needed to achieve economic growth and social progress. A contending view, held by Madam Aung Sang Suu Kyi of Myanmar, is that the length of time it took Western countries to achieve democratisation should not be used as a valid reason for Asian countries to be slow in its implementation.

Indonesia has chosen to take the middle path towards democratisation, as we are aware of the complexity of the effort in realising these twin objectives. If an observer takes into account the complexity of Indonesian society and the complexity of what we are trying to achieve, perhaps a less judgemental view might emerge from our friends and neighbours. Certainly, oversimplifications and stereotypes shed no light and will not help bring about mutual understanding and goodwill.

As to Indonesia's relationship with Australia, it has often been said that no other two countries could be so geographically close to each other and yet be so vastly different from each other. This I do not dispute, for we differ in our historical experiences, in our political system, and in our cultures and social structure, as well as in many other ways. And although we are neighbours, we do not really know each other very well, a state of affairs which I feel needs rectification. This feeling is shared by many Australians, many of whom have gone beyond merely lamenting it to doing something about it, by going to Indonesia and investing there or simply enjoying themselves there. In this respect, the role played by the Australia-Indonesia Institute, and the soon to be announced Indonesia-Australia Institute in Jakarta, is very important in contributing to the promotion of mutual understanding. The organising of the visit by Australian editors to Indonesia a few months ago is an example of a useful and constructive activity initiated by and involving Australians who desire to strengthen our existing bilateral ties.

Australian economic interest in Indonesia has over the years grown tremendously and can be seen from the fact that last year alone, the investment flow from Australia to Indonesia amounted to A\$3.7 billion involving 38 projects, thereby making Australia the ninth largest investor in Indonesia. The number of tourists from each country visiting the other has been constantly on the increase and there appears to be a growing number of Australians who have finally realised that Indonesia has a great deal more to offer for the wholesome enjoyment of the traveller than the beaches of Bali. The number of Indonesian students choosing to study in Australia is continually growing. At any one time, there are some 15,000 Indonesian students enrolled at various educational institutions all over Australia. In addition, I am pleased and impressed by the enthusiastic effort among Australian schools—primary and secondary, as well as tertiary institutions— to teach Bahasa Indonesia. To me, this bespeaks a keen desire to promote the relationship between our two countries and educate students so that any remaining barriers of ignorance can be broken down.

On the other hand, Indonesians feel a growing need to know and understand Australia better. In this, it has been of great help that there are a growing number of literary publications on Australia now circulating in Indonesia. The translation of these reading materials into Bahasa Indonesia has been initiated but needs to be expanded.

What is important is that we should not let the differentiations between our two countries become obstacles in the growth and flourishing of a mutually beneficial relationship. The differences between our systems, our cultures and our respective situations are real and are not easy to bridge, but it may rightly be pointed out that these differences are precisely the ingredients for a synergistic relationship, an effective partnership for economic and social development, as well as a sharing of responsibility for the maintenance of regional peace, security and stability.

Indonesia is a country in transition: economically, it is moving towards industrialisation; politically, it is moving towards greater democratisation. And the nation building process goes on. We are, of course, already a nation but, given our problems and our aspirations, not yet the nation we wish to become.

Indeed, after almost 30 years of rapid economic development and six Five-Year Plans which have brought the Indonesian economy to the take-off stage, and with the rise of a new generation that experienced neither the throes of revolution nor the upheaval of the mid-1960s, Indonesia would seem to be entering a new era. Both forces of continuity and the forces of change are interacting in Indonesia and their interaction should be managed in a creative and constructive way if the future of Indonesia is to be more secure. To be able to do so, we need to share the objective observations and the useful insights that can be provided by solicitous friends such as the Australian National University. That is why it is very important for me, as Indonesia's Ambassador to Australia, to be here listening to and exchanging views with you.

Let me also say this in conclusion: my country is grateful for the attention, patience and understanding, as well as co-operation extended to it by its friends and neighbours. It is also eager to prove that it is worth all that attention, patience, understanding and co-operation, not only by reciprocating bilaterally but, most importantly, by contributing as much as it can to regional and global peace, stability and equitably shared prosperity. That is the constitutional mandate of the Government of Indonesia. That is also the sentiment of the Indonesian man in the street.

Thank you.

1

Introduction

Gavin W. Jones and Terence H. Hull

Thirty years ago, the Indonesian economy was in an abysmal state, poverty was endemic, levels of health and nutrition were very poor, and in general Indonesia appeared to have been left behind by its more prosperous neighbours—Malaysia, Thailand and the Philippines. The changes since that time have been dramatic. Indonesia has almost closed the gap on the Philippines in the per capita income stakes, and according to almost any indicator of development that might be chosen, its position has improved sharply. It will be the purpose of this book to link these changes with changes in Indonesia's demography and human resource development. Such an assessment was carried out ten years ago.[1] Even at that time, it proved a major challenge to draw out the relationship—both as cause and effect—of social and economic change and the changing population situation.

If we thought that change was rapid ten years ago, how much more so is this the case today! We have witnessed unprecedented rates of economic growth in Indonesia over the past decade, with the result that Indonesia is now approaching middle income status on a world development scale. We have witnessed a notable shrinking of the numbers of people in poverty (a group which by 1990 represented only 15 per cent of the population, according to official statistics) and an expansion of the middle class. In education, great advances have been made over the past decade. In health, life expectancy has risen and the infant mortality rate has probably been halved over the past 25 years, judging from the evidence presented in Table 1.1.

---

[1] See Hugo *et al.*, 1987. This book documented the changing demography of Indonesia, set it in historical context and assessed its relationship to the economic and social changes taking place in Indonesia.

TABLE 1.1: Selected demographic and human resource parameters for Indonesia

Population 1980 (millions)			147
Population 1995 (millions)			195
Projected population 2010 (millions)			240
% increase of population 1980-90			22
Projected % increase of population 1990-2000			17
Urban population as % of total population 1970			17
Urban population as % of total population 1990			32
Singulate mean age at marriage for females 1980			20.0
Singulate mean age at marriage for females 1990			21.6
Total fertility rate 1980			4.7
Total fertility rate 1994			2.9
Infant mortality rate 1970			118
Infant mortality rate 1992			66
Net primary school enrolment rate 1975			72
Net primary school enrolment rate 1991			98
	Male	Female	Total
Secondary school enrolment rate 1970	22	11	16
Secondary school enrolment rate 1991	49	41	45

Sources: Various surveys and census reports from the Biro Pusat Statistik (BPS).

These trends are cause for great satisfaction. Yet the undoubted improvement in living conditions shown by the statistics should not lead to euphoria. The Indonesian man or woman in the street (or in the paddy fields) is not satisfied with the income distribution, nor are they convinced that poverty is disappearing. They are dissatisfied with the state of health services and with the education their children are receiving at school; so too, perhaps more importantly, are prospective employers. There is a danger in emphasising macro statistics and ignoring the understandings of people on the ground. There is danger, too, in measuring progress only by local standards. For example, while Indonesia's infant mortality rate of 66 in 1992 appears far more satisfactory than the three digit level of the early 1970s, it appears less satisfactory when compared with the current rate of 26 in Thailand or 14 in Malaysia.

While generalisations are always dangerous, let us make one for which we think the evidence is quite strong. While the New Order government has given single-minded attention to reducing rates of population growth by lowering fertility, it has been less single-minded about reducing mortality. Vaccination campaigns have certainly been conducted with some enthusiasm, but budgetary figures reveal very low proportions of government budgets devoted to health by regional standards and an overemphasis on expensive curative facilities in the large cities at the expense of an effective system of primary health care and efficient referral. The results are clear in Indonesia's comparatively greater success in reducing fertility than in reducing mortality. There is an urgent need to allocate more resources to health and improve the effectiveness of the health sector.

There is little doubt that human resource development has played an important role in the East Asian economic miracle, notwithstanding the poor economic performance of one of the region's best-educated countries, the Philippines (Ogawa, Jones and Williamson 1993). The Philippines story is more testimony to the 'spoiler' role of poor policies (including excessive reliance on import substitution industrialisation), nepotism and mismanagement rather than to the lack of importance of human resource development. Human resource development is playing and can play a major role in future economic development in Indonesia.

The chapters that follow, after the two that deal with recent developments in political and economic conditions in Indonesia, are all on aspects of population and human resource development in Indonesia. In this preface we will paint the picture of the Indonesian population situation in the mid-1990s with very broad brush strokes, as a framework for the more specific analyses. The appendix tables (Tables 1A.1-1A.4) that follow this Introduction give the interested reader the latest statistical information on Indonesia's demographic situation.

The demise of the Soviet Union had the effect of boosting Indonesia from fifth to fourth place among the world's nations in terms of population size. Indonesia's success in population control and the failure of Pakistan and Nigeria to contain their fertility rates probably mean that Indonesia will not retain fourth place beyond about 2020 or fifth place beyond about 2040. Nevertheless, it is a major nation by virtue of its population size and will become a potent economic power if it can manage to sustain current economic growth rates for another two decades or so. Indonesia's population probably passed the 200 million mark in 1996, but more importantly, it passed this milestone at a slowing rate of population growth. The prospect is that population growth will be down to about 1 per cent per annum by the time the population reaches the 250 million mark in about 2014. The deceleration in population growth rates results from the substantial decline in fertility since the mid-1960s (see Chapter 12). This is leading to an age structure that is much more conducive to rapid economic growth than the age structure of the 1970s: 63 per cent of the population was in the working ages (15-64) in 1995, compared with 55 per cent in 1970.

Over a long period, population growth has been slower in Java than elsewhere in Indonesia, with the result that Java (including Madura) now contains slightly less than 60 per cent of Indonesia's population, compared to 69 per cent in 1930. Java's population density, of course, continues to far exceed that of any other major region of Indonesia (see Table 1.2). Indonesia is urbanising quite rapidly; over a third of its population now lives in urban areas. The proportion is even higher in Java, where the rural population has actually started to decline. The human resource development issues Indonesia now faces, then, are in the context of an urbanising and industrialising economy, but one which faces stiff economic competition from countries such as China, Vietnam and the Philippines.

Chapter 2 by Greg Fealy summarises the political situation and the issues facing Indonesia. It notes that despite increasing concern in many quarters over the issue of presidential succession, there are no signs that President Soeharto intends to step down in 1998. The President is increasingly remote, intolerant of opinions contrary to his own, and through actions such as the removal of Megawati Sukarnoputri from leadership of a main opposition party (PDI), the broad crackdown on opposition groups and the award of the national car licence to his son, has convinced many observers that his judgement is

TABLE 1.2: Population of Indonesia, 1995

Province	Area Thousand km^2	Population (thousands)	Average annual growth rate 1980-90	Average annual growth rate 1990-95	Density (person/ sq. km)
Java	135	114,733	1.7	1.3	850
Sumatra	541	40,830	2.7	2.2	75
Kalimantan	551	10,471	3.1	2.7	19
Sulawesi	228	13,732	1.9	1.8	60
Nusatenggara[a]	93	10,959	1.9	1.5	118
Maluku and Irian Jaya	497	4,029	3.2	2.9	8
Indonesia	2,045	194,755	2.0	1.7	95

[a]Including Bali and East Timor.

Source: Biro Pusat Statistik, Indonesia, 1996.

seriously impaired. His hold on power is secure only so long as he continues to deliver economic growth and social stability. The risks of instability associated with the succession are very great.

Anggito Abimanyu (Chapter 3) highlights some of the key economic trends in Indonesia. Economics and politics are always closely linked in Indonesia, and some of the key economic issues are of a 'political economy' kind. These include nagging problems of inflation and current account deficit, the obvious impact of vested interests in the process of economic restructuring, and inability of the government to deal comprehensively with polluters and abusers of economic regulations.

Following these two introductory chapters, the book turns to the main theme of the Update, i.e. the population and human resource development situation. John C. Caldwell (Chapter 4) introduces this section of the book by setting Indonesian population in comparative perspective, showing both the substantial progress made by Indonesia and the magnitude of the task remaining.

Three chapters deal with population mobility and urbanisation. Indonesia is witnessing rapid change in mobility patterns. As Graeme Hugo (Chapter 5) documents, the overall propensity of Indonesians to move on both a permanent and temporary basis has increased over the past two decades, especially the propensity for non-permanent movement, movement within and between urban areas, and international labour migration. Women are increasingly involved in autonomous movement. Hugo documents regional patterns of movement, and the deceleration in net redistribution of people from Java to the Outer Islands. The movement from Java to the outer islands remains a rural-oriented movement, whereas migrants to Java are predominantly moving to the cities, especially Jakarta and its fringe areas located in West Java.

The 1980s was a period of rapid urbanisation unparalleled in Indonesia's history. By 1994, 40 per cent of Java's population lived in urban areas. Outside Java, the figure was only 26 per cent, although two provinces, Sumatera Utara and Kalimantan Timur, matched or exceeded Java's urbanisation level. Much of this urbanisation has been due to reclassification of previously rural areas as they adopted urban characteristics, as stressed in Peter Gardiner's paper (Chapter 7). The lateral extension of Indonesia's urban areas has tended to occur in corridors along major transport routes between major cities, suggesting that mass transportation along these corridors will be very important in regional development. Jakarta is becoming one of the world's megacities, the Jabotabek region now containing about one fourth of Indonesia's urban population. Jakarta attracted half of the investments approved by the Coordinating Agency for Investments in recent years. But as Tommy Firman (Chapter 6) points out, by 1990 Indonesia had seven cities with populations exceeding one million, and this number is projected to reach 23 by 2020.

Gardiner raises doubts (as does Geoffrey McNicoll in Chapter 11) about the necessity for government programs to move people away from Java. Rough projections of labour demand and supply indicate that the expected differential growth of job opportunities in favour of the outer islands will be roughly matched by the faster growth of their labour force through natural increase alone, thus not requiring net migration. As McNicoll notes, population density contrasts between Java and elsewhere in Indonesia have—for no valid reason—tended to be seen as 'a kind of affront that calls for policy action, as if they violated some ideal norm of uniformity'.

Human resource development probably holds the key to Indonesia's longer-term economic prospects, as well as to the possibility of holding a disparate polity and society together. Three provocative chapters are included in the HRD section of the volume—dealing with education, ageing and women's role. Oey-Gardiner's chapter (Chapter 8) raises some disturbing issues about educational developments. Whereas a steady and uninterrupted progression might have been expected from the achievement of universal primary education to the achievement of universal nine years' education, consistent with government policy on this matter, the reality is very different. Not only has universal primary education not yet been fully achieved—as high dropout rates during primary school in the more isolated areas testify—but also the progression rates from primary to secondary school declined during the 1980s and have not increased since. Such a decline was perhaps to be expected, since near-universal primary education meant that the pool of primary graduates eligible to progress has widened from a fairly elitist group before 1980 to include many more from poor and disadvantaged backgrounds. Nevertheless, the implication is that universal lower secondary education will not be achieved simply because the government wishes it, but will require a public perception that it is in the family's interests to keep their children in school for these additional years, with all the costs that this involves.

Despite such troublesome evidence, the underlying demographic circumstances are clearly favourable to the achievement of the government's goals. Declining fertility since the late 1960s has led to a levelling off in numbers reaching school age, meaning that school building and teacher training programs are no longer under much pressure in meeting primary education targets, and attention can be shifted to quality improvement and expansion of secondary education. Turning to equality of access to education, the gender gap at the primary level has practically closed and is narrowing at the secondary level as well. By contrast, the gap in access according to socio-economic background, as in most countries, is proving far more difficult to close.

Indonesia's underutilised resource, women, face many obstacles to full involvement in academic, business and community life. Official ideology continues to give priority to their role in preparing the next generation by nurturing the family. Yulfita Rahardjo (Chapter 9) notes a lag between socio-economic changes (including the closing of the gender gap in education, resulting in a dramatic increase in numbers of educated women) and changes in traditional gender roles. Thus obstacles continue to be placed in the path of women's more effective participation in all areas of life. The answer, she argues, is largely in women's own hands. They must demand greater involvement in the identification of their own problems, and in planning for change, rather than in merely implementing programs established by others.

Ananta *et al.* (Chapter 10) have some important observations to make about ageing in Indonesia. The proportion of elderly in Indonesia's population is not yet very high, but it will inevitably increase. By 2020, the proportion of population aged above 65 in Central Java, Yogyakarta, East Java and Bali will have reached 10 per cent, almost as high a proportion as in Australia, Canada and New Zealand in 1993—and at lower levels of per capita income. This requires long-term planning, not alarm. What must be kept in mind is that there is no choice about an ageing population; if Indonesia is to enjoy low mortality and low or zero population growth, then an ageing population is the inevitable concomitant. Appropriate pension and superannuation programs need to be put in place now, since those who will be elderly in 2020 are already in the workforce. Public perceptions of the elderly need to be changed, so that instead of being regarded as dependants and a burden on the community they can continue to play an active role in society and their abilities be more effectively utilised.

Like their counterparts in developed countries, Indonesians most often link the idea of population ageing with the concept of individual ageing, and in considering this place emphasis on the problems of illness and death. Just as the Ananta *et al.* chapter tries to show that an ageing population can become a positive resource rather than a burden by stressing policies which give better roles for the older people, so Meiwita Iskandar (Chapter 11) argues that the challenges of morbidity and mortality are changing and require greater government attention to consolidate the gains made to date. As the death rate falls, young people are less likely to fall ill, and much more likely to have increased years of life free from the burden of infectious and parasitic diseases. The weight of these diseases is similarly lifted from the middle-aged and older population, yet in its place there is growing awareness of other disease and disability burdens, such as cardiovascular disease, cancers, and the problems of accidents and violence which extract a heavy toll on people of the working age groups. Iskandar reviews the details of these challenges, but shows how frustrating it is for the analyst to raise questions of adult mortality under conditions where data sources are both very limited and very flawed. Her chapter is a plea for greater government attention to the generation of reliable data on health and mortality.

Sri Moertiningsih Adioetomo (Chapter 12) is well placed to see the big picture of fertility and family planning in Indonesia. Based at the Demographic Institute of the University of Indonesia, she leads a number of research projects evaluating the impact of the national family planning program and exploring future directions for fertility change. In her PhD thesis at the ANU a few years ago she argued that the program had effected a major change in attitudes about family size by mobilising a range of community institutions to persistently, consistently and thoroughly promote approval for contraceptive methods, and acceptance of the benefits of small family sizes. This view of the Indonesian family planning program stands in dramatic contrast to the notions of coercion and chaos which have been attributed to programs in other Third World countries. While there has been occasional criticism of the Indonesian approach, the more common reaction has been admiration at the rapid spread of birth control and the reduction of fertility rates. Adioetomo's measured praise for the program makes her argument for program improvements even more cogent. Today, she says, the need is for improvements in the quality of family planning services to encourage women who have dropped out of the program to rejoin by accepting other methods, or by realising that some of the problems they experienced with methods can be overcome through more caring clinical and community services. Improvement of program approaches might also attract the participation of the large numbers of women and men who have thus far lacked interest in contraception, and help the many contraceptive users with problems to become more effective and satisfied program clients. This emphasis on quality, combined with the move toward greater privatisation of services, provides the key to making family planning both self sufficient and sustainable.

Two commentators on the mortality and fertility papers brought complementary perspectives to the Update presentations. Firman Lubis (see Chapter 13) first practised medicine in the opening days of the New Order government, and still remembers a time of great shortages in hospitals, and utter hopelessness in the face of many comparatively simple medical problems. His experience motivated a career devoted to the control of infant and maternal mortality, and helps to explain the concentration which his generation brought to consideration of medial priorities. While not contradicting Iskandar's call for greater concern with the measurement and treatment of the causes of adult mortality, Lubis reminds us of the very reasonable concerns which served to narrow perspectives in the past. Similarly his comments on the Adioetomo chapter strengthen the case for improvement by reminding the reader just how much progress has been made in the last three decades. Gour Dasvarma (Chapter 14) has taught and collaborated with Indonesians for over fifteen years, and in his look at the current situation of fertility and mortality he uses the perspectives of his students to draw attention to the benefits of applying careful scientific investigation to particular regions or data sets. The theses he summarises represent significant, if unpublished, Indonesian contributions to demographic literature. For the foreign reader the findings shift thinking laterally from the question of what is happening to fertility and mortality, to the puzzle of why so little is known of Indonesian demographic studies outside of Indonesia. Language is one barrier, but today there are numerous Indonesians who have achieved overseas degrees. Lack of an outward-looking professional organisation certainly inhibits international publication. Yet still there is a nagging suspicion that these are not sufficient explanations. Perhaps Dasvarma's review will help to break down some of these barriers, and make Indonesian demographic studies more accessible.

The Update was concluded with a symposium to explore the future of Indonesia's population. McNicoll (chapter 15) opened the proceedings with a careful, broad-ranging and insightful analysis of the potentials and pitfalls involved in the process of population projection. This is a paper that will repay more than a cursory reading. The following speakers considered the impact of potential population trends on ageing, education, and the welfare of the people. Agus Dwiyanto (Chapter 17) made a strong case for a major shift in policy from fertility-control policies to quality-oriented human resource development policies. He further argued that wide variation in population and human resource issues among provinces and areas requires the government to decentralise its policy-making, in order to be more responsive to local problems and approaches. Terence Hull (Chapter

16) referred back to the earlier chapters to raise questions about Indonesian data needs, and suggested that the combination of bureaucratic rivalry and illusions of accuracy may lead to the degradation of the very systems of data collection which are needed to understand demographic trends.

Finally the audience was treated to the whimsical reading of a letter from Aris Ananta's friend from the year 2020 (Chapter 20). How, the friend from the future asks, could people have been so silly in making projections of population which turned out to be so totally wrong. Ananta's answer is both timely and timeless. It is timely in warning his audience to take care in their reading of any projections, and to look closely at the assumptions they contain. But it is timeless in its reminder to demographers that the projections are made to promote changes in policy and behaviour which will ensure that the assumptions do not come true. The projections are useful only if they can be made to be wrong. Ultimately Ananta's lesson is applicable to many of the chapters in this volume which mark out the trajectory of social and economic changes on the basis of recent events and current trends. These are not forecasts to narrow the pathway of future generations as much as they are chances to see what might happen if current trends continue unrevised. They are motivations to work for revision.

APPENDIX

TABLE A1.1: Population of Indonesia by province, 1971, 1980, 1990 and 1995

Province	Population			
	1971	1980	1990	1995
1. Daerah Istimewa Aceh	2,008,595	2,611,271	3,416,156	3,847,583
2. Sumatera Utara	6,621,831	8,360,894	10,256,027	11,114,667
3. Sumatera Barat	2,793,196	3,406,816	4,000,207	4,323,170
4. Riau	1,641,545	2,168,535	3,303,976	3,900,534
5. Jambi	1,006,084	1,445,994	2,020,568	2,369,959
6. Sumatera Selatan	3,440,573	4,629,801	6,313,074	7,207,545
7. Bengkulu	519,316	768,064	1,179,122	1,409,117
8. Lampung	2,777,008	4,624,785	6,017,573	6,657,759
9. DKI Jakarta	4,579,303	6,503,449	8,259,266	9,112,652
10. Jawa Barat	21,623,529	27,453,525	35,384,352	39,206,787
11. Jawa Tengah	21,877,136	25,372,889	28,520,643	29,653,266
12. DI Yogyakarta	2,489,360	2,750,813	2,913,054	2,916,779
13. Jawa Timur	25,516,999	29,188,852	32,503,991	33,844,002
14. Bali	2,120,322	2,469,930	2,777,811	2,895,64915
15. Nusa Tenggara Barat	2,203,465	2,724,664	3,369,649	3,645,713
16. Nusa Tenggara Timur	2,295,287	2,737,166	3,268,644	3,577,472
17. Timor Timur	n.a.	555,350	747,750	839,719
18. Kalimantan Barat	2019.936	2,486,068	3,229,153	3,635,730
19. Kalimantan Tengah	701,936	954,353	1,396,486	1,627,453
20. Kalimantan Selatan	1,699,105	2,064,649	2,597,572	2,893,477
21. Kalimantan Timur	733,797	1,218,016	1,876,663	2,314,183
22. Sulawesi Utara	1.718.543	2,115,384	2,478,119	2,649,093
23. Sulawesi Tengah	913,622	1,289,635	1,711,327	1,938,071
24. Sulawesi Selatan	5,180,576	6,062,212	6,981,646	7,558,368
25. Sulawesi Tenggara	714,120	942,302	1,349,619	1,586,917
26. Maluku	1,089,565	1,411,006	1,857,790	2,086,516
27. Irian Jaya	923,440	1,173,875	1,648,708	1,942,627
INDONESIA	119,208,229	147, 490, 298	179, 378, 946	194, 754, 808

Note: Including non-permanent residents (homeless people, sailors, boat people and remote area communities
    n..a. = data not available

Source: 19971, 1980, 1990 Population Census, and the 1995 Intercensal Population Survey.

TABLE A1.2: Population growth by province

Province	Average annual population growth rate		
	1971-80	*1980-90*	*1990-95*
1.Daerah Istimewa Aceh	2.9	2.7	2.4
2. Sumatera Utara	2.6	2.1	1.6
3. Sumatera Barat	2.2	1.6	1.6
4. Riau	3.1	4.3	3.4
5. Jambi	4.1	3.4	3.2
6.Sumatera Selatan	3.3	3.2	3.7
7. Bengkulu	4.4	4.4	3.6
8. Lampung	5.8	2.7	2.0
9. DKI Jakarta	3.9	2.4	2.0
10. Jawa Barat	2.7	2.6	2.1
11. Jawa Tengah	1.6	1.2	0.8
12. DI Yogyakarta	1.1	0.6	0.0
13. Jawa Timur	1.5	1.1	0.8
14. Bali	1.7	1.2	0.8
15. Nusa Tenggara Barat	2.4	2.2	1.6
16. Nusa Tenggara Timur	2.0	1.8	1.8
17. Timor Timur	n.a.	3.0	2.4
18. Kalimantan Barat	2.3	2.7	2.4
19. Kalimantan Tengah	3.4	3.9	3.1
20. Kalimantan Selatan	2.2	2.3	2.2
21. Kalimantan Timur	5.7	4.4	4.3
22. Sulawesi Utara	2.3	1.6	1.3
23. Sulawesi Tengah	3.9	2.9	2.5
24. Sulawesi Selatan	1.7	1.4	1.6
25. Sulawesi Tenggara	3.1	3.7	3.3
26. Maluku	2.9	2.8	2.4
27. Irian Jaya	2.7	3.5	3.3
INDONESIA	2.3[a]	2.0	1.7

Note: [a] Excluding Timor Timur

n.a. = data not available.

Source: 1971, 1980, 1990 Population Census, and the 1995 Intercensal Population Survey.

TABLE A1.3 Official estimates of total fertility rates (TFR) by province

Province	1971 PC (67–70)	1980 PC (76-79)	1985 IPS (81-84)	1990 PC (86-89)	1991 IDHS (87-90)	1994 IDHS
1. Daerah Istimewa Aceh	6.265	5.235	4.790	4.367	3.760	3.30
2. Sumatera Utara	7.195	5.935	5.125	4.289	4.170	3.88
3. Sumatera Barat	6.180	5.755	4.805	3.890	3.600	3.19
4. Riau	5.940	5.435	4.705	4.088	n.a.	3.10
5. Jambi	6.390	5.570	4.620	3.759	n.a.	2.97
6. Sumatera Selatan	6.325	5.585	4.780	4.223	3.430	2.87
7. Bengkulu	6.715	6.195	5.135	3.969	n.a.	3.45
8. Lampung	6.355	5.750	4.795	4.054	3.200	3.45
9. DKI Jakarta	5.175	3.990	3.250	2.326	2.140	1.90
10. Jawa Barat	6.335	5.070	4.305	3.468	3.370	3.17
11. Jawa Tengah	5.330	4.370	3.820	3.049	2.850	2.77
12. DI Yogyakarta	4.755	3.415	2.930	2.082	2.040	1.79
13. Jawa Timur	4.720	3.555	3.200	2.456	2.130	2.22
14. Bali	5.955	3.970	3.090	2.275	2.220	2.14
15. Nusa Tenggara Barat	6.655	6.490	5.735	4.975	3.820	3.64
16. Nusa Tenggara Timur	5.960	5.540	5.120	4.608	n.a.	3.87
17. Timor Timur	n.a.	n.a.	n.a.	5.729	n.a.	4.69
18. Kalimantan Barat	6.265	5.520	4.980	4.437	3.940	3.34
19. Kalimantan Tengah	6.825	5.870	4.765	4.029	n.a.	2.31
20. Kalimantan Selatan	5.425	4.595	3.740	3.238	2.700	2.33
21. Kalimantan Timur	5.405	4.985	4.160	3.275	n.a.	3.21
22. Sulawesi Utara	6.790	4.905	3.585	2.687	2.250	2.62
23. Sulawesi Tengah	6.530	5.900	4.855	3.853	n.a.	3.08
24. Sulawesi Selatan	5.705	4.875	4.125	3.538	3.010	2.92
25. Sulawesi Tenggara	6.445	5.820	5.660	4.908	n.a.	3.50
26. Maluku	6.885	6.155	5.610	4.593	n.a.	3.70
27. Irian Jaya	7.195	5.350	4.835	4.701	n.a.	3.15
INDONESIA	5.605	4.680	4.055	3.326	3.020	2.85

Note: The figures are given to the number of decimal places published by BPS.

n.a. = data not available.

Source: Central Bureau of Statistics website, 2 January, 1997: *http://www.bps.go.id/ pop_emp/ptable.html#table7*

**TABLE A1.4: Infant mortality rate (IMR), by province,
1967, 1976, 1986, 1994**

Province	Infant mortality rate			
	1967	1976	1986	1994 (IDHS)
1. Daerah Istimewa Aceh	143	93	58	58
2. Sumatera Utara	121	89	61	61
3. Sumatera Barat	152	121	74	68
4. Riau	146	110	65	72
5. Jambi	154	121	74	60
6. Sumatera Selatan	155	102	71	60
7. Bengkulu	167	111	69	74
8. Lampung	146	99	69	38
9. DKI Jakarta	129	82	40	30
10. Jawa Barat	167	134	90	89
11. Jawa Tengah	144	99	65	51
12. DI Yogyakarta	102	62	42	30
13. Jawa Timur	120	97	64	62
14. Bali	130	92	51	58
15. Nusa Teng4gara Barat	221	189	145	110
16. Nusa Tenggara Timur	154	128	77	71
17. Timor Timur	-	-	85	46
18. Kalimantan Barat	144	119	81	97
19. . Kalimantan Tengah	129	100	58	16
20. Kalimantan Selatan	165	123	91	83
21. Kalimantan Timur	104	100	58	61
22. Sulawesi Utara	114	93	63	66
23. Sulawesi Tengah	150	130	92	87
24. Sulawesi Selatan	161	111	70	64
25. Sulawesi Tenggara	167	116	77	79
26. Maluku	143	123	76	68
27. Irian Jaya	86	105	80	61
INDONESIA	145	109	71	66

Source: 1971, 1980, 1990 Population Census and the 1994 Indonesian Demographic and Health Survey (IDHS).

PART A: POLITICAL AND

ECONOMIC DEVELOPMENTS

2

Indonesian Politics, 1995-96:
The Makings of a Crisis*

Greg Fealy

When will Soeharto stand down as President?
Oh, ninety-eight.
So, only two more years to go?
No, not 1998; when Soeharto is ninety-eight!

The issue of presidential succession has dominated Indonesian politics for almost a decade. Soeharto, now 75, has held office for 30 years, making him one of the longest-serving leaders in the world. With each passing year there is growing speculation over when he will retire from politics, who will replace him and how the transition to a post-Soeharto era will be handled. The president refuses to disclose his plans, saying somewhat disingenuously that his future will be decided by the People's Consultative Assembly (MPR). Meanwhile, he and the other forces in Indonesian politics, such as the armed forces, the bureaucracy, the business community and various religious and social organisations, compete to maximise their control over or influence upon the succession.

The events of the past twelve months have added greatly to the tensions and uncertainty surrounding his future. The above joke, which enjoyed great popularity in Jakarta political circles in early 1996, satirises the speculation over Soeharto's intentions: once again he has confounded those who expected or hoped that he was soon to

* The fieldwork for this article was undertaken in Jakarta and Yogyakarta during June-July 1996. I am grateful to the organising committee of the Indonesia Update 1996 for providing financial assistance which enabled me to conduct this research.

leave office and instead plans to rule for decades. The joke is apt because there are two striking and contradictory features of the past year. On the one hand, the president has moved determinedly, and at times ruthlessly, to ensure his re-election for a seventh five-year term; on the other hand, there is a growing tide of opinion within many sections of Indonesian society and the New Order regime that he should retire when his present term ends in 1998.

This paper will examine Soeharto's efforts to secure his re-election, and the forces opposing him. Although the tumultuous events surrounding the PDI and the 27 July riots will form a significant part of the paper, it is necessary to begin with analysis of a number of less sensational but important political developments. These concern three key groups: Golkar, the armed forces (ABRI), and Islam. Golkar and ABRI are especially critical to Soeharto's strategy; Golkar because it is his electoral vehicle which will provide him with the large and loyal parliamentary majority which he needs to implement his plans, and ABRI because it provides the coercive power upon which his rule is ultimately based.

Golkar

Soeharto's aim is once again to build momentum for his renomination by engineering a substantial Golkar victory at the 1997 general election. There are, however, considerable obstacles to achieving this. Golkar's vote fell by 5 per cent to 68 per cent in the 1992 election, a loss of seventeen seats, though this was still its second highest result in the five elections of the New Order period.[1] It is generally conceded that the party will face an even more volatile and critical electorate in 1997. Rising educational standards and urbanisation along with access to wider sources of information are producing more independent-minded electors. There is also a record number of young voters participating in the 1997 election. Of the approximately 120 million registered voters, 21.5 million or almost 20 per cent will be voting for the first time (this compares with seventeen million new voters in the

---

[1] This left Golkar with 282 of the 500 seats in the DPR or national parliament. The other two parties, the PPP and the PDI, hold 62 and 56 seats respectively. The remaining 100 seats are held by ABRI (armed forces) representatives.

1992 election).[2] Indications are that disaffection with the government is high within this group. Research conducted by Golkar, for example, has revealed that many younger members of the 'Greater ABRI Family' (that is, the wives and children of serving and retired military personnel) have a declining allegiance to the government party. This group would normally be regarded as core supporters.

Soeharto's efforts to revive Golkar's electoral fortunes began three years ago with the appointment of a new board under the chairmanship of Harmoko, the long-serving Minister for Information. Known for his unswerving loyalty to the president, Harmoko distinguished himself during the previous two elections as an indefatigable and effective grassroots campaigner. He has also used his Information Ministry to ensure extensive media coverage of Golkar activities. Importantly, he is the first civilian to chair Golkar and his appointment signalled a diminution of ABRI influence in the party's leadership. Also appointed were the president's eldest daughter, Siti Hardijanti Rukmana ('Mbak Tutut'), who became first deputy chair, and his second son, Bambang Trihatmodjo, who became treasurer.

Further dramatic changes to the face of Golkar were foreshadowed in December 1995 with the announcement of new regulations preventing the renomination of members of parliament who had already served four five-year terms or who were 65 years of age or older. This will effectively force the retirement of about 60 per cent of Golkar MPs at the national and regional levels. The regulations will not only allow regeneration within Golkar's ranks but also vastly expand Soeharto's opportunities for co-optation. In recent years there has been fierce competition amongst party cadres for the few available parliamentary positions. It is expected that many of the vacancies will be filled by younger high-profile leaders from mass organisations who can maximise Golkar's appeal to the under-40s voters who constitute a majority of the electorate. A further attraction of the new regulations for Soeharto is that they will remove many of the party's

---

[2] *Media Indonesia*, 30 March and 21 May 1996; and *Media Indonesia Network*, 22 May 1996. Any civilian over 17 years of age or married can register to vote in the elections. According to law, voting is not compulsory, but the government disapproves of non-participation. There was a 92 per cent participation rate in the 1992 general election.

older, more critical parliamentarians such as Jakob Tobing and Kharis Suhud.[3]

Golkar has also significantly intensified its campaign activities over the past eighteen months, despite a government prohibition on electioneering outside the formal campaign period. Harmoko and Tutut have spearheaded these 'pre-campaign' activities. Both have toured widely and dispensed unprecedented sums to bolster Golkar's grassroots support. This has included channelling money to an array of educational, welfare, religious, cultural and infrastructure projects. Tutut, for example, has dispensed more than Rp5 billion to Islamic boarding schools (*pesantren*) in East Java during the past year.[4] Selected Muslim groups have been funded to undertake the pilgrimage to Mecca and popular local PPP and PDI leaders (and, in several notable cases, entire branches) have been 'enticed' to join Golkar. The most flagrant of the party's campaigning activities has been that of *kuningisasi* (literally, 'yellowisation') in which villages receive favourable treatment in return for painting buildings, houses and fences yellow, the colour of Golkar.

ABRI

Soeharto continued to use his influence over military promotions to appoint loyalists to key posts in the armed forces. These promotions came at an unprecedented rate. There are normally two rounds per year but there were five in 1995 and another four in February and March of 1996 alone.[5] Many of those promoted have been younger officers who graduated from the military academy during the 1970s and are personally known to Soeharto through family or collegial connections or through service on the palace staff. The president apparently regards these 1970s-generation officers as more politically biddable than those from the late 1960s.

---

[3] *Gatra*, 23 December 1995; and *Forum Keadilan*, 1 January 1996, p. 23.

[4] *Media Indonesia Minggu*, 23 September 1995.

[5] *Republika*, 26 December 1995 and 19 March 1996; and *Surabaya Post*, 15 March 1996.

Four names have stood out amongst this merry-go-round of appointments and transfers: Prabowo Subianto, Wiranto, Subagyo Hadi Siswono and Soesilo Bambang Yudoyono. Prabowo, Soeharto's son-in-law and the son of Professor Soemitro Djojohadikusumo, was given command of Kopassus (Red Berets) in November 1995, thus continuing his rapid ascent through the ranks. He has risen from colonel to major-general in just ten months, and at 44 years of age is the youngest two-star general in ABRI history. Prabowo is highly intelligent and a brave and resourceful field commander but has a volatile temperament. He claims to have no political ambitions. Wiranto is one of many former Soeharto adjutants to enjoy swift advancement. In March 1996 he was appointed Kostrad (Green Berets) commander —a position usually occupied by a major-general — at the rank of lieutenant-general. There is growing speculation that he is being groomed to become the next army chief-of-staff.[6] Subagyo was Wiranto's predecessor at Kostrad and now holds the critical post of commander of the Diponegoro division in Central Java. He is a former presidential bodyguard and continues to enjoy Soeharto's trust. Yudoyono, the son-in-law of the late Lt-Gen. Sarwo Edhie, was promoted from chief of staff of the Jakarta region to commander of the Sriwijaya division in south Sumatra.[7]

The most controversial issue involving ABRI in the past year was its political role in the next election and particularly its relations with Golkar. The relationship between the two organisations has been strained since 1993. The appointment of Harmoko and the growing influence of the powerful Minister for Science and Technology, Dr B. J. Habibie, in party affairs were the main causes of this tension, but sections of the military were also displeased that ABRI's quota of seats in the national parliament was to be reduced from 100 to 75 after the next election. These measures were seen as increasing Soeharto's influence at the expense of the military's. As a result, it was expected that ABRI would again adopt a largely neutral stance in 1997, as it had at the two previous elections.[8]

---

[6] See, for example, *Gatra*, 23 March 1996.

[7] *Suara Pembaruan*, 8 August 1996; and *Forum Keadilan*, 9 September 1996, pp. 12-19.

[8] *The Australian*, 16-17 March 1996; and *Tempo Online*, 23 March 1996.

In March, however, the army chief of staff, Gen. R. Hartono, publicly declared ABRI's allegiance to the government party. At a rally of Golkar cadres attended by Tutut, with whom he has a close relationship, Hartono donned a yellow jacket and stated that 'every ABRI member is a Golkar cadre' who would give unquestioning loyalty to the party. He went on to say: 'As a Golkar cadre, it is legally binding for me to accept the advice and guidance of the Golkar board chair, Mbak Tutut'.[9] His remarks created a furore. PPP and PDI leaders as well as many political commentators condemned them as partisan and a return to the politics of the 1970s when ABRI intervention underpinned Golkar's electoral success.[10] Hartono's statement also embarrassed and angered many of his fellow officers. Most believe his public declaration to have been a foolhardy act which compromised ABRI's attempts to portray itself as an independent and impartial force. A commonly-held suspicion was that he had placed his personal career and desire to demonstrate his loyalty to Soeharto and Tutut above the institutional interests of the armed forces. In the following weeks the ABRI commander, Gen. Feisal Tanjung, the Defence Minister, Gen. Edi Sudradjat, and Lt-Gen. Syarwan Hamid, the head of the Armed Forces' Social and Political Affairs section, were forced to 'clarify' Hartono's remarks, explaining that they only applied to the Greater ABRI Family and reassuring other parties that the armed forces would remain neutral.[11]

Despite assurances to the contrary, the available evidence suggests that ABRI will adopt a pro-Golkar stance during the election. Many of the younger ABRI officers known to be antipathetic to the government party have been shifted to less politically sensitive positions and observers report increased support by regional military commands for Golkar activities.

Islam, ICMI and Habibie

Much has been written about the religious and cultural revival of Islam from the early 1980s and the accompanying 'santri-fication' (literally, becoming more Islamically devout) of Indonesian society in

---

[9] *Jakarta Post*, 15 March 1996; and *Forum Keadilan*, 8 April 1996, p. 100.

[10] *Jakarta Post*, 15 and 20 March 1996.

[11] *Antara* and the *Straits Times* 17 March 1996; and *Republika*, 26 March 1996.

general and the New Order elite in particular. Growing numbers of avowedly *santri* Muslims (as opposed to nominal or *abangan* Muslims) now occupy positions in cabinet, the senior bureaucracy and ABRI leadership. Soeharto himself has also adopted a more devout lifestyle. *Santri*-fication has been both a consequence and a reflection of a political rapprochement between Islam and the New Order since the late 1980s. The main symbol and vehicle for this reconciliation has been ICMI (Ikatan Cendekiawan Muslimin se-Indonesia: Association of Indonesian Muslim Intellectuals), which was established in 1990 under the chairmanship of Habibie. ICMI has become a major source of career opportunities and financial patronage for educated middle-class Muslims.

Despite this cultural efflorescence, the events of the past year have confirmed impressions that ICMI cannot yet be regarded as a distinct and autonomous political force. There are two main reasons for this. First, ICMI is heavily dependent upon Habibie and ultimately Soeharto for its present favoured position. It is Habibie's access to the palace and ability to secure financial and bureaucratic benefits which is the key to ICMI's success. As one ICMI leader said: 'Habibie is our [ICMI's] ticket to Soeharto and the corridors of power. Without him we are back on the fringes'. If either Habibie or Soeharto were to leave office, ICMI's immediate future would be uncertain. Secondly, the main beneficiaries of ICMI have been politically conservative Muslims from bureaucratic and technological backgrounds, rather than the more critical or reform-minded intellectuals and social activists. Indeed, most of those promoted by Soeharto and Habibie to cabinet or senior bureaucratic positions would not, prior to the 1980s, have been regarded as 'Muslim leaders' as they lacked both religious learning and a background of activism in Islamic organisations. These factors reveal the president's desire to promote 'development-minded' Islam whilst subordinating politically assertive Muslims.

Soeharto's determination to ensure ICMI's political subservience was apparent at the organisation's second national congress held in Jakarta in December 1995. Leading intellectuals and activists, unhappy at what they saw as ICMI's overly compliant relations with the government, insisted that Adi Sasono, a prominent NGO leader and government critic during the 1980s, be appointed as secretary-general. Soeharto reluctantly accepted the proposal but responded by appointing half the cabinet and a range of ICMI antagonists and

Habibie adversaries to the new 114-member board.[12] His actions not only diluted the influence of intellectuals and activists within the ICMI leadership but also served to deflect criticism that the organisation had become a vehicle for militant Muslims.

This was not the only recent setback to be suffered by ICMI. In early December, the Trade minister and Habibie confidante, Satrio Budiardjo ('Billy') Joedono, became the first minister in 29 years to be removed from office mid-term. Joedono's departure was ostensibly to allow the merger of the Trade and Industry departments. It was widely acknowledged, however, that he had performed poorly in his portfolio. He was criticised for torpid policy-making, for failing to arrest the decline in non-oil export growth, and for not maintaining good relations with the business community. His refusal to grant favours to powerful and well-connected entrepreneurs, including members of the Soeharto family, was also rumoured to have hastened his removal.[13] Another ICMI minister, Haryanto Dhanutirto, was also embroiled in controversy after the press published details from a leaked inspector-general's report to Soeharto. The report accused the minister of misusing his office for personal gain and catalogued 392 'violations' over the past twelve months totalling Rp9 billion (US$4.5 million). Although sections of the report were later shown to be incorrect Haryanto's reputation was seriously tarnished by the affair. There is much uncertainty about Soeharto's role in orchestrating this controversy, but his responses following publication of the report were seen as a warning both to ICMI ministers and to the rest of the cabinet of the power which he held over their careers.[14]

---

[12] Among the Habibie opponents appointed to the board were Professor Soemitro Djojohadikusumo, Lt-Gen. (ret.) Wahono, Lt-Gen. (ret.) Soerono and the Coordinating Minister for Politics and Security, Soesilo Sudarman. A good account of the ICMI congress can be found in *Forum Keadilan*, 1 January 1996, pp. 14-16.

[13] *Jakarta Post*, 8 December 1995; and *Far Eastern Economic Review*, 21 December 1995, p. 60. According to a number of senior financial journalists in Jakarta, the president was annoyed at Joedono's reluctance to grant the 'national car' licence to his youngest son, Hutomo Mandala Putra ('Tommy').

[14] *Republika*, 22, 23, 27, 28 and 29 December 1995, and 3 and 8 January 1996; and *Antara*, 26 December 1995.

New political movements

The past year has been notable for the emergence of a variety of political reform movements challenging key aspects of the status quo. It saw the establishment of two nascent political parties, as well as a number of quasi-parties and 'rainbow' organisations. The most radical of these new organisations are the two self-declared parties, PRD (Partai Rakyat Demokratik: the People's Democratic Party) and PUDI (Partai Uni Demokrasi Indonesia: the Indonesian Democratic Union Party)—the first new parties of the New Order period.[15] Both parties are in direct contravention of Ordinance no. 3, 1985 which limits the number of parties to three: Golkar, PPP and PDI. PRD is the more militant of the two. It openly challenges key elements of New Order orthodoxy by advocating, amongst other things, self-determination for East Timor, the introduction of a social democratic political system, a review of *Pancasila* as the sole ideological foundation (*asas tunggal*) of all social and political organisations, and immediate improvement in workers' wages and conditions. It has also bestowed 'Democracy Awards' to the Fretilin guerilla leader, Xanana Gusmao, and the novelist, Pramoedya Ananta Toer. At the core of the PRD is a group of student and labour activists led by Budiman Sudjatmiko.[16] PUDI was founded by the former PPP politician, Sri Bintang Pamungkas, in May 1996. It claims to be in the *golput* (*golongan putih*; literally, 'blank group') tradition, a reference to those electors who, in protest at what they see as an iniquitous political system, have abstained from voting. Its manifesto describes the New Order as 'totalitarian' and refers to Soeharto's own 1967 speech to the national assembly (MPR) in promising to correct the abuses of the Sukarno regime.[17]

---

[15] The only other party to be formed during the New Order, Parmusi in 1968, was not so much a new party as a resurrection of Masyumi which had been dissolved by Sukarno in 1960.

[16] PRD was originally founded in 1994 but transformed itself into a party in April 1996. *Tempo Online*, 3 June 1996; and *Forum Keadilan*, 12 August 1996, pp. 18-19.

[17] *Kompas*, 29 May 1996; and *Asiaweek*, 1 June 1996.

In addition to these two parties, there were three new quasi-parties formed in October and November 1995. All brought together disaffected older generation politicians with younger NGO activists. Each took the initials of a Sukarno-era party, though carefully avoided use of the word 'party' in their name. PNI (Persatuan Nasional Indonesia), commonly known as 'PNI Baru', was chaired by Madame Supeni, a former ambassador from the early 1960s; Masyumi Baru (Majelis Syarikat Umat Muslimin Indonesia) was founded by the former PPP and thwarted Golkar politician, Ridwan Saidi; and Parkindo (Partisipasi Kristen Indonesia) was led by Sabam Sirait, a PDI leader who had been secretary-general of the original Parkindo prior to its merger with PDI in 1973.[18] The emergence of these parties prompted considerable discussion about the return of sectional or *aliran* politics.

The third category of new organisations are the so-called 'rainbow groups' (*kelompok pelangi*), a reference to their diverse membership. Of these, PCPP (Persatuan Cendekiawan Pembangunan Pancasila: Association of Pancasila Development Intellectuals) and YKPK (Yayasan Kerukunan Persaudaraan Kebangsaan: National Brotherhood Reconciliation Foundation) are the most overtly political. Both organisations share similar origins and memberships, though their fates have differed markedly. They have brought together retired ABRI officers, academics, and religious and political figures who are concerned at the recent direction of New Order politics. A major source of anxiety is the growing state sponsorship of Islam, and particularly ICMI. They regard this as a reversion to the divisive religious and primordial politics of the Sukarno era. Both organisations have therefore emphasised national unity and reconciliation. PCPP was formally established in June 1995 but was quickly brought under Soeharto's control. Following the 'taming' of PCPP, many of its more critical members founded YKPK in October. It is led by two former

---

[18] *Tiras*, 9 November 1995; *Republika*, 17 and 25 November 1995; and *Surabaya Post*, 25 November 1995. Masyumi Baru is the exception of these three parties in that none of the surviving Masyumi leaders from the 1950s became involved. This was nicely summed up by the PPP chair, Hasan Ismail Metareum, who said: 'There are no old Masyumi leaders in the New Masyumi and none of the New Masyumi leaders were in the old Masyumi'. *Republika*, 28 November 1996.

generals, Bambang Triantoro and Kharis Suhud, but attracted support from an array of Muslim and Christian organisations as well as NGOs.[19]

The most recent rainbow organisation is KIPP (Komite Independen Pemantau Pemilu; Independent Election Monitoring Committee) which was formed in March 1996 under the chairmanship of former *Tempo* editor, Goenawan Mohammad. Modelled on organisations such as Namfrel in the Philippines and PollWatch in Thailand, KIPP's main aim is to monitor all aspects of the election process and to report on any irregularities. It attracted support from an impressive array of liberal intellectuals, human rights campaigners, Muslim and Christian leaders and politicians. Although avowedly non-political, KIPP nevertheless serves to highlight disillusionment with the lack of electoral probity in New Order politics. One of its undeclared objectives was to minimise regime manipulation of the PDI vote, in anticipation that Megawati would attract a significant increase in support. Although welcomed by the PPP and PDI, KIPP has faced government harassment.[20]

A number of conclusions can be drawn about these new organisations. First, with the exception of PRD, these groups are largely the product of intra-elite political tensions rather than genuine grassroots movements. Secondly, the impact of these organisations to date has been minimal. All remain small (usually less than a few hundred members) and poorly funded and few have succeeded in building branch networks outside of Jakarta. Many of their founders indeed anticipated that the political restrictions of the New Order would make rapid expansion impossible in the short term. As one YKPK leader said, 'We are awaiting the winds of change which will blow us into the political mainstream'. But they have, nonetheless,

---

[19] 'PIPA', on Apakabar, 27 October 1995; *Tiras*, 2 November 1995, pp. 19-29; *Republika*, 13 November 1995; and *Suara Independen*, no. 5, October/November 1995.

[20] *Kompas*, 16 and 27 March 1996; *Republika*, 26 March 1996. Harassment of KIPP included disruption of its meetings in a number of regional cities and the formation of anti-KIPP groups in Surabaya and Jakarta. *Republika*, 26 and 27 March 1996; and *Gatra*, 13 and 20 April 1996.

succeeded in focusing attention on important issues such as restrictions on the number of parties, the linkage between democratisation and *aliran* politics, and the need for greater electoral transparency.

Megawati and PDI

The most potent reform figure to emerge in recent years has been Megawati Sukarnoputri, who was elected as chair of PDI in December 1993. She is a unique and in many ways an unlikely political leader. She is the first popularly-elected party leader of the New Order period, but she also lacks many of the skills usually found in a successful politician. She is not a strong orator, appears to have little grasp of policy details, and has poor organisational and tactical skills. She does, however, possess a number of significant assets, the most obvious of which is the name Sukarnoputri—literally, 'the daughter of Sukarno'—a name which still has an almost magical resonance within many sections of Indonesian society. She also has a deep sense of moral conviction and has repeatedly demonstrated her uncompromising stance on issues of justice, equity and fairness.

Megawati has strengthened PDI's tradition of populist egalitarianism. She has persistently criticised the government over issues such as corruption and cronyism, social and economic inequalities, and restrictions on freedom of speech and association. But by far her most significant decision has been to allow sections of PDI to propose her nomination for the presidency in 1998. Although this was welcomed by many proponents of political reform, some of her closest advisers warned that it would trigger government retaliation which could ruin her career. She refused to reject the nomination, however, claiming that every member of the MPR had a constitutional right to propose presidential candidates.[21] It may also be that Megawati, mindful of the indignities which Soeharto inflicted upon her late father, relished the opportunity to aggravate his successor.

Megawati's actions in challenging Soeharto polarised Indonesian politics. The government and its supporters were dismissive of her nomination and intensified their efforts to destabilise her leader-

---

[21] *Surabaya Post*, 26 and 30 January 1996; *Forum Keadilan*, 12 February 1996, pp. 100-107; and *Gatra*, 24 February 1996.

ship. For the fragmented opposition movement, though, she became a symbol around which they could rally. Especially as government attempts to remove her from office became more blatant, many opposition and reform groups from outside PDI joined in a loose pro-Megawati alliance. This took on a tangible form with the establishment of MARI (Majelis Rakyat Indonesia: Indonesian People's Council) in June 1996. MARI comprised about fifty activists representing 28 organisations, including PRD, PUDI, Masyumi Baru, PNI Baru, the Legal Aid Institute, the independent trade unions, SBSI and PPBI, the Petition of Fifty group, and various church and Muslim students' groups.[22]

Removal of Megawati and crackdown on opposition

These developments greatly increased the government's determination to remove Megawati from formal politics. Almost since she came to power there had been various regime-sponsored attempts to undermine her leadership. These had included fomenting divisions in the East Java branch, assisting a rival board led by Yusuf Merukh, and accusing various pro-Megawati PDI leaders of having links to the (now defunct) communist party (PKI). But in early May events were set in train which would lead to her ouster. Soerjadi, the PDI chair from 1986 to 1993, and Fatimah Achmad, the head of PDI's parliamentary faction, were recruited to lead the campaign within PDI, and military officials began pressing local branches to call for an extraordinary congress. This eventually took place in Medan, 20-23 June and saw Soerjadi re-elected as PDI chair.

Megawati remained defiant, refusing to attend the congress or recognise Soerjadi's authority. She also launched legal proceedings against the government and the new board, and her supporters refused to vacate the PDI headquarters in Jakarta. On 27 July, pro-government thugs and police stormed the headquarters, sparking the worst riots seen in Jakarta for twenty-two years. Official estimates put the number of dead at five, though many observers believe the real figure to be much higher. Twenty-two buildings and over one hun-

---

[22] *Jawa Pos*, 31 July 1996; *Forum Keadilan*, 12 August 1996, pp. 13 and 19; and *Tapol*, no. 136, August 1996, p. 5.

dred vehicles were also destroyed. In the aftermath of the rioting the government launched an extensive crackdown on opposition groups. It accused the PRD of master-minding the violence and likened its ideology and activities to the PKI. Various PRD and MARI activists, including Budiman Sudjatmiko and Mochtar Pakpahan from SBSI, were arrested and charged with subversion, and many others have been called in for interrogation and warned to refrain from anti-government activities.

Much of the motive force behind both the toppling of Megawati and the clampdown on opposition groups came from Soeharto himself. He had disapproved of Megawati's elevation to the PDI leadership in 1993 and had sanctioned the destabilisation campaign against her. But the prospect of Megawati challenging for the presidency would have greatly hardened his resolve to remove her. He has always insisted upon being re-elected unopposed, thereby maintaining an image of overwhelming endorsement of his rule. To be challenged in 1998 after three decades in office and six successive elections by acclamation would be taken by Soeharto as a deep personal affront. That the challenger should be a Sukarno would only serve to deepen his irritation; Soeharto has long resented the enduring public affection for his predecessor. Some observers have even suggested that such is Soeharto's aversion to competing in a presidential ballot, he would feel compelled to withdraw his nomination rather than endure the humiliation of even a small percentage of the votes being cast against him.

In addition to complicating his own re-election plans, Soeharto may also have regarded Megawati as a threat to Tutut's political fortunes. As Golkar's first deputy chair, she had responsibility for its campaign in East Java, the province where the party faced its heaviest challenge from PDI. At the 1992 election, it lost ten seats in East Java, nine of which went to PDI. For the 1997 election, it was expected that Megawati would be PDI's number one candidate in the province. A poor showing by Golkar in East Java would undoubtedly have tarnished Tutut's political reputation and undermined any plans which Soeharto may have for her to hold high political office.[23]

---

[23] There is considerable speculation in political circles that Soeharto is grooming Tutut for the vice-presidency, with the the intention that she will be his eventual successor.

Soeharto's role in generating the crackdown on opposition and reform groups and use of anti-communist rhetoric has also been noteworthy. During the past year he has repeatedly rejected the need for change to Indonesia's political system[24] and linked opposition to his rule with subversive activities. This began with his warning, in early October 1995, about 'formless organisations' (*organisasi tanpa bentuk*, or OTB) which were spreading communism.[25] The day before the attack on the PDI headquarters Soeharto made the extraordinary statement that there were 'bald devils' (*setan gundul*) riding on the back of the PDI.[26] A week after the riots, the president called a full cabinet meeting at which he described the PRD as anti-government (*makar*) and accused it of having 'methods of thinking and acting like the PKI'.[27] Most recently, he took the unusual step of using his Independence Day speech to declare that PKI-style thinking still 'manifests itself in Indonesia' and that the PRD had used the PDI to spread insurrection.[28] The degree to which Soeharto believes there is a genuine communist threat is a matter of debate but there can be little doubt of his resolve to use it as an instrument of repression.

Some observers have argued that the removal of Megawati and subsequent crackdown was yet another masterful display of authoritarian political management by Soeharto. Once again he has seized the initiative, demonstrated the awesome coercive powers at his disposal, and left his rivals in disarray.[29] Megawati and most of her supporters have been driven from formal politics, and the PDI, now

---

[24] See, for example, *Kompas*, 24 May 1996 and the *Straits Times*, 13 June 1996.

[25] Soeharto's remarks were made public by the Minister for Youth and Sports, Hayono Isman. *Kompas*, 16 October 1995; and *Tiras*, 26 October 1995.

[26] Myths about fearsome bald demons are commonplace amongst Javanese farmers. BBC evening Indonesian-language broadcast, 26 July 1996, and *Far Eastern Economic Review*, 8 August 1996, p. 15.

[27] *Jawa Pos*, 8 August 1996; and *Republika*, 9 August 1996.

[28] *Suara Pembaruan*, 16 August 1996; and Voice of America English-language broadcast, 16 August 1996.

[29] An example of this view is Michael van Langenberg's article, 'Can Indonesia look forward to a more democratic future?', *The Australian*, 13 August 1996, p. 11.

deeply divided and under pro-government leadership, has been disabled as an electoral threat to Golkar. The violence of 27 July has also served to remind the anxious business and professional classes of the continuing need for a strong, military-backed government to maintain order. Last of all, by invoking the spectre of communism, the regime has a pretext for sweeping retaliation against its opponents. Having branded the PRD as 'subversive' and 'PKI-like', the government can now impugn and intimidate the broad coalition of pro-Megawati forces, and indict some of its most vocal critics. Even outspoken retired generals such as Rudini, Wahono, and Bambang Triantoro are to be investigated by Pepabri, the Association of Former Armed Forces' Officers.[30] In short, according to this interpretation, Soeharto has further entrenched his authority and is now free to manage the succession as he sees fit.

In the short term, there is some validity in this interpretation. In the longer term, however, these events have seriously undermined confidence in the regime's competence and harmed the prospects for a smooth transition to a post-Soeharto era. There are several reasons for arguing this. First, there is a strong perception within politically informed sections of Indonesian society that the PDI affair and ensuing unrest were crises of the regime's own making. Indeed, they can be seen as the culmination of three years of inept management of PDI by various ministers and senior ABRI officers. These officials have seemed ill-informed or heedless of the mood within the party, repeatedly backed weak candidates such as Budi Hardjono and Latief Pudjosakti for leadership positions, lost control of two party congresses (that is, the Medan congress of July 1993 and the Surabaya congress in December the same year), and until April 1996, supported Yusuf Merukh's unpopular rival board. The failure of these measures has locked the regime into a cycle of ever-more forceful and legally dubious actions to impose its will on PDI, of which the June 1996 Medan congress and the storming of the PDI headquarters stand as

---

[30] *Media Indonesia*, 3 August 1996.

stark testimony.[31] As a result, unfavourable comparisons are frequently made between the performance of current high officials such as the Internal Affairs Minister, Yogie S. M., Feisal Tanjung, Hartono, Syarwan Hamid, and the chief of general staff, Lt-Gen. Soeyono, and Soeharto's earlier political managers such as Ali Moertopo, Soedjono Hoemardani and Benny Moerdani.

Secondly, the resort to communist conspiracy theories to explain the violence of 27 July is widely seen as spurious and anachronistic. Despite regime claims to the contrary, there has been no verifiable organised communist activity in Indonesia since the late 1960s, and attempts to paint the small and politically marginal PRD as a reincarnation of the PKI have been met with well-deserved scepticism. The incitement of communist-phobia is also increasingly at odds with Indonesia's post-Cold War diplomatic initiatives which have included supporting Vietnam's admission into ASEAN and normalising relations with the People's Republic of China. Not only is the raising of the communist spectre unconvincing for politically-informed Indonesians, there are also strong indications that sections of the cabinet and ABRI leadership are increasingly perturbed by the air of unreality surrounding the government's crackdown.

Soeharto's hardline strategy carries a high level of risk because it fails to address underlying socio-economic problems, and indeed, probably exacerbated tensions by suppressing dissent and vilifying government critics. Growing inequalities of wealth are a key source of resentment, particularly amongst the urban poor. The dangerous level of tension is evident not only in the July violence in Jakarta but also in rioting which broke out in the cities of Purwokerto, Pekalongan and Ujung Pandang during the past year.

---

[31] Another organisation which proved resistant to the regime's political designs was Nahdlatul Ulama (NU). In January 1996, sections of the government endeavoured to oust NU's outspoken chair, Abdurrahman Wahid, by sponsoring an extraordinary congress which duly elected a rival NU board under the leadership of Abu Hasan. The rival board collapsed within three months.

As a result there is heightened anxiety within many sections of the regime and its support base over the prospects for an orderly succession. Fear of social unrest is especially strong amongst the political elite and middle classes. Such unrest would not only imperil Indonesia's continued economic growth but would also threaten the existing structures of social and political power. Within these groups there is a widespread belief that reform is essential if disorder is to be avoided during the transition. This reform process should be gradual and cautious in order to satisfy community demands for political change without jeopardising the privileged position of key elements within the regime such as the armed forces, the oligarchy of elite families, the bureaucracy and the business community. These reforms would include strengthening existing institutions such as parliament and the legal system as well as reducing the endemic levels of corruption and cronyism.

It is for this reason that many of the New Order's more liberal thinkers regarded Megawati's removal as a grave miscalculation. The basis of their argument is that she was a greater political asset than she was a threat. They asserted that in Indonesia's tightly controlled electoral system, a Megawati-led PDI had little chance of increasing its vote sufficiently to challenge Golkar's parliamentary majority.[32] Furthermore, if her presidential nomination had proceeded, she would only have attracted support from a small minority of MPR members. Allowing her to remain as party leader would, however, have signalled a growing political openness and maturity.

Soeharto's determination to tighten further his hold on power and repress reform movements therefore places him at odds with many in his own regime. The dangers of this ever-greater dependence upon one man have been highlighted in recent months by increasing doubts over his judgement and health. Aside from Megawati's removal and the suppression of opposition groups, the president's continued tendency towards arbitrary and nepotistic policy-making remains a major cause of concern. His decision in February to award the

---

[32] Even if the PDI vote increased to 20-25 per cent of the national total, it would still leave Golkar with about 60 per cent, approximately the level of support it enjoyed during the 1970s.

sole 'national car' licence to his youngest son, Hutomo Mandala Putra ('Tommy'), was a particular source of dismay. The decision gave massive tax concessions over three years to one of Tommy's companies to build and market the first 'Indonesian-produced' car, effectively a re-badged Kia sedan from South Korea. Tommy's company had no automotive manufacturing or retailing experience and was later permitted to assemble the car in South Korea using Indonesian labour. The new policy has caused extensive disruption to existing automotive producers and cost the government heavily in forgone tax revenue.[33] Concerns about the president's health arose in July when he went to Germany at short notice for medical tests and treatment. Although he is in relatively good health for a man of his age,[34] there is mounting apprehension about how long he can maintain his present heavy work load. The death of Ibu Tien Soeharto, his wife of 49 years and trusted counsellor, in April also drew attention to his mortality and will to continue as president. Were Soeharto to die in office or become incapacitated the possibility of an intra-elite power struggle and social unrest remains high.[35]

---

[33] *Jakarta Post*, 29 February and 1 March 1996; *Gatra*, 9 March 1996; *Indonesia Media Network*, 29 March 1996; and *Suara Pembaruan* and *Jawa Pos*, 30 May 1996. Whilst there is considerable debate amongst economists on the merits of the 'national car' policy, there was near-unanimity that Tommy should not have been awarded the licence. Soeharto apparently chose Tommy because he felt his youngest son had received fewer lucrative business opportunities than his siblings, Tutut and Bambang.

[34] Soeharto suffers from diabetes, kidney stones and a leaking heart valve, though none of these is deemed serious enough to force him to curtail his official duties.

[35] According to article 8 of the 1945 Constitution, 'should the President die ... or be unable to execute his duties during his term of office, his office shall be taken by the Vice-President until the expiry of that term'. Regardless of who assumes the acting presidency, there is likely to be a power vacuum following Soeharto's departure, as various political forces compete for influence and seek new alliances.

Conclusion

It would be premature to describe the events of mid-1996 as a crisis for the New Order regime, but they have the makings of one. Much depends upon Soeharto. It may be that having reasserted his authority, he will institute measures to ensure a smooth transition at a time of his choosing. Some observers even speak hopefully of the president pursuing the 'Lee Kuan Yew Option' of standing down mid-term and handing power over to a trusted successor. The prospects of this, however, would seem slight. Soeharto gives no sign of preparing to surrender power and indeed, appears to regard himself as indispensable to the prosperity and good order of the nation. He is increasingly remote and intolerant of opinions contrary to his own, and refuses to disclose his plans for the succession or allow candid public debate about political change. He furthermore seems unwilling to curb the vaulting and kleptocratic commercial ambitions of his family and cronies, despite the obvious harm done to his own reputation and that of the New Order political system.

Soeharto's control over the army leadership, the bureaucracy and the political system has virtually ensured his re-election in 1998, though disillusionment and uncertainty over his rule and the direction of the regime continue to mount. At the present time this intra-regime disaffection is held in check by fear of presidential reprisals and a reluctance to deepen divisions within key pillars of the New Order such as ABRI, Golkar and the bureaucratic elite. But Soeharto's hold on power is only secure so long as he continues to deliver economic growth and social stability, the two central planks of his legitimacy. Should he suffer further health problems or commit major errors of judgement which lead to serious social unrest or undermine economic confidence, then pressures will build for him to stand down or be forced from office. The risks of such a confrontation are extreme.

3

Recent Economic Events in Indonesia: From Rapid Economic Growth to National Car Policy

*Anggito Abimanyu**

Introduction

What is driving Indonesia's rapid economic growth? In 1995 the gross domestic product (GDP) grew 8.1 per cent, up from 7.5 per cent in 1994. This trend is expected to continue in 1996, with growth in GDP estimated at 7.5 to 8 per cent. Deregulation of industries has spurred investment in the growing private sector. One of the biggest deregulations of the past year was the floating of Indonesia's Telekom stocks on international stock exchanges to raise funds for servicing development. Since the number of telephones per capita in Indonesia is very low, this move gave a large boost to funds. Foreign participation is needed in highly capital-intensive industries with long pay-back periods, because the domestic market alone cannot supply such massive investments.

Foreign investments flowed in at a record rate of US$39.9 billion for 1995, up from the US$23.7 billion record in 1994. In 1996, however, it is projected that foreign investment approvals are likely to drop by 30 per cent to US$27 billion. During the same year cancellation of

* The author would like to thank Arti Adji, Rio Quiserto, Elan Satriawan, Sari Sitalaksmi and Yenny Ting for their contributons and helpful advice.

foreign investment reached US$458 million—far above the cancellation value for 1995. In an attempt to increase the value of foreign investment for the coming year, the government has introduced selective fiscal incentives for foreign investors.

The direction and pace of deregulation however is currently being questioned by international investors. This policy is looked down upon by World Trade Organisation(WTO) representatives from Europe and US as Indonesia stubbornly thrusts itself into the automobile manufacturing industry (PT Timor case), with the aid of Korean technology.

Concern about Indonesia's current account deficit and inflation has arisen after the current account deficit reached US$6.5 billion, or 3.8 per cent of GDP, in March 1996. The deficit is expected to widen to US$9.2 billion in 1996, and US$7.9 billion in 1997, driven by increasing demand for imported raw materials and capital goods as a result of high foreign investment. During the election year, 1997, greater pressure for expansionary spending from both a strong private sector and the public sector will be evident. This burden however, has been eased by other capital inflows, in the form of portfolio investments and off-shore loans. Meanwhile, inflation is another factor testing Indonesia's impressive record of macro-economic control. Inflation seems to be under control in recent years: down from 9.6 per cent in 1994 to 9.0 per cent in 1995, it may drop to less than 8 per cent in 1996.

Per capita GDP and per capita consumption have improved in every province, an improvement confirmed by social indicators. The incidence of poverty has also declined in all provinces. The growing income inequality between income groups, however, is still an issue which recently reached especially violent proportions. Rioting severely shook the town of Timika, where the difference in welfare between employees of the American-owned mining firm PT Freeport and local residents incited a rampage of destruction. The riots demonstrated the residents' frustration over how the profits, reaped from local resource extraction, are monopolised by the firm and the central government, while redistribution for more employment creation and public services at the point of extraction is ignored.

This chapter reviews major economic events in Indonesia during the August 1995-96 period. High economic growth, recent debates about overheating, the political economy of the 27 July riot and the future of the national car policy are given attention. Despite greater political uncertainty and a slowdown in export performance, current development suggests that strong growth will continue throughout 1996.

Economic growth and sectoral contribution

Indonesian GDP rose in 1995 by 8.1 per cent, compared to 7.5 per cent in 1994. The 1995 growth was again led by domestic demand. The manufacturing and construction sectors continued to expand rapidly, while agriculture, trade and utilities also accelerated. The non-oil GDP aggregate grew 9.0 per cent. GDP from agricultural growth rebounded from the drought-depressed rate of 1994, especially food crops, while non-rice production continued to be much stronger than rice. Meanwhile, forestry was stagnant, owing to weak export demand and supply problems attributable to unsustainable sectoral policies. Within manufacturing, the export-oriented sector grew slowly, while those sectors oriented toward domestic consumption grew more rapidly (see Table 3.1).

TABLE 3.1: Real growth in national output and expenditure (1993 prices, per cent per year)

	1993	1994	1995
GDP	7.3	7.5	8.1
Non-oil & LNG GDP	8.1	7.9	9.0
Agriculture	1.7	0.5	4.0
Non-oil/non-agric. GDP	9.8	9.7	10.1
Manufacturing	13.2	13.5	13.0
Utilities	11.1	12.7	15.5
Construction	14.5	14.9	12.9
Final domestic demand	7.1	8.5	10.2
Consumption	7.4	7.0	9.1
Fixed investment	6.6	12.6	12.9

Source: World Bank (1996) based on data from Biro Pusat Statistik (BPS).

Final domestic demand on the expenditure side has led growth in GDP for the second year in a row. Reflecting the strength in construction, foreign investment and domestic investment approval (up by 33 per cent in 1992-95), fixed investment rose by 13 per cent. The rapid growth of private consumption (compared to growth in GDP) may be attributed to continued sustained real wage growth and the 1995 tax cuts. In contrast, government consumption rose only by 3 per cent in 1995.

Macro-economic policy performance

This section discusses recent macro-economic policy and problems, particularly those associated with monetary and fiscal policy, inflation and the current account deficit. Indonesia has gained a well deserved reputation for sound macro-economic management. In the last ten years, policy adjustments have dealt effectively with a wide range of shocks: the loss of oil revenues after 1985; overheating from the surge in oil revenues and mega-projects in the early 1990s; and fallout from the Mexico crisis in 1995. Although the nature and causes of the past overheating are debatable (see Bird 1996), the economy showed signs of beginning to overheat again in 1995. Increases in consumption and construction demand led to higher non-oil import growth. Despite tightening monetary and fiscal policies, the current account widened markedly, although the inflation rate is predicted to decline to the 7-8 per cent range this year.

Monetary and fiscal policy

There were two important monetary policies made by Indonesia's central bank, Bank Indonesia (BI), between 1995 and 1996, designed to help create macro-economic stability. First, effective from 1 February 1996, BI both increased the reserve requirement from 2 per cent to 3 per cent of banks' current liabilities, and excluded cash from the definition of 'reserves', for the purpose of fulfilling the requirement. If the monetary authorities hold the supply of base money constant, banks will have to reduce their portfolio of loans and deposits significantly to comply with the new reserve ratio, and this will tend to slow monetary expansion. Second, from 1 January 1994 to December 1995 BI widened the exchange rate band of the rupiah several times; BI has increased the band about Rp56 (10 to 66 rupiah). A wider band would reduce incentives for hot money flows thereby also reducing the swings in capital movements. This change of the band would also give BI more control over reserve money.

Indonesia's government has not been as active in the implementation of fiscal policy as it has in monetary policy. In 1994, there was a tax reform that was intended to make Indonesia's tax rates competitive with other Southeast Asian countries. Another aim of this new tax was to help stimulate investment and growth in the more remote regions of the country. In 1995 and 1996, under its tax incentive program, the government tried again to boost investment by granting a tax holiday. Indonesia's economic performance since the tax reform of 1986 suggests that higher taxes and the absence of tax incentives have not been the only factors involved in luring new investment. Other more important policies, such as providing infrastructure to support business, building roads, providing electricity etc., are better lures for potential investors than those mentioned above.

In a traditional closed market economy, a combination of tighter monetary and fiscal policy would be suggested for stabilising economic conditions on a macro scale. Indonesia is, like so many other countries in the world, opening its doors to the global marketplace. In an open economy, managing the money and credit aggregates is difficult, owing to interest-elastic capital flows which tend to offset open market operations. Changes in domestic credit can be offset by changes in international reserves; this will reduce the effect on reserve money.

In the short run, the central bank may still be able to strengthen monetary policy's impact on the domestic economy by widening the intervention band. However, in the long run monetary policy has its limitations. BI will find it difficult to sustain an interest rate which differs greatly from international rates. Attempts to maintain an interest rate much below world levels will eventually exhaust the finite stock of international reserves. If Indonesia's central bank chooses to pursue a tight money policy this will result in an increase in domestic interest rates. Given expectations holding the rate of depreciation of the rupiah against the US dollar constant, high domestic interest rates will attract capital inflow from abroad, offsetting the original contraction of money.

Taking into account the limitations of monetary policy, used in isolation, in orchestrating change in an open economy, a proper mixture of both monetary and fiscal policy needs to be developed which fits that country's specific needs. In the case of Indonesia, government should make fiscal policy more contra-cyclical, which means running small overall surpluses during times of cyclical upturns and strictly earmarking these surpluses to undefined long-term liabilities, such as the civil servants' pension funds or debt prepayments.

Inflation

Consumer prices in 1995 rose by 9.0 per cent (see Table 3.2), the fifth time during the past six years that increase in consumer prices has been between 9 and 10 per cent. In 1995, slower growth in housing prices, in part reflecting a slowdown in Jakarta's real estate boom, accounted for a large proportion of the decline in inflation, compared to the previous year's figure. Inflation accelerated in the first and second quarter of 1996. Flood-related supply disruptions were a factor, but all major categories (except energy) also rose sharply. The high demand for foodstuffs around Idhul Fitri (end of the fasting period) contributed to the inflation rate in the first quarter of 1996. In April the government announced increases in transportation tariffs that will put additional upward pressure on inflation. Price increases for the rest of the year will need to average around 0.5 per cent per month to keep inflation below 10 per cent during 1996. The last Economic Ministries Meeting in October 1996 (Sidang Kabinet Menteri EKUWASBANG) announced an August inflation figure of -0.68 per cent.

The current account deficit

The current account deficit rose from 2 per cent of GDP in 1994 to about 4 per cent, or US$7.9 billion in 1995. The current account deficit will swell to US$8.8 billion (4 per cent of GDP) in this fiscal year. Both macro-economic and structural factors underlie this current account imbalance. Essentially, it occurs because investment expenditure is in excess of domestic savings, leading to an inflow of capital to finance the difference. In other words, the deficit reflects an excess of expenditure over income. Concern over the current account deficit is justified if investment financed by foreign sources is inefficient and non-productive (James 1996).

TABLE 3.2: Indonesian inflation rate, 1994-96
based on Consumer Price Index

Group	1994	1995	1995 Jan-July	1996 Jan-July
General	9.24	8.64	6.09	4.71
Food	13.93	13.32	9.68	4.32
Housing	9.09	5.67	4.11	3.33
Clothing	6.08	6.50	4.43	4.55
Others	4.89	7.00	4.53	7.31

Source: BPS (July)1996. *Buletin Ringka*s.

Indonesia's growth rate of exports in 1995 was low compared to that of some neighbouring countries. However during the first semester of 1996, Indonesian export growth has held up as well as, or better than, most other Asian countries. Non-oil exports grew by 15 per cent in 1995, and have maintained growth of 13 per cent in the first semester of 1996. Mining and a wide variety of industrial products, including processed rubber, paper, electrical goods, and ores and metal products have been the major contributors to this rapid growth. Major agriculture commodity exports such as coffee, cocoa, and tea declined in 1995, principally owing to failing international commodity prices. Manufacturing products, notably plywood and to a lesser extent garments, continue to suffer from the same problems as last year.

In the capital account, increased foreign direct investment and other capital inflows financed the wider current account deficit and build up of reserves. Portfolio investment has also stimulated the growing private sector, particularly the telecommunication sector. PT Telkom and PT Indosat, together with PT Timah (Tin company), have raised capital for servicing development through international stock offerings. Part of these funds (US$1.5 billion) was used to pay back existing foreign debt (*Presidential Speech*, August 1996).

Industry, trade and deregulation

Recent trade and industrial performance

The decline in growth of Indonesian exports during the past year is not unique, as export growth across Asia has slowed significantly since the first half of 1995 (see Table 3.3). Compared to other Asian countries (see figures on China, Japan, Singapore, and Thailand for example), Indonesia's growth rate of exports shows a better performance. The causes of slowing export growth are mainly linked to external conditions, and panic over this trend should be avoided.

Yet the decline of export growth rates in the current year, like last year, was also due to internal problems such as the weak competitive performance of leading commodities, bureaucracy, high costs and illegal payments (bribes) (*Warta Ekonomi*, 7 October 1996: 11). The competitiveness of 10 leading commodities in the international market is now being questioned for future sustainability. Continued deregulation and a sound macro-economic environment will provide investors with the stable and predictable conditions they require to compete successfully in international markets. On the other hand,

TABLE 3.3: Asian economies' export growth slowdown (per cent change)

Country	1996 Jan-June	1995 Jan-June	1995 Year
China	-8.2	44.8	23.1
Hong Kong	6.1	18.0	14.6
Taiwan	6.4	22.7	20.0
Indonesia			
(non-oil exports)	10.5	15.4	13.3
	13.1	15.2	15.1
Japan	-7.9	18.2	12.1
Korea	12.0	33.5	30.5
Malaysia	16.5	30.4	25.9
Philippines	20.0	31.5	28.4
Singapore	7.4	15.8	22.6
Thailand	6.0	31.7	23.1

Source: IMF, DOTS *World Total Exports*.

special fiscal or financial incentives such as import restrictions are likely to be ineffective or even counter-productive.

Table 3.4 shows that textile exports increased by 8.2 per cent, from US$2,269 million in January-June 1995, to US$2,455 million in January-June 1996. Exports of a number of other products grew much more rapidly than this, though from a lower base. The only negative export groth recorded was for processed wood (-0.05 per cent).

TABLE 3.4: Growth and composition of 10 leading non-oil exports (US$ million)

Commodity	1995 Jan-June	1996 Jan-June	Growth 1995-96 (%)
Textile	2,269.0	2,455.9	8.2
Wood products	2,199.6	2,198.6	-0.05
Rubber	902.9	964.5	6.8
Electronic	889.4	963.8	8.4
Leather, leather goods and shoes	918.1	937.3	4.3
Steel and machinery	623.3	939.7	50.8
CPO	573.4	715.2	24.7
Pulp and paper	499.1	554.2	11.1
Food and beverage	239.2	337.8	41.2
Gold, silver and metal	183.9	334.7	82.1
Total 10	9,297.8	10,421.7	12.1

Source: Deperindag (MITI), September 1996.

On the import side, between January and May 1996, the total value reached US$17,247 billion, of which the import of raw materials (US$12,327) accounted for around 71 per cent (Table 3.5). Meanwhile, imports of capital goods topped 20 per cent (US$3,440) and consumption goods about 9 per cent. Rapidly expanding imports, especially those of raw materials, indicate the fragility of Indonesia's supporting industries, since the increased imports were mainly goods used by downstream industries, which were unable to obtain necessary materials domestically. Import of raw materials in the food sector grew by 147 per cent, while processed raw materials grew by 3.8 per cent. Despite contributing only a small amount to total imports (9 per cent),

**TABLE 3.5: Imports by broad economic categories, Jan-June
1995-96 (US$ million)**

Month	Consumer Goods		Raw Materials		Capital Goods	
	1995	1996	1995	1996	1995	1996
Qrt-I	521	763	6,626	6,978	1,794	1,875
April	227	307	2,213	2,648	646	734
May	222	408	2,310	2,701	733	831
Total	970	1478	11,149	12,327	3,173	3,440

Source: BPS (August)1996. *Indikator Ekonomi* [Economic Indicators].

imports of consumption goods grew 40 per cent in May 1996 compared to the same period a year before.

The food sector accounted for the largest share of consumption
imports (US$647,791 million), a hike of 71 per cent. Non-durable
goods came in second, reaching US$106,913 million. During the first
quarter of 1996, imports of capital goods reached US$2,610 million or
an increase of 6.9 per cent—far below imports of raw materials
(*Kompas*, 6 August 1996).

The above figures on export and import performance show a
spillover of rising demand into imports because of short-term
domestic production. Domestic industries still depend heavily on
imports. Imports of raw materials have been growing rapidly, while
imports of capital goods have been sluggish. Augmentation of capital
goods is the engine of production, since without it there would be no
increase in production. Sluggish growth in production capacity will
widen the gap between aggregate demand and supply, in turn leading
to a higher value of imports. Capital injection via new foreign
investment appears to be the solution to this problem. Nevertheless,
attracting foreign investment is not easy, as investors emphasise the
rate of return of the firms they invest in. In line with today's increasing
globalisation, investors no longer care about nationalist issues but
focus their funds where they will reap the highest return. Many

investors claim the Indonesian investment climate is challenged by complicated bureaucracy and lack of transparency. In 1996, the cancellation of foreign investment reached US$458 million (25 projects) far above the cancellation value for 1995 of only US$29.3 million (8 projects). Most projects are cancelled at the request of prospective investors.

Trade deregulation

In a bid to encourage export competitiveness, the government announced a deregulation package in January 1996. This package reduces tariffs on 428 products by 5 to 15 percentage points. This will facilitate cost decreases for imported raw materials used in producing export products. This package also allows foreign firms to export farm, forest, fish, mining, and manufactured products. Furthermore, foreign firms are allowed to be involved in the distribution of goods used by producers in the special export processing zones, i.e. Kawasan Berikat (KB) and Entrepot Produksi Tujuan Ekspor (EPTE). Goods supplied to producers in these zones are also granted an import duty facility.

In February 1996, the government announced a policy on the automotive industry. This policy is aimed at enhancing the production of a national car. This led to an acrimonious debate between the government, especially the Ministry of Trade and Industry, and economists, and is discussed later in this paper.

In June 1996, the government announced another deregulation package scheduling tariff reduction, simplifying the import distribution system and establishing an anti-dumping committee. The June deregulation, which contains 11 outward-oriented steps aimed at achieving better non-oil and gas export performance, might appear to counter the current account deficit. Nevertheless, this deregulation contains discriminatory elements by facilitating only certain exporting firms in certain industrial sectors. This exception would be generally accepted if there were a logical economic reason behind it, but unfortunately, such a reason cannot be found. Despite the discriminatory elements, the establishment of an anti-dumping committee was a good step, as Indonesia has been a target for the dumping of products, but there has been no action to counter dumping because of the lack of an institution with the authority to handle this problem. On the other hand, Indonesia is facing the European Community's charge of dumping footwear and textile goods. It is now the duty of the anti-dumping committee to overcome this charge.

Vested interests challenge Indonesia's industrial performance. Although in September 1995, the government refused PT Chandra Asri Petrochemical Centre's request for protection, the refusal was withdrawn in February 1996. The government raised the tariff rate on propylene and ethylene imports by 20 percentage points. This protection will affect industries that use propylene and ethylene-derived inputs. Other key industries affected are plastics and imitation leather footwear. Meanwhile, the phenomenon of rent-seeking action continues to appear. All pesticide producers are required to have stickers which guarantee their product safety. Economically, it is fine to sticker the products, but it is disconcerting that the right to sell the sticker is not decided through a transparent competitive process. The private company which sells the stickers will certainly profit from their sale and, in turn, this will increase the price of pesticides borne by farmers (Bird 1996).

The anti-competitive phenomenon in industrial performance has been attracting economists' attention in recent years. The presence of monopolies and oligopolies is one of the favourite topics of industrial economists. A study by Abimanyu and Xie (1995) concludes that industrial concentration in Indonesia remains high and there is no indication of a long-term decline. They suggest, however, that concentration ratios alone are not sufficient to infer the lack of competition in an industry. It is possible for an industry to achieve competitive pricing of products although it is highly concentrated over time. The sheet glass industry is a highly concentrated industry with competitive pricing products (Xie and De Bruynkops 1995). Recently, public attention has been paid to the behaviour of Indonesian oligopolies, whose price-setting behaviour is suspected of disadvantaging consumers. A highly concentrated industrial sector is suspected of contributing to the rate of inflation.

Does industrial concentration in Indonesia induce inflation? A study has been conducted aimed at analysing the impact of industrial concentration upon price adjustment in Indonesia. Using an error-correction estimation, this study found that a one per cent increase in ratio of concentration (CR4) leads to a 0.69 per cent increase in price adjustment. Using the Hirschman-Herfindahl Index as a measure of industrial concentration, this study yielded consistent estimates. Indonesian industrial data (3-digit and 5-digit ISIC, 1975-94) suggest that co-operation between sellers is more effective where industrial concentration is high. In highly concentrated sectors which are characterised by low costs of search and communication among sellers, price changes can be effectively co-ordinated and thus the process of adjustment to equilibrium can be speeded up. Prices in highly concentrated oligopolistic sectors have shown a tendency to move in parallel fashion. Imperfect co-operation may impede price change at low levels of concentration, but oligopolistic co-ordination may improve as concentration rises. Therefore, the rate of industrial price adjustment is positively and consistently related to concentration (Adji 1996).

Timor case

The Minister for Trade and Industry gave a tax exemption to a new company owned by Tommy Soeharto, PT Timor Putra Nasional (PT. Timor). PT Timor was granted a monopoly preferential status for national car production in co-operation with Kia Motors from South Korea and the car will sell at a price of Rp35 million, 30 per cent or more below that of competitors in the same vehicle size category (Manning and Jayasuria 1996). According to Inpres 2/1996, a national car is one produced by a 100-per cent Indonesian-owned company and must contain 60 per cent domestic components. PT Timor, however, will utilise only 20 per cent of domestic components in the first year of production, 40 per cent in the second year, and 60 per cent in the third year. Timor, the brand name of the prospective national car, will be exempt from 35-per cent luxury tax and import duty on components for three years. The production of Timor will begin in 1998. At the beginning, Timor will not be produced domestically. For the first year, PT Timor will import completely assembled sedans from Kia until it builds a components factory. On 4 June the president decreed that PT Timor can import 45.000 cars until June 1997. It seems that PT Timor cannot pull together the production line and tools needed for domestic production (Bird 1996; *Business Asia*, 25 March, 20 June 1996).

The special treatment awarded to PT Timor angered foreign auto companies, especially those of Japan and USA. During the past two decades, Japanese auto industries have maintained a 90 per cent share of the auto market in Indonesia. Foreign companies cannot qualify for tax exemption and import duty reduction. Following the presidential decree stating that Timor can be assembled in South Korea and exported back to Indonesia for a maximum period of a year while enjoying tax exemption (*Japan Times*, 1 June 1996), Japan and the US announced that they would bring Indonesian auto policy before the WTO by September 1996. The MITI of Japan has argued that the decree deviated from fair, non-discriminatory and liberal trade under the WTO. The aim of the Indonesian government to produce national cars does not deviate from free trade. Yet its strategy to produce national cars, namely the special facility awarded to PT Timor, contravenes the spirit of free trade. Meanwhile, the Indonesian government argues that the policy on the national car is conducted because during two decades of foreign involvement in the domestic auto industry, there has not been a transfer of technology. It seems that the Indonesian government will not step back and review its controversial national car policy. Therefore, there is little possibility for the two parties to bridge the gap between their different views.

Foreign companies were not the only parties bitter over the 4 June decree. PT Bimantara, owned by Tommy's older brother, Bambang Trihatmodjo, had hoped to produce a national car in cooperation with Hyundai from South Korea. On economic grounds, PT Bimantara would have been a better choice than PT Timor. It already has an assembly factory and access to Hyundai technology. Economists could not see logical economic reasons to explain the choice of PT Timor over PT Bimantara to head the national car program. Nevertheless, without the privilege of tax exemption, PT Bimantara plans to continue its production of national cars, Cakra and Nenggala. A top executive of Bimantara says that it will take three years for the company to achieve 60-per cent domestic components, a level with zero per cent of import duty. Its Elantra sedan has already reached 17.2 per cent domestic components, and it will reach 60 per cent after completing a 100,000 unit a year assembly line in 1998 (*Far Eastern Economic Review*, 20 and 27 June 1996).

The national car program does have an impact on the domestic auto market. Domestic consumers are in doubt about whether to buy new cars. They expect the auto price to decrease owing to the national car policy. In 1996, figures for auto sales decreased 10-15 per cent. Meanwhile, in September 1997, PT Bakrie Motor plans to launch a multi-purpose van under the brand of Bakrie. The leader of the Bakrie group says that in the first year, the van will reach 40 per cent of local content, 45-50 per cent in the second year, and 60 per cent in the third year, a level at which component duty falls to zero. The Bakrie group says that it will not ask for government facilities. Yet, using the presidential decree as the benchmark, Bakrie should receive tax exemption after reaching 60 per cent local content *(Kompas,* 5 August 1996).

In only two months after the Presidential decree on the national car was announced, more than two auto companies other than PT Timor have responded by launching their own national cars. The consumers seem to approve: two or three players are better than one and consumers may gain even more, at least in the short term. The producers, on the other hand, may be the big losers, particularly if their sales are significantly affected.

To sum up, there is still an ambivalence in government policies. On the one hand, it continues to conduct packages of deregulation to increase export competitiveness in anticipation of a freer market. On the other hand, policies such as the national car policy fly in the face of economic liberalisation.

Regional development, labour and environmental issues

Although per capita CDP and per capita consumption have improved in every province, together with a consistent decline in the incidence of poverty in all regions, a number of challenges remain. Disparities in poverty levels persist. Some social indicators remain similar to those in low-income countries. The numbers of the poor remain large in Java and Sumatra, and poverty incidence is high in the eastern part of Indonesia. Decentralisation, backed by resource mobilisation by 'subnational' administration would help to meet these challenges, particularly helping the off-Java provinces grow faster and reduce the need for large-scale transfer. In many cases, however, the government of Indonesia's limited decentralisation initiatives were taken within the constraints of a heavily centralised system (Kuncoro 1993).

The government announced that the daily minimum wage would rise by an (unweighted) average of 10.6 per cent in 1996. The increases in the heavily industrialised areas of West Java were near 13 per cent; in total they ranged from 5.4 per cent in East Java to 14.3 per cent in Central Sulawesi. The minimum wage, however, is not an appropriate tool for poverty alleviation because it covers only formal-sector employees. The government has now continued and expanded its poverty alleviation program through the Inpres Desa Tertinggal (IDT) project.

The quality of growth is an issue in Indonesia today. Although Indonesia has made significant progress in its regime of industrial control, this progress has met legal, institutional and technical barriers, limiting the effectiveness of industrial pollution control. Beyond command and control type instruments, Indonesia now utilises an instrument of company rating to control pollution. In June 1995, Indonesia launched a program to publicly disclose the performance of environmental polluters. This initiative, called the Program for Pollution Control, Evaluation and Rating (PROPER), is expected to promote compliance with existing regulations and reward firms whose performance exceeds regulatory standards. Under PROPER, polluters are assigned a colour rating from gold (excellent) to black for very poor (Table 3.6). The table shows that domestic and public companies performed relatively poorly in comparison with foreign firms. PROPER ratings were publicised, allowing readers to make their own judgment on which firms comply with the environmental regulations. Firms will be rated in coming years to give them an ongoing incentive to reduce pollution.

TABLE 3.6: Business performance rating based on 187 polluting facilities in Java and Sumatra, 1995

Ranks	Domestic Firms (PMDN)	Foreign Firms (PMA)	Public Companies (BUMN)
Gold	0	0	0
Green	0.8	7.4	2.8
Blue	30.3	70.7	50.0
Red	65.9	19.5	47.2
Black	3.0	2.4	0
Total	100.0	100.0	100.0

Source: BAPEDAL (National Pollution Control Agency) 1996.

APPENDIX

The impact of the 27 July riot on the economy

That the Indonesian economic ground is strong should be questioned again now that political issues such as succession and, particularly, the 27 July riots have shaken the stability of the economy. However, it seems that the investment climate and local exchange rate against the US dollar in the markets have returned to normal. At the end of July, local exchange rates against the greenback fell from Rp2,338 per dollar to 2,357 per dollar. By August 5, the rate had risen to Rp2,343. Meanwhile the Jakarta Stock Exchange Cumulative Stock Price Index fell by 20.57 points on 28 July 1996 but had risen again by 20.18 points at the beginning of August 1996.

The 27 July riot is a caution for foreign investors. 'The country risk profile is much higher now', said Carey Humprey, the president of emerging markets at Foreign & Colonial in an interview with *Warta Ekonomi* in August 1996.

Foreign investors will probably hold up investment until the end of 1996 or reduce their portfolios in Indonesia. Hence, investment will slow down for some time. Since the incident resulted from political matters, monetary policy might not affect the shaky ground of the Indonesian economy. It is therefore important for the government to take political action to stabilise the economy (*Kompas*, August 1996).

Although foreign investors will now be more careful in investing in Indonesia, government and local entrepreneurs appear to be very confident about the positive trend of Indonesia's business climate. Nevertheless, other political incidents in the future will greatly affect the business climate. As the Asian Executives Poll in the *Far Eastern Economic Review* (August 1996) shows, in Indonesia the political situation is seen as critical to economic stability.

Anggito Abimanyu

FIGURE A3.1: Exchange rate of Rupiah against the US dollar before and after the 27 July riot.

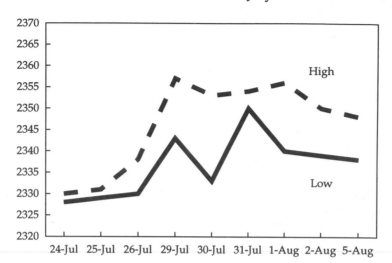

FIGURE A3.2: Cumulative Stock Price Index on the Jakarta Stock Exchange before and after the 27 July riot.

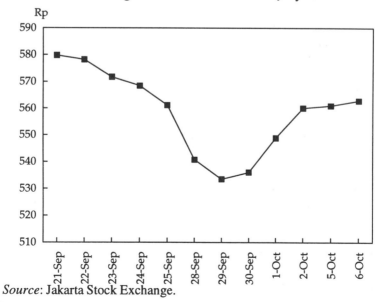

Source: Jakarta Stock Exchange.

PART B: POPULATION AND
HUMAN RESOURCE
DEVELOPMENT

4

Population and Human Resources: Indonesia's Demographic Place in the Larger Scene

John C. Caldwell

This brief introduction will assign Indonesia a place in the global demographic transition, which is converting the world from a place of high birth and death rates to one where both levels are low. For countless millennia life expectancies at birth were little more than 20 years. Now some countries, including Australia, have reached 78 years. Even the lowest level in the world now exceeds 40 years. Similarly, total fertility rates (the average number of live births per woman over a lifetime at current annual rates) probably exceeded six for aeons. Now, levels around one, or half that needed for long-term replacement, are being recorded for the first time. Nevertheless, some countries still exhibit total fertility rates over six. They are mostly in sub-Saharan Africa but four are found in ESCAP Asia and another four in Western Asia.

Table 4.1 shows that Indonesia, with a population around 200 million, is a giant in this part of the world. It is the home of over two-fifths of the population of South East Asia and has eleven times the population of Australia. In comparison with the real giants of Asia, China and India, Indonesia is small and its population constitutes only 6 per cent of that of the whole continent. The three other large countries of South East Asia, Vietnam, Philippines and Thailand, together add up to approximately the same population as Indonesia.

TABLE 4.1: Indonesia in perspective, 1995

		Population	Per capita income
	Indonesia	198 m	US$730
Comparisons:[a]	South East Asia	41%	68%
	Asia	6%	37%
	World	3%	16%
	Australia	11 times	4%
Three other largest	Thailand	60 m	US$2,040
South East Asian	Philippines	68 m	US$830
countries	Vietnam	75 m	US$170

[a] Indonesia as a fraction of the other listed areas.
Source: PRB 1995.

By Asian standards, Indonesia is relatively poor with a per capita income only two-thirds of that of South East Asia as a whole. It might be noted that the total economy of Indonesia is less than half the size of that of Australia.

Mortality

Indonesia, like most of the rest of the world, has enormously reduced its mortality since the end of Second World War (Table 4.2). A life expectancy of 38 years in the first half of the 1950s increased over the next four decades by 25 years, showing an average gain of almost 0.6 years for every elapsed year. During this period, Indonesia slowly reduced the gap between its mortality level and that of both South East Asia and Asia as a whole and also that of the world. Its performance compared with Thailand and Vietnam and was significantly better than the Philippines. It has not yet reached the much slower rate of improvement that characterises low-mortality countries such as Australia. Infant mortality rates fell during those decades to two-fifths of the earlier level.

TABLE 4.2: Mortality

	1950-55	1965-69	1995
Indonesia			
Life expectancy (years)	38	46	63
Infant mortality rate			
(per 1,000 live births)	160	124	64
1995 life expectancy comparisons			
South East Asia	41	49	64
Asia	41	54	65
World	46	56	66
Australia	70	71	78
Thailand	47	57	70
Philippines	48	56	65
Vietnam	40	48	65

Sources: United Nations 1995c; PRB 1995.

The onset of fertility transition

In most Western countries, including Australia, fertility began to fall during the last third of the nineteenth century and is now below long-term replacement levels. Table 4.3 shows that the Indonesian decline began around 1970, fairly typical of Asia and the Third World as a whole. Propelled by a highly organised family planning program from the late 1960s, fertility decline has been steeper than anything known in the Western experience. The current total fertility rate of 2.8 is slightly below that of Asia as a whole and considerably below the Third World average. It is also below the South East Asian average. The United Nations (1995c) Medium Population Projections show Indonesia's fertility reaching long term replacement about twenty years from now, although the momentum of growth will probably ensure continued natural increase for another half-century with stationary population probably not being achieved under 350 million people.

TABLE 4.3: Fertility (total fertility rates)[a]

	1950-55	Last year before onset of marked fertility decline		1995
		Year	TFR	
Indonesia	6.4	1970	5.5	2.8
Thailand	6.6	1965	6.4	2.2
Philippines	7.3	1965	6.6	4.1
Vietnam	6.1	1980	5.6	3.7
Singapore	6.4	1958	6.0	1.8
Hong Kong	4.4	1958	5.3	1.2
South Korea	5.2	1965	6.1	1.6
Taiwan		1965		1.8
Malaysia	6.8	1965	6.7	3.3
India	6.0	1965-70	5.7	3.4
Bangladesh	6.7	1975	7.0	4.3

[a]Average life-time births per woman if the fertility levels for the specified period are held constant.

Source: United Nations 1995; PRB 1995.

Indonesia's fertility decline has been impressive compared with the Philippines and Vietnam, although the latter is now catching up by employing a somewhat coercive national family planning program with a considerable level of legal abortion. Richer South East and East Asian countries have achieved lower fertility. The country that has done better than Indonesia, and has achieved replacement fertility with no real government pressure, is Thailand. There, a demographic revolution has clearly accompanied a largely spontaneous economic one.

TABLE 4.4: Contraception, 1994

	% using FP[a]	1st method	2nd method	3rd method
Indonesia[b]	50	Pill (15%)	Other supply (15%)	IUD (13%)
Thailand	66	Fem. sterilisation (23%)	Pill (19%)	Other supply (9%)
Philippines	40	Other non-supply(25%)	Fem. sterilisation (12%)	Pill (9%)
Vietnam	53	IUD (33%)	Other (15%)	Other supply (15%)
Singapore	74	Condom (14%)	Fem. sterilisation (22%)	Pill (12%)
South Korea	79	Fem. sterilisation (35%)	Male sterilisation (12%)	Condom (10%)
Malaysia	48	Other non-supply (17%)	Pill (15%)	Condom (6%)
India	43	Fem. and male sterilisation(30%)		Condom (5%)
Bangladesh	40	Pill (14%)	Fem. sterilisation (9%)	Other non-supply (9%)

[a] Percentages using each method are percentages of all couples where the wife is of reproductive age.

[b]Female sterilisation = 3%; male sterilisation = 1%; condom = 1%.

Source: United Nations 1994b.

Indonesia has achieved its family planning success in spite of the need to overcome considerable obstacles. Most successful Asian family planning programs have relied on methods which need infrequent contact with family planning workers. The backbone of these programs has been female and male sterilisation, intra-uterine contraceptive devices (IUDs) and often abortion (Table 4.4). The Indian program has been driven by sterilisation which has changed its focus over the decades from males to females. Excluding abortion because of its unsatisfactory statistics, sterilisation and the IUD have accounted for nearly 90 per cent of all fertility control in rural India and rural

China. The two very successful early programs, those of South Korea and Taiwan, were originally largely IUD programs. China and Vietnam employ abortion as a major back-up service, and it has long provided much of Japan's fertility control.

Indonesia has found sterilisation and abortion to be largely culturally unacceptable, although there is a cautious movement towards menstrual regulation. In contrast, half of all control of fertility in Indonesia is achieved by hormonal methods, the pill and more recently Norplant. This has meant an expensive program with intensive use of labour. Indonesian resources have been devoted to the family planning program in a way that they have not been to health services.

Marriage and early fertility

The Indonesia fertility transition has not been preceded or accompanied by a dramatic rise in female age at marriage, as was the case, for instance, in Sri Lanka and parts of the West. The Demographic and Health Surveys of the late 1980s showed that half of Indonesian women were still marrying before 20 years of age, compared with little more than one-third in Thailand and one-quarter in Sri Lanka (Table 4.5). In fact, Indonesia compares with Pakistan where the relative position of women to men and women's educational levels are much inferior to those of Indonesia.

TABLE 4.5: Marriage and early fertility

	% of women 20-24 marrying before 20 years	% of women 20-24 giving birth before 20 years	% of ever-married women married more than once
Indonesia	51	36	16
Thailand	37	24	9
Sri Lanka	28	17	2
Pakistan	49	30	2

Source: Westoff *et al*. 1994.

Indeed, over one-third of Indonesian women still give birth to their first child before 20 years of age, a higher level than even in Pakistan and more than double the Sri Lankan level.

A striking aspect of marriage among both Indonesians and Malays has been the high level of divorce. These levels have been declining rapidly but divorce in Indonesia is still well above other Asian levels and compares with the contemporary situation in much of the West.

Comparisons

Table 4.6 attempts to place Indonesia in comparative perspective by employing ranking scales where performance of countries is ranked from the best to the worst in developmental perspective.

TABLE 4.6: Indonesia's comparative demographic rankings, 1995[a]

	Area of comparison		
	World[b]	ESCAP Asia[c]	Southeast Asia[d]
Per capita income	79	15	6
Life expectancy	90	17	7
Infant mortality rate	88	15	7
Total fertility rate	59	10	3

[a]Rankings from best to worst (best − highest p.c.i., and life expectancy; lowest infant mortality rate and total fertility rate).

[b]Out of 133 countries with populations exceeding one million.

[c]Out of 33 countries from Iran to Japan.

[d]Out of 10 countries (Brunei, Cambodia, Indonesia, Laos, Malaysia, Myanmar, Philippines, Singapore, Thailand, Vietnam).

Source: World Bank 1996; ESCAP 1995.

Of the 133 countries with populations of more than one million identified by the World Bank , Indonesia's per capita income is at the 79th rank or about three-fifths of the way from top to bottom. Thus, if income is to be the chief determinant of demographic change, Indonesia does relatively poorly in terms of health with life expectancy ranked 90th. On the other hand, it has done relatively well with regard to fertility where its relatively low fertility compares with Latin American levels.

With regard to mortality, Indonesia performs only a little below expectations based on income when the comparison is made with ESCAP Asia or South East Asia. Though its health performance is rather average, its low fertility is quite outstanding in either of these comparisons.

Overview

Indonesia's demographic transition is well under way. Like much of Asia it has added 25 years to its life expectancy over little more than four decades. Yet it is salutary to realise that United Nations Demographic Projections do not anticipate a life expectancy at birth of 75 years until the middle of next century. The somewhat mediocre improvement in health compares with one of the world's better records in reducing fertility and hence natural increase. Nevertheless, the failure of infant and child mortality to fall particularly fast may begin to place a constraint upon how fast fertility can contrive to fall. Partly because of this, and partly because the 1994 Cairo International Population and Development Conference's *Programme of Action* places an emphasis not only on better reproductive health but also on better health in general, Indonesia might well consider the advisability of placing as much emphasis on health services as on family planning.

Population Mobility and

Urbanisation

5

Changing Patterns and Processes of Population Mobility

Graeme Hugo

Introduction

While Indonesia has been experiencing rapid social and economic change over recent years, Indonesians' movement on a permanent or temporary basis has changed significantly in scale, nature, spatial patterning and composition. The relationships between these changes and wider social, economic, political and demographic change is complex, two-way and little understood. This paper seeks to document some of the major shifts which have occurred in population mobility in Indonesia over the last decade or so, paying particular attention to the contemporary period. In undertaking this task a range of sources are accessed. These include the 1990 Census and other national statistical data sets but substantial use is also made of the growing body of case studies of the causes and consequences of population movement in Indonesia. The latter reflect a growing recognition within Indonesia of the economic, social and political significance of population mobility, not only by researchers but also by policy makers and planners.

The paper demonstrates, insofar as is possible with the available data, that the overall propensity of Indonesians to move on both a permanent and temporary basis has increased over the last two decades, and that the movement has become more complex with respect

* The fieldwork for this article was undertaken in Jakarta and Yogyakarta during June-July 1996. I am grateful to the organising committee of the Indonesia Update 1996 for providing financial assistance which enabled me to conduct this research.

to the types of movement taking place. This especially has involved increasing levels of non-permanent movement, movement within and between urban areas, and international movements, especially labour migration. It is demonstrated also that population movement has become less selective with respect to gender, age, region of origin and class. The ethnic dimension in Indonesian mobility is discussed, along with the greatly increased significance of female migration. Some important shifts in the spatial patterning of population movement are observed, including increased levels of rural to urban movement and a reversal of the trends of the 1960s, 1970s and early 1980s of increasing net redistribution of population from Inner Indonesia to Outer Indonesia.

The causes of the changing patterns, levels and composition of mobility are addressed in terms of a number of theories of internal migration. Clearly, the pace and nature of economic and social change in Indonesia have been of critical significance in reshaping population mobility. However, it is argued also that labour market segmentation, network and institutional factors all have been of significance as has government intervention. It is considered that the trends identified in Indonesia with respect to population mobility in the early 1990s are likely to intensify rather than change fundamentally in the second half of the decade.

Some data considerations

Any assessment of population mobility in Indonesia is constrained by the limited nature of the sources of data available for such an analysis. The main sources of such data are the decennial national censuses and these have been critically assessed elsewhere (Hugo 1982a). The main limitations can be summarised as follows:

- Internal migration data collected in the census only relate to interprovincial migrations which constitute less than a fifth of all permanent moves made in the country.
- The census data fail to detect most non-permanent migration.
- Since the origin of migrants is only coded to the provincial level, migration cannot be categorised into rural-urban, rural-rural, urban-urban and urban-rural migrations.
- The census does not collect data on international labour migration out of the country.

Most concerted efforts to overcome these limitations were made in the 1995 Intercensal Survey (SUPAS) which included more questions on migration than any previous census or national survey including one on place of residence five years previously (October 1990) coded down to *kelurahaan* and differentiated by rural and urban character.[1] Unfortunately, the results of SUPAS were not available at the time of writing the present paper. This is doubly unfortunate since it is argued in this paper that a significant reconfiguration of interprovincial migration has occurred in Indonesia in the last decade and that this has become especially pronounced in the period since the 1990 Census. The 1990 Census data which are presented and discussed here do, however, give strong indications of these changes.

While there has been little change until the 1995 SUPAS in the nature of national migration data collected in Indonesia, our knowledge of the patterns, processes and impacts of population mobility more broadly defined has been considerably extended via a number of detailed case studies and subnational surveys. Many of these studies are used here in an attempt to present a comprehensive portrait of contemporary and emerging trends in Indonesian population mobility.

A specific form of population movement which is increasing in significance in Indonesia is international labour migration out of, and into, the nation. Here again the data sources are somewhat limited. The Department of Labour maintains records of workers moving temporarily overseas and expatriates coming to Indonesia to work. However, such records only reflect official registrations and ignore the clandestine movement which is significantly greater in volume than that which is registered (Hugo 1996a).

Changing levels of population mobility

There can be no doubt that individual mobility of Indonesians has greatly increased over the last two decades as both a cause and a consequence of the substantial social and economic change that has occurred and with a veritable revolution in transportation improve-

---

[1] Other migration questions included in SUPAS were (BPS 1995b): place of birth coded to *kotamadya/kabupaten*; last place of residence coded to *kotamadya/kabupaten*; length of time at present place of residence; and reason for migrating in the last five years.

TABLE 5.1: Measures of migration, 1971-90

	Migration Measure	Males	Females
1971	Per cent ever lived in another province	6.29	5.06
1985	Per cent ever lived in another province	8.37	7.29
1985	Per cent intra-province migrants	7.04	6.75
1985	Per cent five-year migrants:		
	interprovincial	2.07	1.85
	intra-provincial (between *kabupaten*)	1.97	1.89
1990	Per cent ever lived in another province	10.62	9.03
1990	Per cent five-year migrants: interprovincial	3.54	3.12

Source: Indonesian Censuses of 1971 and 1990; Intercensal Survey of 1985.

ments. Nevertheless, this transformation in Indonesia remains difficult to quantify. Census data relating to migration over the last two
decades are presented in Table 5.1. These data, as was alluded to
above, only show the tip of the iceberg of mobility, reflecting only
more or less permanent *interprovincial* migrations.

Nevertheless, even this limited measure shows that over the last
two decades there was a 69 per cent increase in the proportion of
Indonesian males who had ever lived in a province other than that in
which they were living at the time of the census. The equivalent figure
for women was 79 per cent. Further evidence of both the increasing
tempo of movement and the narrowing of the gap between male and
female migrants is provided by the five-year migration data for 1990
in Table 5.1. Although female interprovincial migration rates in Indonesia remain below those of males, increased involvement of women
in autonomous, often long-distance migration is one of the most salient
changes in population mobility in Indonesia over the last decade or so
(Hugo 1992).

To even the most casual observer of Indonesia over the last two
decades, one of the most striking changes has been the proliferation of
motor vehicles, both public and private. In Java virtually every community is now served by motorised public transport. It is not exagger-
ating to say that individual mobility has been transformed with greater

TABLE 5.2: Number of persons per motor vehicle, 1940-93

	Including Motor Cycles	Excluding Motor Cycles
1940	823	991
1950	1507	1691
1956	446	735
1961	263	447
1966	191	375
1971	129	300
1976	63	193
1978	46	144
1980	38	123
1985	24	80
1990	20	64
1993	17	55

Source: BPS publications on Motor Vehicles and Length of Roads.

ownership of motor cycles and motor cars but especially the rapid development of public transport. This is reflected in Table 5.2 which shows that there has been a very dramatic decrease in the number of persons per motor vehicle in Indonesia over the last two decades.

By 1993 there were only 17 Indonesians per registered motor vehicle (including motor cycles), less than a tenth the number two decades earlier. When only four or more wheeled vehicles are considered, the ratio has fallen from 300 persons per vehicle to 55 in 1993. While Java accounted for only 60 per cent of the national population in 1993, it had 66 per cent of the motor cycles and 73 per cent of other vehicles. It is not only in the land transport area that there has been a parametric increase in movement of people but also by air and sea as Table 5.3 indicates. This reflects the fact that mobility in Outer Indonesia has also greatly increased, especially through the rapid expansion and development of the ferry system.

The picture which emerges from the above is of a society which has a high level of spatial mobility and one in which the level of average individual mobility has increased massively over the last two decades. The relationship between this shift and the rapid social and economic change which has swept Indonesia is complex and two-way. Personal travel has become more accessible and relatively cheaper and enabled most Indonesians to range more widely than ever before in searching for work and education. This process has been bolstered by expansion of education and virtual total penetra-

TABLE 5.3: Changes in numbers involved in various kinds of movement, 1968-92

	1968	1992	Change (%)
Passengers transported by ferry	6,780,000	46,637,000	+588
Domestic air passengers	382,285	3,746,075	+880
Overseas air passengers	68,170	2,238,442	+3184
Foreign tourists	86,100	2,569,870	+2885
Number of *haj* pilgrims	20,555	104,861	+410

Source: Republic of Indonesia 1993.

tion of the country by mass media[2] which has informed Indonesians of job opportunities and different ways of living in distant potential destinations.

International migration

One of the most striking changes in the Indonesian population mobility scene over the last two decades has been the growth in significance of international population movements, especially those involving labour migration, usually on a non-permanent basis. Figure 5.1 shows the exponential increase which has occurred in the number of overseas contract workers deployed through official auspices over the Five Year Plans in Indonesia between 1979 and 1995.

---

[2] At the 1990 Census, 25.7 per cent of Indonesian households had television sets and 57 per cent radios. The 1994 Indonesian Demographic and Health Survey found that 68.5 per cent of women interviewed had watched television in the week before interviews and 56.5 per cent listened to the radio daily (DHS 1995: 31).

In the first Repelita only 5,624 were sent overseas and in subsequent plans this increased to 17,042; 96,410; and 292,264. In Repelita V (1989-94) the government set a target of 500,000 workers to be sent overseas and this was far exceeded (652,272). Repelita VI is even more ambitious with a target of 1.25 million. In the first year of the plan a record number of 176,187 official workers were deployed. However, these official registered international labour migrants are only a minority of Indonesian workers overseas. There is substantial undocumented labour migration out of Indonesia, most of it focused on East and West Malaysia (Hugo 1993a), although illegal movement to other destinations like Singapore, Hong Kong, Taiwan, Saudi Arabia and perhaps Australia is on the increase (_Jakarta Post_, 18 April 1995). While measurement of undocumented movement is extremely problematical, an amnesty in Peninsular Malaysia has given an indication of the scale of the movement. Indeed, the undocumented migration from Indonesia to Malaysia is perhaps the second largest such stream after the Mexican immigration to the United States. Table 5.4 presents my estimates of the numbers of Indonesians working overseas on a temporary basis in 1995. This represents 1.5 per cent of the total Indonesian labour force at any one point in time.

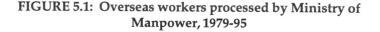

FIGURE 5.1: Overseas workers processed by Ministry of Manpower, 1979-95

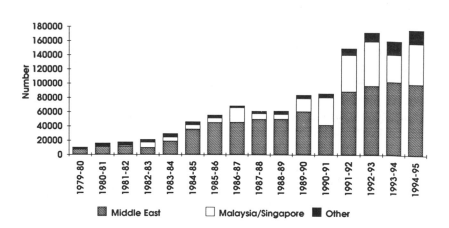

**TABLE 5.4: Estimated numbers of Indonesian workers abroad
in 1995**

Type of migrant worker	Estimate	Source
Official OCWs	224,364	Ministry of Labour
Clandestine workers in Peninsula Malaysia	600,000	Amnesty data
Clandestine workers in Sabah/Sarawak	350,000	*Forum Keadilan* 26, 12 April 1995: 50-55
Other illegals (HK, Japan, Australia etc.)	20,000	Various sources
Trainees	20,000	Hiebert 1995: 54 Furuya 1995: 9
Total	1.214.364	

The major features of contemporary labour migration out of Indonesia have been summarised elsewhere (Hugo 1996a) but some of the main elements are as follows:

- The legal movement is still dominantly directed toward Saudi Arabia and mainly involves women who work as housemaids.
- Housemaid migration is increasing to Singapore, Hong Kong and Malaysia.
- Indonesian international labour migration predominantly involves unskilled workers.
- The movement to Malaysia is overwhelmingly male but female migration is becoming more important.
- Some longstanding migrants to Malaysia are settling permanently there.
- While Java, especially West Java, provides the bulk of official labour migrants, many of those going overseas as undocumented workers come from Eastern Indonesia, South Sulawesi and Sumatra, although East Java is also an important origin.
- There are no accurate data on remittances but official data on transfers indicates that US$1.2 billion were sent back to Indonesia

by migrants during Repelita V. This, however, is only the tip of the iceberg of such flows since the bulk of remittances are sent through unofficial channels.

It is also relevant to point out that there has been an increase in the flow of expatriate workers into Indonesia in recent years which is on a scale unprecedented since the colonial era. This is a function of the rapid economic growth which has created significant shortages in high skilled and specialised areas of engineering, accountancy, management etc. The existence of some mismatch between the training and education system on the one hand and the skill needs of the labour market on the other has led to this paradoxical situation in a country where a third of the labour force is underemployed (Hugo 1993b). Official registrations of new international workers residing in Indonesia doubled from 20,761 in 1990 to 41,422 in 1994.[3]

Interprovincial migration

Former President Soekarno frequently articulated Indonesia's population problem as being one of 'unbalanced' distribution rather than excessive growth. There is a marked difference in population density between 'Inner Indonesia' (Java, Bali and Madura) which in 1990 supported 61.5 per cent of Indonesia's population on 6.9 per cent of the nation's land area, and Outer Indonesia. However, this contrast to a large degree reflects the actual variation in resource endowments and ecological situations between the nation's provinces. Moreover, perceptions of Outer Indonesia as being 'empty' are far from accurate—if Sumatra were a separate nation its 37 million inhabitants would make it the world's 28th largest nation. While there are parts of the Outer Islands which have potential for development, policies which seek to solve the population growth problem by 'evening out' the distribution of Indonesia's population through massive migration programs are not feasible either in terms of the potential of the destination areas to absorb them or in terms of the logistic costs of transferring millions of people out of Java and settling them elsewhere.

---

[3] These data indicate new registrations only and do not include people who had registered in earlier years. They also exclude large numbers of people who came to Indonesia on a short-term basis or who enter Indonesia on a non-working visa and subsequently obtain employment. The source of this information is the Directorate General Binapenta in the Ministry of Labour.

Indonesia has had a transmigration program to transfer p[ ]
Inner to Outer Indonesia, although its goals are now predominantly
articulated in terms of regional development in the Outer Islands
rather than demographic redistribution. Nevertheless, the uneven
distribution of population in Indonesia is one of the most salient
features of the nation's demography.

For most of this century, Java's population has been growing
more slowly than that of Outer Indonesia. Hence Table 5.5 shows that
the proportion of Indonesians living in Java has declined from around
two-thirds at the time of Independence to 60 per cent at the 1990
Census. This was given particular impetus in the late 1970s and early
1980s when some 1.29 million families (around 5 million people) were
moved under the auspices of the transmigration program. However,
the shift in government policy in the late 1980s to facilitate international and domestic private investment and industrialisation is tending to favour growth in Java. Between 1985 and 1990 the number of
people moving into Java (773,789) was almost as great as the number
moving in the opposite direction (973,340).

TABLE 5.5: Population of Java and other islands, 1900-90

	Java		Other Islands		Total
	('000)	%	('000)	%	('000)
1900	29,000	72.0	11,150	28.0	40,150
1920	34,984	71.0	14,171	29.0	49,155
1930	41,718	69.0	19,009	31.0	60,727
1961	62,993	64.9	34,026	35.1	97,019
1971	76,102	63.8	43,130	36.2	119,232
1980	91,270	61.9	56,220	38.1	147,490
1985	99,853	60.9	64,194	39.1	164,047
1990	107,574	60.0	71,748	40.0	179,322

Source: Hugo et al. 1987: 31; BPS 1991a.

It was pointed out earlier that Indonesian census data are only able to detect the more or less permanent migration *between* the nation's 27 provinces. Nevertheless, the spatial patterning of this mainly long distance movement has important demographic, economic and social implications. Figure 5.2 depicts the major migration flows between provinces at the 1990 Census. Central and East Java are clearly the major origins of migrants with substantial flows to a range of Outer Island destinations (especially in Southern Sumatra) and to Jakarta. The large flow from Jakarta to West Java has increased greatly in recent years and reflects largely the overspill of the rapidly expanding city of Jakarta into adjoining West Java province (Hugo 1996b).

Jakarta is a major focus of migration from all provinces, not only within Java but in the Outer Islands as well. These migration patterns are the major reason for the significant interprovincial differences in population growth depicted in Figure 5.3, although the fertility and mortality differentials are also important.

The major regional differences in population growth are as follows:

- *Java's* population grew at very low rates during the 1980s—1.8 per cent per annum in the early 1980s (compared with 2.2 per cent for Indonesia as a whole) and 1.5 per cent in the late 1980s (compared with 1.8 per cent). This was partly a function of the lower fertility in Java than elsewhere but also due to net outmigration from Java to the Outer Islands.

- *Jakarta* recorded a very low rate of population growth in the late 1980s—0.9 per cent, compared with rates of around 4 per cent per annum over the previous half century. It is clear, however, that this understates the true rate of growth of Jakarta because:

    -    Jakarta's residential development has overspilled into the adjoining West Java *kabupaten* of Bogor, Tanggerang and Bekasi. It is estimated (Vatikiotis 1991: 35) by Jakarta's government that half a million workers each day commute into Jakarta from adjoining areas. A great deal of Jakarta's new manufacturing employment has also been established in these 'overspill' areas.

    -    Many residents of Jakarta have recently migrated to the capital but have not registered locally and will have indicated in the census that their home area was their usual place of residence.

    -    In addition, many people engage in circular migration whereby they work much of the year in Jakarta but keep their family and their stated place of usual residence in their home

FIGURE 5.2: Major interprovincial migration according to province of previous residence statistics from the 1990 census

Source: Indonesian Census of 1990.

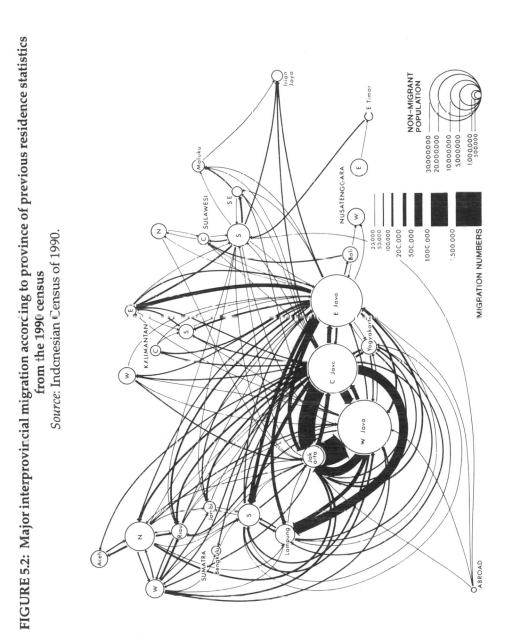

FIGURE 5.3: Average annual growth rate by province, 1980-90
Source: Calculated from Indonesian Censuses of 1980 and 1990.

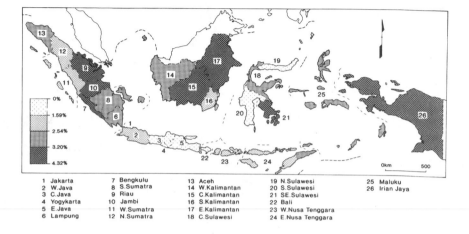

1	Jakarta	7	Bengkulu	13	Aceh	19	N.Sulawesi	25	Maluku
2	W.Java	8	S.Sumatra	14	W.Kalimantan	20	S.Sulawesi	26	Irian Jaya
3	C.Java	9	Riau	15	C.Kalimantan	21	SE.Sulawesi		
4	Yogykarta	10	Jambi	16	S.Kalimantan	22	Bali		
5	E.Java	11	W.Sumatra	17	E.Kalimantan	23	W.Nusa Tenggara		
6	Lampung	12	N.Sumatra	18	C.Sulawesi	24	E.Nusa Tenggara		

village. Hence, while they are part of Jakarta's labour force, they are not counted as Jakarta residents at the time of the census (Hugo 1978, 1982a).

- *West Java*, on the other hand, grew at well above the national average in the late 1980s (2.8 per cent) and more than twice the rate of other Java provinces. This was partly due to its higher fertility levels but also due to the 'overspill' from Jakarta. West Java was the only Java province to increase its rate of growth between the early 1980s and late 1980s.
- *Elsewhere in Java* growth rates were very low. In particular, Yogyakarta's population actually recorded a decline between 1985 and 1990. These low growth rates were a function of both low fertility and outmigration to the Outer Islands and to the Jakarta-West Java urban complex.
- In *Sumatra*, a diversity of patterns of growth is in evidence. Especially striking here is the fact that *Lampung's* population barely

grew at all between 1985 and 1990 after several decades of growth rates in excess of 5 per cent per annum. This dramatic change was partly due to the government's decision in the early 1980s to stop transmigration from Java to Lampung. Indeed, Lampung now is similar in many ways to the areas in Java which the transmigrants originally left. Other reasons for the lack of growth of Lampung include the opening of a new road to neighbouring *Bengkulu* which has facilitated outmigration and resulted in Bengkulu having one of the fastest rates of growth in the nation in the 1980s. In fact, in the late 1980s, Bengkulu grew at 4.6 per cent per annum, second only to Riau. Another element in Lampung's population stability is that, like rural Java which it is increasingly coming to resemble, Lampung is losing migrants to large urban areas, especially in nearby Jakarta-West Java. Hence Lampung has gone from being the nation's most consistently fast growing province for the first 85 years of this century to having the second slowest growth rate in the nation in the late 1980s.

- Rapid rates of population growth were recorded in *Riau* where oil-related employment is increasingly being supplemented by the industrial developments in Batam and Bintan. The latter are associated with the *Growth Triangle* concept which sees the development of urban Singapore overspilling into adjoining areas of Malaysia (Johore Baru) and Indonesia. Other provinces in Sumatra to record high rates of growth included the provinces with substantial natural resource exploitation projects—Jambi, South Sumatra and Aceh. West and North Sumatra continue to be major areas of outmigration and their populations grew at rates below the national average.

- *Sumatra's* overall rate of growth in the late 1980s was 26 per cent lower than in the early 1980s and 32 per cent lower than in the 1970s. Its growth was slower than at any time in the Independence period and while it is still growing at above the national average, it would seem that lower fertility and perhaps reduced inmigration from elsewhere in Indonesia (especially that associated with land settlement) are bringing about a new era of reduced population expansion in Sumatra.

- In *Kalimantan* the picture is quite different with population growth being higher than all of the other islands of Indonesia and being almost double the national average in the late 1980s. It was especially high in Central (4.5 per cent per annum) and East (4.4 per cent) Kalimantan. This is obviously associated with continued and expanded exploitation of natural resources as well as increased focusing of transmigration on Kalimantan.

- *Sulawesi's* population, on the other hand, grew only slightly faster than that of Java in the late 1980s. This was mainly because the provinces of South and North Sulawesi, traditionally areas of significant outmigration, grew at well below the national average. On the other hand, the frontier provinces of Central and Southeast Sulawesi grew quite rapidly with the expansion of land settlement and, to a lesser extent, resource exploitation activities.
- *Bali's* low fertility is reflected in one of the slowest rates of population growth in Indonesia in the late 1980s (1 per cent per annum).
- In the other islands of Indonesia, *West Nusa Tenggara* has grown at slightly above the national average while *East Nusa Tenggara's* rate is just below that figure. *Maluku* has maintained a high growth rate while *Irian Jaya* and *East Timor* have grown considerably faster than the nation as a whole. In the latter two areas especially, there have been substantial inmigrations from elsewhere in the nation, especially South Sulawesi and, to a lesser extent, Java.

With respect to the longstanding concern with the 'balance' of population between Inner and Outer Indonesia, it is clear that the last decade has seen a slowing down in the *net* redistribution of people out of Java and into the Outer Islands. The government's Transmigration Scheme was given great impetus in the late 1970s and the first half of the 1980s by large infusions of funds generated by oil revenues and from the World Bank. Hence as Figure 5.4 shows, the large numbers of families who were moved from Java-Bali to the Outer Islands in Repelita III and IV differed greatly from those moved in the previous Repelita. However, it will be noted in Figure 5.4 that Repelita IV saw a substantial decline in the numbers of transmigrant families funded by the government and an increase in the number of spontaneous (*swarkasa*) transmigrants. This pattern was even more pronounced with the economic crunch of the mid-1980s; funding of transmigration was cut back so that the numbers of families moved in Repelita V did not approach the ambitious target of 550,000. Indeed, sponsored families numbered around a fifth of that target. Nevertheless, there are some indications of a possible upswing in transmigration in Repelita VI (1993-98).

**FIGURE 5.4: General and spontaneous transmigrants,
Repelita I-Repelita V**
Source: Unpublished Indonesian Census data.

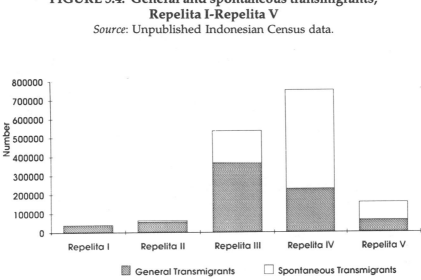

Figure 5.5 shows the provinces of origin and destination respectively of transmigrants during the first five Repelita. The dominance
of Central and East Java as origins is clearly apparent. Sumatra remains the predominant destination of transmigrants accounting for
57.8 per cent during the first four Repelita and 54.3 per cent in
Repelita V. However, Lampung's declining attraction is apparent in
the fact that it was the second most important province of destination
during Repelita II-IV, accounting for 11.1 per cent, but it absorbed
only 6.7 per cent of transmigrants in Repelita V. Meanwhile, the
proportions settling in Eastern Indonesia (mainly Irian Jaya) increased
from 6.8 per cent to 10.1 per cent, in Kalimantan from 22.2 to 23.1 per
cent and in Sulawesi from 8.5 to 12.5 per cent.

FIGURE 5.5: Origin and destination of transmigrants, 1968-93
Source: Republic of Indonesia 1993.

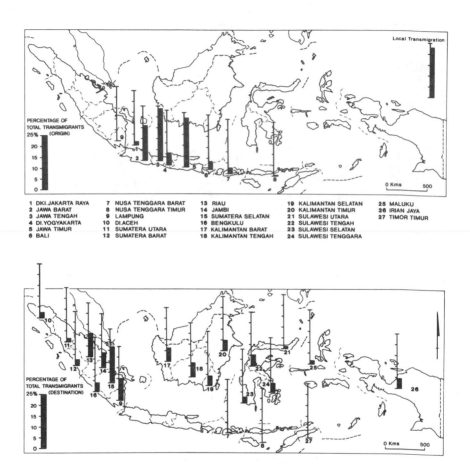

Transmigration, however, is only one element (and not the largest one) in a substantial migration from Java to the other islands. Table
5.6 shows that the number of people living in the Outer Islands but
who had migrated there from Java increased by 73 per cent between
1971 and 1980 while the number who had moved in the opposite

direction increased by only 15 per cent. Hence there was a net migration loss to Java overall of 2.4 million people. However, during the
1980s there has been a distinct change. There was a net increase of
migrants from Java residing in the Outer Islands in the 1980s
(1,576,910), a similar magnitude to that recorded in the 1970s
(1,510,354), although the percentage increase of 44.1 per cent was
lower than that recorded in the 1970s. Hence, although there was a
quite significant increase in outmigration from Java in the 1980s, it
was somewhat lower than some projections had anticipated on the
basis of the 1970s experience. The most striking change, however, in
Table 5.6 is in the number of migrants from the Outer Islands residing
in Java—this doubled between 1980 and 1990. As a result there was
only a comparatively small (15.7 per cent) increase in the overall
lifetime net migration loss from Java, from 2.35 million in 1980 to 2.71
million in 1990.

TABLE 5.6: Migration into and out of Java, 1971, 1980 and 1990[a]

	1971	1980	1990	% Change	
				1971-80	1980-90
Total outmigrants	2,062,206	3,572,560	5,149,470	+73	+44.1
Total inmigrants	1,067,777	1,225,560	2,434,719	+15	+98.7
Net migration	-994,429	-2,347,000	2,714,751	+136	+15.7

[a]Based upon 'most recent' migration data using census question on province of
previous residence.

Source: 1971, 1980 and 1990 Censuses of Indonesia.

It is interesting to pursue this change a little more by examining
the extent to which migrants between Java and the Outer Islands
settled in urban and rural destinations. Table 5.7 shows that two-
thirds (65.7 per cent) of migrants from the Outer Islands who have
settled in Java lived in urban areas. Indeed, when only urban-destined
migrants between Java and the other islands are considered, Java

records a net gain. On the other hand, more than three-quarters (76 per cent) of Java people living in the other islands in 1990 resided in rural areas. Hence while urban-destined migrants from Java to the Outer Islands are by no means insignificant in number (1.2 million), they are outnumbered three to one by rural-destined movers and the net rural flow is heavily in favour of the Outer Islands.

TABLE 5.7: Migration into and out of Java by urban-rural destination, 1990[a]

	All migrants		Migrants aged 5+ arriving 1985-90		
	Urban	Rural	Urban	Rural	Total
Total outmigrants	1,233,874	3,915,596	361,857	601,483	963,340
Total inmigrants	1,600,333	834,386	464,739	309,050	773,789
Net migration	+366,459	-3,081,210	+102,882	-292,433	-189,551

[a]Based upon 'most recent' migration data using census question on province of previous residence.

Source: 1990 Census of Indonesia.

One interpretation of the above would be that the mid-1980s saw a significant shift in interprovincial migration patterns in Indonesia. In the early 1980s there was a continuation of the pattern of the late 1970s with a substantial net outmigration from Java to the Outer Islands. This was fuelled not only by the huge investments in transmigration but also by government policy which stressed natural resource exploitation and export. However, in the later 1980s with the decline in transmigration, but especially the shift in government policy toward encouragement of foreign and domestic investment in manufacturing, this pattern changed. The bulk of manufacturing investment was focused on Java, especially in and around Jakarta. This led to not only a reduction in the flow of Javan residents to the Outer Islands, but also an increase in the numbers of Outer Island residents migrating to Java, attracted by the rapidly expanding urban-based job opportunities. Some evidence to support such an interpretation is provided by data from the 1990 Census question which asked Indonesians their province of residence five years prior to the census. These are provided in Table 5.7 and show that over the 1985-90 period the net migration loss to the Outer Islands was quite small (-189,551), especially in relation to the total volume of movement occurring between Inner and Outer Indonesia. It seems certain that these trends have continued apace since the 1990 Census so that the 1995 SUPAS results may well show that between 1990 and 1995 there were more people who moved from the Outer Islands to Java than moved in the opposite direction.

The substantial shifts which have occurred in interprovincial migration patterns over this century can be discerned by comparing the 1990 pattern shown in Figure 5.2 with those found in earlier censuses. Hence the patterns of interprovincial lifetime migration evident at the 1930 Census (see Hugo 1979: 180) show a dominance of the colonial contract coolies from Java to the province of North Sumatra. On the other hand, the pattern evident at the 1971 Census (*ibid.*: 181) shows two major flows, both with their origins in West, Central and East Java. The first is a focus of migration on Southern Sumatra with the increasing significance of transmigration and resource development and the second is the expanded movement to the Jakarta capital city district. These patterns become even sharper in the 1980 Census. However, the 1990 map (Figure 5.2) reveals a diminished significance of Java to Outer Islands flows compared with the earlier maps.

The dominant flows are toward Jakarta and from Jakarta to West Java, the latter reflecting the suburbanising movements of Jakarta residents into Bogor, Bekasi and Tanggerang as the rapidly expanding capital overspilled its boundaries (Hugo 1996b). These shifts are even more apparent in Figure 5.6 which shows the main five year flows between provinces for the five years preceding the 1980 and 1990 Censuses. (Note that in Figure 5.6 the increased volume of movement necessitated a change in scale between the maps showing 1975-80 and 1985-90 movement.)

FIGURE 5.6: Major interprovincial migration streams, 1975-80 and 1985-90
Source: Indonesian Censuses of 1980 and 1990.

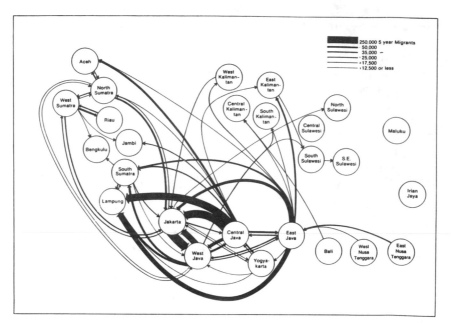

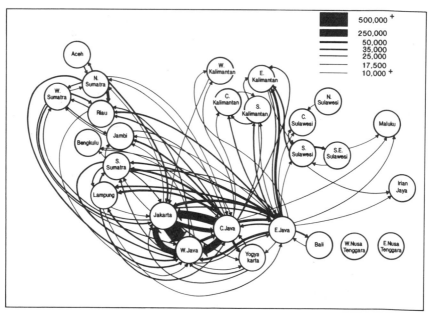

The shift away from Java to Outer Island flows and toward intra-Java flows is readily apparent. In 1980 there were 1,107,035 persons living in the Outer Islands who had been living in Java five years previously, whereas in 1990 the number had declined to 963,340. On the other hand, in 1990 there were 701,715 persons in Java who had been living in the Outer Islands five years previously compared with only 456,910 persons in 1980. Hence in 1975-80 there was a net loss of 650,125 from Java but this declined to 189,551 in 1985-90.

Non-permanent migration

It was mentioned earlier that non-permanent migration is widespread in Indonesia but is not detected in any of the standard data collections such as the census. One form of such movement is the international labour migration referred to earlier. However, similar forms of migration are occurring within the nation. Field studies in the early 1970s (Hugo 1975, 1978) demonstrated the widespread incidence and socio-economic significance of circular migration and commuting from rural to urban areas in Indonesia. While there are no substantiating data collected in censuses or national surveys it is clear that the tempo of non-permanent movement has greatly increased over the last two decades. There are a number of case studies which demonstrate this. In particular studies which resurveyed villages studied in the early 1970s discovered a substantial increase in non-permanent moves (e.g. Keyfitz 1985; Singarimbun 1986) and found that this change had been fundamental in improving the economic situation in those villages through a substantial inflow of remittances. Quotations from two such studies will suffice to document this pattern of an increasing tempo of temporary migration out of Javan villages over the last two decades. Edmundson and Edmundson (1983: 53) in their comparison of two East Java villages in 1969 and 1981 found that in one of their villages

> The mid 1980 Census included 630 urban workers who retained village residence cards but they were only present on weekend visits. This intermediate category of part-time migrants forms an important new group whose freedom of movement and social adaptability represent a significant change in attitude from the traditional and highly territorial thought patterns of older villagers.

Manning's (1986: 28-31) report of the Agro-Economic Survey's studies in six West Java villages from 1976 to 1983 concludes that

Despite substantial increases in rice production and incomes, there appear to have been relatively few jobs created in rural areas. Quite a substantial proportion of rural households seem to have benefited from the 'trickle down' of urban income growth through entry largely into self-employed activities in transport and petty trade. This has been a major factor influencing agricultural income change in the survey villages over the seven year period studied ... permanent movement to urban areas and movement out of agriculture was not a dominant pattern.

More than a decade ago the World Bank (1984: 20) estimated that at least 25 per cent of rural households on Java have at least one family member working for part of the year in urban areas. This would imply that at least 3.75 million people are involved in this form of migration on Java, equivalent to just over 50 per cent of the measured 1980 urban employment in Java. Of course, since migrants are only working in the cities for part of the year the average effect is less than this, but it is not unlikely that about one-sixth of the average daily urban workforce consists of temporary migrants not included in official employment figures. A series of studies sponsored by the Ministry of Population and Environment (Mantra and Molo 1985) examined circular migration and commuting in six Indonesian cities. In addition to establishing how significant and widespread this mobility was in cities of varying sizes in both Inner and Outer Indonesia it was found that the great majority of these movers had only been circulating to those cities since 1980. It would appear that this pattern of an increasing tempo of non-permanent migration has continued over the last decade and became of even greater significance with improvements in transport, advances in education, changes in the roles of women, and increased urban and industrial development.

Perhaps the strongest evidence of a pattern of continued increase in the scale and significance of non-permanent migration in Java during the period since the first study in West Java carried out in 1973 (Hugo 1975) is derived from a comprehensive longitudinal study of 37 villages in Java carried out over the period 1967-91. In that study Collier *et al.* (n.d.: 1) concluded that:

Twenty five years ago many of the landless labourers on Java had very few sources of income ... Now most of the landless rural families on Java have at least one person who is working outside of the village, and in a factory or service job.

In all of the villages in the 1992-93 resurvey, massive migration out of the village to jobs in the larger cities and towns was recorded and only 20 per cent of households depended on agriculture for their total livelihood. The bulk of the movement recorded was on a temporary basis. The fact that those villages were deliberately selected to be representative of villages both in highly accessible and low accessibility areas suggests that the scale of non-permanent rural-urban movement from Javan villages has increased exponentially in recent years and that such movement still far outweighs permanent relocation from village to city. Moreover, with further labour--displacing developments in agriculture (Hugo 1995), it seems likely that this movement will continue to be of great significance in Indonesia. The reasons for opting for a non-permanent migration strategy over permanent relocation have been explored elsewhere (Hugo 1978, 1982b, 1985) and include the following elements:

- This type of mobility strategy is highly compatible with work participation in the urban informal sector since the flexible time commitments allow time to circulate to the home village. Similarly, the ease of entry to the urban informal sector is a factor.
- Participation in work in both the urban and rural sectors spreads the risk by diversifying families' portfolio of income-earning opportunities.
- The cost of living in urban areas (especially Jakarta) is considerably higher than in rural areas so that keeping the family in the village and 'earning in the city while spending in the village' allows earnings to go much further.
- Many urban jobs, especially those in the informal sector, can be readily combined with regular visits to the home village.
- Java's transport system is cheap and diverse, and allows workers to get to their home village quickly.
- Job options in the village, especially during seasonal increases in demand for labour (such as harvesting time), are able to be kept open. Hence risk can be spread over several sources of income.

- Many informal and formal sector employers in large cities, especially Jakarta, provide barracks-type accommodation for workers.
- Often the movement is part of a family labour allocation strategy in which some members are sent out of the village to contribute to the village-based family's income.
- In many cases there is a social preference for living and bringing up children in the village where there are perceived to be fewer negative, non-traditional influences.
- Social networks are crucial in the development of this form of migration. Most temporary migrants make their initial movement with other experienced migrants or join family or friends established at the destination.
- As is the case with international migration, recruiters and middlemen of various types have played a significant role in the increasing rural to urban migration in Indonesia. As Collier *et al.* (n.d.: 41) point out ..... 'Often a factory manager will meet with the head of the village to recruit young people for his factory. They sometimes would send a bus in the morning to pick up the workers'. Such a pattern of strong *mandor* (foremen), *calo* (recruiter) and *taikong* (agents) has a long history in Java and has become even more significant in recent years in encouraging migration to both formal and informal sector jobs based in urban areas. Firman (1991), for example, has demonstrated the critical role played by *mandors* in the construction industry in urban Indonesia.

While there are many similarities in the contemporary situation with respect to patterns and processes of non-permanent migration compared with the 1970s, there also have been some significant changes. Paramount among these is the increasing involvement of women in both permanent and temporary movements, especially those directed from village to city. Another change is that the increasing size of the formal sector in Indonesian cities, especially Jakarta and other large cities in Java, has led to an increasing number of migrants having to be more or less permanently settled in the city and not free to come and go to their village as frequently and readily as was possible when they worked in the informal sector. In many cases, for example with many of the young women working in factories in and around cities like Jakarta and Surabaya, there are intentions to eventually return to settle in their village but the fixed time commitments of their work prevent them circulating to and from the village on a weekly, fortnightly or monthly basis.

It is also readily apparent that Indonesia has become a much more urbanised society over the last two decades. In the 1980s, not only was the rate of urban growth more than six times greater than that of the rural population but the absolute growth of the urban population (almost 23 million) was twice that of the rural population (11.8 million). If we examine *urbanisation*, however, the gains have been more modest than those in urban growth with the percentage of Indonesians living in urban areas increasing from 22.4 in 1980 to 30.9 per cent in 1990. While urbanisation has been taking place throughout the post-Independence period in Indonesia, the 1980s represented a period of rapid urbanisation unparalleled in Indonesia's history.

A substantial part of the increase in urbanisation between 1980 and 1990 in Indonesia was due to reclassification of areas from rural to urban. Gardiner and Oey-Gardiner (1991) report that the number of rural *desa* classified as urban almost doubled between 1980 and 1990 from around 3,500 to approximately 6,700. It is apparent that not only have Indonesia's urban areas recorded massive population gains during the 1980s but also there has been a huge increase in the lateral extent of urban areas. This lateral extension of Indonesia's urban areas has tended to occur in corridors, along major transport routes radiating out from (and linking) major urban areas (McGee 1991b; Firman 1989, 1991, 1992). In addition to the population classified as urban in the census, however, there are large numbers of rural residents, especially in Java, who work in non-agricultural occupations often based in urban or peri-urban areas by virtue of circular migration or commuting. The blurring of the distinction between urban and rural areas in Indonesia, especially Java, which was apparent in the early 1970s (Hugo 1975, 1978) has become even more apparent over the last decades. Indeed, McGee (1991b, 1992) has coined the term *kotadesasi* to describe the process whereby extensive areas have a complex mix of urban and rural activities.

Explaining changing population mobility in Indonesia

The literature relating to the nature, causes and consequences of population mobility within Indonesia has expanded greatly in recent years (e.g. see Bandiyono 1987, 1993; Mantra and Kasai 1987; Kasai 1988; Rietveld, Sadyadharma and Sudarno 1988; Sjahrir 1989; Hetler 1990; Gardiner and Oey-Gardiner 1990; Firman 1991, 1994; Wahyuni 1991; Gunawan and Erwidodo 1993; Tirtosudarmo and Meyer 1993;

Keban 1994; Leinbach and Smith 1994). The causes of population mobility are complex and all that can be attempted here is to summarise the major elements in the constellation of forces increasing levels of mobility and reshaping its spatial patterning and composition. Clearly, the sustained high levels of economic growth and the substantial economic restructuring have been of crucial importance. The shift in economic policy since the mid 1980s to massively increase foreign and domestic investment via a package of deregulation measures and relaxation of foreign ownership rules has obviously been of fundamental importance in the increasing rural to urban migration and the greater focusing of migration on Java.

Economic change is the key driving force in Indonesian population movement but it is not only growth which is involved but also the considerable restructuring of the economy. Table 5.8, for example, shows that during the 1980s agriculture's share of Indonesia's workforce fell below half for the first time while its share of GDP fell below a fifth. Moreover, it is anticipated that Indonesia's agricultural workforce will begin to decline in numbers in the late 1990s (Hugo 1993a: 75) and declines are already apparent in some provinces. The 1970s saw a number of modernising and commercialising changes in agricultural technology and practice in Indonesia (White 1979; Hugo 1985: 59-62) which led to some displacement of workers from agriculture. These changes were associated with the adoption of the High Yielding Varieties of rice and the package of innovations known as the 'Green Revolution'. The changes having labour-displacement effects in Indonesia, especially Java, included:
- A change from traditional labour organisation to wage labour which limited access to agricultural work.
- Change from traditional forms of harvesting (using an *ani ani* or small blade) to use of the sickle.
- Increased use of tractors.
- Replacement of hand milling by mechanical hullers.

It would appear that in the 1990s a new round of labour-displacement innovations is occurring in agriculture in Java (Naylor 1992: 28). These include:
- A recent drive to mechanise rice cultivation and threshing on Java through making subsidised loans available.
- Movement toward direct seeding of rice which will mean that all of the labour associated with transplanting will be lost.

TABLE 5.8: GDP and labour force in agriculture

	Agri-cultural GDP (Rp billion at constant 1983 prices)	Agri-culture's Share of GDP (%)	Agri-cultural Labour Force (million)	Agri-culture's Share of Labour Force (%)	Agri-cultural GDP/ Agricultural Labour (Rp '000 per person at constant 1983 prices)
1980	16,399	25.0	28.8	55.9	569
1985	19,300	22.7	n.a.	n.a.	n.a.
1990	22,357	19.4	35.5	49.2	626

n.a. = not available.

Source: Tomich 1992: 9.

- Increased use of herbicides displacing labour originally associated with weeding.

Naylor (*ibid.*) quotes research indicating that the latter two innovations will reduce total labour use by around a third in rice cultivation in Java while another third would be lost if mechanised cultivation and threshing became widespread. She indicates that the total effect of these innovations would reduce labour hours per hectare from 1,460 to 625 per year. This would have very dramatic impacts on agricultural employment in Java, especially the women, and put great pressure on the other sectors to absorb labour. Structural change in Indonesia will therefore continue to see a significant redistribution of labour between sectors and, associated with this, increased labour mobility.

The manufacturing sector has been one of the most dynamic in Indonesia in the second half of the 1980s and early 1990s, growing at over 10 per cent per annum in most years, well above the average for all sectors. This is particularly true of the non-oil and gas manufacturing subsector. In 1991 the share of the economy made up by manufacturing exceeded agriculture for the first time in the nation's history. As Hill (1992: 5) points out

> This is an historic turning point in Indonesia's economic development. Although the event was hastened by poor rice harvests, its fundamental origins lie in the impressive export-oriented industrial growth which has occurred since 1986. The speed of the structural change in the last quarter century is revealed in the fact that over the period 1966-91 the share of manufacturing in GDP has risen from 8 per cent to 22 per cent while that of agriculture has declined from 51 per cent to 19 per cent.

The growth in this sector is reflected in employment. In the 1980s employment in large and medium sized manufacturing enterprises increased by 117 per cent but that in small enterprises also expanded by a very healthy 62.6 per cent (*ibid.*: 38). Indeed, in the late 1980s small-enterprise employment grew as fast as that in large and medium sized enterprises. Java had 76.2 per cent of all manufacturing employment in large and medium enterprises in 1990. The proportion of small-enterprise employment in Java was even higher (77.2 per cent). The fact that much investment in manufacturing since 1990 has been in and around Jakarta would suggest that manufacturing employment has become even more concentrated in Jakarta, especially that in large enterprises. Table 5.9 shows that in the first three years of the 1990s employment in large and medium-scale manufacturing enterprises increased by almost a third—with a higher rate of increase in Java than in the Outer Islands. These changes have been fundamental in shaping population mobility patterns.

Social changes have also impinged significantly upon population mobility within Indonesia. The role and status of women is one element in this as are the shifts in the structure and functioning of families in Indonesia as the extended family gives way to a dominance of emotionally nucleated families.

The enormous expansion of education has undoubtedly encouraged mobility. Almost all Indonesian children gain at least some primary schooling and it is intended that three years of secondary schooling become compulsory by the end of the century. The impact of increased education on population mobility is well exemplified in the remarks of Keyfitz who returned in 1985 to a village in East Java

TABLE 5.9: Change in registered manufacturing enterprises, Java and other islands, 1989-90 to 1992-93

	1989-90	1992-93	% Growth
Number of enterprises			
Java	68,414	80,835	18.2
Other islands	48,324	67,007	38.7
Total	116,738	147,842	26.6
Number of employees			
Java	3,188,824	4,280,461	34.2
Other islands	1,772,947	2,312,544	30.4
Total	4,961,771	6,593,005	32.8

Source: Indonesia, Department of Labour 1995.

where he had lived in 1953-54. One of the major changes he noted was that in a village that formerly was without a school, now virtually all children of school age start school. He further observes:

> The youngster who has learned to read and write and is intro-duced to the issues of the nation and the world is not happy to serve his parents in the old way. At school he comes under a different line of authority from the parental and finds much less reason to respect those who traditionally are his elders and betters. He develops needs for recreation and ambition for advancement in life that go far beyond anything his parents have visualized and beyond anything the village can offer. He urgently wants work and a career that correspond to his training. We were told that few graduates of the high school return to the village (Keyfitz 1985: 704-705).

Similarly, the impact of mass media remarked upon earlier in this paper has been significant. Again Keyfitz's (*ibid.*: 707-708) obser-vations graphically portray the massive dimensions of the change that has occurred:

In 1953 contact with the outside world among even the upper
level of citizens was confined to what they learned from the
headman at a weekly meeting of the village elders. The headman
in turn obtained his information from a daily paper he had
brought by messenger from Gondonglegi ... Our recent visit
shows that the media have taken the place of much of the earlier
face-to-face communication. Everyone can find out what is
happening for himself, on his own transistor radio ..... The
national electricity grid reached the village in 1982 and with it
came television—there are now some 60 receivers in the village.

The impact of mass media in informing villagers of economic
and social opportunities elsewhere is underestimated. It is the present
writer's field experience that increased mass media penetration has
played a significant role in changing the attitudes and expanding the
horizons of many village-dwellers in Indonesia. The role of these
changes in migration decision making can be seen in a study of labour
migrants to Saudi Arabia from Central Java and Yogyakarta (Mantra,
Kasnawi and Sukamandi 1986) which found that a majority of respondents first learned of job opportunities through the mass media or
government sources.

The proliferation of all forms of public transport, road improvements etc. demonstrated earlier in this paper and the associated
enormous increase in personal mobility has had very large direct (in
facilitating movement) and indirect (through expanding knowledge
of job opportunities elsewhere) effects on population movement.
Leinbach (1983) shows conclusively in a sample survey of communities influenced by new and upgraded feeder roads in Indonesia that
such developments are followed by greatly expanded population
mobility and an enlargement of the employment fields of rural
dwellers.

The influence of government policy upon population mobility is
another element which needs to be considered in the Indonesian
context. It is clear from the earlier discussion that the Indonesian
government's economic policies have had a large indirect impact
upon levels and patterns of movement. However, a distinctive feature
of Indonesia's demography over a long period has been substantial
attempts by government to directly intervene to influence population
mobility (Hugo 1988). Although the transmigration program referred
to earlier was the most prominent, there have been several other

programs which seek to encourage migration. These include attempts to sedentarise tribal groups in Irian Jaya and Kalimantan and to attract labour to Batam in the Sijori Growth Triangle. In recent years the involvement of government in the promotion, control and regulation of international labour migration has been substantial (Hugo 1995).

As was indicated earlier, there are several elements in Indonesia which have sustained and enhanced population mobility flows once they have been established. Central here is the role of social networks. Once a 'pioneer' migrant is established at a destination all the family members and acquaintances of that migrant acquire a piece of social capital (Hugo 1993a). In both internal and international migration, most migrants move to areas where they have friends and relatives who assist them in entering the labour and housing markets at the destination, as well as adjusting more generally to that context. Such chain migration is not only of critical significance in the migration process but is instrumental in the process of labour market segmentation in destination areas, especially cities. Migrants from particular regions tend to cluster in particular occupations and reside in particular areas because in most cases relatives and others from the same origin area are instrumental in assisting newly arrived migrants to obtain work and housing.

Another important element in understanding contemporary internal and international labour migration in Indonesia is the growing institutionalisation of much of that movement. Most significant here is the role of a whole group of recruiters, brokers, agents, middlemen etc. variously known as *calo, taikong* or *mandor*. These are highly organised and greatly facilitate and not only encourage much of the migration to overseas destinations, especially Malaysia (*ibid.*), but also are often involved in the rural to urban migration process as was pointed out earlier.

Conclusion

Indonesia is experiencing economic and social change at an unprecedentedly rapid rate and this is both reshaping, and in turn being influenced by, substantial shifts in the level and pattern of population movement. Forces of globalisation are impinging upon this movement in a myriad of ways as foreign investment levels rise, multinationals set up factories in Indonesia, global mass media reach into most Indonesian households and political and economic relationships with neighbouring and other nations develop and change. Within Indonesia, increasing commercialisation of agriculture, structural shifts in the economy, achievement of more or less universal education, widespread radio and television ownership, changes in the structure and functioning of the family and shifts in the role and status of women are all interrelated with increasing levels and complexity in population mobility. Nevertheless our knowledge of the shifts in population movement and its linkages with economic and social change still remains very limited despite a burgeoning of the literature on this topic over the last decade. The inclusion of more detailed migration questions in the 1995 Intercensal Survey should provide some new insights into the dynamics of mobility within provinces.

It appears certain that population mobility will continue to increase in scale as well as in economic and social significance in Indonesia in the remainder of the 1990s. It is difficult to see any substantial change occurring in the major trends identified in this paper. Despite rapid and far-reaching change, Indonesia remains a labour-surplus country in which poverty and underemployment remain high and there is a net increment in the labour force of more than 2 million each year. Spatial inequalities are substantial and new job opportunities are highly concentrated. Economic growth rates remain high, structural shifts in the economy continue apace as does social change. It would, therefore, seem that in the second half of the 1990s Indonesians will become even more mobile, their internal and international movements will become more complex in their spatial patterning and a wider spectrum of the population will become involved.

6

Patterns and Trends of Urbanisation: A Reflection of Regional Disparity

Tommy Firman

Urbanisation is defined as the level of urbanity of a community or nation. Demographically, the level is measured by the urban population's proportion of the total population (Goodal 1987: 492). Urbanisation should be distinguished from urban population growth, which is measured by the rate of annual increase of the urban population, either of individual cities or of the entire urban population. Usually, although not always, there is a close relationship between urbanisation and the urban population growth rate.

Although in a narrow sense, urbanisation can be viewed as a demographic phenomenon, in a broader sense it has social, economic and political dimensions. Sociologically, urbanisation is the transformation from a rural life style to industrial ways of living.

Urbanisation is a process that is closely related to other processes of socio-economic development. The advanced countries, especially North America and Western Europe, Australia, Japan and New Zealand, for example, have a much higher proportion of urban population than developing countries, such as Indonesia (Table 6.1). Meanwhile, the newly industrialised countries, South Korea and Malaysia, for instance, have shown a distinct transition towards an urban society.

Although urbanisation is a universal process, and a reflection of social and economic development, there are various problems with specific aspects of the process being faced by developing countries. One of the prominent characteristics is the high concentration of urban population in certain cities only, especially the large cities, and lately this tendency has been developing at an increasingly faster rate (see ESCAP 1993).

TABLE 6.1: **Urbanisation trends in some countries in Asia
and the Pacific, 1979-90**

Country	1970		1980		1990	
	Total Pop. ('000)	% Urban	Total Pop. ('000)	% Urban	Total Pop ('000)	% Urban
ASEAN						
Brunei Darusallam	130	61.7	185	59.9	266	57.7
Indonesia	120,280	17.1	146,776	23.4	179,321	30.9
Malaysia	10,852	27.0	13,763	34.6	17,567	43.0
Philippines	37,540	33.0	48,317	37.4	62,413	42.6
Thailand	35,745	13.3	46,718	17.3	55,701	22.6
Other Southeast Asian countries						
Myanmar	27,102	22.8	33,821	24.0	41,675	24.8
Cambodia	6,938	11.7	6,400	10.3	8,246	11.6
Laos	2,713	9.6	3,205	13.4	4,139	18.6
Vietnam	42,729	18.3	53,700	19.3	66,693	21.9
ASIA						
China	830,675	17.4	996,134	19.6	1,139,060	33.4
India	554,911	19.8	688,856	23.1	853,094	27.0
Afghanistan	13,623	11.0	16,063	15.6	16,557	18.2
Bangladesh	66,671	7.6	88,219	11.3	115,593	16.4
Pakistan	65,706	24.9	85,299	28.1	122,626	31.0
South Korea	31,466	50.1	37,436	68.8	43,411	79.8
Developed countries						
Australia	12,552	85.2	14,695	85.8	16,873	85.5
Japan	104,331	71.2	116,807	76.2	123,460	77.0
New Zealand	2,820	81.1	3,113	83.3	3,392	84.0

Source: ESCAP 1993: II-11.

The present urbanisation processes in the developing countries in Asia are different in a number of respects from the experiences of the industrialised countries about one century ago. As stated by McGee (1991a, 1991b) and Lin (1994), the distinction between 'rural' and 'urban' is blurred in contemporary urbanisation processes in Asia. Both agricultural and non-agricultural activities occur side by side in the surrounding areas of the urban centres. This 'blurring' is indeed a product of rapid economic development and modern technology advances. Another aspect of the present urbanisation trend in Asia, especially in South East Asia, is the integration of cities into the global economy, boosted by capital accumulations at a global scale (McGee 1995; Douglass 1995; see also Rimmer 1995). The process is called 'mega-urbanisation' (McGee and Robinson 1995).

At present, advances in transportation and communication technologies are greatly facilitating the flow of capital, people, and information from foreign countries to Indonesia. The flow of investment from foreign countries, especially from transnational corporations in advanced countries as well as the newly industrialising countries, is profoundly influencing Indonesia's economy. Current developments in production technologies have greatly facilitated the horizontal and vertical divisions of industrial production processes, thus establishing what is called the new international division of labour. These developments have in turn become the prime mover for the integration of the large world cities, including Indonesian cities, in the global economic system (see Fujita 1991; Knock 1994; Sassen 1994).

In the light of this background, the present chapter will discuss the pattern of urbanisation in Indonesia. After reviewing briefly the factors enhancing urbanisation, two queries are raised for starting discussion: first, what are the patterns of demographic development and spatial urbanisation in Indonesia? Secondly, what will be the future trends of urbanisation in Indonesia?

Factors enhancing urbanisation

Urbanisation and development of cities are induced mainly by economic developments. Industry and services are the main economic activities that affect development of cities. These activities tend to take place in large cities owing to 'urbanisation economies' that can be simply defined as the economic advantages of a city, notably a large city, that attract the establishment of economic undertakings in the city. These are for example, the availability of utilities such as electricity, water and ports; concentration of markets and also of skilled labour. An illustration of how large cities in Indonesia can attract various economic activities is the fact that until July 1995, about half of the foreign (PMA) and domestic (PMDN) investments approved by the Coordinating Agency for Investments (BKPM) were concentrated in Jabotabek or Metropolitan Jakarta (PMA US$109.3 billion and PMDN Rp. 322.9 trillion respectively: Firman 1995).

In the Jabotabek area, the present foreign investment is dominated by Japan and the newly industrialised countries, such as South Korea, Hong Kong and Singapore. The strategy of these countries is to relocate their industries to countries with low labour cost, such as Indonesia. By the middle of 1995, Japan's cumulative share of investments in Indonesia since the early 1970s had reached 15 per cent of the total amount of foreign investments, followed by Hong Kong, Taiwan and Singapore, with 11.9 per cent, 6.7 per cent and 5.3 per cent respectively. However, it is worth noting that the foreign invested industries are in general 'footloose' in character, having very little linkage with the local economy (*ibid.*).

This means that the Jabotabek as well as the national economy is greatly influenced by the economic decisions of Tokyo and to a lesser extent, Hong Kong. In terms of the global urban system this will also mean that Jabotabek is being oriented to Tokyo.

So far, foreign involvement in the Indonesian economy has been not only in the sector of industry, but also in the sectors of finance and other services. Developments in the financial sector include a growing number of foreign banks operating in Jakarta. In 1992 there were already more than 100 foreign banks in operation, comprising head offices, branch offices and agencies, including the leading foreign banks, such as Bank of America, Citibank, Bank of Tokyo and others (*ibid.*). Money market activities have also grown rapidly. In 1988 there were no more than 25 companies registered in the Jakarta Stock Market, whereas in 1993 there were already more than 160 companies (Sjahrir 1993).

Developments in the sectors of industry, finance and services in Jabotabek and the other large cities like Surabaya, Bandung and Medan, have in turn encouraged developments in the property sector, especially the construction of luxurious housing estates in new towns in the outskirts, shopping centres, hotels and other buildings. The property sector has become a big business in the large cities.

Economic activities have recently become increasingly concentrated in large cities, mainly owing to the many deregulation policies in the sectors of industry and finance. The policies have been launched by the government to enhance performance efficiency in the economic sectors and to promote export of non-oil commodities, and these will in turn be expected to increase the national economic growth rate. Although deregulation policies are essentially economic policies, and are not intended to influence urban development and urbanisation, their impact on urban development is nevertheless considerable. To a large degree the deregulation policies spurred development of large cities, especially the cities in Java, rather than the small towns. This is because the big cities are better equipped with the needed infrastructure and facilities for developing economic activities.

Demographic dimensions

The population censuses of 1980 and 1990 defined a locality as 'urban' when it complied with the three following requirements (BPS 1988; see also Firman 1992): (1) having a population density of 5000 people or more per square kilometre, (2) having 25 per cent or less of the households working in the agricultural sector; (3) having eight or more kinds of urban facilities).[1]

On the basis of the above criteria, the Biro Pusat Statistik (BPS) uses a more technical scoring system (see *ibid.*) to define a locality as being 'rural' or 'urban'. Such a system has its weaknesses (Rietveld 1988: 75-6; Firman 1992). For example, the indicator for urban facilities is arbitrarily defined and does not consider the differences in quality of the facilities. Besides, the blurred distinction between 'urban localities' and 'rural localities', especially in Java, has reduced the relevance of the above criteria (Hugo, forthcoming). Nevertheless, the classification system is still very useful in studying urbanisation at the macro level of analysis.

---

[1] These facilities include primary school or equivalent; junior high school or equivalent; senior high school or equivalent; cinema; hospital; maternity hospital/mother-child hospital; primary health care centre/clinic; road that can be used by three- or four-wheeled motorised vehicles; telephone/post-office agency, market with buildings, shopping centre; bank; factory; restaurants; public electricity; party-equipment renting services.

Based on the above-mentioned classification system, the urbanisation level of an area can be identified. In Indonesia, there has been a steady increase in urbanisation since 1920, when the level of urbanisation had only reached 5.8 per cent (Soegijoko and Bulkin 1994). The proportion of the population living in urban localities reached 22.3 per cent in 1980, and had increased to 30.9 per cent in 1990, and to 34.3 per cent according to the 1994 National Social and Economic Survey (Susenas) (Table 6.2). This is running ahead of Hugo's (forthcoming) prediction that by the year 2000, about one-third of the Indonesian population will live in the urban areas, and there will be a substantial number of rural people working and finding their living in the urban areas through circular migration and commuting. According to a recent projection (Ananta and Anwar 1995) the urban population in Indonesia will reach 116.5 million and 140.3 million people respectively by the years 2010 and 2020, indicating that the level of urbanisation will increase to 50 per cent and 55 per cent respectively. For comparison, the urban proportion of the world population at that time will reach 56.5 per cent and 62.8 per cent respectively (ESCAP 1993: II-35).

Indonesia is indeed undergoing a rapid increase in the level of urbanisation, although it still belongs to the group of countries with low urbanisation. According to Hugo (forthcoming), out of the 19 countries with a population of above 50 million people, Indonesia's level of urbanisation is one of the lowest, just above Thailand, Vietnam and Bangladesh.

In the past two decades, the urban population in Indonesia had grown at a rapid rate. In the 1971-80 period the growth rate reached 4.60 per cent per year, and this increased to 5.36 per cent per year in the 1980-90 period. For comparison, growth of the total population had reached a rate of 2.34 per cent per year in the 1971-80 period and the rate had decreased to 1.97 per cent per year during the 1980-90 period.

As for the components of urban population growth in Indonesia during 1980-85, according to the United Nations (ESCAP 1993: II-16), more than one-third (35.2 per cent) was due to natural increase, and the remaining 64.8 per cent was due to migration and reclassification. It was expected that in the 1990-95 period the figures would be much the same: 37.0 per cent for natural increase and 63 per cent for migration and reclassification.

TABLE 6.2: Urban population in Java and the Outer Islands, 1980-94

	Java	Outer Islands
1980		
Urban population ('000)	22 929	99 916
Urban proportion of population	0.251	0.177
Share of urban population (%)	69.8	30.2
1990		
Urban population ('000)	38 341	17 092
Urban proportion of population	0.357	0.238
Share of urban population (%)	69.2	30.8
Annual rate of urban pop. growth 1980-90 (%)	5.29	5.60
1994		
Urban population ('000)	44 960	20 294
Urban proportion of population	0.398	0.263
Share of urban population (%)	68.8	31.2

Sources: BPS 1991b, 1992a, 1995c.

In 1950, there was only one city with a population of more than one million people, namely Jakarta. In the year 1980 however, the number had increased to four, with the addition of Surabaya, Bandung and Medan. Then, in 1990, the number had increased again to seven, with the addition of Semarang, Palembang, and Ujung Pandang, whose population was just a shade under one million people. By the end of the PJP II (Second Long Term Development Phase), that is, the year 2020, the number of cities having more than one million people is projected to increase to 23, eleven of them with a population of more than five million people, including Jabotabek, which is predicted to reach a population of 35 million people at that time (Kartasasmita 1995: 5).

Spatial patterns and distribution

In terms of absolute numbers, the urban proportion of the total population and the share of urban population, the island of Java is still
dominant (Table 6.2). Java's estimated share of Indonesia's total urban
population in the year 1994 had already reached 69 per cent, leaving
only 31 per cent in the islands outside Java. These shares appear to
have remained constant since 1980. Meanwhile, the urban proportion
of the population in Java had reached 40 per cent, whereas outside
Java it was only 26 per cent. However, a more detailed analysis
indicates that there is a very high proportion of urban population in
two provinces outside Java, namely Sumatra Utara (North Sumatra)
and Kalimantan Timur (East Kalimantan), the proportions in 1994
being 40 per cent and 50 per cent respectively. These two provinces
have experienced rapid economic development when compared to
the other provinces in Indonesia (Firman 1996b).

A simple indicator frequently used to analyse the distribution of
urban population is the primacy index, that is, the ratio of the population of the largest city over the second largest (Goodal 1987: 225) or
alternatively the ratio of the population of the largest city over the
total population of the next three largest cities. An analysis of the
primacy index in Indonesia, using the second method of analysis
(Firman 1996a), namely the ratio of the Jabotabek urban population to
the total urban population of Gerbangkertasusila (Metropolitan
Surabaya), Bandung Raya (Metropolitan Bandung) and Mebidang
(Medan-Binjai-Deli Serdang: Metropolitan Medan), shows a ratio of
1.27 in the year 1980 and 1.39 in the year 1990. Meanwhile, it may also
be recorded that the share of the Jabotabek population in the total
urban population in Indonesia had reached 23.5 per cent in 1980 and
23.6 per cent in 1990. On the whole, this indicates the dominance of
Jabotabek as a concentration of urban population in Indonesia. This
pattern is also reflected in the disparity of Gross City Product per
capita in some cities in Indonesia, where in 1992 the highest (Jakarta)
reached US$2,843, almost three times the figures of US$1,085 for the
second highest—Surabaya City (Table 6.3). Nevertheless, the degree
of concentration is not as high as for example in Thailand, where the
Bangkok Metropolitan Area is a highly dominant primate city, or the
Philippines, where Metro Manila is quite dominant.

The spatial development of cities in Java tends to be in the form of corridors that connect the large cities (Firman 1992; Firman and Dharmapatni 1995). The main urban corridors include those of Jakarta-Bandung; Cirebon-Semarang; Yogyakarta-Semarang; and Surabaya-Malang. Most significant in the corridor development is the increasing mixture of urban economic activities, especially industry, with rural economic activities, namely agriculture, which in turn has caused a blurring of the distinction between 'rural' and 'urban', both physically as well as social-economically. This indeed reflects increasingly intensive links between the cities and the villages (Firman 1996a), in line with McGee's (1991a) argument that urban development and urbanisation in regions with high population densities, such as the island of Java, South Korea or Taiwan, should be region-based and not city-based.

The present developments of large cities in Java are notably characterised by internal restructuring, both physically as well as social-economically. One of the striking characteristics of restructuring in Metropolitan Jabotabek is the changing function of the core area, from being a centre of manufacturing activities to become a centre for finance and services, whereas the manufacturing activities are shifted to the fringe areas (Firman 1995).

The restructuring process is physically characterised by the conversion of land in the outskirts or fringe areas as well as in the town centres. In the fringe areas there is an immense conversion of agricultural land to non-agricultural land uses, especially large-scale housing developments, including the mushrooming development of new towns, industrial estates and even golf courses. There are now 26 new towns and prospective new towns in the Jakarta surroundings with land areas of over 500 hectares (*Majalah Properti Indonesia*, March 1996). Meanwhile, in the core areas of Jakarta City, slum areas are being converted into a business zone, with shopping centres, hotels, offices, condominiums, and the like. This is a reflection of the development of the sector of finance and service, which has in turn encouraged the booming of the property sector in large cities, notably Jakarta, Surabaya, Bandung, Medan and others.

Up to August 1995, the Kantor Badan Pertanahan Nasional(KBPN) or the National Land Administration Office had issued the location permits for land development in the Bogor-

TABLE 6.3: Cities in Java and Outer Islands with population between 50,000 and 1,000,000, 1980 and 1990 (thousands)

	Province	Population in 1980	Population in 1990	Growth Rate (%)
Java				
Semarang	Central Java	820.1	1,003.6	2.0
Yogyakarta	Yogyakarta	395.0	412.1	0.4
Malang	East Java	470.1	649.7	3.3
Surakarta	Central Java	469.5	503.8	0.7
Cirebon	West Java	223.5	244.9	0.9
Kediri	East Java	173.4	235.3	3.1
Pekalongan	Central Java	132.4	227.3	5.6
Tegal	Central Java	131.4	215.6	5.6
Madiun	East Java	145.6	165.8	1.3
Pasuruan	East Java	91.3	133.7	3.9
Probolinggo	East Java	98.1	131.1	2.9
Magelang	Central Java	123.4	123.2	-
Sukabumi	West Java	109.9	119.9	0.9
Blitar	East Java	75.5	113.0	4.1
Salatiga	Central Java	81.7	98.0	1.8
Outer Islands				
Palembang	South Sumatra	757.5	1,085.5	3.7
Ujung Pandang	South Sulawesi	638.8	912.9	3.6
Padang	West Sumatra	296.7	477.0	4.9
Bandar Lampung	Lampung	284.2	457.9	4.9
Banjarmasin	South Kalimantan	330.1	443.1	3.0
Pontianak	East Kalimantan	276.7	387.4	3.4
Pekanbaru	Riau	186.2	341.3	6.3
Samarinda	East Kalimantan	182.5	334.9	6.3
Balikpapan	East Kalimantan	208.0	309.2	4.0
Jambi	Jambi	155.8	301.4	6.8
Manado	North Sulawesi	217.1	275.2	2.4
Ambon	Maluku	111.9	205.2	6.3
P. Siantar	North Sumatra	150.3	203.8	3.1
Donggala	Central Sulawesi	73.0	168.5	8.7
Bengkulu	Bengkulu	32.5	146.4	16.2
Banda Aceh	Aceh	71.9	143.4	7.2
Kupang	East Nusa Tenggara	87.9	141.7	4.9
Jayapura	Irian Jaya	81.5	130.1	4.8
Tebing Tinggi	North Sumatra	69.6	116.8	5.3
Pangkal Pinang	Riau	86.9	108.4	2.2
Kendari	Southeast Sulawesi	43.1	103.0	9.1
Tanjung Balai	North Sumatra	41.8	101.6	9.3
Palangka Raya	Central Kalimantan	51.7	99.7	6.8
Gorontalo	North Sulawesi	63.6	94.0	4.0
Pare-Pare	South Sulawesi	63.1	84.1	2.9
Bukit Tinggi	West Sumatra	55.6	72.1	2.6
Sibolga	North Sumatra	59.5	71.6	1.9
Payakumbuh	West Sumatra	24.6	50.5	7.5

Source: BPS 1991b.

Tangerang-Bekasi (Botabek) region to developers, to already cover an area of 81,200 hectares. However, the land acquisition process is proceeding slowly, and developers have been able to acquire only 41 per cent or about 33,275 hectares (*Kompas*, 6 December 1995). Of the already acquired land, only about 13,000 hectares are already being developed, whereas the remaining areas are left unattended or neglected. Furthermore, there are at present application documents being processed to obtain the Decree Letter for land authority for thousands of hectares in the region (Hidayat 1995). At the present time, the government is also preparing plans for land reclamation for town development at two locations, namely the Jakarta Waterfront City and Teluknaga in the district (*kabupaten*) of Tangerang.

The Biro Pusat Statistik recorded the change of land use from agricultural to non-agricultural uses in Indonesia as a whole between 1991 and 1993 to total 106,424 hectares, covering 57,987 hectares (54.0 per cent) for housing; 16,542 hectares (15.7 per cent) for industry; 5,210 hectares (4.9 per cent) for offices and the remaining 25 per cent for other uses (*Kompas*, 7 November 1995). Of the total conversion, that of 54,722 hectares (51 per cent) took place in Java.

The other conspicuous phenomenon in the development of cities in Indonesia at the moment is the rapid increase of the urban population and non-agricultural workers in the fringe areas of big cities. For example, in the period 1980-90, the annual population growth rates in the districts of Tangerang, Bogor and Bekasi which are the fringe areas of Jakarta, were 20.9 per cent, 11.7 per cent and 19.9 per cent respectively (Firman 1992). This was due to the migration of newcomers from various areas, even from outside Java, into the districts which are now the largest industrial centres in Indonesia. Of course the number of inmigrants is larger when the number of non-permanent dwellers, who have no intention of becoming permanent citizens in the districts, are included. Another perspective on these trends is given by the number of non-agricultural workers in Botabek, which in 1971 numbered 584,000 workers but had increased to 2,360,000 workers in 1990 (Hugo, forthcoming). Even more striking, Jones and Mamas (1996: 51) found that during 1980-90, while employment in DKI Jakarta rose by only 52 per cent, in its inner ring (the part of Botabek which had been influenced directly by the expansion of Jakarta City), employment increased by 425 per cent, or about eight times as rapidly. In addition, the educational attainment of the workforce in the inner ring also increased dramatically.

Part of this process was the movement of many DKI Jakarta residents to the outskirts due to the thriving development of new housing complexes in the area. This is reflected by the fact that there are at present about 400,000 people residing in Bekasi who are still holding the Residency Card (*Kartu Tanda Penduduk*) of DKI Jakarta (Firman and Dharmapatni 1995). A study on the fringe areas of Jakarta carried out by Browder, Bohlan and Scarpaci (1995) revealed that many residents of the fringe areas were people with middle and higher income levels from the core city area, i.e. Jakarta, and in contrast there were very few people from the rural areas. At the moment, the fringe areas have been integrated, spatially as well as functionally, into the economy of Metropolitan Jakarta, and have very few linkages with the rural economy.

It is also worth noting that owing to the rapid population growth in the fringe areas, the DKI Jakarta population as a proportion of Jabotabek had decreased from 54.6 per cent in 1980 to 43.2 per cent in 1990 (Firman 1995). The same is also happening in the Metropolitan Bandung area (Firman and Dharmapatni 1995; Firman 1996b).

The other conspicuous aspect is the flow of commuters between the outskirts and the core city areas. It is estimated that at the moment there are about 350,000 people commuting between the city of Jakarta and the districts of Serang, Tangerang, Bogor, Bekasi and Karawang (*ibid.*). It is expected that the number will increase to half a million people by the year 2010 (JMDP 1992).

The next question is regarding the functions and developments of small and medium towns, namely the towns with a population between 50,000 and 1 million people. An attempt to answer the question is by using simple data, namely the population growth rate of the towns, although the data are obviously far from adequate to be used for addressing the question. On the whole one can say that the population growth rates of these small and medium towns in Java are relatively low, far below the average urban population growth in Java, that was 5.29 per cent per year, with the exception of Malang, Kediri, Pekalongan and Tegal (Table 6.4). Nevertheless, one should study further whether the increase is due to inmigration and natural increase or due to the extension of the administrative boundaries of these small and medium towns. The municipalities of Blitar and Pasuruan experienced a high rate of population growth, although the absolute numbers involved were not very large. Meanwhile, the municipality of Magelang experienced a decrease in its population.

TABLE 6.4: Gross city product per capita of selected cities, 1992
(US$)

	Gross City Product Per Capita
Jakarta	2,843
Surabaya	1,085
Bandung	739
Medan	925
Semarang	576
Banjarmasin	809

Source: *National Report for Habitat II*, Annex I, Final Draft, February 1996.

The study by Titus (1993) in Central Java on the small towns of Banjarnegara, Wonosobo, Purworejo and Purbalingga revealed a very weak role of the small towns as centres for collection and distribution of goods, because the rural population are dealing directly with the tradesmen, suppliers as well as wholesalers, from the large cities, thus bypassing the small towns. Apart from that, Titus (*ibid*: 25) also argues that the policies and programs aimed at agriculture and village development are directly defined and decided at the national level, hence greatly reducing the roles of these small towns as centres for agricultural development. It appears in this case, that the small towns are only serving the rural community groups with middle and higher levels of income. On the basis of this observation, Titus (*ibid*: 26) concluded:

Thus, the potential role of the small-town as a regional service centre (Rondinelli and Evans, 1983) is mainly reduced to that of a regional service centre, following passively the developments and structural changes induced in its hinterland by external forces originating at the national level and in higher order centres.

In contrast, the increase of population in small and medium towns outside Java during 1980-90 was higher than in towns in Java, and much higher than the national population growth rate of 1.97 per cent per year. Several cities even had a higher growth rate than the average urban population growth rate in Java during that period of time (5.4 per cent) or the annual national average urban growth rate of 5.6 per cent (Table 6.3). Most interesting to observe is that the highest growth rates in outer island cities were in some of the smaller cities, with less than 400,000 people (Table 6.4). A dramatic example was the city of Bengkulu, having an average growth rate of 16.2 per cent per year. However, this case should be taken with caution, as the sharp increase might be due to the expansion of the town administrative boundaries.

In general, the very limited data have shown that the population growth of small and medium towns outside Java was much faster than that of such towns in Java. It appears that the small and medium towns outside Java are playing a more significant role and function as centres for regional economic activities compared with the small and medium towns in Java, owing to the dominant roles of the large cities in Java.

Conclusion

Referring to the first query posed at the beginning of this chapter, that is, regarding the demographic and spatial patterns of urbanisation in Indonesia, first of all it can be concluded that, as in most developing countries, urbanisation in Indonesia is still highly concentrated in large cities. At the moment, about one-fourth of the Indonesian urban population is centred in Jabotabek. The primacy index also indicates the dominance of Metropolitan Jabotabek as the largest concentration of urban population in Indonesia. Overall, these patterns reflect a regional disparity in Indonesia, between Jakarta and the other cities; between large and small cities; and between Java and the outer islands.

Secondly, the spatial development of cities in Java is forming a corridor connecting certain of the large cities. The most significant characteristic of this development is the blurring of the distinction between the 'urban' and the 'rural' areas. This is a manifestation of the increasingly intensive links between towns and villages in Java. In the meantime, the fringe areas are experiencing very rapid population growth, whereas the core city is experiencing a decrease in population growth. This is illustrated, for example, by the decreased proportion of Jakarta population in the Metropolitan Jabotabek region. It is obvious that in this relation, the cities in Java can no longer be viewed as individual cities, in the sense that these cities must always be seen in relation to their surrounding quasi-urban areas and also in relation to other cities with which they have close links. Meanwhile, the nearby fertile agricultural areas have been converted at a remarkable pace into urban housing areas, industrial estates and the like, a feature of the process of mega-urbanisation in South East Asia (McGee 1995).

However, this does not mean that the rural-urban distinction should be completely disregarded, rather that urbanisation should be seen in regional perspective. Therefore, a regional development framework is needed for a broader context of urban planning on the island (see also Jones 1988: 141).

The population growth rate of the small and medium towns outside Java is relatively high when compared to the small and medium towns in Java. Although growth rates are only a rough indicator, it seems that the small and medium towns outside Java are playing a more significant role as centres for development as compared to the towns of that size in Java. As Titus (1993: 26) maintains,

> ... the recommendations of the National Urban Development Strategy Report (NUDS 1985), aimed at the stimulation of small and intermediate urban centres [notably in Java], should be considered with caution.

Thirdly, it should be admitted that urbanisation is a natural and inevitable process , along with the social and economic development of the nation. The cities are indeed playing a very important role in the economic development process, in line with the World Bank's observation that 40 to 60 per cent of the Gross Domestic Product (GDP) of developing countries is produced in the urban areas. In fact, in Indonesia the contribution of urban economy sectors to the national GDP is estimated to have reached 50 per cent, and is expected to increase to 75 per cent in the future (*National Report for Habitat II*, 1996, Final Draft: Annex I). Not surprisingly, the higher the proportion of urban population in a region, the greater the contribution of urban economy sectors to the regional economy (Table 6.5). Thus, urbanisation should not be viewed as something negative, but should be directed as a means of attaining broader national development goals.

Fourthly, present development policies which stress the export of non-oil products are greatly influencing the process of urbanisation and urban development. The large cities, especially those in Java, are

TABLE 6.5: Contribution of urban sector to GDP
(per cent)

	Contribution of Urban Sector to GDP (1990)	Proportion of Urban Population (1993)
Java	68.1	38.4
Sumatra	15.9	27.3
Indonesia	50.0	34.0

Source: National Report for Habitat II, Annex I, Final Draft, February 1996.

promoted by the policies, as the cities are better prepared with the supporting facilities and infrastructure. In the short run, it seems that the regulations tend to widen the disparities between small towns and intermediate cities, on the one hand, and large cities, especially those in Java, on the other hand; and the disparities between Java and the outer islands.

Given the patterns of urbanisation and urban development discussed above, there should be a fundamental change in the practices and institutional mechanisms of urban management in Indonesia. The existing bureaucratic practices of urban management obviously cannot cope with the unprecedented fast growth of urban areas in Indonesia, and therefore, there should be innovative management in infrastructure provision, environmental development, financing, housing and land development, otherwise the socio-economic as well as land-use and infrastructure problems in the cities will become even worse, especially in the large cities.

The management of urban development should be perceived as the responsibility not only of the government, but also of the private sector and the urban communities, as the government alone obviously does not have enough resources to meet the demands for urban development. Therefore, there is a need to establish a good governance for urban development that involves all the actors, notably the local government, private sectors, and communities, in the spirit of equal 'partnership', not one subordinated to another.

It should be added that owing to the emergence of urban corridors joining large cities, notably in Java, spatial planning should take this phenomenon into account. For instance, mass transport development along the urban corridors seems destined to be a very important element in urban and regional development in Java.

The development of small towns and intermediate cities in the outer islands is still very relevant, since those cities play a significant role as growth centres in regional development. At this point, decentralisation from Jakarta as the national centre to the outer islands is considered to be one of the keys to encourage small towns and intermediate cities in the outer islands.

7

Migration and Urbanisation: A Discussion

Peter Gardiner

Introduction

The studies of geographic mobility of population and urbanisation have historically been the poor stepchildren of Indonesian demography. Yet it must be emphasised that the extent to which they have achieved prominence has been, in no small measure, a result of the influence of the authors of the previous two chapters. Dr Hugo taught us many years ago that permanent migration (what is more or less measured by the censuses) is only the tip of the iceberg. There is an even more intense pattern of shorter-term mobility which links people and places across quite a broad expanse of geographic space. On Java, the evolution of widespread and relatively inexpensive transport networks means that today there are very few rural villages which do not have at least some fairly strong economic or social linkages with the outside world. And this outside world is expanding. As recently as fifteen to twenty years ago this world might have been limited to a few nearby urban centres; today, it often encompasses foreign economic opportunity in places like Malaysia or the Middle East.

Migration

Interest in internal, and particularly interregional, flows of population has, of course, been stimulated by the Indonesian government's longstanding policies to shift population from the densely populated heartland of Java and Bali to the, at least perceived, wider open spaces of the Outer Islands. The result has been the well-known and often controversial Transmigration Program which, although subject to considerable shifts in policies and organisation over the years, still enshrines the questionable mission of saving Java from impoverishment due to overpopulation and the even more debatable premise that lack of sufficient numbers of people constitutes the major development constraint in many other parts of the country.

Demographically it has long been clear that numerical impacts of transmigration on Java have been relatively small. Declining fertility has played a much more significant role in curbing overall rates of population growth. In some Outer Island provinces with small base populations, however, the impacts have been more substantial, accounting, during the 1980s, for the great majority of inmigration and perhaps as much as 25 to 30 per cent of overall population growth.

In terms of internal interregional mobility, current policies are clearly designed to continue fostering outward movement, even if the Transmigration Program itself increasingly relies on self-sponsored (*swarkasa*) movement to fulfil its targets. The concepts of Western and Eastern Indonesia (Indonesia Bagian Barat and Indonesia Bagian Timur) are now enshrined in long-term development planning and ways are being sought to encourage investment and relatively more rapid development in the Eastern Islands.[1] Population movement, designed in part to address perceived imbalances in labour supply, is seen to be an important element in this process.

Yet it is not clear if such heavy emphasis on population mobility is well founded, and here two questions can be raised. The first has to do with the nature of much of the Outer Islands economy and the relation of labour and land, and the second has to do with demographic forces themselves and the pace of 'natural' growth of the labour supply in relation to possible regional-specific trends in labour demand.

---

[1] While 'Inner' and 'Outer' Indonesia generally differentiates between the islands of Java, Madura and Bali and the rest of the country, IBB *and* IBT includes Sumatera and Kalimantan along with Java as parts of Western Indonesia with Nusa Tenggara, Sulawesi, Maluku and Irian comprising the Eastern zone of the country.

With the exception of a few relatively diversified metropolitan centres and industrial enclaves, Outer Indonesia is characterised by a resource-based economy focusing on agricultural and forest products and minerals. Many of these activities involve extensive claims to land and involve very low man-land ratios in terms of labour requirements. The claims emanating from these sources are large and growing—the rapid expansion of estate crops such as palm oil, and the quite massive areas now being allocated for commercial tree farms (primarily for the pulp and paper industry) are cases in point. The point is, of course, that land use (along with land capability) is an important factor in determining what relevant population densities are likely to be, or should be, sustained. If these demand very low densities, then claims of distortions simply because densities are low, along with claims of need to bring in increasing volumes of new population, may not make very sound economic sense.

Land extensive claims in the economy also need to be considered in terms of land requirements to meet environmental concerns, for maintenance of biodiversity and, not least, to meet needs of indigenous populations which are still generally growing faster (on the basis of natural increase alone) than in the Inner Islands where the demographic transition started earlier. The end result is thus a question, not just of environmental carrying capacity, but also of economic carrying capacity which needs to be more carefully addressed in setting policies on population redistribution and in using public resources (as opposed to improved and more open labour market mechanisms) to influence where people go.

In looking at labour markets, one simple, although somewhat hypothetical exercise is to compare labour demand and supply derived, on the one hand, from regional economic projections and, on the other, from demographic projections incorporating various assumptions on interregional migration.

Here, Table 7.1 provides a few alternative projections of population and labour supply (here proxied by the working age population) between 1990 and 2020 for Inner Indonesia (Java, Madura and Bali) and for the Outer Islands. Both projections are derived from official projections made by the Indonesian Central Bureau of Statistics (Biro Pusat Statistik — BPS); one assuming trends in interprovincial migration according to levels observed in the late 1980s and the other assuming no net interprovincial migration and only incorporating the fertility and mortality assumptions used by BPS.

TABLE 7.1: Population ratios (2020/1990) for total and working-age population for Inner and Outer Islands based on alternative migration scenarios

	Migration assumption	Population ratio	Growth rate
Total population			
Inner Islands	Trend migration	1.30	0.9
	No migration	1.35	1.0
Outer Islands	Trend migration	1.71	1.8
	No migration	1.56	1.5
Working age population			
Inner Islands	Trend migration	1.56	1.5
	No migration	1.62	1.6
Outer Islands	Trend migration	2.17	2.6
	No migration	1.97	2.3
Labour demand			
Inner Islands		1.71	1.8
Outer Islands		2.11	2.5

Sources: Trend Migration Projections are from Biro Pusat Statistik (Proyeksi Penduduk per Propinisi 1990-2020, Jakarta, 1994). No migration projections were prepared by the author using BPS fertility and mortality assumptions. Labour demand projections are from BAPPENAS.

First, it can be easily seen that even without any interregional migration between Inner and Outer Indonesia, there is still a substantial difference in growth. This is largely a result of historical lower fertility and the earlier start of the demographic transition in the inner part of the country. Under this 'no migration' scenario, population in Inner Indonesia would grow by about 30 per cent between 1990 and 2020 compared to close to 56 per cent in the Outer Islands. On the other hand, the 'trend migration' scenario results in a slight reduction in growth on Java/Bali and a substantial increase in growth for the Outer Islands.

Age structure effects mean that the working-age population (a reasonable first proxy for growth in labour supply) will grow faster than population as a whole, but the ratios also imply a gradual decline in growth rate of the working-age population from that observed in the recent past (nationally, this was close to 3 per cent annually during the 1980s). Growth in the working-age population in Inner Indonesia would be around 1.6 times over the 30-year period compared to between 2.0 and 2.2 times in Outer Indonesia depending on which migration assumption is used.

These growth rates can be compared with labour demand estimates from a regional econometric model developed by the National Planning Agency (Bappenas). These estimates are based on projections of sectoral output by province and labour coefficients (employment elasticities) which are allowed to change to reflect improvements in productivity over time. It should also be noted that these projections include quite optimistic assumptions on patterns of investment and export growth *vis-à-vis* the Eastern Islands as opposed to Java. They are hardly precise, but they do lead to one quite interesting observation; over the longer term represented here, the natural growth (no migration) scenario appears to come closer to a labour market balance between Inner and Outer Indonesia than the trend migration projection prepared by BPS. In other words, the difference in natural growth in the labour supply between Inner and Outer regions is almost sufficient, in itself, to provide for the greater relative increase in employment opportunity projected to occur in the Outer Islands under the economic model.[2]

This also raises questions about the economic efficiency of pushing people away from Java. The likelihood, of course, is that some movement will happen in any case as the structure of labour markets will be different in different regions. However, the potential for increasing relative migrant flows toward Java, in spite of government policies, should not be discounted.

---

[2] The fact that growth in the working age population is slower than that of labour demand is also indicative of future tightening of labour markets as a result of age structure effects of slowed population growth. The gap in growth would logically be met by changes in labour force participation, in unemployment, possibly by some foreign labour, and hopefully by declines in underemployment leading, independent of technological change, to increased productivity on a per-worker basis.

Urbanisation

Urbanisation has also received increasing prominence as an issue in Indonesia's overall development. Although levels of urbanisation in Indonesia have historically remained low compared to some other large developing countries, the policy debate has been fuelled in recent years both by high recorded overall urban population growth rates and by perceptions of increasing concentration toward the largest metropolitan centres, particularly those located on the densely populated core island of Java.

Urban definitions are, in fact, quite country-specific, so that precise international comparisons are often difficult. Even internal comparisons are clouded by the need to take account not only of natural increase and net migration (the bread and butter of demographers), but also of *reclassification*—the process by which spatial units (in the case of Indonesia, administrative villages or *desa*) and the people within them change in status from rural to urban over time.

Factoring out reclassification is important since it is rural-urban migration which is often seen as one of the most salient issues and a reflection of relative disparities between city and countryside. Clearly, if most of the 65 per cent of urban growth not accounted for by natural increase (see Firman, this volume p. 100) were accounted for by net rural-urban migration it would tell quite a different story than if most were accounted for by reclassification of areas and people who were actually there all along.

Results of my own work in several of Indonesia's largest metropolitan regions confirm the degree to which reclassification has played a significant role in urban growth over the past few decades. In Jabotabek,[3] for example, of the recorded 1980-90 urban growth rate of 5.8 per cent, about 35 per cent was due to natural increase, about 30 per cent to reclassification and about 35 per cent to net rural-urban migration (Table 7.2). Jabotabek, however, is clearly atypical. Similar analyses of metropolitan Surabaya, metropolitan Bandung and Met-

---

[3] The national capital region includes the administrative cities of DKI Jakarta, Bogor and Tangerang and the administrative regions (*kabupaten*) of Bogor, Tangerang and Bekasi.

ropolitan Medan indicate substantially smaller net migration effects—
and correspondingly larger reclassification effects—on urban growth.[4]

A more pertinent question might be why isn't rural to urban
migration higher? Poverty remains largely a rural phenomenon and
virtually all critiques of current calculation methods would tend to
increase the rural share of poverty, not make it smaller. There is little
evidence of real deterioration in urban employment opportunity—
higher urban unemployment rates are mainly among educated first-
time job-seekers. They may be indicative of difficulties of finding a
'suitable' job, but they are not indicative of a chronic pool of labour
who cannot find any work at all. While the informal sector remains
significant, formal wage or salaried employment is absorbing an increasing proportion of the urban workforce, in spite of rapid urban
growth. One explanation might lie in levels of 'circular' migration
which is largely unrecorded in the census. In any case, the important
observation seems to be that actual mobility does not appear to be far
out of line with growth in urban economic opportunity. It may well be
that urban jobs are contributing significantly to declines in rural poverty through remittances and fewer 'rural' mouths to feed, although
formal research in this area still remains limited.

The evidence of reclassification impact does, however, open up
another area of interest and that is the nature of transformation of
space in and around urban centres—what we can see in processes of
urban expansion, sub-urbanisation and, in some of the major metropolitan areas, growth of satellite towns on the urban fringe. How cities
grow—economically, socially and environmentally—has long been a
topic of study in the Western world. It is relatively new to Indonesia.
Nevertheless, it constitutes an important area of work and, particularly when addressed in distinct spatial terms, has obvious implications for the planning and design of a wide range of urban facilities
and services.

---

[4] Reclassification also affects analysis for larger units. Thus, Firman's (in this
volume) analysis of growth of municipalities (*kotamadya*) between 1980 and
1990 is affected by the fact that about 20 per cent of these units underwent
boundary changes resulting in area expansion during the decade. Lack of a
common area definition can clearly lead to misleading estimates of growth
relative to *kotamadya* which maintained constant boundaries throughout the
period.

TABLE 7.2: Decomposition of growth rates in four major metropolitan regions, 1980-90

	Jabotabek (1)	Surabaya (2)	Medan (3)	Bandung (4)
Recorded growth rates				
Urban	5.8	4.5	5.1	4.8
Rural	-1.4	-1.8	-3.9	-0.7
Total	3.5	2.3	2.8	2.4
Constant area growth rates				
1980 urban area	2.3	1.0	1.7	1.6
Expansion area	7.9	7.2	5.8	5.2
1990 urban area	3.6	2.5	2.7	2.4
Rural area	3.3	1.7	3.2	2.4
Effect of:				
Reclassification	30.3	39.6	40.5	43.2
Natural inc. (5)	34.5	43.9	48.4	46.8
Net migration	35.3	16.4	11.1	10.0

(1) Jabotabek—DKI Jakarta; Kodya. Bogor, Tangerang; Kab. Bogor, Tangerang, Bekasi.
(2) Metropolitan Surabaya—Kodya. Surabaya; Kab. Sidoarjo, Gresik.
(3) Metropolitan Medan—Kodya. Medan, Binjai; part of Kab. Deli Serdang.
(4) Metropolitan Bandung—Kodya. Bandung; Kab. Bandung, part of Kab. Sumedang.
(5) Assumed annual rates—Jabotabek (0.18), Metropolitan Surabaya (0.18), Metropolitan Medan (0.22), Metropolitan Bandung (0.20).

Computer-based graphic techniques allow us to demonstrate a telling story. This is enhanced by an ability to map at least some characteristics down to very local (*desa*) level which, when combined on a larger-scale metropolitan frame, permits analysis of patterns of distribution and change in a meaningful way. As an example, Map 7.1 shows a graphical breakdown of administrative areas for the national capital region, Jabotabek. This is expanded in Map 7.2 into a base map, including overlays for main roads and rivers, which provides a frame for subsequent analysis.

Some idea of the nature of urban expansion can be gained from Map 7.3 which shows, for Jabotabek, the location of *desa* units which were classified as urban in 1980 and 1990 according to the censuses. To the degree that urban definitions actually reflect the 'urban' nature of population and space, the patterns of urban expansion, spreading out beyond the existing administrative boundaries of the city of Jakarta into the surrounding areas of West Java, are immediately clear.

An even more direct indication of the expansion process can be obtained by plotting the change in population between 1980 and 1990 at the *desa* level (Map 7.4). This not only documents the dominance of the urban fringe in absorbing population increase, but also the negligible (in some cases negative) growth which characterised the central city core. At least for the larger cities in Indonesia, the story of urbanisation is only partly one of rural-urban migration; an equally, if not more, powerful component has to do with the transformation of space, and the use of space within the metropolitan sphere.

From a planning perspective, a major concern lies in documenting and analysing the factors (or actors) determining these processes of spatial change. Individual and household decisions are, of course, at the base of it all, but evidence suggests that these are increasingly being conditioned by a range of other factors: land prices, location of major infrastructure (particularly road networks), location of industrial and large-scale commercial job opportunity and, in some of the large metropolitan areas, location decisions now being made by the private real estate sector. Again, graphic techniques offer a source of opportunity since, given suitable data, most of these factors can also be mapped and their relation to patterns of demographic change assessed. As an example, Map 7.5 shows patterns of employment in medium and large-scale manufacturing in 1995 in Jabotabek. The spread of industry away from historical concentrations in North and East Jakarta along major lines of access is clearly evident.

A final map, Map 7.6, shows a time trend of spatial change in population distribution for Jabotabek; starting with historical change between 1980 and 1990 and progressing to a projection up to the year 2010 which was prepared for the Jabotabek Metropolitan Development Plan Review (JMDPR) Project carried out in 1992/93. The projection was, in fact, based on a *desa*-level model which estimated growth as a function of population density and the existence

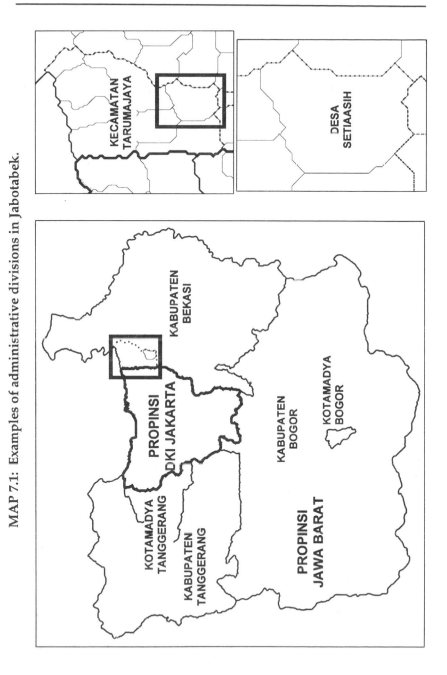

MAP 7.1: Examples of administrative divisions in Jabotabek.

MAP 7.2: Metropolitan Jakarta (Jabotabek), base map.

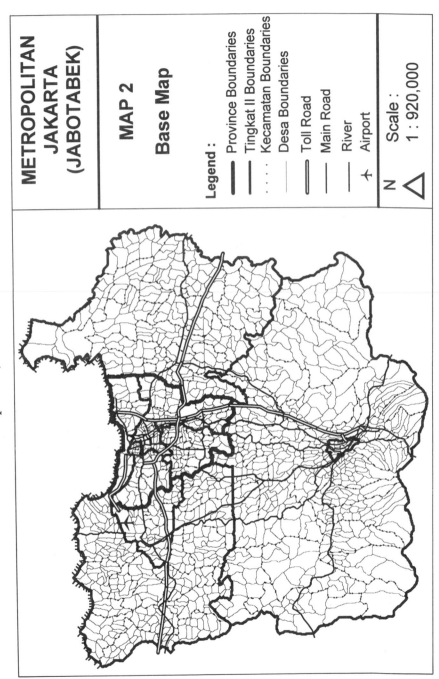

METROPOLITAN JAKARTA (JABOTABEK)

MAP 2

Base Map

Legend :

▬ Province Boundaries

▬ Tingkat II Boundaries

⋯ Kecamatan Boundaries

— Desa Boundaries

═ Toll Road

— Main Road

— River

✛ Airport

N △

Scale :
1 : 920,000

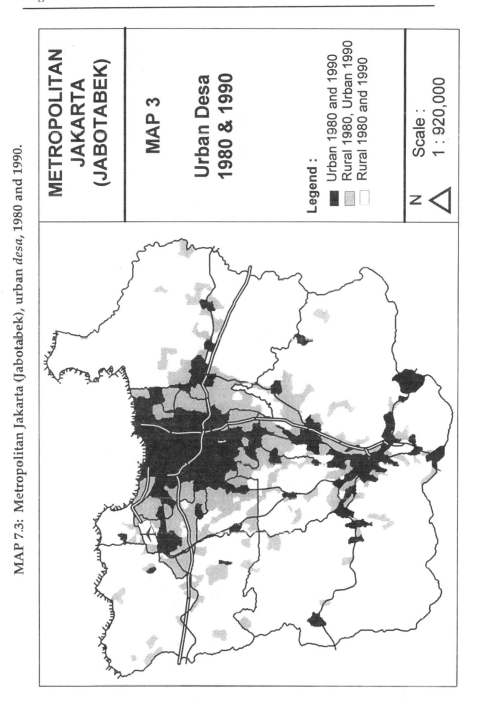

MAP 7.3: Metropolitan Jakarta (Jabotabek), urban *desa*, 1980 and 1990.

METROPOLITAN JAKARTA (JABOTABEK)

MAP 3

Urban Desa 1980 & 1990

Legend :
Urban 1980 and 1990
Rural 1980, Urban 1990
Rural 1980 and 1990

N

Scale :
1 : 920,000

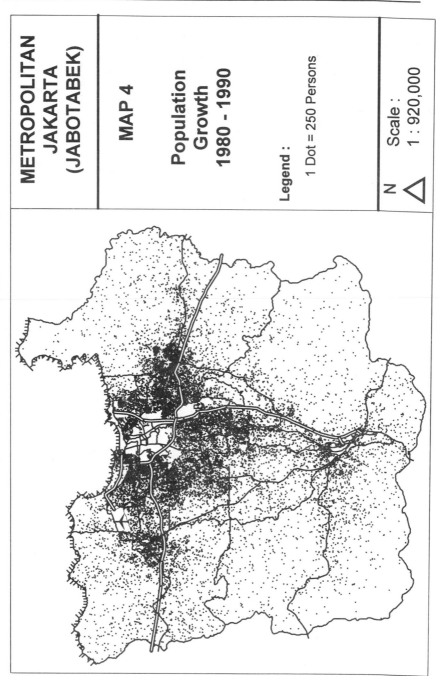

MAP 7.4: Metropolitan Jakarta (Jabotabek), population growth, 1980-90.

METROPOLITAN JAKARTA (JABOTABEK)

MAP 4

Population Growth 1980 - 1990

Legend :

1 Dot = 250 Persons

N

Scale : 1 : 920,000

MAP 7.5: Metropolitan Jakarta (Jabotabek), medium and large-scale industrial employment, 1995.

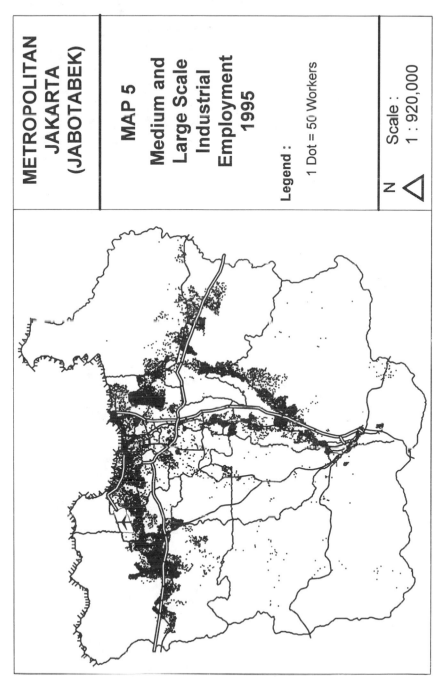

METROPOLITAN JAKARTA (JABOTABEK)

MAP 5
Medium and Large Scale Industrial Employment 1995

Legend :

1 Dot = 50 Workers

N

Scale :
1 : 920,000

MAP 7.6: Population of Jabotabek, 1980, 1990 (actual),
2000, 2010 (projected).

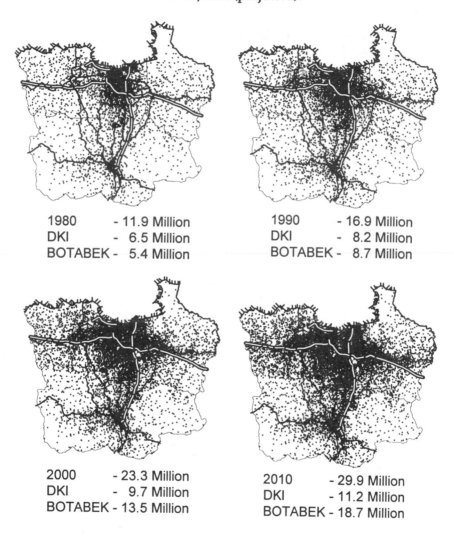

1980	- 11.9 Million
DKI	- 6.5 Million
BOTABEK -	5.4 Million

1990	- 16.9 Million
DKI	- 8.2 Million
BOTABEK -	8.7 Million

2000	- 23.3 Million
DKI	- 9.7 Million
BOTABEK -	13.5 Million

2010	- 29.9 Million
DKI	- 11.2 Million
BOTABEK -	18.7 Million

1 Dot = 2000 persons

of a range of factors (infrastructure, economic activity, private sector development intentions, environmental constraints) which were seen to favourably or unfavourably affect growth potential in one area as compared to another. This kind of picture serves to demonstrate the inbuilt momentum in the current pattern of spatial development toward continuing expansion of the metropolitan area.

My own feeling is that this kind of work needs to be expanded, particularly in a world (which does include Indonesia) where environmental and social concerns are assuming an ever-increasing prominence. Where and how are environmental problems emerging—not only industrial pollution, but also impacts of households in areas of rapidly increasing density and where municipal services (e.g. water supply) are still not available? How are developers' and other claims on land influencing or limiting choices of where people can, or can afford to, live? In Jabotabek and other major urban centres the classic view of economically heterogeneous (but ethnically homogeneous) urban villages seems to be giving way to patterns of spatial segregation based more on lines of social or economic class, but we still have only limited knowledge of how this is happening in terms of urban space. How are job locations, for example the growth of labour intensive industrial employment on Jakarta's urban fringe, affecting residential growth and perhaps formation of new urban *kampung* in places that only a few years previously were largely rural and agricultural in nature?

Firman reflects on a number of the salient issues associated with this process; the depopulation of the urban core and the rush to suburbia, a situation fostered both by extremely high central-city land values and the rapid growth of large-scale real estate development on lower-priced fringe-area land. Jakarta does seem to be going the way of many Western cities where the core areas are dedicated primarily to public and high-value commercial use and where commuting, often over long distances, is increasingly becoming the norm. Unfortunately what does not yet characterise Indonesian cities are adequate road networks and public (including mass) transport. This is likely to be a major problem in the future and one which could influence the nature of development in the core areas (in Jakarta, increasingly a place of five-star hotels and 'Central Business Districts' comprising shining towers of glass and steel) in competition with more 'user-friendly' locations on the fringe.

Aspects of Human

Resource Development

8

Educational Developments, Achievements and Challenges

Mayling Oey-Gardiner

Introduction

Indonesia has progressed from being one of the poorest countries in the world some three decades ago to a ranking as one of the high-performing Asian economies, enjoying high and sustained growth (World Bank 1993a). Economic growth has been fairly robust for the past 35 years, and during the early 1990s, the country enjoyed an average growth of close to 7 per cent per annum. Part of this high and sustained growth has been attributed to investments and developments in human resources, including education. Even with Indonesia's vast population, enrolment rates at the primary and secondary levels are well beyond those of other countries at similar levels of income (*ibid.*).

With rich natural resources, good fortune and good macro-economic management, not only consumption poverty but also human resource poverty is being rapidly reduced. The proportion of the population below the poverty line declined from 60 per cent in 1970 to about 14 per cent in 1993 (World Bank 1994b: 30). Oil revenues during the oil boom years of 1973-82 funded the development of the physical and social infrastructure. Both education and health sectors were the largest beneficiaries. Teaching and health work became important sources of employment. Vast public investments, particularly in elementary education, have resulted in changes in the valuation placed on education over time. The successes achieved at the primary level—in only one decade the proportion of children of primary school age attending school rose from 60 per cent to 94 per cent—led to optimism. In 1990, a new goal was set. Nine years compulsory basic education, six years in elementary school and three years at lower secondary school, was to be achieved in three planning periods or fifteen years. On 23 May 1996, the Coordinating Minister for Social Welfare (Menko Kesra) announced in closing a National Working Meeting of the Ministry of Education and Culture (MOEC, also referred to as the DPK), that the president had decided to accelerate the achievement of compulsory basic education. Instead of fifteen years it is to be achieved in ten years. The consequent budgetary requirements are also being adjusted (*Kompas*, 24 May1996[1]).

On the global scene, relatively high and rapidly rising educational qualifications of Indonesia's population and workforce have been hailed as important contributors to the nation's high and sustained economic growth (World Bank 1993a). In looking towards the future, however, within the regional and national context there remains cause for concern. Education levels are still low and weaknesses continue to be pointed out in the fields of science and technology and management (Abeng in *Jakarta Post*, 26 May 1996[2]; Gunawan in *Jakarta Post*, 26 May 1996[3]; Widiadana in *Jakarta Post*, 26 May 1996[4]). The purpose of this chapter is to trace the developments and achievements in Indonesia's world of education with an emphasis on the recent past, and then to examine the challenges facing the nation as it looks into the future.

The school system

The formal school system in Indonesia is both simple and complex. Simplicity is found in the basic levels, of which there are four. Complexity lies in the fact that many government agencies are involved in the provision of educational services.

---

[1] 'Penuntasan Wajib Belajar Dipercepat Jadi 10 Tahun' [Completion of Compulsory Education Is to Be Accelerated to 10 Years], p. 11.

[2] 'Tanri Abeng Works Without Stress', p.11.

[3] 'Indonesia Lacks Home-grown Managers', p.6.

[4] 'MBA Certificate No Longer Ticket to Instant Success', p.6.

The four levels of the formal education system consist of six years primary, three years each of lower and upper secondary, and tertiary education. Each of these are separated by national final examinations. Tertiary education varies greatly—from one to four years non-degree programs, known as either D (for diploma) or S0 (for non-*sarjana*) programs, to at least four-year S1 or undergraduate programs. Thereafter one can attend S2 programs (equivalent to masters programs) and the highest level is the S3 or doctorate program. Besides, professional specialist programs are known as SP I and SP II (Figure 8.1).

The above description refers to the system under the aegis of the MOEC. These are secular schools where religious education is offered as a compulsory course. Depending on their sources of funding, these schools are distinguished between public and private schools, even though many private schools are also beneficiaries of public subsidies in one form or another, in return for which they have to conform to government set rules and regulations on standards. While secular primary schools are mostly public, starting at the lower secondary level there are more private than public schools, and the higher the level the greater the role of the private sector in the provision of education.

Then there is the religious school system, mostly Islamic, which is allowed to devote up to around 40 per cent of its curriculum to religious teachings. While these schools are the responsibility of the Ministry of Religious Affairs, MORA, they also follow the curriculum set up by the MOEC for their secular subjects.

While there are only two ministries—MOEC and MORA—responsible for the delivery of primary education, there are many other ministries providing vocational training at the secondary and tertiary levels.

The data

The data used for analysis in this paper are mainly those collected by the MOEC and Central Bureau of Statistics (CBS, or Biro Pusat Statistik [BPS]). Data collected by the ministry are based on school statistics, while it is the business of the BPS to regularly conduct national surveys, several of which are population based. In addition, some discussions will also be based on the results of a recently completed Indonesian Family Life Survey (IFLS).

FIGURE 8.1: Indonesian education system

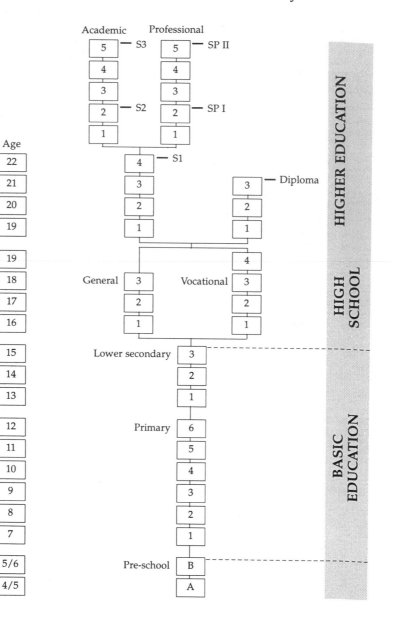

These two sources are used here to complement each other. On the one hand, MOEC collects fairly detailed statistics on the schools which are its responsibility, and these constitute the majority. Since, however, other ministries also provide education services, these data are mostly not captured by the MOEC statistics.[5] Besides, those statistics requiring populations at risk are usually based on projections, and available data are not broken down by gender.

To help overcome these limitations in the school statistics we also rely on national population statistics. As BPS does not conduct special education surveys but education information is often collected during other population and socio-economic surveys, these data sources are equally limited. On the other hand, BPS is more likely to publish gender and residence-specific data. It is the combination of the two sources therefore which will enrich our analysis.

School attendance

As more and more children attend school, they also stay in school longer on average. But, of course, not all school-age children benefit equally from available services. Even though declining, gender differences persist and widen with rising levels of schooling. Far more pronounced are differential access between income classes, residence and region.

Through a combination of good luck and favourable macro-management, the poor in Indonesia have also benefited significantly from development—growth with equity—as public investments were also directed at developing social infrastructure. Education in particular has benefited from windfall profits resulting from sudden rises in oil prices during the early 1970s. With an emphasis on primary education and provision of at least one primary school per village, attendance among primary school-age children rose dramatically. Over time, children have remained in school longer and girls have generally benefited disproportionately. As primary school attendance was already almost universal—around 90 per cent—in the mid-1980s (BPS 1987), optimism grew, leading to rising expectations, and the setting

---

[5] As non-MOEC education programs are usually rather small (except for those that are the responsibility of MORA), we suggest that the overall impact on society is also limited.

of the new goal of at least nine years of basic education. In the meantime, gaps persist, especially by income and urban-rural residence.

Rapid growth in school attendance

Following on from a cardinal belief of Indonesia's founding fathers, education has always been regarded as a basic human right. Thus the constitution guarantees all citizens the right to an education (Article 31(1)). 'Education at all costs, even bad education is better than no education at all', has been the principle in rapidly expanding Indonesia's education system. Thus, politically, numbers have always been important and equity has mainly been translated in quantitative and regional terms.

The earliest estimate after Indonesia declared independence in 1945, was for 1950 when some 5 million children were enrolled in primary schools but another 6 million children were not enrolled (Kelabora and Orr, 1977:97). Even under fairly poor and deteriorating socio-economic conditions thereafter, which culminated in an aborted coup in 1965, numbers of children attending school continued to grow rapidly. When the New Order government took over in 1966, the primary concern was to bring order and stability in all walks of life. For the first year of Indonesia's First Five-year Development Period (1969-74), known as Repelita I, already some 12.8 million children were attending primary schools. Two decades later, the number had already more than doubled to 26.2 million children. Similarly, the growth in numbers of students at higher levels has also been phenomenal —lower secondary school students increased fivefold from 1.1 million to 5.7 million, and upper secondary students eightfold, from 0.46 to 3.72 million, during the same period.

A sudden rise in the number of primary school students can be observed starting in 1974 (Figure 8.2). This was the first year when the primary school special program, known as SD Inpres (for primary school presidential instruction), was implemented. The goal was to achieve universal enrolment during Repelita IV of 1984-89. For that purpose the policy is rural-based as more than 80 per cent of the population still lived in rural areas at that time. Every village was to have at least one primary school. In 1977, tuition fees at public schools were abolished for grades 1-3 and the following year for grades 4-6.

Apparently, not much effort was needed to convince parents of the benefits of educating not only sons but also daughters, at least at

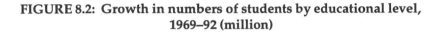

FIGURE 8.2: Growth in numbers of students by educational level, 1969–92 (million)

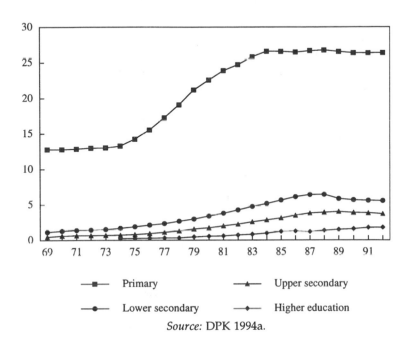

Source: DPK 1994a.

the primary level. As the network of schools became denser, schools became located closer to home. Only a decade after introduction of the special primary school program, enrolment had risen from 60 to 94 per cent. The number of primary school students started to decline towards the end of the 1980s. For the past few years, every new school year the media reports on closure of some schools. Part of this decline can be attributed to the successes achieved by a very active national family planning program.[6]

---

[6] Although the total population growth rate has only declined to 1.6 per cent per annum from its peak of 2.36 per cent per annum between 1971 and 1980, the impact of declining fertility has been much sharper at the school-going ages. The number of primary school-aged children had stopped increasing by about the mid-1980s.

The numbers and growth in students at higher levels are far lower (Table 8.1). There are a number of factors which account for this difference. First, there are six grades in primary school and only three in lower and upper secondary schools. Second, continuation rates beyond primary school are still fairly low—from primary to lower secondary school only 60 per cent early this decade. Educational costs are a strong deterrent to continuing children's education after elementary school, as annual lower-secondary school expenditures incurred by families have been found to be almost three times as much as expenditures for primary school (BPS 1994b, Table 33: 108-109). Whereas primary school fees are still affordable even for the poor, this is not the case for lower secondary school (Serrato and Melnick 1995: 96-97). As constraints are even greater at higher levels, enrolments at this level are much lower. Considering the far greater annual fluctuations in the number of students attending higher education institutions, recorded by the MOEC, and a rather rapid growth in the number of institutions, interpretation at this level is difficult.

Over time there has been a secular decline in the growth and ultimately in absolute numbers of students, which picked up again starting in 1993 (Table 8.1). At the primary level high growth occurred mainly during Repelita II of 1974-79 and slowed down substantially thereafter to even negative growth in Repelita IV. At the lower-secondary school level, considering that the numbers of students are still relatively small, one would have expected still continuing high growth. Instead, the period of high, double-digit, growth lasted for two planning periods only, of Repelita II and III, after which there occurred a slowdown in the growth, and actually absolute declines from 1988 to 1992. Enrolments picked up again starting in 1993. A similar pattern also characterises the growth in the numbers of upper-secondary school students. This slowdown and even absolute declines in the numbers of secondary school students during the latter part of the 1980s and early 1990s was also observed by Booth (1994), who concurred with the argument posed in the LPK (1994) and also supported by the BPS (1994b) findings that far higher educational costs constitute the major deterrent for continuing education. But differential costs between primary and secondary education may not be the only reason, as the numbers of students rose again starting in 1993. In light of the new policy to have all children of the relevant ages complete nine years of schooling by 2004, further investigation on who continues and who drops out of the system is urgently needed.

TABLE 8.1: Growth in numbers of students (in thousands) by educational level, 1969-92/93

	Number of students				Annual change (%)			
	Primary	Lower Secondary	Upper Secondary	Higher Education*	Primary	Lower Secondary	Upper Secondary	Higher Education*
1969	12,802	1,127	463					
1970	12,822	1,292	598		0.2	14.6	29.2	
1971	12,896	1,401	652		0.6	8.4	9.0	
1972	13,031	1,444	665		1.1	3.1	2.0	
1973	13,069	1,518	684		0.3	5.1	2.9	
1974	13,314	1,691	724	232	1.9	11.4	5.9	
1975	14,280	1,900	795	250	7.3	12.4	9.8	7.8
1976	15,550	2,136	933	275	8.9	12.4	17.4	10.0
1977	17,265	2,340	1,108	306	11.0	9.6	18.8	11.3
1978	19,075	2,674	1,290	306	10.5	14.3	16.4	0.0
1979	21,166	2,983	1,574	458	11.0	11.6	22.0	49.7
1980	22,552	3,412	1,751	543	6.6	14.4	11.3	18.6
1981	23,862	3,809	2,022	597	5.8	11.6	15.5	9.9
1982	24,700	4,273	2,261	718	3.5	12.2	11.8	20.3
1983	25,804	4,758	2,588	824	4.5	11.4	14.5	14.8
1984	26,568	5,189	2,856	977	3.0	9.1	10.4	18.6
1985	26,551	5,670	3,131	1,218	(0.1)	9.3	9.6	24.7
1986	26,445	6,132	3,499	1,265	(0.4)	8.2	11.8	3.9
1987	26,650	6,422	3,818	1,179	0.8	4.7	9.1	(6.8)
1988	26,725	6,447	3,919	1,357	0.3	0.4	2.7	15.1
1989	26,529	5,853	4,031	1,486	(0.7)	(9.2)	2.9	9.5
1990	26,348	5,686	3,901	1,591	(0.7)	(2.9)	(3.2)	7.1
1991	26,326	5,605	3,841	1,773	(0.1)	(1.4)	(1.5)	11.4
1992	26,340	5,576	3,715	1,794	0.1	(0.5)	(3.3)	1.2
1993*	26,320	5,841	3,783	2,043	(0.1)	4.8	1.8	13.9
1994*	26,200	6,392	4,042	2,230	(0.5)	9.4	6.9	9.2

Source: Ministry of Education and Culture 1994a; * raw data provided by Ministry of Education and Culture.

Extending schooling

Similar patterns are also shown by data obtained from population surveys. Rapid rises in enrolment ratios occurred during the decade of the 1970s, which were, however, not continued during the 1980s.

With rapidly rising numbers of students at all levels, there has been a tendency to extend school life (Figure 8.3). The age-specific enrolment ratio curves for 1961 and 1971 are practically superimposed, but the curve shifted dramatically higher by 1980, with only a slight further rise, concentrated at younger ages, between 1980 and 1990. Thus, while over time more children stay in school longer, during the decade of the 1980s there appears to have been a slowdown in the rise in enrolment of children beyond primary school age.

The impact of the special primary school program is very noticeable. Without special public intervention, as was the case during the 1960s, very little change in age-specific enrolment occurred, meaning that student growth was basically a function of population growth. Attendance ratios of children aged 7-12 years[7] rose dramatically during the second half of the 1970s when widespread public investments in primary schools were made, and slowed down during the 1980s as most primary school-age children were already attending school. Actually, during the 1980s, the upsurge continued among the younger primary school-age children, reflecting the fact that increasingly parents are sending their children at younger ages.

Though the school enrolment of primary school-age children continues to be very satisfactory, with a few regional exceptions, the rather sluggish growth in school attendance ratios of lower secondary school-age children, aged 13-15 years, during the 1980s requires serious attention. This phenomenon is particularly worrisome in light of the recently set target of achieving nine years' compulsory basic education early in the next century. While decennial census results may mask the intercensal changes, they are also fairly consistent with the MOEC statistics. The slowdown in enrolment increases in the mid-

---

[7] When the special primary school program was introduced, the backlog led the government to raise the entrance age from 6 to 7 years. Hence, the ideal primary school ages became 7-12 years. Now that practically universal enrolment has been reached, the entrance age has again been reduced to 6 years.

FIGURE 8.3: School attendance ratios by age, 1961–90

Sources: BPS, Population Censuses 1961, 1971, 1980 and 1990.

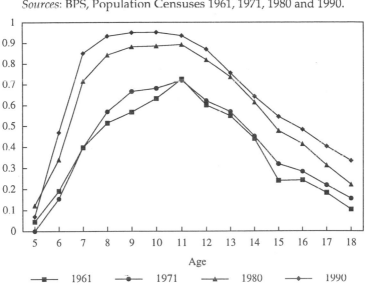

1980s, culminating in actual decline in enrolments in the late 1980s, coincided with declining continuation ratios between primary school and lower secondary school from the peak reached in 1979-80, when about 74 per cent of primary school graduates continued to lower secondary school, to a low of around 60 per cent in the early 1990s (Figure 8.4). The trend for relatively fewer children to continue to lower secondary school flies in the face of the government's declaration of compulsory basic education as a medium term goal. Poverty, both absolute and relative, and unattractive opportunity costs, may well have contributed to this phenomenon.

Gender gaps

... the Ministry of Education and Culture does not distinguish students by gender. In reality, however, the data show that educational opportunities for girls are relatively more limited than for boys (Departemen Pendidikan dan Kebudayaan 1994b).

FIGURE 8.4: Crude continuation ratios from primary to lower secondary school, 1974–93[a]

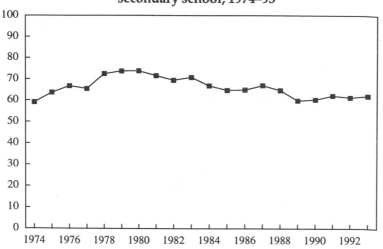

[a]Continuation ratios refer to the ratio between the first year lower-secondary school students over primary school graduates for the same year. Though admittedly rather crude, they are sufficiently indicative. *Source*: DPK 1994a: 156.

If there are gender differences, these occurred accidentally, and if gender gaps narrowed, this was not by design but rather by default. It was due to the very rapid expansion in the education system that girls benefited relatively more than boys over the course of Indonesia's social development during the last 25 years. Quantitatively, gender gaps are rapidly narrowing and this phenomenon extends throughout higher levels of education.[8] This phenomenon has been observed earlier (Oey-Gardiner 1989, 1991), and is found in many other parts of the world as well (World Bank 1993a). To the extent that gender gaps persist, this is basically the result of selective admission, as once in the system, girls tend to do as well as, if not better than, boys.

---

[8] This phenomenon has been observed earlier and others as well (Oey-Gardiner 1989, 1991a, Hatmadji, Widyawati and Herdiana 1993; Suleeman 1993).

Even though stereotypical socialisation patterns continue to distinguish between social roles for daughters and sons, when possible, parents are willing to invest equally in their children of both sexes. It is therefore not surprising that the gender gap has practically been eliminated among primary school-age children and is rapidly narrowing for older children as well. In 1971, even among primary school-age children, aged from nine years onwards, there was still a visible gender gap which widened with age, but by 1990 the gap had practically been closed. As a consequence of developments at the primary level, the observable narrowing in the gender gap for children aged 13 years on has occurred mostly during the 1980s (Figure 8.5).

The above census results are further confirmed by rapidly rising gender ratios (F/100 M) among students. The gender ratio at the primary level was already fairly high in the mid-1970s, 86 per cent and from the late 1980s to the early 1990s it has remained fairly stable at around 93 per cent (Table 8.2). At the lower-secondary level, the gender ratio rose by 22 percentage points from 65 to 87 per cent. Most striking has been the progress at the upper-secondary level. In the mid-1970s there were only slightly more than half as many girls as boys attending upper secondary schools, while by 1993 the ratio had already risen to 84 per cent, almost the same level as among primary school students in the mid-1970s.

One would expect that rising gender ratios in the total student body are being fuelled by similarly rising gender ratios at entrance and continuation to subsequent levels. However, we suggest that underrepresentation of girls among students is a function of differential access at entrance. The trends are not very clear, as gender ratios for first-grade primary school students remained fairly stable or even declined during the early 1990s (Table 8.3). Gender ratios of continuation rates from primary to lower secondary school have risen only slowly during the last decade. No clear pattern can be observed in gender ratios of continuation from lower to upper secondary school.

While gender ratios among students are improving, gender differences continue, in quantitative as well as qualitative terms. Even though the numbers of students entering at each level continue to be somewhat smaller for girls than boys, girls appear to perform better in school than boys. Repeater rates are slightly lower for girls than boys. During 1992/93, repeater rates were as follows: at the primary level

FIGURE 8.5:　Male and female school attendance ratios by age, 1971, 1980 and 1990

Male

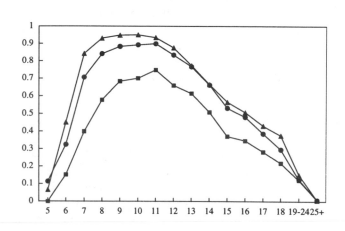

Female

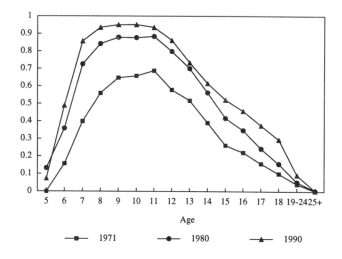

Age

|　| 1971 | 1980 | 1990 |

Sources: CBS; Population Censuses.

TABLE 8.2: Sex ratios (females/100 males) of students by level, 1976-93

	Primary	Lower Secondary	Upper Secondary
1976	85.9	65.1	56.7
1983	91.0	74.0	69.3
1987	92.3	80.8	75.8
1988	93.5	81.9	77.0
1989	93.5	82.7	81.1
1990	94.4	84.2	79.1
1993	93.3	87.0	84.0

Sources: Ministry of Education and Culture, various publications.

8.8 and 8.8 per cent for girls and boys, at the lower secondary level 0.7 and 1.3 per cent for girls and boys, and 0.5 and 1.2 per cent for upper-secondary school girls and boys. A recent study[9] shows that 21 per cent of girls as opposed to 24 per cent of boys at elementary school failed a grade (Serrato and Melnick 1995: 92).

As a result there is greater age-level consistency for girls than boys, as indicated by the ratio between net and age-specific enrolment ratios. Whereas age-specific enrolment refers to the percentage of the age group attending school, net enrolment refers to the proportion of the age group attending the ideal or proper level of schooling.

---

[9] Results of the Indonesian Family Life Survey, a national household survey and matched community survey, representing about 83 per cent of the Indonesian population, conducted in 1993 and 1994 by RAND in conjunction with Lembaga Demografi at the University of Indonesia.

TABLE 8.3: Sex ratios (females/100 males) of Grade 1 primary
school students, and continuation rates from primary to lower
secondary and from lower to upper secondary, 1983-93

	Grade 1	Continuation rate (%)	
	Primary	Primary to Lower Secondary	Lower Secondary to Upper Secondary
1983	92.1	85.8	93.7
1984	91.4	87.2	91.7
1988	92.8	87.4	85.9
1989	91.1	86.3	98.7
1990	92.0	92.9	96.7
1991	91.4	88.2	89.0
1992	89.7	89.3	87.3
1993	90.2	89.0	93.5

Sources: Ministry of Education and Culture, various publications.

The ratio between the net and age-specific enrolment ratios indicates
the level of consistency between age and level of schooling. Though
not the case at the primary level, at higher levels these ratios are
higher for girls than boys (Table 8.4). This implies that girls progress
'faster' for their age than boys or that boys are more likely to be older
for their level beyond primary school.[10] This difference can partially
be attributed to gender differences in continuation, initially between
primary and lower secondary school, leading to greater selectivity
among girls than boys in continuing beyond primary school.

---

[10] Interestingly enough, this seems to be a widespread phenomenon (see
Knodel and Jones 1996)

TABLE 8.4: Age-specific (AS) and net (N) enrolment by gender
and N/AS ratio, 1992-94[a]

	Age-Specific	Net	N/AS
Females			
7 - 12	94.2	92.1	0.98
13 - 15	71.2	50.0	0.70
16 - 18	43.2	32.4	0.75
19 - 24	10.8	7.2	0.66
Males			
7 - 12	93.9	92.2	0.98
13 - 15	73.5	50.0	0.68
16 - 18	47.4	34.0	0.72
19 - 24	15.0	8.8	0.58

[a] Age-specific enrolment ratios refer to the proportion of an age group attending school, regardless of level; net enrolment ratios refer to the proportion of an age group attending school at the ideal or proper level of schooling (see Figure 8.1 for ideal age-level consistency); and N/AS ratio refers to the degree of consistency between age and ideal level of schooling.

Sources: BPS, special tabulations from Susenas 1992-94 (National Socio-economic Surveys), which are now conducted annually.

In sum, it has been shown above that gender differences in access to education have been declining rapidly over time, a worldwide phenomenon. On the other hand, however, girls are still less likely to attend and continue school than boys. The reason for such gender differentials cannot be attributed to academic performance, as girls perform better in school than boys. Girls are less likely to fail a grade or repeat a grade and girls are more likely to be younger or the right age for the level of schooling than boys. Instead, the reasons may well lie in the socio-economic environment which favours sons. The labour market also rewards men more than women even for the same level of education: on average women make only about two-thirds of men's earnings (BPS 1995a). As such signals are also recognised by parents, it is not surprising that priority in education continues to be given to sons.

Income gaps

Much more striking are the income gaps in access to education. Even the lowest level of education is still not accessible to the very poor. Some of the poor have to withhold their primary school-age children from attending school. The older children get, the more of them are withheld from attending school. Schooling is simply not yet a priority among many people in Indonesia. Even among the wealthiest, sub-stantial proportions of children are withheld from attending school.

Results of a recent survey show striking poverty gaps in access to education. The gap widens with age (or implied level). Even among the wealthiest group, enrolment among upper secondary school-age children is still rather limited (Figure 8.6). Among the 7-12 year olds, the difference in enrolment between the poorest and wealthiest quintiles is 13 percentage points; at the next level of education, or among 13-15 year olds, the difference has widened to 37 percentage points, and among the next age group of 16-18 years it is an extraordinary 52 percentage points, representing a fourfold difference between 17 and 69 per cent.

The above findings suggest that poverty and financial pressures are major constraints, but they are not the only deterrent to attending school. There are other factors which affect the demand for education, particularly the rather low valuation placed on education for older teenagers.

Although the overall gender gap is far less pronounced than the poverty gap, at older ages the gender gap also rises. The results of the IFLS show that among 7-12-years-old children, 92 and 93 per cent of girls and boys were enrolled in school, among 13-15-year-olds the comparable figures were 65 and 69 per cent and among the 16-18-year-olds the figures were 36 and 46 per cent. More striking are the gender differences among the poorest and the wealthiest groups (Figure 8.7). While it is usually said that when household finances are a constraint, sons are given priority in schooling, these data seem to imply that other values enter parents' considerations. Not just the poor but the rich too seem to discriminate between their daughters and sons.

FIGURE 8.6: Age-specific enrolment rates by per-capita
expenditure quintile[a]

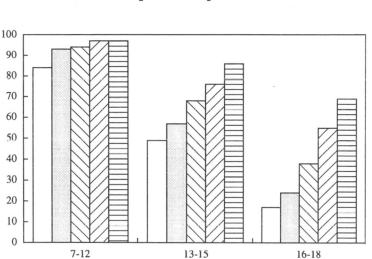

FIGURE 8.7: Age-specific enrolment rates by sex and per-capita
expenditure quintile[a] (per cent)

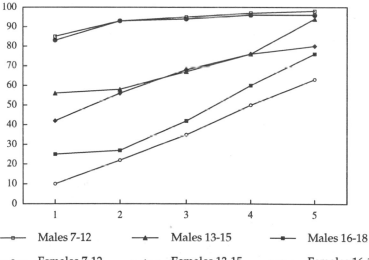

[a]Quintiles are numbered from 1 (the poorest) to 5 (the wealthiest).
Source: Serrato and Melnick 1995, Table 4.3: 86.

More worrisome were the trends noted for the later 1980s. Between 1987 and 1989, up to the fourth decile, gross enrolment declined at all levels as opposed to continuing rises for the higher income groups. Besides, even at the lower secondary level, less than 20 per cent were attending school while among the top decile practically all children were attending school. Of course even greater discrepancies were recorded for upper secondary school attendance— in 1989 only about 2 per cent among the lowest but almost all among the highest income decile were attending this level of schooling (World Bank 1993a:15-16).

Compared to gender, poverty is a much stronger deterrent to accessing education, particularly beyond the primary level. This is consistent with 'no money' being the most common reason given for non-continuation of schooling among the population aged 5-29 years (48.6 per cent).[11] If the disturbing patterns of declining numbers of students, particularly at lower and upper secondary schools, and very slight intercensal growth in enrolment ratios of children of the relevant ages between 1980 and 1990 as shown earlier, are the result of the poor withdrawing their children from school, this has serious implications for the government's efforts to reduce consumption poverty.[12]

Urban-rural gaps

Urban residents have more favourable access to educational opportunities than rural residents; they are more likely to attend school and they are also more likely to attend school longer. But the enrolment

---

[11] Other reasons included 'sufficient education' (11.1 per cent), 'not capable' (6.6 per cent), 'distance to school' (2.7 per cent), 'not accepted' (1.4 per cent), 'looking for work' (7.7 per cent), 'house-keeping' (4.5 per cent) and 'others' (17.4 per cent). (BPS 1992e, Table 6.3: 46-47.)

[12] There are currently two large-scale poverty reduction programs. The first is known as the IDT for Inpres Desa Tertinggal, a special program for backward villages (numbering some 20,000 villages), managed by Bappenas. The second program has just been initiated by a presidential decree (January 1996), as an additional 2 per cent tax on companies and individuals earning more than 100 million Rupiah, the proceeds of which are to be controlled by a foundation headed by the president for the benefit of poor households residing outside the IDT villages.

trends have been rather similar (Figure 8.8). A noticeable difference can be observed in enrolment ratios starting with children aged 12 years and over, which are much higher in urban than rural areas. These differences in enrolment ratios among children of LSS and USS ages reflect widening of differentials in availability (physical availability of schools) at higher levels of education and to a lesser extent differential accessibility (cost of education).

The impact of the special primary school expansion program which is rural-based (every village is to have at least one primary school) has been significant, particularly in raising enrolment ratios between 1971 and 1980 among children between the ages of 7 and 11 years.[13] Regrettably, however, these efforts have not been continued and adjusted according to the needs of the children as they aged, during the following decade of the 1980s. Hence, hardly any growth occurred in age-specific enrolment among the population beyond primary school age between 1980 and 1990. This is true not only for the rural population but even for the urban population. In an era when there is a great deal of discussion of the need to develop human resources, these trends should be seriously attended to.[14]

More interesting are the trends by gender (Figure 8.9). As observed earlier, gender differences have been narrowing. There is a wider gender difference in urban than rural areas, which became very pronounced by 1990. These patterns are attributed to differences in opportunity cost. In rural areas young adult males are not as likely to continue school, but instead go in search of employment; in urban

---

[13] The decline in enrolment ratios between ages 11 and 12 may well be a function of the census date which is October 1, while graduation is in June. A proportion of children aged 12 should then be continuing to LSS, but as noted earlier there is a substantial drop in attendance of LSS due to much higher school-related expenditures, which especially the poor can hardly afford.

[14] Of concern is the focus in the discussions on the need to develop Indonesia's human resources. Most of the emphasis, where education is becoming a rapidly growing business, has in the recent past been at higher levels. Concerns are, for instance, expressed with regard to the future of international trade, for the need for more and better managers and engineers and the like. Regrettably, insufficient attention is being paid to the fact that higher education is dependent on what happens at lower levels.

FIGURE 8.8: Urban and rural enrolment ratios by age, 1961-90

Urban

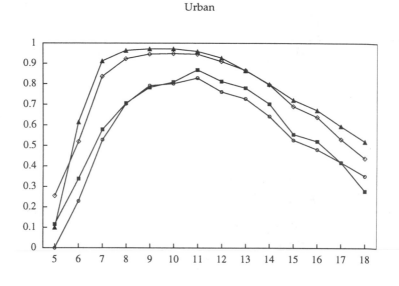

Rural

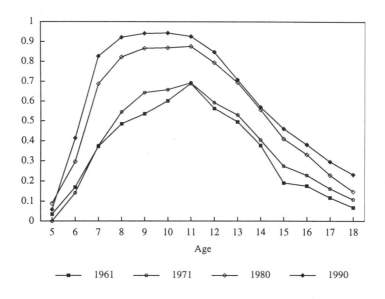

Age

■— 1961   ─○─ 1971   ─◇─ 1980   ─◆─ 1990

Sources: CBS, 1961, 1971, 1980; 1990 Population Censuses.

FIGURE 8.9: Age and gender-specific enrolment rates by urban-rural residence, 1961, 1971, 1980, 1990

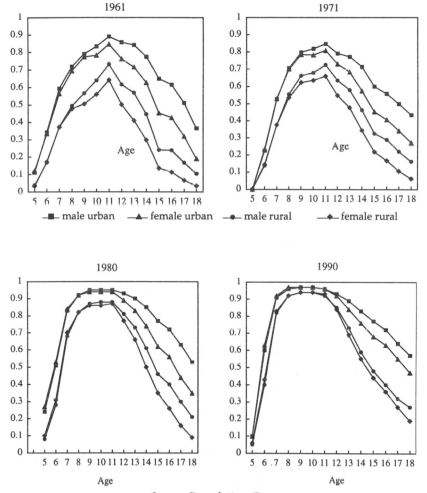

Source: Population Censuses.

areas it is the opposite, girls are more likely to join the workforce. Especially since the 1980s, Indonesia has increasingly attracted both domestic and especially foreign investments in light and labour-intensive manufacturing industries producing for export. Numerous factories have been set up in and around major urban centres. Many of these manufacturing industries rely on young girls to work in their factories. When standing along roads towards industrial estates at opening and closing hours, one can meet literally thousands of young women going or coming from work. Anecdotal evidence suggests that schools in the vicinity of large industrial estates have had to close their doors for want of students.

While the gender gap in urban areas narrowed, the same cannot be said of rural residents. In 1971 there was a 17 percentage points difference (40 and 57 per cent respectively for females and males) and in 1990 the difference had declined to only 10 percentage points (65 and 75 per cent). In rural areas at the start the difference was 12 percentage points (16 and 28 per cent) and two decades later it had become 11 percentage points (39 and 50 per cent respectively). These patterns may be a function of responses to the labour market created in and around urban areas as a result of employment opportunities created through industrialisation as well as in service industries. As mentioned earlier, Indonesia is currently a rapidly growing economy where economic growth is increasingly led by labour-intensive and export-oriented industries, where not only men but large numbers of women have found paid employment (World Bank 1996: Chapter 3). The rapidly expanding middle class is concentrated in urban areas. They are also more likely to rely on household help, further expanding the labour market for females.

The greatest contrast is of course that between rural females and urban males. Even by 1990 only about one out of every 10 rural females had completed lower secondary school, while 46 per cent of urban males claim such qualifications.

Higher education

Little has been said about higher education so far, the main reason being the weaknesses in available quantitative data (Table 8.1). Yet it is the outcome of this part of the education system which constitutes the main focus of discussion on the quality of Indonesia's human resources.[15] As numerous deregulation measures have been introduced since the mid-1980s, the private sector has become an increasingly dominant force in the national economy, creating more formal-sector jobs which demand different qualifications from those required by the public sector. Whereas fields of study seem to have mattered little in the public sector, which differentiates and ranks employees by degree and seniority (Clark and Oey-Gardiner 1991), private sector employers find quality managers,[16] accountants, engineers and other professionals to be in short supply.

Irrespective of the unreliability of available quantitative data,[17] the higher education system has clearly expanded very rapidly since the mid-1980s and continues to expand. The upward movement from mass primary education through the SD Inpres program started to

---

[15] The issue of the quality of the Indonesian higher education system has been widely discussed. A team at the Center for Policy and Implementation Studies conducted research on this topic for several years (Keyfitz *et al.* 1988a, 1988b). Quality in higher education was also the theme of the *Indonesia Assessment 1991* (Hill 1991), in which various aspects of the system which contribute to poor quality were discussed. The debate continues and in June 1996 the media widely discussed plagiarism of undergraduate (*S1*) student *skripsi* (thesis) by *dosen* (teaching staff) to obtain their research credit points for promotion (*Kompas* , 27 May 1996, 'Ratusan dosen di Jatim jiplak skripsi', 27 May 1996, p.1).

[16] Writing in 1991 about business education in Indonesia, Habir (1991) noted the very rapid growth in the number of business schools (from 8 in 1987 to 20 in 1991). As the demand for managers was not met by the existing pool and the price of managers skyrocketed, the market responded with a proliferation of business schools, some of which produced graduates of questionable quality. Some programs held classes only once a week and others took high school graduates as their MBA candidates. The shortage of quality managers continues to constrain domestic business development (T. Sima Gunawan in *Jakarta Post,* see footnote 2; Tanri Abeng in the *Jakarta Post,* see footnote 1). Today many discover that MBA certificates are no longer tickets to instant success (Widiadana in *Jakarta Post,* see footnote 3).

[17] The reason for severe up and down swings in the numbers of students may well be that these data constitute a result of individual institutions reporting the requested data which are then collated by the Ministry. Hence the quality of the information is subject to the reporting quality of the institutions and data processing at the Ministry.

affect the intake into the higher education system around that time. The mid-1980s also marked the beginning of the introduction of de-regulation measures when formal sector jobs, including those for higher education graduates, were created by the private sector. De-mand for such credentials has therefore risen. As demand for manag-ers in particular grew, the private sector took the lead and responded by opening numerous MBA programs, which only later were fol-lowed by postgraduate management programs at public institutions of higher education or PTN (Habir 1991).

Education is increasingly becoming good business. Initially, the government responded to rising demand by increasing the intake of new students into the existing public system or PTN,[18] to which in 1984 was added only one open university. Government policy continues to be to hold constant the number of public institutions. As there is rapidly growing excess demand, the private sector has responded favourably by opening new institutions of higher education. Conse-quently the higher education system has become increasingly domi-nated by the private sector. In the mid-1970s the public system was still dominant in terms of student body, graduates and lecturers—one-half to two-thirds were in PTN. Today only about one-third of the total post-secondary student body attend PTN. The same is true of graduates and lecturers (Departemen Pendidikan dan Kebudayaan 1994a, Tables 3.14 - 3.16: 164-166).

In the past, when the higher education system was still domi-nated by the public system, concerns were expressed about the qual-ity of the output of the system;[19] today the saga continues. Most of the blame, however, is now placed on the private schools, which are said

---

[18] Which currently consists of 43 conventional public institutions of higher education or PTN (30 universities, 3 technical institutes and 10 IKIP or teacher training institutes), one open university and five arts institutes and/or academies.

[19] Poor quality output of the PTN system has been attributed to very sudden and rapid expansion of the system without the necessary preparation to maintain some kind of quality. During the 1960s, 29 new PTN were added to an existing pool of nine. Worse, this occurred during a time when Indonesia suffered from extremely rapid economic deterioration (Keyfitz *et al.* 1988a, 1988b).

to have made education a business rather than a contribution to idealised social services. Quality issues arise partly from the fields of study. While it is often said that private schools establish themselves by selecting 'cheap programs' in the 'soft sciences' of education, social science and law, public schools have actually done the same. For instance, in 1987, only 22 per cent of the study programs at PTN were in the non-education sciences (Oey-Gardiner 1988).[20] The proportion may be even smaller in PTS. It is therefore not surprising that the private sector claims there are too few engineers and skilled workers with science and technology backgrounds.

Achievements

As the expansion in the education system has led to practically universal enrolment of the primary school-age population, the working-age population is rapidly becoming better educated.[21] For all the quantitative advances made during the past two decades, however, overall levels of education remain fairly low in the nation's bid toward industrialisation and in facing globalisation of the economy. With a lag, the trends in educational achievements have followed similar patterns to those shown for school attendance. Not only are education levels rising, the gender gap is also narrowing and so is the urban rural gap. However, unlike the case with school attendance which showed fairly rapid narrowing of the gaps, in the case of achieved education, the gaps remain much wider. Owing to the relative recency of the education expansion, rising education qualifications are concentrated among the youth, especially those living in urban areas.

---

[20] As unemployability of teacher education graduates has become a problem, a recent policy has been introduced for IKIP or teacher education institutions to change into universities.

[21] Within the South East Asian context, Indonesia's educational progress is said to have been remarkable not only in terms of quantitative performance but also as regards efficiency and equity (Pernia 1991).

Amount of schooling

As the special primary school program was socially oriented, to more equitably spread the benefits of social development, a prime target has been those who would otherwise not have attended school. It is therefore no surprise that the biggest impact of the special primary school program has been on rapidly reducing the proportion of the population that has never attended school. Because enrolment of females and rural dwellers had been particularly low, it was among females and rural residents that the decline in the percentage who had never attended school was sharpest.

Only two and one-half decades ago, four out of every ten persons aged 10 years and over had never attended school; by 1990 this was true of only 16 per cent of the population. We suggest that it was due to availability (physical distance) and accessibility (cost, free tuition) that parents were willing to give their daughters equal opportunity with their sons to attend school, with a consequent more rapid decline in the proportion of females compared to males who had never attended school. For females the decline was from about one-half to less than one-quarter, or some 29 percentage points, while for males the decline was from 29 to 11 per cent, or 18 percentage points. Closer proximity and accessibility were particularly important in enabling rural parents to send their children to school. In 1971 only 22 per cent of the urban population 10+ had never attended school; two decades later this proportion had shrunk to 8 per cent. In rural areas the decline was from 44 to 20 per cent.

Two decades ago only one out of every four persons had completed at least their primary education. Today it is every other person. At this level at least, the gender gap is narrowing, albeit still only slightly. Similar to the pattern for the total population, for females too, two decades ago only one out of every four had completed primary school and today it is already every other person. For males the rise was from 35 to 58 per cent.

Of course greater advances have been made by urban residents. In urban areas school density is usually much higher and residents also place greater value on education. As well, the educated and those seeking education are more likely to be concentrated in urban areas. Thus even two decades ago, already half the urban population 10+ had completed their primary education, but today, seven out of every

10 persons had similar qualifications. Among rural residents the increase was from only 22 to 44 per cent. Over time the urban-rural gap has actually widened.

To be educated is to be young

Considering the relative novelty of the policies to achieve universal enrolment at the primary level, it is not surprising that even by 1990 the effects are still concentrated on young adults aged less than 25 years. That is not to say that no older people were educated, but rather that among older people education was far more elitist in nature. While Indonesian girls have benefitted disproportionately, most girls, and young girls too for that matter, have completed only primary school and even lower secondary schooling is not yet very common.

The gains during the latter 1980s have been quite striking among teenagers aged 15-19. In 1980 slightly more than half this age group had completed at least primary school, but a decade later almost nine out of every ten persons had such qualifications. Interestingly, the age-specific pattern for those with at least lower secondary schooling in 1990 closely resembles the pattern for those with at least primary schooling in 1970; clearly, even lower secondary education is still not widely accessible to the masses. The highest proportion with completed lower secondary schooling is recorded for those aged 20-24 (45 per cent), and this proportion declines rapidly among older age cohorts.

As a result of mobility towards urban areas among the better educated, the urban-rural gap in educational achievement is widening. Increasing concentration of the educated in urban areas is not just a phenomenon of the youth. It cuts across all ages, and is evident not only among men but even more so among women. This condition is of course closely related to the greater dynamism in the urban labour market, where most jobs requiring education are located. Among young adult urban residents (20-24 years old) three-fifths (60 per cent) of females and three-quarters (75 per cent) of males had completed lower secondary education. The urban-rural gap is greater among females than males and the pattern holds for all age categories. Education, especially lower secondary or more, is a ticket for leaving their rural environs in search of urban employment and life styles. Even though the overall educational qualifications of the rural population are also improving, the pace of change appears to be rather slow.

Challenges

The emphasis above has been on Indonesia's quantitative achievements in education. While education is widely regarded as a ticket to a good job, the probability of obtaining desirable jobs is declining rapidly with rising open unemployment, particularly among those with high school and tertiary education. Yet the needs of the private sector for skilled workers are not being met, and the numbers of expatriate workers are rapidly rising, attracted by Indonesia's booming economy.[22] This is causing alarm for the Minister of Manpower.[23]

In the past, education provided a means of social mobility through improving access to paid employment in the formal sector, normally the public sector. Until about a decade ago the public sector was the major employer. While such remains the situation in most areas of the country, it is no longer the case in large and economically vibrant cities, such, as, for instance Jakarta, the nation's capital, and a few other smaller cities. Starting in 1993 the government has declared zero growth for the civil service, leaving the private sector to take the lead in employment creation for an ever more 'educated' workforce.

Concerns about open unemployment are relatively recent in origin, dating from the mid-1980s. Until 1980, open unemployment figures were generally low in Indonesia, only around 2-3 per cent. Development, however, brought with it an anomaly: more resources were available to invest not only in physical but also in social infrastructure, especially in education. The results have been shown before. As education became more widespread, however, the value of education as a passport to obtaining paid employment in the formal sector in fact diminished. While graduates of a particular level of schooling still expect to find better paying or at least similar jobs to those of their counterparts a generation before them, they soon find out that such jobs have become relatively scarce.

---

[22] *Jakarta Post*, 'RI Economic Boom Draws Expatriates', 26 May 1996, p. 1.

[23] The monthly wage bill for foreigners reached US$200 million in 1995. Not only are high-level positions of managers and professionals being filled by expatriates, but 41 per cent of all 57,177 foreign workers in 1995 who were recorded by the Tax Directorate General were operatives (*Jakarta Post*, 26 May 1996, p.1).

Even though rates of open unemployment rose between the last two censuses, the level was still rather low (1.7 and 3.2 per cent in 1980 and 1990 respectively).[24] This low level has been attributed to Indonesia's labour force still being predominantly agrarian and second, the absence of social security, rendering open unemployment a luxury the majority cannot afford, especially when they are poor.[25]

Of concern, however, is not the overall open unemployment rate but rather the education-specific levels, which, according to the 1990 census results rose fairly dramatically with education, more so among females than males and more strikingly among urban than rural residents. Double-digit open unemployment rates for females with upper secondary (14 per cent) and higher education (10 per cent), especially among urban women, are alarming.

Even though it is acknowledged that these high unemployment rates refer mainly to the young and first-time job seekers (about three-fourths), these results do send signals to the consumers of education, especially when they are poor. These could well be the signals which, as noted earlier, have led to a slowdown in the growth in enrolment of the lower-secondary age groups, probably especially among the poor.

Thus, whereas the supply of the educated labour force is rising rapidly, the demand for existing and available skills is not expanding at an equal pace. Will parents and their children wish to continue schooling to higher levels, or will there be a further slowdown in

---

[24] While Independent Indonesia has, in fact, already conducted four population censuses, comparable unemployment figures are only for the last two censuses. The 1971 Census results suffer from changes in imputation rules, which did not follow the logical sequence of the questionnaire, thereby raising the overall unemployment rate from 2 to 9 per cent in different publications (Series C and Series D and E). Later analyses recognised that in fact open unemployment rates for a basically agrarian society with no social security should, in fact, be low. Hence, later data collections on the labour force were no longer subject to such imputation rules. Second, there are in fact other data sources on the labour force, which are not presented here for reasons of incompatibility. Specialised labour force data collection exercises have consistently resulted in higher rates than recorded by the census.

[25] The 'safety valve' is the large proportion of the labour force categorised as unpaid family workers.

attendance, especially among the poor? The answer to this question will only be found in a few years time, as several large-scale projects are in the pipeline to bring lower secondary education closer to home, as happened at an earlier stage with primary education.

In a nutshell the challenges facing Indonesia's world of education as we are approaching the 21st century of globalisation and free trade are twofold. At the lower end it is the realisation of basic education for all, while at the upper end it is the need to meet the skill and professional requirements of the time.

9

Women's Role in Demographic Transition and Human Resource Development

Yulfita Raharjo

Background

The numerous policies and programs for human resources development (HRD) that have been implemented over the years by the Indonesian government have heavily concentrated on the supply side.
However, it is becoming clear that supplying facilities is not necessarily sufficient. This is particularly true for women, since there is no
guarantee that all women will be able to, or even want to, fully
participate in HRD programs. Socio-cultural factors, including gender
stereotypes depicting women as passive, dependent and inferior to
men, as well as the existing economic, political and legal arrangements are significant obstacles. Unfortunately, policy-makers and
planners have not yet fully identified the obstacles to women's participation. However, one key strategy to address the situation seems to be
the encouragement of a demand, a desire and a need by women to
participate in development programs. The other component must be
the encouragement of women's ability to operationalise these decisions.

Introduction

Since Repelita V there has been a reorientation of development efforts
in favour of social development. This is partly in response to a growing awareness that the development achieved in the last few Repelita
did not necessarily benefit the majority of the people. It is also partly a
recognition that development indicators emphasising economic and

statistical measures are too narrow. The facts show that the continued economic growth experienced by Indonesia is no guarantee of ordinary people receiving an equal share of the outcomes of national, regional or local development.

The critical importance of a human face for development is not a new idea for Indonesia. It is stated clearly in the national ideology of *Pancasila* and in UUD 45, Article 33: the people's welfare is the ultimate objective of the development process. However, this objective has acquired new urgency in recent years, mostly related to the growing problem of human resources failing to meet development requirements. This urgency is also related to the tough competition that Indonesia is expected to face in the era of globalisation. Furthermore, with the introduction of labour-saving technologies, it is imperative for Indonesia to upgrade its human resources to meet different industrial and small business demands.

Despite a population of 200 million people and rich natural resources, Indonesia remains largely unawake. The challenge is how to raise the productivity of 200 million Indonesians, men and women, in this time of rapid global socio-economic change. In response to this challenge, and in parallel with relatively high economic growth (average 6 per cent per annum), in the last two decades the Indonesian government has continued to invest not only in the productive sectors but also in HRD and social services through various programs and interventions, such as the provision of health care and facilities, education and economic opportunities. The result has been that HRD, in general, shows an improvement, as demonstrated by some key indicators (see Table 9.1).

While progress has been made, the level of Indonesia's human resources development is among the lowest in Asia (Table 9.1). Furthermore, as will be discussed below, if the development record is then broken down by sex, it shows that HRD among women is inadequate, and even lower than for men.

The Indonesian government realises the importance of women's strategic position. In particular the national ideology stresses women's social function in preserving and continuing cultural values; women's critical role in influencing the quality of human resources of succeeding generations, and women's important contribution to demographic transition. Over the last two decades the Indonesian government has been making special efforts to promote policies, programs and interventions for the enrichment of women's HRD. The impact of develop-

TABLE 9.1: Selected HRD indicators, 1980-90:
selected ASEAN countries

Country	Expectation of life at birth		Literacy rates		Second-level gross enrol-ment ratio (females)	GNP per capita
	1985	1990	1985 Male/ Female	1990	1988-90	1992
Indonesia	56	61.5	80/64	71.8	41	670
Malaysia	68	70.1	83/65	74.0	58	2,790
Philippines	63	64.2	88/87	87.7	75	770
Thailand	64	66.1	95/87	90.7	32	1,840

Sources: United Nations Development Programme 1991, 1993; UNICEF 1991; World Bank 1994b.

ment-induced changes, such as smaller families, widespread primary schooling, access to health facilities, declining fertility and infant mortality rates and older age at marriage, has deeply affected the lives and behaviour of Indonesian women. The impact of such changes has been much greater on women than on men despite the persistent discrepancy between socio-economic changes and cultural values which inhibit women from fully participating in the development process. Unfortunately, in implementing human resources programs, this essential cultural aspect is frequently overlooked.

In most cases, we have even failed to identify the obstacles to women's participation in the development process. This provides the explanation for the low level of utilisation of human development opportunities among women, which in turn reinforces the low quality of life of Indonesian women. It is a vicious circle. Providing promising and well-intended policies, programs and interventions for women is not enough: we need to encourage a need, a desire, indeed a demand by women to participate in development programs. We need to actively involve them in the development process. This is the problem we must solve.

The situation of women's human resource development in Indonesia

The First World Women's Conference was conducted by the United Nations in Mexico in 1975, followed by the declaration of 1975-85 as the United Nations Decade for Women. The aim was to advance the role and participation of women in the development process. In 1980, a mid-term review was conducted in Copenhagen. After that, the document *Forward-Looking Strategies for the Advancement of Women* (see Fraser 1987) was issued at the Second World Women's Conference in Nairobi, as a means of evaluating the achievements of the Women's Decade. In that conference various indicators and strategies were developed to cope with the constraints faced. The Fourth World Women's Conference in Beijing in 1995 proposed a 'Platform for Action', with the theme *Equality, Development and Peace*. In between, several relevant conferences were conducted, including the Convention on the Elimination of All Forms of Discrimination against Women (CEDAW)(1979) and the Cairo International Conference on Population and Development (1994), to mention just two.

Indonesia as an active member of the international community has been involved in and committed to this global women's movement. Its involvement in the international arena has also influenced national policies on women. As a follow up to the 1975 World Women's Conference in Mexico, a junior Minister for the Role of Women was appointed in 1979, whose main function was encouraging the role of women in the development process. This position was upgraded in 1983 to become the State Minister for the Role of Women. However, as an office of the State Ministry without portfolio, the office is not directly involved in implementing the programs. Its coordination role very much depends on the 14 implementing sectors. In general, there are no comprehensive women's programs, limited funds are available, and the results, not surprisingly, are disappointing.

In general, women's human resource development shows some concrete improvements, especially recognising the late start and the extent of the initial lag behind men. However, despite considerable changes to the lives of Indonesian women, in various situations a gender gap still persists. Here follow four important aspects of women's situation in Indonesia which illustrate where women stand now.

Education

Education and information are urgently needed as investments in human resources. The Program of Action of the International Conference on Population and Development focused on education as one of the most important means of giving people knowledge, skill and, in particular, self-confidence and access to information. Over the last 20 years, the Indonesian government has implemented widespread basic education programs for all and specific education intervention programs for rural areas. The result is that Indonesia has made some significant gains as measured by indicators of educational participation (see also Chapter 8, this volume). For example, the percentage of illiterate 15-24 year olds has declined sharply, from 26 per cent (females) and 13 per cent (males) in 1970 to 18 per cent (females) and 10 per cent (males) in 1990. Although in older age groups (25 years and above) the illiteracy figures are still high, they do show improvement, i.e. from 68 per cent (women) and 37 per cent (men) in 1970 down to 54 per cent (women) and 28 per cent (men) in 1990. The continuing high illiteracy rate among older people is due to the long-term results of having limited educational opportunity. Interestingly, the percentage of female illiterates declined faster than the male percentage.

One special education program, known as Program SD Inpres, was introduced in 1973. This was an instruction, based on a presidential decree, to build at least one primary school in each village. The impact was impressive. According to the 1990 Population Census, more than 90 per cent of children of primary school age were able to go to school. The program has also had an impact on women's education, as can be seen from the considerable improvement in the percentage of girls in primary school. In 1980 only 58 per cent of primary school aged girls attended school, but this had risen to 92 per cent in 1990. With the new nine years compulsory education policy, it is

expected that Indonesia will have more and more people with basic
education.

However, despite improving women's participation in basic
education, marked gender inequalities still persist in higher education. As shown in Table 9.2, the ratio of female to male enrolment
indicates a dramatic inequality of access to tertiary education.

**TABLE 9.2: Indonesia: illiteracy and education indicators
for males and females**

	Males	Females
% illiterate 15-24, 1990	2.6	4.9
% illiterate 25+, 1990	15.8	33.5
Combined first and second-level gross enrolment ratio		
1980	79	65
1990	85	78
Third-level enrolment per 100,000 population, 1990	1,789	280
Females per males enrolled 1990		
Second level	81	
Third level	48	

Sources: United Nations, 1995a.

Health (see also Chapter 11, this volume)

There has also been significant progress in improving the health status of the population in general and women's health in particular over
the last two decades. Health policy goals have aimed to achieve the
maximum coverage of basic health services. Major health endeavours
stressed the provision of a vast health infrastructure through commu-
nity-level primary health centres (*Puskesmas*). The specific strategy was
to improve coverage rates of immunisation and maternal and child
health care. Various health development policies, programs and interventions were introduced, and focused on public health, family plan-

ning services and children's health. As a result, the growth in the number of *Puskesmas* has been dramatic. There were 1,227 *Puskesmas* at the beginning of Repelita 1 (1968), which increased to 6,227 *Puskesmas* and 17,116 *Puskesmas Pembantu* (health subcentres) by the end of Repelita V. *Puskesmas* are relatively evenly distributed throughout the country.

In response to the acute shortage of medical personnel, especially in remote rural areas, in 1991/92 the government introduced a community service program for medical graduates on short-term contracts, known as the *dokter PTT* program. This was in addition to the existing *dokter Inpres*, a program requiring young graduate doctors to serve the community in remote rural areas for 2 or 3 years.

As a result, the health status of Indonesians is much better than before. In the period 1971 to 1994, the infant mortality rate declined from 145 infant deaths per thousand to 56. During the same period, life expectancy at birth increased from 46 years to 63 years (males 62 years and females 65). Nevertheless, despite improvement in nearly all aspects of health status, the key health indicators remain unsatisfactory, especially in comparison with other Asian countries (Table 9.3).

TABLE 9.3: Key health indicators in selected Asian countries

	Indonesia	Philippines	Thailand	Malaysia
1994 Infant mortality rate	56	39	34	14
1993 Under 5 death rate	111	59	33	17
1994 Life expectancy	62/65	64/68	66/71	69/73
1993 Maternal mortality	390	74	37	26

Sources: IMR and Lo: ESCAP 1994.
          Under-5 Death Rate: United Nations Development Programme 1995.
          MMR: World Bank 1993b.

As shown in Table 9.3, maternal mortality in Indonesia is extremely high. According to the Indonesian Health and Demographic Survey of 1994, the current maternal mortality rate (MMR) is still 390 per 100,000 live births for the period of 1989-94. The growing literature on women's health in the developing world indicates that there are complex issues of interaction between bureaucratic approaches (providers, services) and socio-cultural factors, which may contribute to the problems of maternal mortality. This is also true for the Indonesian case. One explanation for the high MMR in Indonesia is that a large numbers of births are not attended by trained personnel, especially in remote rural areas. In addition, there are few backup services (including a lack of treatment for medical complications), a persistence of improper treatment and shortages of staff and supplies, particularly for high-risk pregnancies.

In responding to this situation, one of the health policies announced in Repelita V is for the placement of at least one trained midwife (*bidan desa*) in each village. The midwife is to be the health services manager and hopefully she will support the delivery of health services for mother and child, including family planning work and simple clinical services. Certainly there is the potential for the *bidan desa* to assist in the improvement of local health conditions, especially through health services for the mother and child. In the last five years about 19,400 *bidan desa* have been trained and posted nationwide.

However, in improving women's health, especially dealing with maternal mortality and reducing their reproductive burden, the problem is not only access to appropriate health services, but is also linked to women's poor reproductive rights,[1] which in turn reflect women's low social status, specifically linked to gender inequalities which disadvantage women.

Although women may not have power in terms of the control of their reproduction, they still take the greater responsibility in family planning and family planning messages in Indonesia are directed to them. Within Asian countries, Indonesian men's use of contraceptives

---

[1] Reproduction rights have to do with the right to be informed and have access to safe, effective, affordable and acceptable methods of family planning of their choice, and the right of access to appropriate health care services that will allow women to go safely through pregnancy and childbirth.

is the lowest, i.e. 4 per cent, compared with 9 per cent and 24 per cent in Thailand and the Philippines, respectively (IPPF Medical Bulletin, 1988).

The main causes of death among women are indeed those which relate to their reproductive function. Gynaecological infections, chronic anaemia and malnourishment are suspected as contributing to pregnancy complications and maternal and neo-natal death. A woman needs more nutritious food, especially during pregnancy and breast feeding, but iron deficiency is chronic among Indonesian women of reproductive age. Traditional practices or beliefs related to food, dietary habits, weaning, ante- and post-natal care and delivery often have negative impacts on women's health.

Diet and nutritional status are influenced by beliefs and tradition but also by the availability of food. In most families, priority is given to the husbands/men in the household. Women traditionally sacrifice themselves for their families, putting themselves after other members of the family. From an early age, women are discriminated against, and yet girls/women contribute to the family and work long hours. If women are overburdened and inadequately nourished, their physical development is limited. This in turn affects their health and threatens their ability to give birth to healthy babies. Discriminatory attitudes also have a bad impact on women's health, especially if combined with poverty and ignorance. This darker side of women's life in turn influences the quality of women's resource development.

The government of Indonesia has accepted the reproductive health concept adopted at the 1994 International Conference on Population and Development (ICPD) in Cairo, which stated that improvement in reproductive health is a pre-requisite for sustainable socio-economic development. However, so far there has been no particular effort in terms of developing comprehensive policies, programs or actions, although recently there have been growing initiatives among academics and NGOs to conduct advocacy, research and seminars on reproductive health, reproductive rights, gender awareness and other social factors. Given that the health system in Indonesia is still uni-focus in its approach and perceives reproductive health as a clinical issue, there is a need to further examine the relationship between political, economic and socio-cultural factors, on one hand, and women's health and reproductive health on the other. It is clear that women's health cannot be improved if no supporting interventions are made.

Economic activities

Since 1970 women's share in the labour force has been increasing. More and more women are working outside the home. Along with increasing labour demands, there are several reasons for women to enter the labour market, such as economic need and the desire for self-articulation. Other women have an interest in social-voluntary work. According to the 1990 population census, female labour force participation was 37 per cent.

In fact, it is hard to know how many women are actually in the labour force. Because of the nature of their work, usually centred in the home, frequently interspersed with daily housework tasks, it is difficult to measure women's work precisely. The official concept and definition of work used in the population census contributes to bias when dealing with women's different range of activities, especially in the informal sector and in family businesses, which are a vital part of household survival strategies. Besides, women themselves often do not consider their economic activities as work, even if they produce goods for the market. As a result, numerous women's economic activities are concealed and overlooked. It can therefore be assumed that in reality women's labour force participation is much higher than is reported. And yet women workers are not considered important or even to exist. One important implication is that gender differences are not fully considered in small business development designs, for example. Women's difficulties in gaining access to credit for capital investment are a good example of gender discrimination.

Even though Indonesia ratified the Convention on the Elimination of all Forms of Discrimination against Women in 1979 and then operationalised it in various laws, regulations, decrees, and across various sectors, in the labour market Indonesian women still face gender discrimination in terms of wages and non-gender-sensitive work conditions. More women than men are employed on a contractual basis. They may be paid on a daily basis without any social security. Since they lack economic access and networks, they also lack opportunities to develop their own human resources. Occupational segregation can be seen in the types of occupation showing a concentration of women, e.g. the informal sector. As a result, women are not protected in terms of labour laws (e.g. wages, occupational health).

In the last two decades, especially as a consequence of slower economic growth after the end of the oil boom, there has been a flow of labour from Indonesia to other countries such as Malaysia, Singapore, Hong Kong and also the Middle East. It should be emphasised that the number of undocumented and illegal labour migrants, including female workers, has been increasing at an alarming rate. Despite success stories, it is also creating many problems in the foreign countries (sexual abuse, violence, imprisonment, etc) and at home (spouse remarriage, neglected children etc). One study indicated that instead of buying nutritious food, the remittances had been spent on motorbikes, house renovations and the like (Purwaningsih, forthcoming). Most of these workers are unskilled and innocent, lack knowledge of their rights and responsibilities, and have no experience of contracted jobs. Therefore, they are easily victimised and abused by the system, the recruiters as well as the employers. In the long run, these problems are likely to further impact on human resource development.

Women's perspective on demographic transition and human resource development

Human resources development and demographic transition are closely interconnected. The following section discusses the role of Indonesian women in these processes.

Fertility change

Population growth rates are subject to changes in fertility, mortality and migration, all of which play a crucial role in the complex process of demographic transition. Compared with the experiences of Western countries, demographic transition in Asia is proceeding relatively rapidly. It is also important to note that in contrast with industrialised countries, evidence indicates that in many Asian countries fertility decline can occur even at a relatively early stage of development. The experiences of many Asian countries question the validity of the 'classical' model of demographic transition that regards socio-economic development as a primary prerequisite for fertility transition (Ogawa and Tsuya 1993: 32-33). In Indonesia there has been a deliberately organised effort to control fertility, especially through the national family planning program, that started in the early 1970s.

Since the mid-1970s, the magnitude and tempo of fertility transition in Indonesia (and the underlying process) have been unique in the developing world. The total fertility rate has dropped from 4.1 in 1985 to 2.9 in 1995, while the annual population growth has declined from 2.2 per cent in 1985 to an estimated 1.7 per cent in 1995. Although there has been no consensus among developmentalists on how women's role affects demographic transition, it is obvious that women have contributed much to the remarkable change in fertility in Indonesia. As already acknowledged, the major role of women in reducing the fertility rate was through their active participation in family planning programs. However, the ineffectiveness of interventions aimed at male participation suggests the need for further improvements in the family planning programs, especially since the current family planning approach is through *keluarga sejahtera* (family welfare). Therefore, women should not be the only 'objects' in the development of reproductive health and reproductive rights: men should also be involved and have equal responsibility in these matters.

Mortality changes

Mortality decline occurred in Indonesia without prior substantial socio-economic development. Besides the transfer of medical knowledge and technology from the industrialised countries, the mortality change in Indonesia is mainly due to the long history of government public health and hygiene programs starting from the colonial period. As a consequence, life expectancy at birth for both sexes has increased substantially. However, life expectancy at birth is a summary measure of mortality at all ages in a population. Therefore, the figures of 62 for males and 65 for females need clarification. Note that a careful examination of mortality changes is needed, for although the tempo of improvements and the degree of absolute gains are relatively similar for each sex, there still remain crucial differentials between the two, if we consider age specific groups.

Indonesia has introduced various health programs for infants and children under five. This may be explained by the fact that Indonesia could realistically make substantial reductions in infant mortality. However, there are no such programs for youth, adolescence, middle or old age. Similarly, until recently, Indonesia has had no particular policies or actions regarding reproductive health and reproductive rights.

Educational changes

Primary education has become almost universal in Indonesia. As a result, the proportion of the population with primary education appears to be increasing steadily. As a further step, recently the government announced a policy of nine years of compulsory education. Rising enrolments have led to a better educated labour force and later marriage as the longer students stay at school, the higher the age of marriage, especially among girls. Supported to some extent by the impact of a government regulation on the minimum age of marriage, the speed and the extent of the increase in the age of marriage for boys and girls has been remarkable.

In contrast with primary and secondary education, however, substantial differences can be found among both sexes at tertiary level. As noted earlier, females lag far behind. The obvious impact is reflected in the quality of the female labour force. Firms will be more willing to employ males, especially in higher positions, leaving women marginalised, i.e. in the informal sector with limited access to training and further education. This is reflected in the quality of Indonesian women's resources in general.

Changing patterns of labour force participation

Labour force participation rates of women in Indonesia have increased substantially and are expected to increase further, until at the beginning of the 21st century (in the year 2003), the labour force participation of Indonesian women is expected to reach 50 per cent. Women's economic participation is concealed and overlooked, because they are much more likely to be categorised as family workers. However, structural changes in the economy are causing a substantial reallocation of unpaid family workers or self-employed workers towards paid work as employees. This is certainly true for women. The changes reflect the shift away from employment in the primary sector (agriculture) towards employment in secondary and tertiary sectors. In general, the young (women) workers who are mobile leave traditional agricultural employment. Nearly all of them lack skill and knowledge. Therefore, even though they change jobs they do not change their plight.

Conclusion

In recognition of the importance of women's role in demographic transition and human resource development, the Indonesian government has made impressive efforts over the last two decades to promote policies and development programs intended specifically for women. At the same time, the impact of development changes, such as declining infant mortality, smaller families, widespread health facilities and almost universal primary schooling, has triggered profound changes in the lives of Indonesians, and particularly Indonesian women. To mention just a few, the age of marriage among Indonesian women is rising; women's literacy, participation in education, health status, labour force participation and life expectancy have also increased. And women have become agents of change themselves, for example in the Family Planning Program where women's involvement has been crucial to the dramatic decline in the national fertility rate.

It must be stressed, however, that despite considerable changes in the lives of women, their quality of life remains relatively low and in some aspects of human development, they lag well behind men. Future Indonesian generations will depend on these women. The question is, why have such promising and well-intentioned policies and programs for women failed to produce the expected results? Policy makers, planners, researchers and implementers need to examine more thoroughly the factors which restrict women's access to HRD and their opportunity to make free and informed choices about fertility, migration, education, work and life-threatening health matters. HRD and demographic change are interconnected and we need to know better how to support women in improving their quality of life.

10

Some Economic Demographic Aspects of 'Ageing'

*Aris Ananta, Evi Nurvidya Anwar
and Diah Suzenti*

Baby boom and old people boom

Those who were born in the 1950-70 period in Indonesia are called the 'baby boom' generation. The fertility rate was relatively high in this period. Since 1970 the fertility rate has shown a rapidly declining trend, though the number of births still rose because although the number of children per woman declined, the number of women was still on the rise. The number of births started decreasing only after 1980.

The baby boom generation always brings its own problems. When they were born, they crowded the facilities related to pregnancies, deliveries and child care. When they were school children, they crowded the school and other educational facilities. When they entered the labour market, they crowded job markets for first time workers. When they were married, they crowded the housing market. When they had health problems, they crowded the health facilities. And when they are old, they will crowd the limited facilities for old people. In other words, this baby boom generation will become the old person boom generation. This old person boom generation will be prominent from 2010 to about 2030.

This chapter attempts to show some potential issues of the future old people boom, viewed from a demographic perspective. Section 2 discusses the 'state of ageing' in Indonesia using both the commonly used definition of old people (65+) and the officially used definition of old people (60+). The discussion employing the commonly used definition is to allow some international perspective on the issue of old people in Indonesia. Comparison of the two definitions (see Table 10.1) reveals that more than 30 per cent of the officially defined old people are still in the age group 60-64, who are not yet called 'old' in advanced countries.

The remaining sections follow the official definition of old people. Section 3 discusses the 'quality' of the old people, in 1990 and in the future. Quality is here simply defined as their education and health condition. Section 4 discusses participation of old people in the labour market and their level of urbanisation. It also speculates about the pattern of mobility of old people for selected provinces in 1975-80 and 1985-90. Section 5 concludes the chapter by discussing policies that will turn old people into assets, rather than burdens for economic development.

State of 'ageing' in Indonesia

There are many ways to define how old a population is. One way is to use the percentage of old people, usually defined as those aged 65+. A population with less than 5 per cent old people is said to be a young population; with more than 10 per cent, an old population; and, in between 5 per cent and 10 per cent, an intermediate population. According to this definition, Indonesia in 1990 was still classified as a 'young population,' because only 3.8 per cent of its population was aged 65+. In 2020 Indonesia will be an 'intermediate population' with 7.2 per cent of its population consisting of people aged 65+. Thus, within this 30 year span, Indonesia is said to be 'ageing'—a population experiencing a process of getting older (indicated by a rising percentage of old people).

As shown in Table 10.1, most of the provinces also still have a young population. Intermediate populations are seen only in Yogyakarta (7.3 per cent aged 65+) and Bali (5.4 per cent). Central Java (4.7 per cent) and East Java (4.8 per cent) have almost 'graduated' to intermediate populations. In the year 2020, East Java will be the only province already classified as an old population, but Central Java, Yogyakarta and Bali will be close to an old population, with more than 9 per cent of their population already aged 65+. Thus, in the year 2020, Yogyakarta will no longer be the province with the oldest population. Yet all provinces will have experienced an ageing process, i.e. a rising percentage of old people.

TABLE 10.1: Percentage of elderly and children under five by province, 1990 and 2020

	60+		65+		(60-64)/65		Under 5	
	1990[a]	2020[b]	1990[a]	2020[b]	1990[a]	2020[b]	1990[a]	2020[b]
D.I. Aceh	5.3	9.3	3.1	5.9	41.1	36.6	14.0	8.0
North Sumatra	5.2	9.2	3.2	5.6	39.3	38.8	13.8	8.6
West Sumatra	7.3	11.5	4.4	7.3	40.0	35.9	12.4	7.4
Riau	4.0	9.0	2.3	5.4	43.6	39.8	13.9	7.8
Jambi	3.9	9.1	2.1	5.5	45.4	39.6	13.3	8.3
South Sumatra	4.0	9.6	2.8	5.9	41.0	39.0	13.8	8.0
Bengkulu	4.7	8.7	2.8	5.1	40.8	41.3	13.6	7.9
Lampung	4.7	10.4	2.6	6.5	44.6	38.0	13.2	6.9
DKI Jakarta	3.2	11.3	1.7	7.0	46.4	38.3	10.1	7.2
West Java	6.0	10.1	3.6	6.3	40.5	38.1	12.1	7.3
Central Java	7.8	14.9	4.7	9.6	40.5	35.6	10.9	6.3
Yogyakarta	11.0	19.9	7.3	9.5	34.3	34.1	7.8	5.8
East Java	8.0	15.7	4.8	10.2	39.7	35.1	9.5	5.9
Bali	8.3	14.6	5.4	9.4	35.0	35.4	9.1	6.0
West Nusa Tenggara	5.4	9.1	3.4	5.9	37.3	35.0	14.3	8.7
East Nusa Tenggara	6.3	10.3	3.9	6.5	38.1	36.5	14.3	8.3
East Timor	3.6	7.3	2.0	4.4	44.5	40.2	18.0	10.6
West Kalimantan	4.4	9.7	2.6	6.0	41.5	38.1	13.9	8.2
Central Kalimantan	4.1	9.1	2.4	5.5	41.8	39.9	13.7	8.0
South Kalimantan	5.1	11.3	2.9	7.1	43.3	37.2	11.6	7.2
East Kalimantan	3.5	9.4	2.0	5.4	43.0	42.1	12.4	7.2
North Sulawesi	6.3	13.7	4.0	8.7	36.5	36.4	10.2	6.0
Central Sulawesi	4.3	9.1	2.6	5.6	39.6	38.8	13.1	8.2
South Sulawesi	6.1	11.4	3.7	7.6	39.0	33.6	11.8	7.3
South East Sulawesi	4.3	7.9	2.7	4.9	38.4	38.2	15.5	9.7
Maluku	5.1	8.7	3.2	5.3	37.8	39.1	14.6	8.2
Irian Jaya	1.8	8.6	0.9	5.2	49.6	40.2	15.9	8.3
Indonesia	6.3	11.3	3.8	7.2	40.1	36.7	11.7	7.0

[a]Calculated from the 27 publications of the 1990 Population Census , by province series, published by Biro Pusat Statistik in 1992.

[b]Calculated from 27 publications in the Population Projection Series published by Demographic Institute, Faculty of Economics, University of Indonesia.

Though the Indonesian population will be ageing, the percentage of old people in the year 2020 will still be far below 17.5, the percentage of old people in the 'oldest country', Sweden. Thus Indonesia, and even its four oldest provinces (Yogyakarta, Bali, Central Java and East Java) will probably still be far from the 'ageing of the aged society', where there is a rapid rise in the percentage of people aged 80+. In terms of this percentage, then, Indonesia in the year 2020 will probably still be in the category of 'young aged society.'

Yet, as shown in Table 10.2, the percentage of old people in these four provinces in the year 2020 is very close to the percentage of old people in four advanced countries (Canada, Australia, New Zealand and Iceland) in 1993. On the other hand, the projected income per capita in these four provinces is still much lower than the income per capita of the four advanced countries in 1993. Note that the projection of income in the four provinces uses an optimistic assumption, that the economy grows by an annual rate of growth of 10 per cent and that future economic growth follows an exponential, rather than geometrical, curve. With a less optimistic scenario, the income per capita in these provinces will be smaller, and, thus, the problems will become harder.

Thus, these four provinces will face, in the year 2020, the same issues of ageing as the four much more advanced countries face in 1993, but the four provinces will have to handle the issues with much fewer economic resources. Worse, the absolute number of old people in these four provinces (7.9 million in 2020) will be much bigger than the absolute number of old people in the four advanced countries in 1993 (about 5.8 million). Thus, the relatively large number of old people and the relatively low income per capita are the two crucial issues relating to ageing in Indonesia.

It is also interesting to note that Indonesia will experience an absolute increase in old people of 11.5 million within 30 years from 1990—from 6.7 million in 1990 to 18.2 million in 2020 (see Figure 10.1). This addition of old people is as big as the total population of Sulawesi in 1990 or 0.64 times the current Australian population.

A slightly different picture emerges if another definition of old people is used. Indonesia officially defines people 60+ as old people. With this definition, the percentage of old people in 1990 was already 6.3 and will be 11.3 in the year 2020. In absolute terms, with this definition, there will be an addition of 20.1 million old people in the

TABLE 10.2: Ageing and the economy: a crude comparison

	Population aged 65+ (%)	Population aged 65+ (million)	Income per capita (1993 constant price) (US$)
Indonesian province (2020)			
Central Java[a]	9.6	3.33	7,043
Yogyakarta[b]	9.5	0.38	6,535
East Java[c]	10.2	3.83	8,441
Bali[d]	9.4	0.35	8,940
Advanced country (1993)[e]			
Canada	11.6	3.34	19,970
Australia	11.5	2.02	17,500
New Zealand	11.3	0.40	12,600
Iceland	10.6	0.03	24,950

Sources:

[a]Sugihardjo, Chotib and Setiadi 1995.

[b]Ananta, Sugihardjo and Prihastuti 1995.

[c]Ananta, Sugihardjo and Setiadi 1995.

[d]Ananta, Chotib and Setiati 1995.

[e]UNDP 1996.

1990-2020 period. This number is about 1.1 times the current Australian population.

According to the official definition, in the year 2020, the percentage of people 60 and over in Central Java, Yogyakarta, East Java and Bali will already be about 15 per cent. The low percentage in DKI Jakarta will rise rapidly to about 11.3 in the year 2020. Yogyakarta will still be the province with the oldest population.

Table 10.3 shows that the percentage of population aged 65 and over will surpass the percentage of children under five in 2020 (or in 2010 if 'old people' is as officially defined: the population 60+). Note,

FIGURE 10.1: Number of elderly population: Indonesia, 1990-2020

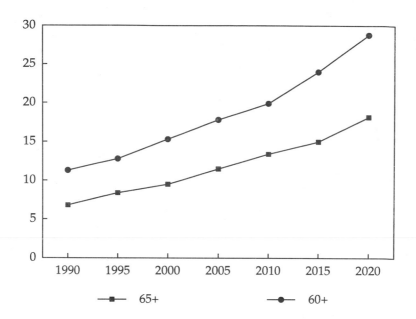

—■— 65+   —●— 60+

TABLE 10.3: Proportion of elderly and children under five, 1990-2020 (per cent)

	60+	65+	Under 5
1990	6.3	3.8	11.7
1995	6.6	4.3	11.2
2000	7.3	4.6	10.1
2005	8.0	5.2	9.1
2010	8.5	5.7	8.4
2015	9.8	6.1	7.7
2020	11.3	7.2	7.0

Source: Calculated from Ananta and Anwar 1995a.

however, that the number of old (65+) people will only exceed the number of children under five in the provinces of Central Java, Yogyakarta, East Java, Bali, North Sulawesi and Indonesia as a whole.

The dependency ratio will decline from 67.8 in 1990 to 41.4 in 2020 (Ananta and Anwar 1995a), but the composition of the dependent population will also be changing. The young dependency ratio will decline from 61.5 in 1990 to 31.2 in 2020, and the old dependency ratio will rise from 6.3 in 1990 to 10.1 in 2020. This implies that the dependency burden of the economy will come increasingly from the old people. In the 1960s and 1970s Indonesia had a relatively large number of young people who already consumed but did not produce. Within the next 25 years, there will be an increasingly greater number of old people, who still consume but no longer produce.

Who should finance the consumption of these old people? Spending for consumption of the young population will get 'results', meaning that the young population will some day become the labour force. A better labour force will produce a larger output. Thus, spending on the youth can be seen as an investment for the economy. On the other hand, spending on the old cannot be seen as an investment. Most of them will not produce, whatever the amount spent on their consumption.

Who will care for the old people? The old people in the year 2020 will have a smaller number of children than did the old people in 1990, though they may still have about three or four children. Further, these children are mostly those born after 1980 and hence they are better educated and, consequently, more mobile geographically. In the year 2020, these children may no longer reside with their parents. In this case, the old people will not be able to depend on their children (or their children-in-law) to take care of them. Nor can they depend on their nephews and nieces since their nephews and nieces are also similar to their children: the younger relatives will all be relatively very mobile and may also reside elsewhere. Neither can they depend on the children of their friends.

Thus, these old people will have to depend on someone else, someone who is not their relative or the children of their friends. Their children may support them financially but may not be able to support them physically.

Because Indonesia consists of 27 different provinces, the discussion of ageing at the national level may not well reflect the condition at provincial or even at lower administrative levels. Therefore we will present more detailed discussion on three provinces expected to provide better 'representativeness' of the 27 provinces, even though these three provinces may still hide many important and interesting features of ageing at the provincial level. The provinces are selected so that they represent provinces with the most advanced state in ageing (Yogyakarta), the 'medium' state (East Nusa Tenggara) and the 'low' state (South Sumatra). The differences in shape of the population pyramid of these provinces in 1990 and 2020 are shown in Figures 10.2 and 10. 3.

Health of the elderly

It is unfortunate that there are no data on the health status of the population in general or, even worse, of old people.[1] Thus, the following discussion is largely qualitative. The only quantitative information is from Table 10.4, showing the life expectancy at birth and at the beginning of old age. Indonesian people (and also older people) are expected to live longer and longer. Advances in medical technology may have contributed to this lengthening of life. In 1995, a woman just entering 'old age', or just turning 60, is expected to live about another 17 years; a man, 15 years. In the year 2020, such a woman will be expected to live another 18 years; and a man, 17 years. Therefore, within the next 30 years, an old woman will still be expected to live longer than an old man, though the gap in life expectancy will be decreasing.

However, the classic question arises, 'Will Indonesians simply add years to their life or will they also add life to their years?'. Will they live long but in poor health or will they live long with good health? Will old women, then, 'suffer' more than the old men? Issues of divisions of jobs at a younger age may reappear, with many different dimensions, in old age.

---

[1] There are no quantitative data, either at present or even for the future, on the health status of old people in Indonesia, compared to the health status of old people in the developed countries at the present time. Qualitatively, it is even more difficult to speculate on the health status of the older people in Indonesia, relative to that in advanced countries.

FIGURE 10.2: Age pyramids of Indonesia, Yogyakarta, South Sumatra and East Nusa Tenggara, 1990 (%)

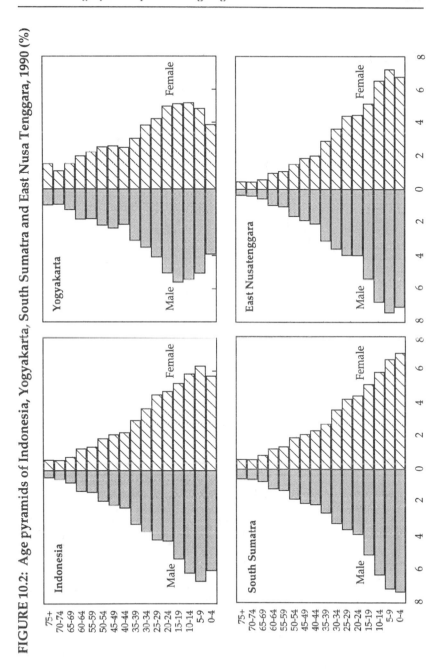

FIGURE 10.3: Population Pyramid: Indonesia, Yogyakarta, South Sumatra and East Nusa Tenggara, 2020

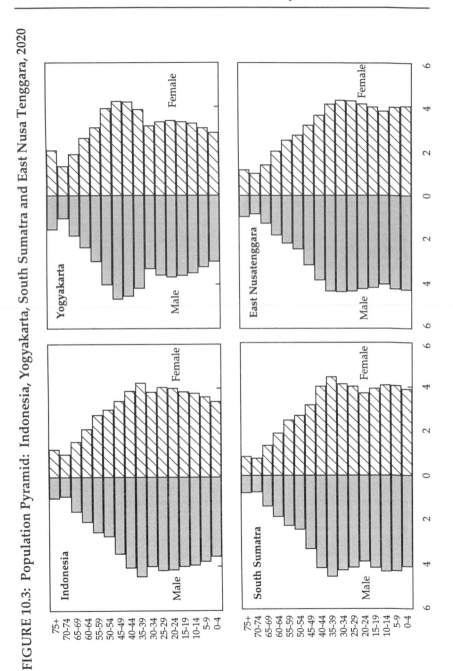

TABLE 10.4: Life expectancy of females and males at birth (e_0) and at 60 (e_{60}) by region, 1990-2025

	1990-95	2005-2010	2020-2025
Life expectancy at birth (e_0)			
Indonesia			
Females	64.4	68.7	71.3
Males	61.3	66.4	69.1
Yogyakarta			
Females	69.4	73.1	75.2
Males	67.7	72.0	74.0
South Sumatra			
Females	61.4	66.1	69.5
Males	60.5	66.1	69.9
East Nusa Tenggara			
Females	60.8	68.2	72.7
Males	59.9	67.6	71.9
Life expectancy at 60 (e_{60})[a]			
Indonesia			
Females	16.7	17.5	18.0
Males	15.0	16.1	16.7
Yogyakarta			
Females	17.5	18.7	19.5
Males	15.7	17.4	18.3
South Sumatra			
Females	16.7	17.1	17.5
Males	15.0	15.7	16.7
East Nusa Tenggara			
Females	16.3	17.5	18.0
Males	14.7	16.1	17.4

[a]Calculated from Coale and Demeny (1983).

Sources: Ananta and Anwar 1995a; Ananta, Sugihardjo and Widyawati 1995; Ananta, Sugiharjo and Prihastuti 1995; Anwar, Chotib and Prihastuti 1995.

With data from the US until the latter part of the 1980s, Crimmins, Hayward and Saito (1994) found that reduction in mortality caused a big increase in the length of dependent life —a higher proportion of non-functioning old individuals. People can experience more years of life, but with worsening health. This is because the reduction in mortality was attributable to mortality due to chronic diseases, in particular if the society was in the early stages of declining mortality from chronic diseases.[2] In other words, lengthening in years of life is not necessarily accompanied by an improving quality of life for the old people. Indeed, the lengthening of old people's lives may increase the economic burden on the society, which, either in the form of family or government, must take care of these old people who no longer produce but still consume (and consume more and more if they are not in good health).

On the other hand, experiences in OECD countries have shown that recently there has been a happily reversing trend, that there are more and more healthy and fewer disabled old people. This is because of the success in postponing the onset of chronic disease and the advances in medical technology to restore the health of patients. Yet experiences in those countries also reveal that the progress in medical technology in lengthening the life of the people is much faster than the progress in raising the age at the onset of chronic disease and the progress in restoring the health of the patients. As a result, the average span of life in disability still continues (Hennessy 1994).

If Indonesia follows the US trend of mortality-morbidity, then the rising expectancy of life among the Indonesian population will also mean decreasing the health of those who survive longer and longer. It implies that the old people will increasingly become a burden on the economy. To overcome this tendency, policies should be introduced in an effort to raise the age of onset of chronic disease or to enhance the ability to cure the diseases such that health can be fully

---

[2] For further discussion of the negative association between mortality and morbidity, see Chapter 18, this volume.

or almost fully restored. Efforts are also needed to find means for people to die more peacefully at cheaper cost. Spiritual life and more attention to non-Western technology may also be re-examined for possible means to simultaneously reduce the cost of taking care of the old people and raise their quality of life.[3] Otherwise, the Indonesian economy has to anticipate a rising economic burden resulting from the booming numbers of old people. Yogyakarta will face this issue earlier than East Nusa Tenggara because it will experience ageing sooner.

Education of the elderly

Education is here simply defined as formal education—educational attainment. Just as education in general is rising, so is the education of the old people, as a result of the movement into the elderly population of better educated younger cohorts. As shown in Table 10.5, in 1990 74 per cent of old women and 42 per cent of old men in Indonesia had no education. The percentage is higher in Yogyakarta (86 per cent for females and 49 per cent for males) and East Nusa Tenggara (75 per cent for females and 54 per cent for males), but lower in South Sumatra (67 per cent for females and 27 per cent for males). The pattern of educational attainment of old people is, as expected, worse than that of the population aged 25-59. The younger generation has better education and thus, when they are old, they will also have better education than the elderly cohorts they replace. The gender difference in education is also less in the younger population, so this will result in faster improvement in the educational attainment of the elderly female population than of the elderly male population in the future.

Table 10.6 shows the rising educational attainment of the old people in the 30-year period from 1990 to 2020, for both males and females. Row 'a' in the table shows the conventional measurement of

---

[3] This thought is still very speculative and thorough studies on this topic are worth pursuing.

TABLE 10.5: Educational attainment of females and males aged 60+, 25-59 and 25+ by region, 1990

	No schooling	Some primary	Primary	Secondary+	Total
60+					
Indonesia					
Females	73.8	16.2	7.8	2.2	100
Males	41.6	31.7	20.2	6.6	100
Yogyakarta					
Females	85.7	7.4	4.6	2.2	100
Males	49.2	23.8	20.0	7.0	100
East Nusa Tenggara					
Females	74.8	18.6	6.0	0.7	100
Males	53.9	31.4	11.8	2.9	100
South Sumatra					
Females	66.7	23.5	7.9	1.9	100
Males	27.4	42.9	22.5	7.3	100
25-59					
Indonesia					
Females	27.8	30.3	26.1	15.9	100
Males	12.9	28.6	31.1	27.4	100
Yogyakarta					
Females	31.6	21.5	24.0	23.0	100
Males	11.8	22.2	31.2	34.7	100
East Nusa Tenggara					
Females	31.1	30.7	28.3	10.0	100
Males	18.7	32.4	28.2	20.8	100
South Sumatra					
Females	17.0	40.8	27.2	15.1	100
Males	6.5	34.8	32.2	26.5	100
25+					
Indonesia					
Females	34.6	28.2	23.4	13.8	100
Males	16.9	29.0	29.6	24.5	100
Yogyakarta					
Females	43.8	18.3	19.6	18.3	100
Males	20.0	22.6	28.8	28.7	100
East Nusa Tenggara					
Females	37.6	28.9	24.9	8.6	100
Males	24.2	32.3	25.6	18.0	100
South Sumatra					
Females	23.0	38.7	24.8	13.5	100
Males	9.0	35.8	31.1	24.2	100

Source: Calculated from Biro Pusat Statistik 1992 (a,b,c,d).

TABLE 10.6: Educational attainment of females and males aged 60+, 1990, 2005 and 2020

	Scenario	No schooling	Some primary	Primary	Secondary+	Total
Females						
1990	a	73.8	16.2	7.8	2.2	100.0
	b	12.5	2.6	1.2	0.4	16.7
	c	75.1	15.4	7.4	2.1	100.0
	d	11.9	2.5	1.3	0.4	16.1
	e	71.9	16.1	9.1	3.0	100.0
2005	a	54.5	25.0	14.4	6.1	100.0
	b	10.0	4.2	2.4	1.0	17.5
	c	57.2	23.9	13.4	5.5	100.0
	d	9.5	4.1	2.4	1.0	17.0
	e	52.8	24.2	15.6	7.4	100.0
2020	a	29.2	30.6	25.8	14.4	100.0
	b	6.0	5.3	4.3	2.4	18.0
	c	33.2	29.7	24.0	13.1	100.0
	d	5.5	5.2	4.4	2.6	17.8
	e	28.6	28.4	26.5	16.6	100.0
Males						
1990	a	41.6	31.7	20.2	6.6	100.0
	b	6.5	4.6	2.9	1.0	15.0
	c	43.1	31.0	19.6	6.3	100.0
	d	6.1	4.6	3.0	1.0	14.7
	e	38.5	30.4	22.7	8.5	100.0
2005	a	25.7	32.8	25.6	15.9	100.0
	b	4.4	5.3	4.0	2.4	16.1
	c	27.6	32.9	24.8	14.7	100.0
	d	4.1	5.0	4.0	2.5	15.6
	e	23.3	30.7	27.2	18.9	100.0
2020	a	13.6	29.2	31.6	25.6	100.0
	b	2.6	4.9	5.1	4.0	16.7
	c	15.6	29.7	30.7	24.0	100.0
	d	2.3	4.7	5.1	4.3	16.3
	e	12.2	26.1	31.9	29.8	100.0

(continued on p.196)

<u>Notes to Table 10.6:</u>

a: Percentage distribution across educational attainment categories as conventionally measured.

b: Expected years of life lived by persons in each educational attainment category on the assumption that level of mortality is the same for all levels of education.

c: Percentage of life expectancy by educational attainment category.

d: Expected years of life lived by persons in each educational attainment category on the assumption that mortality is higher with lower education.

e: Row 'c' is further adjusted allowing for mortality differential by education: assuming higher mortality rate for those with lower education.

---

educational attainment. It indicates that there will be a big reduction in the percentage of old people not having any education. For the female old people, for example, the percentage will decline from 73.8 in 1990 to 29.2 in the year 2020, while the percentage of old people with at least secondary school will rise from 2.2 in 1990 to 14.4 in the year 2020.[4]

However, the above measurement is a crude one because it has not been adjusted for age structure of the population aged 60 and over. Being age-standardised, row 'b' shows the decomposition of the life expectancy at age 60 (the beginning of the elderly life of the old people). The female population age 60 in 1990, for example, has an expectancy of life as long as 16.7 years. These person-years are expected to be distributed as follows: 12.5 years by those with no schooling,

---

[4] We assume that people will not change their educational attainment after age 25. Thus, we use a cohort method to arrive at educational attainment of population age 65+. For example, the educational attainment of male population age 65-69 in 2020 is assumed to be the same as the educational attainment of males aged 35-39 in 1990.

[5] We multiply the educational attainment in each five-year age group with the $_5L_x$ (number of years lived in a life table) in the corresponding age group. We sum up the results and we get the expected years filled with each educational attainment. The results are shown in row 'b'. From this row, we calculate the percentage composition of each educational attainment, shown in row 'c' In this exercise, we use the West Family in the Coale-Demeny Life Table (1983).

4.2 years by those with some primary, 2.4 years by those with primary school, and 1.0 year by those with at least secondary education.[5]

The life expectancy will rise to 18.0 years in the year 2020. The female population aged 60 will experience a lengthening of life by 1.3 years during the next 25 years. As shown in Table 10.6, row 'b', they will also be better educated. The 18 years of life available, on average, after age 60 for the female population in the year 2020 will be distributed as follows: 6.0 years (instead of 12.5 years in 1990) by those with no schooling and 2.4 years (instead of only 0.4 years in 1990) by those with at least secondary education. Row 'c' in Table 10.8 simply shows the percentage composition of the life expectancy at age 60 by educational attainment. Similar analysis and conclusions follow for the male elderly.

Thus, even with the refinement in the measurement, the old people will be better educated. Further refinement is shown in rows 'd' and 'e' in Table 10.6. With this refinement, mortality rates vary with educational attainment and mortality is assumed to be higher, the lower the educational attainment.[6]

With this further adjustment, as shown in row 'd' in Table 10.6, expectancy of life for females aged 60 in 1990 is only 16.1 years. The smaller number of years in row 'd' than in row 'b' reflects the fact that a large portion of the population still has low education and those with low education have a higher mortality rate. A 'loss' of 0.7 years is the result of this further refinement. In the year 2020, the loss is only 0.2 years. With simple refinement (row 'b'), expectancy of life of the female population at age 60 is 18.0 years and it declines to 17.8 years with further refinement. The decrease in the loss reflects a decreasing portion of the female old population with low education.

Yet comparison of rows 'b' and 'd' reveals that though expectancy of life is smaller with further refinement, the years spent by those with at least secondary education are longer with further refinement. In the year 2020, the years spent by those with primary school education are also longer with further refinement. Row 'e' can be compared with row 'c'. They show the proportion of years lived in old age by

---

[6] This measurement is similar to the age-adjusted refinement. The difference is only in the use of the mortality rate. If the first refinement assumes the same mortality level across different educational attainment, here each educational attainment has a different mortality level, where higher educational attainment is associated with lower mortality rate.

those with different levels of education, according to different as-sumptions.

The rising education of the old people implies that they will also have higher aspirations. They will be more demanding in fulfilling their needs, especially their health needs. They will also be more concerned about their welfare than the old person of the present time or of ten or twenty years ago.

It should also be noted that the educational gap by gender will decrease, whatever approach is used in Table 10.6. From row 'e', the age-mortality-adjusted educational attainment, it is shown that in 1990, 71.9 per cent of female old people had no education, and for males only 38.5 per cent. In the year 2020, the percentage for females declines to 28.6 per cent, while the males' percentage declines to 12.2 per cent.

Table 10.7 shows that the number of old people without any education is very large, about 6.5 million in 1990, equivalent to about one-third of the current total Australian population or more than three times the total Australian elderly population. This number will rise to 7.3 million in 2005 and 2010. It will then decline to about 6.6 million in the year 2015 and 2020. The relatively low quality of old people, compared to that in advanced countries, will become another crucial aspect in the ageing issue in Indonesia.

It should be noted, however, that by the year 2020 Indonesia will also have almost the same number of old people with at least junior high school education—about 6.3 million, as with no education—about 6.6 million. The rising number of relatively better educated old people may also bring its own problem: they will be more demanding. If they can only consume, without producing anything, then their more sophisticated demand for services may impose additional prob-lems for the economy. Thus, the economy needs to be able to find jobs and induce as many as possible of those relatively educated old per-sons to work and contribute to the economy.

In the three selected provinces —Yogyakarta, East Nusa Teng-gara and South Sulawesi—the absolute number of old people without any education in the year 2020 will be smaller than that in 1990, despite the great increase in the size of the elderly population. Fe-males in the East Nusa Tenggara will be the only exception; the number of uneducated among elderly females there will continue to grow. The gap between the sexes in the number of uneducated old people will decrease in the provinces of Yogyakarta and South

TABLE 10.7: Population aged 60 and over
by educational attainment, 1990-2020[a]
(number)

	No schooling	Some primary	Primary	Secondary+	Total
1990[b]	6,585,692	2,653,538	1,542,389	485,928	11,277,557
1995	6,857,099	3,315,997	1,907,974	697,142	12,778,212
2000	7,339,643	4,195,945	2,525,924	1,200,688	15,262,199
2005	7,308,074	5,083,574	3,479,067	1,896,994	17,767,709
2010	6,938,496	5,797,728	4,467,338	2,733,333	19,936,895
2015	6,560,388	7,159,351	6,234,662	4,038,152	23,992,553
2020	6,622,001	9,368,572	9,012,043	6,311,458	31,314,073

[a] We use the cohort method to project the number of old people by educational attainment. The assumption is that people will not change their educational attainment and that they will follow the educational pattern of 1990 Population Census.

[b] Calculated from Biro Pusat Statistik 1992a.

Sumatra, but will increase in East Nusa Tenggara. In general, therefore, the education status of elderly females will still be lower than that of elderly males. This is simply a reflection of the general educational differential by sex. Thus, if considered along with the discussion about 'health' in the previous subsection, the conclusion is that female old people will live longer with less education than male old people.

**TABLE 10.8: Participation in the labour force of elderly
by age and sex, 1995-2020
(per cent)**

	1995	2005	2020
Females			
60-64	44.1	50.6	58.3
65+	26.2	30.8	36.1
Total	32.3	37.6	44.1
Males			
60-64	80.7	81.2	81.8
65+	59.9	60.9	62.2
Total	67.1	68.2	69.5

Source: Compiled from Ananta and Anwar 1995a.

Market participation and the urbanisation of old people

Using past experience, the projections show that the labour force participation rate of the elderly will rise. As with the young labour force, the female rate is also rising faster than the male rate. Table 10.8 indicates that the male rate will remain almost constant at about 80 per cent for age 60-64 and about 60 per cent for age 65+. The female rate will jump from about 44 per cent in 1995 to about 58 per cent in 2020 at age 60-64 and from about 26 per cent to about 36 per cent for ages 65+.

The question is whether the future will really follow this path. Why did old people participate in the past? Why will the female old people be increasingly involved in the labour force? Did they participate in the past because of their poverty? If so, then, with the rise in income per capita, there will be fewer and fewer old people participating in the labour market because their children can support them. However, if they participated because of their aspiration to work, they will continue to participate in the market. This path also assumes the disappearance of the value that old people should not work. (When old people are working they are considered poor.) It is desirable that in future, old people will still be able and willing to work.

Further, at least until 1985-90, Indonesian old people do not seem to have been mobile. Rogers *et al.* (1984) show a general age-specific migration pattern which includes a rising outmigration rate by the time people grow old, the peak being reached around retirement age. Yet Irian Jaya is the only province in Indonesia showing such a peak, in particular for males, probaly reflecting the return of transmigrants and government employees to their place of residence before migrating into Irian.

In general, there is no sign in Indonesia (based on the data from 1975-80 and 1985-90) of any tendency for the rate of outmigration of old people to rise. A complete description of the outmigration pattern of the Indonesian provinces in the period of 1975-80 and 1985-90 is found in Ananta and Anwar (1995b). Will other provinces of Indonesia besides Irian Jaya follow the general pattern for a secondary peak, the peak of outmigration at retirement age, to develop? Will there be any rise in outmigration of old people? Further studies should be carried out on this issue, utilising the data from the 1995 Intercensal Survey.

An increasing proportion of the elderly in Indonesia will reside in urban areas: from about 33 per cent in 1995 to 43 per cent in 2005 to about 55 per cent in 2020. Table 10.9 reveals that in 2020 there will be about 15.7 million old people living in urban areas, in contrast to only 13.1 million old people living in rural areas. The number of old people in urban areas in 2020 will be five times as high as that in 1990. This path assumes that past experience can still be used as a good guide and also that the rural population will start decreasing in the year 1995 (see Chapter 18, this volume). There is not expected to be any difference in the urbanisation pattern between male and female old persons. Unfortunately, there is no separate projection, for urban and rural areas, of labour force participation rates. However, we can speculate that the rate will rise in both the rural and urban areas.

Will it be easier for the old people to live and work in urban, rather than rural areas? As the population will reside more and more

TABLE 10.9: Population aged 60+ by age and place of residence, 1990, 2005 and 2020 (number)

	1990	2005	2020
Urban			
60-64	1,192,000	2,808,512	5,877,885
65-69	726,966	2,165,715	4,256,082
70-74	502,517	1,339,824	2,589,616
75+	494,788	1,479,830	2,991,368
Total	2,916,271	7,793,881	15,714,951
Rural			
60-64	3,334,451	3,448,182	4,702,866
65-69	2,022,758	2,841,655	3,686,908
70-74	1,526,509	1,744,816	2,171,173
75+	1,477,568	1,939,175	2,546,981
Total	8,361,286	9,938,828	13,107,928

Source: Compiled from Ananta and Anwar 1995a.

in urban areas, policies may be directed more toward making urban old people productive. The health problems related to living in urban areas must be given special consideration. The coming information era may be utilised to facilitate the greater productivity of old people in Indonesia, through creating and encouraging old-people-intensive technologies.

Old people as assets

The success in reducing fertility and population growth has brought this ageing problem to Indonesia. The provinces of Central Java, Yogyakarta, East Java and Bali, in particular, will face the issues of ageing in 2020. Yet, the ageing issue in Indonesia will be different from that in the more advanced countries. First, Indonesia will face the issue with much more limited economic capabilities. Second, the educational attainment of the Indonesian old people in the year 2020 will still be much lower than that in advanced countries. Third, though the percentage of old people is not as large as in some developed countries such as Sweden (17.5 per cent) and Norway (16.1 per cent) in 1993, the absolute number of old people in Indonesia may become alarming. In 2020, it will be about 9.8 million if we use the international definition of old people as those aged 65+, or about 15.7 million if we use the current official Indonesian definition of the population aged 60+.

Thus, the fertility revolution has relieved the economy by reducing the dependency burden, specifically the youth dependency burden. Yet the fertility revolution also brings the ageing issue, the rising dependency burden of the old. The composition of the dependency burden is shifting away from the young, those who already consume but do not produce, to the old, those who still consume but no longer produce.

If Indonesia's aged are merely consuming (because of their ill health and long life), they will really be a burden on the economy. Thus, Indonesia has to find ways to ensure that more of its old people remain healthy and productive, to avoid excessive health expenditure for old people, and ensure that they are still making a contribution to the economy. The effort should be directed toward those who are still 'young' at the current time. They should be prepared for a better style of life in old age.[7]

---

[7] A better style of life may include better eating, sleeping and exercise habits, and a better spiritual life. Probably, though this is still speculative, we may also start thinking of 'healing' rather than curing in dealing with illness. We may soon start adopting the strategy of maintaining good health, rather than curing sickness, and of maintaining good health until death comes.

Public Health,

Mortality, Fertility

and Family Planning

11

Health and Mortality

Meiwita B. Iskandar

Introduction

This paper reviews major health problems that have affected mortality patterns in Indonesia, in relation to the observed trends in infant, child, and general adult mortality between the 1970s and the 1990s. The discussion will focus on the lack of adequate records of adult mortality (particularly routine reports of death rates by age) and the need for more accurate classification of causes of death. Health and mortality may be influenced by underlying socio-economic factors, so information on health care cost and utilisation, and the socio-cultural aspects of morbidity and mortality will be briefly presented as well.

Although 'health' is defined as a positive state of physical, mental and social well-being, the description of 'health' in national statistics lacks suitable positive indicators (Campbell and Graham 1991: 2). Thus the emphasis of 'health' in this paper is more on the negative aspects of poor health services or 'ill-health' which produce death as a measurable outcome. In taking this perspective, though, we should not forget that many people in Indonesia, as elsewhere in the world, spend much of their lives in a state of generally good, if less than robust, health.

Mortality trends and patterns

Considering the importance of levels and trends of health and death, most countries try to closely monitor mortality data, trends and patterns through established national vital registration systems. Unfortunately, after 51 years of independence, through lack of political and organisational commitment to this goal, Indonesia has yet to establish a reliable basic demographic recording and reporting system. This has resulted in inability to measure at least three types of information that must be recorded precisely in order to monitor mortality trends: (a) the time period to which deaths are referred; (b) the group of people to which deaths refer; and (c) the type or cause of deaths measured (Palmore and Gardner 1994: 1).

Thus infant and child (under five) mortality are currently estimated by direct retrospective questions on the number of live births and infant deaths during a specified period, by indirect procedures based on proportions of children dead to mothers in particular age groups, by analysis of birth cohorts from pregnancy histories, and by reports of the survival status of women's last live birth. Both retrospective and indirect measures are subject to a large number of potential errors of coverage, calculation, and interpretations: which means that they are often not validly comparable, and are subject to fairly wide margins of error.

Therefore, Indonesian mortality measures have to be interpreted cautiously. In addition, as a consequence of different sources and estimation methodologies applied, the reliability and validity of some of the mortality data for the 1980s and the 1990s will differ from those found in the 1950s, 1960s and 1970s. It is unavoidable also that where national data were not available, estimates and projections undertaken by the United Nations Population Division and other internationally produced estimates are used.

1920-50: A brief recapitulation

During the colonial and early Independence period, the available data on mortality were largely limited to Java. An appraisal by van Gelderen based on the 1930 census (total island-wide population of 40.9 million) stated that the crude death rate (CDR) was 23 per 1,000 persons and infant mortality rate (IMR) was as high as 200 per 1,000 births (reviewed by Nitisastro, cited in Utomo and Iskandar 1986: 13). Another crude estimate based on the mean of reported deaths between 1919 and 1921 produced a CDR of 24.3 per 1,000 persons for 1920, and 17.9 per 1,000 persons for 1930 (*ibid.*: 13). According to Nitisastro(cited *ibid.*), the mortality level decreased sharply between 1925 and 1930, was more-or-less constant between 1930 and 1935, and again increased very steeply between 1935 and 1940. It was suspected that the crude mortality level around 1920 was indeed higher than that of 1930 because of the severe influenza epidemic during that period (*ibid.*: 13). During the period 1940-50, the reported principal causes of the excess deaths were the impact of wars (Second World War) including forced conscription for labour, harsh food procurement policies, and the collapse of major agricultural export industries, which brought a rapid decline in the people's living conditions (*ibid.*: 13).

1950-60: The turning point

A turning point that led to a sustained downward trend in the mortality history of Indonesia began in the early 1950s, when the population entered a period of relative peace and improved welfare. Food supplies and other essentials such as textiles recovered from their wartime dislocations. There was also a successful campaign to eradicate malaria. The United Nations estimated that the CDR for Java declined from 30 per 1,000 persons in 1951-52 to 23.5 between 1951 and 1960; while Mamas (1964) calculated a CDR of 27 per 1,000 persons for the whole of Indonesia during the period 1955-60 (Utomo and Iskandar 1986: 14). The actual death rate for the 1950s was uncertain; nonetheless the available estimates and information on the conditions convey the impression that a CDR of 20 to 30 per 1,000 persons and an IMR of 100 to 300 per 1,000 births are likely to be the acceptable ranges (*ibid.*:14). The continuous decline in childhood mortality in several regions of Java, Bali, Sumatra, and Sulawesi was confirmed by the Demographic Institute's 1973 Fertility-Mortality Survey analysed by McDonald, Yasin and Jones (1976: 69).

1960-1970s: The first two censuses as basis of mortality estimates

The 1961 population census was the first modern census in Indonesia. It used a combination of the *de jure* and *de facto* definitions of population to calculate a total of 97,018,829 persons for the whole country, including the disputed territory of West Irian (presumed to have a population of 758,000). The population of Java was 62.99 million. The census was used as a calculation base for more reliable childhood mortality estimates, although data on child survivorship were limited to only three provinces of East Java, Yogyakarta and Jakarta (Utomo

1982). The 1971 census incorporated data on children ever born and surviving, which made it possible to estimate trends between 1961 and 1971.

Results of the 1971 (second) census indicated that the proportion of children that died before age 5 was around 263 per 1000 in Jakarta, 245 in East Java, and 207 in Yogyakarta (analysed by McNicoll and Mamas 1973); and infant mortality rates (IMR) per 1,000 live births were 195 in Jakarta, 115 in East Java, and 113 in Yogyakarta (analysed by Hull and Sunaryo 1978; both studies were cited in Utomo and Iskandar 1986: 15). The IMR for males all over the country was suspected to be 18 per cent higher than that for females (Cho *et al.* 1976: 62, cited in Dasvarma 1986: 64). According to McNicoll and Mamas (1973), childhood mortality in these three provinces declined between 20 and 30 per cent, thus implying a rise of about six years in life expectancy during the 1960s (Utomo and Iskandar 1986: 15).

The 1973 Indonesian Fertility and Mortality Survey data analysed by McDonald, Yasin and Jones (1976: 56-57) focused on the proportion dying before age 2 from 1,000 live births (in the notation of the life table q(2). The highest rates were found in rural West Java (181 per 1,000 live births), followed by rural Central Java (138), with the lowest rates existing in East Java's rural areas (134). Outside Java, q(2) in rural areas was highest in Sumatra (151 per 1,000 live births), followed by Sulawesi (149) and Bali (100). The rate in urban Sumatra for q(2) was 106 per 1,000 live births, which was similar to that in East Java (100) but the q(2) in urban Sulawesi (143 per 1,000 live births) tended to be close to that of urban West Java (125) and Central Java (130) (Utomo and Iskandar 1986: 16).

According to the Biro Pusat Statistik (BPS 1982), the CDR in the 1970s declined 26 per cent from 18.8 per 1,000 persons (1967-70) to 13.9 in 1976-79, with urban areas (12.7) lower than the rural areas (14.5 per 1,000 persons). The BPS considered the urban CDR in 1979 had already achieved a low level, and to push it lower than 10 per 1,000 population would be a difficult challenge for the health system (cited in Utomo and Iskandar 1986: 16).

The 1980 census data, combined with the 1976 Intercensal Population Survey (SUPAS), and the 1979 National Social Economic Survey (Susenas) had produced various IMR estimations for the 1970s. Soemantri (1983) estimated an IMR around 107 per 1,000 live births in mid-1977, ranging from 187 in West Nusa Tenggara province to 62 in

Yogyakarta province; and Dasvarma (1983) concluded that infant mortality based on the survivorship of the last live births was also in the vicinity of 100 (cited in Utomo and Iskandar 1986: 17). According to the 1976 Indonesia Fertility Survey which covered only six provinces in Java and Bali, the IMR estimate for these six more developed provinces was 91 per 1,000 live births (*ibid.*: 17).

The analysis of the situation of children and women in Indonesia by BPS and UNICEF in 1984 concluded that IMR declined from 150 in 1961 to 135 in 1971, representing an average annual decrease of 1.5 per cent. The IMR for 1980 was 98 per 1,000 live births, indicating that IMR decline was twice as fast in the 1970s, about 3.2 per cent per year (CBS/UNICEF 1984: 27).

1980-95: Continuation of IMR and under-five mortality decline

Both IMR and the under-five years of age mortality rate (U5MR) are declining rapidly, and the goals of 45 and 65 respectively, by the year 2000, are feasible to reach. Between 1967 and 1993, IMR decreased from an estimated 145 to 58 per 1,000 live births and U5MR from 218 to 81 per 1,000 live births (GOI-UNICEF 1995a: 3). The 1994 IDHS data also indicate that IMR has declined 24 per cent during the 15 years before 1994, from 75 deaths per 1,000 live births in the period mid-1979 to mid-1984, to 57 per 1,000 in the period mid-1989 to mid-1994. This latter estimate of IMR was confirmed by the BPS calculation of 58 deaths per 1,000 live births using an indirect technique referring to the year 1993 (CBS *et al.* 1995: 137). However, the recorded neonatal mortality rate merely declined 18 per cent, a much lower percentage than the reduction of post-neonatal mortality, child mortality, and U5MR (30, 31 and 26 per cent respectively). Perinatal mortality caused by infections, birth trauma resulting from obstructed labour, and low birth weight or prematurity due to poor nutritional status of the mother accounted for most of the neonatal mortality rate. The probability of dying between birth and the fifth birthday (U5MR) declined from 110 deaths per 1,000 in 1980-84 to 81 per 1,000 live births in 1990-94 (*ibid.*).

Infant and under-five mortality are sensitive indicators of social welfare. Thus, the above reduction in infant and child mortality is not only a successful attainment of a long-term health policy goal, but also an important social policy goal in itself. It indicates that over the past two decades both social and health improvements have been substantial. This advance was achieved primarily by the far-reaching expansion of community health centres built in all 27 provinces during the oil-boom period of the 1970s and early 1980s. When the oil price declined between 1982 and 1988, direct spending on health fell by 45 per cent, cutting the central government support back to the levels attained in the late 1970s (World Bank 1989: 1). Fortunately, progress in the agricultural sector altered the position of Indonesia from the world's largest rice importing country in the 1970s to one of rice self-sufficiency in 1984. Moreover, Indonesia's non-oil sectors grew such that dependency on oil has fallen from a 24-per cent contribution of oil and gas to the national product in 1981 to only 13 per cent by 1992 (GOI/UNICEF 1994: 2).

At the beginning of Repelita I (1969-74), there were only 1,227 health centres. By 1978, the number of health centres had more than tripled, to 4,353, and continued to increase to between 6,588 and 6,954 by mid-Repelita V (1993), accompanied by a rapid growth of the health subcentres from 6,636 in 1978 to 19,977 in 1993 (World Bank 1994a:1, 1995:1). On average, there is now one health centre per 27,000 people compared to about one per 96,000 in 1968. In addition, the number of first-line referral (Class C and D) hospitals was also expanded from 260 (1978) to 300 (1993), which augmented the total bed capacity from 23,962 to 29,449 in this period (*ibid.*: 1).

Recently, considering the limits expected for government funding in future, a policy has been implemented to no longer absorb all graduating health workers automatically into the government system. Thus, it will be a major challenge to protect past gains and improve quality of care in government services, particularly in an estimated 750-1500 *pocket* or *remote* areas (areas with high IMR in 1994) in the country (World Bank 1994a: vi). To retain, or even attain, the reduction of IMR in these areas, greater attention is being paid to protecting them from possible budget cuts even when the public sector can no longer absorb all costs.

Indonesia compared with other Asian countries

Although IMR has declined over 60 per cent for the last 24 years, from 142 deaths per 1,000 live births in 1968 to 57 per 1,000 live births in 1992, Indonesia's IMR is still much higher than the levels achieved by

TABLE 11.1: Infant mortality rate (IMR) in selected Asian countries and per cent decline in 1960-80 compared to 1960-93

	1960[a]	1980[a]	% decline 1960-80	1993[b]	% decline 1960-93
India	165	123	25	81	51
Indonesia	150	98	35	71	53
Burma	158	101	36	81	49
Sri Lanka	71	44	38	15	79
Thailand	103	55	47	27	74
Philippines	106	55	48	45	58

[a]Utomo and Iskandar 1986: 17, Table 2.3.

[b]UNICEF 1995: 72 (see also CBS et al. 1995: 137; UNICEF 1994: 64).

Thailand (27), the Philippines (48), and Sri Lanka (15 per 1,000 live births) (see Table 11.1).

Life expectancy at birth

Heligman (1975) constructed life tables for Indonesia based on the 1961 and 1971 censuses, and calculated a male infant mortality of 151 in 1961 and 132 in 1971, and a female mortality of 136 and 118 respectively (cited in Dasvarma 1986: 64). His estimation concluded that life expectation at birth for 1961 was 40.85 years for women and 35.38 years for men; and for 1971 was 42.96 years for women and 40.15 years for men (Utomo 1982: 308-309; Utomo and Iskandar 1986: 20).

Life expectancy at birth (LEB) for Indonesian women in mid-1967 was 45.6 years according to McDonald (1978) (cited in Dasvarma 1986: 65), and 50.4 years for a sample of ten subdistricts covered by the 1974-77 Sample Vital Registration Project (SVRP) and analysed by

Gardiner. The SVRP also estimated that LEB for women during that period was 2.7 years greater than LEB for men (cited in Utomo 1982: 311; Utomo and Iskandar 1986: 20).

The *1995 Indonesian Health Profile* published by the Ministry of Health reported that LEB changed from 42.2 years in 1967 to 60.79 years in 1993 for males and from 47.17 years in 1967 to 64.54 years in 1993 for females (see Table 11.2a) (DepKes-PusDaKes 1995: 49, Table III.A.7). Overall, there is a consistent increase in LEB for males (37.6 per cent for the period 1967-86 and 44.1 per cent for 1967-93) and females (30.5 per cent for the period 1967-86 and 38.9 per cent for 1967-93), which confirms a slightly faster rate of gain in life expectancy for males (see Table 11.2b).

Life expectancy at age 20: Census 1961 and 1970

Adult mortality can be estimated on the basis of infant and childhood mortality through a set of model life tables, but to apply this to such countries as Indonesia would be full of methodological pitfalls (Utomo 1982: 308-309). There needs to be some basis for selecting particular model patterns, and some confidence that the estimates of infant or child mortality are relatively accurate. These assumptions are not always justified. The only widely quoted calculations of life expectancy not reliant on model life table equivalencies are the estimates of life expectancy at age 20, made by Heligman (1975) from comparisons of age structures and survivors in two censuses. His estimates were 37.54 years for women and 35.38 years for men using the 1961 census; and 38.48 years for women and 36.32 years for men using 1971 census data (cited in Utomo and Iskandar 1986: 20). Compared to estimates of women's and men's LEB which increased by 2 to 5 years between 1961 and 1971, expectation of life at age 20 appeared to have increased by about 1-1.5 years. Heligman (1975) suspected that this was due to a deterioration in public health services and a decline in nutritional standard in 1960s (cited in Utomo and Iskandar 1986: 20). In the absence of more reliable data sources and methodologies these speculations remain virtually unverifiable.

Estimation of death rates by age-groups: 1971-86

A prospective study by Gardiner (1974-77) which examined deaths by age and sex, from a sample of just over 250,000 persons in the Indonesian SVRP, concluded that there was an extremely low mortality in

TABLE 11.2a: Life expectancy at birth by sex in Indonesia 1967-93

	Male	Female	Total
1967	42.20	47.17	45.73
1976	50.64	53.69	52.21
1986	58.06	61.54	59.80
1990	59.59	63.28	61.49
1992	60.42	64.15	62.34
1993	60.79	64.54	62.72

Source: DepKes-PusDaKes 1995: 49, Table III.A.7.

late childhood and early adulthood (age 10-40) relative to the levels of infant mortality. His estimates for male death rates were 154 per 1,000 for infants compared to 21 per 1,000 for children aged 1-4; 4.7 per 1,000 for children aged 5-9; and 2.3 per 1,000 for young adolescents aged 10-14. Female death rates were lower, 130 per 1,000 for infants, followed by 18 per 1,000 for children aged 1-4; 4.9 per 1,000 for children aged 5-9; and 2.0 per 1,000 for young adolescents aged 10-14 (cited in *ibid.*: 21).

Hull and Rohde (1978), using data from a single year, 1972, the year following the 1971 Population Census, calculated death rates at different age-categories by multiplying the estimated population of Java by age and sex at 31 December 1971 and mortality rates from South Model level 14. Death rates (the estimated proportion per 1,000 of people in the age-group who die annually) differed between men and women, with men's rates exceeding women's in almost all age-groups above 15-19 years old. Between the age-categories of 5-9 and 10-14, death rates were similar for men and women, around 2.3 per 1,000 people in the age-group. Then, they increased slightly to about 5 per 1,000 people (in that age-group) between the age-categories of 15-19 and 25-29, with men's rates slightly higher than women's. Compared to women, death rates rose faster among men. Death rates were above 5 per 1,000 people among men at the age-categories of 30-34, 35-39 and 40-44 years, and rose further above 10 per 1,000 people of age-categories 45-49 and beyond. Among women, death rates were above

**TABLE 11.2b: Per cent increase of life expectancy at birth, 1967-86
compared to 1967-93**

	1967	1986	1993	% Increase 1967-86	% Increase 1967-93
Women	47.17	61.54	64.54	30.5	38.9
Men	42.20	58.06	60.79	37.6	44.1

Source: DepKes-PusDaKes 1995: 49, Table III.A.7.

5 per 1,000 people at the age-categories of 35-39, and rose above 10 per 1,000 people at the age-categories 55-59 and beyond (cited in Utomo and Iskandar 1986: 22, Table 2.7). However, to what extent these model figures may represent the actual situation was unknown.

The 1980 Household Health Survey (HHS), executed by the Ministry of Health's Research and Development unit to collect the principal causes of mortality and their distribution by age-group, was a retrospective survey covering six provinces (urban areas of Central Java and South Kalimantan, and rural areas of East Java, North Sumatra, West Java, and South Sulawesi) with a total of 123,258 people as the sample size. Verbal autopsy data were collected by newly graduated doctors and medical interns. The following 1986 HHS covered 2,923,034 people (56,907 households) in seven provinces (Yogyakarta, Bali, North Sulawesi, Bengkulu, West Kalimantan, Maluku and West Nusa Tenggara). Since both HHS 1980 and 1986 calculated death rates by age-groups, comparative mortality patterns and annual reduction rates are compared in Table 11.3a.

The table indicates that overall, crude death rates declined from 12.1 to 7.0 per 1,000 population within seven years between 1980 and 1986. Reduction of death rates occurred in all age-groups, differing only in its annual reduction rate (ARR). For the age-categories of 1-4, 35-44, 45-54 and 55+, ARR was over 12 per cent. But for infants and each of the age-categories 5-14, 15-24, and 25-34 years, ARR was under 10 per cent, with the lowest ARR in age-group 25-34 years (Budiarso 1987: 164).

**TABLE 11.3a: Estimated death rate per 1,000 population
by age-group, 1980 and 1986**

	Death rate per 1,000 people		ARR[c]
	1980[a]	1986[b]	
< 1	104.8[d]	71.8	-6.6
1 - 4	19.6	10.6	12.3
5-14	2.4	1.6	8.1
15-24	2.5	1.8	6.7
25-34	2.7	2.3	3.2
35-44	6.8	3.7	12.2
45-54	15.0	8.1	12.3
55+	44.3	21.7	14.3
All ages	12.1	7.0	10.9

[a]The 1980 HHS covered a total of 121,129 people in six provinces, with 905 deaths analysed.

[b]The 1986 HHS covered a total sample of 56,842 households in seven provinces, with 2,055 deaths analysed.

[c]Annual Reduction Rate.

[d]Budiarso 1981:27.

Sources: Budiarso 1987: 164, Table 5.

Household Health Surveys 1992 and 1995: no more direct estimation of death rates

It is noted that analysis of mortality in the Household Health Surveys of 1992 and 1995 did not attempt to estimate the levels of the death rates any more, instead publishing the proportionate distribution of deaths by age and sex (see Table 11.3b).

TABLE 11.3b: Proportionate distribution of deaths by sex and age, 1992 and 1995

	HHS 1992[a]			HHS 1995[b]		
	Male	Female	Total	Male	Female	Total
< 1	22.4	24.4	23.3	14.7	11.0	12.9
1-4	8.6	7.5	8.1	4.4	4.9	4.6
5-14	3.8	5.7	4.7	4.5	4.0	4.3
15-24	3.8	3.0	3.4	4.8	2.6	3.8
25-34	3.3	5.3	4.3	4.7	7.5	6.0
35-44	6.2	7.3	6.7	7.5	6.3	6.9
45-54	10.9	7.8	9.5	7.3	8.6	7.9
55-64	14.1	10.5	12.4	13.4	12.6	13.0
55+	26.9	28.3	27.6	38.6	42.6	40.5
All ages (n)	100.0	100.0	100.0	100.0	100.0	100.0
	(661)	(561)	(1,222)	(640)	(573)	(1,213)

[a] Balitbangkes-DepKes RI (1994): 38, Table 4.5.

[b] Djaja, Soemantri and Siregar (1996): 6, Table 2. The 1992 HHS was integrated with Susenas 1992. Total sample size was 66,560 households in 27 provinces, with 1,235 deaths analysed. The 1995 HHS was integrated with Susenas 1995 and the 1994 DHS. Total sample size was 206,240 households. Preliminary analysis on mortality only covered 1,757 deaths in Java and Bali.

Principal causes of infant mortality

In 1978, Rohde, Hull and Hendrata examined the mortality pattern for Java using comparative data on cause patterns of mortality in the 1960s which were assumed to be similar to Java's 1972 situation. In the absence of reliable data for Java, they took estimates from Mexico and the Philippines found to be consistent with the limited data on the prevailing levels of mortality and causes of death in Java. The result showed that the three leading causes of infant death in Java were perinatal diseases, pneumonia, and infectious and parasitic diseases.

The five leading causes of death among children aged 1-4 were infectious and parasitic diseases, diarrhoea, pneumonia, violence, while a large percentage of deaths fell into the residual 'others' category which included malnutrition and its complications (Rohde, Hull and Hendrata 1978: 67).

The first HHS) in 1972 and the second HHS in 1980, using the WHO International Classifications of Diseases (ICD) VIII, were able to present causes of infant death in six provinces: three provinces were in Java and three in Sumatra, Kalimantan and Sulawesi. The results showed that in both surveys, the three leading causes of infant deaths were identical: diarrhoea, acute respiratory tract infection (pneumonia), and tetanus; followed by neonatal diseases, meningitis, and other infectious and parasitic diseases (IPDs) (Budiarso, Putrali, and Muchtaruddin 1980: 50).

The HHS 1986 used ICD IX and as a consequence, produced a different classification of diagnoses. The principal cause of infant death was tetanus, followed by perinatal diseases (low birth weight, birth injuries, etc.), diarrhoea, and acute respiratory tract infection (pneumonia), followed by diphtheria, pertussis and measles (Budiarso 1987: 161). In HHS 1992, again based on ICD IX, the most common cause of death was perinatal diseases, followed by: acute respiratory tract infection (pneumonia), 'unknown' causes, diarrhoea, tetanus, and infectious and parasitic diseases (Balitbangkes-DepKes RI/BPS 1994: 42). HHS 1995 was the first Indonesian survey to use ICD X to classify diagnoses of causes of death. The preliminary mortality analysis using this data set included only 1,757 of 2,073 deaths reported in Java and Bali. In this survey perinatal diseases were again the leading cause of deaths among infants, while acute respiratory infection (pneumonia) and diarrhoea were again second and third in order, while the fourth most common cause was the previously insignificant category of nervous system disorders which strangely outranked tetanus (Djaja, Soemantri and Siregar 1996: Table A.1).

Causes of death among children aged 1-4

HHS 1980 listed ten leading causes of death among young children: acute upper respiratory tract infections, skin infections, diarrhoea, bronchitis and pneumonia, measles, helminth infections, eye infections, ear infections and accidental injuries (Budiarso, Putrali and Muchtaruddin 1980: 24).

HHS 1986 listed five major groups of causes of death, with diphtheria, pertussis and measles as a group being listed first followed by diarrhoea, acute respiratory infection, infectious and parasitic diseases and malaria (Budiarso 1987: 161). By 1992 diarrhoea was recorded as taking the greatest toll among children of ages 1-4 and in 1995 the most common cause was listed as respiratory tract infections.

Leading causes of adult mortality

In the Household Health Surveys of 1972 and 1980 the causes of adult mortality were not specifically analysed. Instead the analysts at the Ministry of Health examined lists of causes of all deaths, including infants and children of ages 1-4. Basically, diagnosis of the first five major causes of death for all ages was heavily influenced by the infant and child deaths, and the first and second most common causes were acute lower respiratory tract infections and diarrhoea. The more typically adult causes such as cardiovascular diseases and tuberculosis rank third and fourth on the list of causes across all ages. To be noted was the change in the trend of tuberculosis, which in 1972 was third, becoming fourth in 1980 (Budiarso, Putrali, and Muchtaruddin 1980: 49).

A more detailed breakdown of age groups in presenting causes of death among adults (aged 15-34, 35-44, 45+) was started in HHS 1986 report. This enabled us to observe the changing trend on causes of death among adults in 1986, 1992 and 1995. The following sections on causes of deaths ranked according to age structures 15-34, 44-54, and 55+ will refer to these tables.

Causes of death according to rank for age-group 15-34

In 1986, tuberculosis ranked as the number-one killer among young adults accounting for 15 per cent of all deaths in this age-group. This preventable and curable infectious disease remained a significant killer in 1992 (third in rank) and 1995 (second in rank). Accidents and injuries became first in rank (responsible for 20 per cent of all deaths in this age-group) in 1995. Diarrhoea, which was placed ninth in 1986 and eighth in 1992, jumped into the third place in 1995. Pregnancy, birth, and diseases of the puerperium held fourth position in 1986, rose to second most common reported cause in 1992, but then dropped into sixth place in 1995. Neoplasms (malignancies or cancers) maintained the relatively stable ranking of fifth in 1986 and fourth in 1992 and 1995. Because deaths in the young adult age group are relatively rare, even a very large sample is unable to cover a sufficient number of cases to produce reliable results, and this is particularly likely to affect the enumeration of maternal deaths.

Causes of death according to rank for age-group 35-44

In 1986 and 1992 tuberculosis (TB) was also the leading cause of death among adults of middle age. In HHS 1995 (only Java and Bali), reported deaths caused by TB dropped into second place, replaced by cardiovascular diseases as the most common cause. In third position in 1986, 1992 and 1995 were problems resulting from digestive system disorders. A tremendous change occurred in the fourth place, which in 1986 was held by deaths in pregnancy, birth and puerperium, but in 1992 was replaced by injuries and accidents. It has been suggested that this shift was caused by successful family planning messages to dissuade women aged over 35 from becoming pregnant. Neoplasms or malignancies, placed eighth in 1986, were recorded in second place in 1992, and dropped back to fifth position in 1995.

Causes of death according to rank for age-groups 45-54 and 55+

Cardiovascular diseases have constantly been the primary cause of deaths among older adults in 1986, 1992 and 1995. It is feared that this was due to lack of knowledge and attitudes designed to achieve and maintain a healthy lifestyle, a necessity at ages 45 and above. The changing pattern of mortality from infectious diseases to cardiovascular diseases has been interpreted by experts as evidence of continuing epidemiological transition in Indonesia. A constant killer for all older adults was, definitely, tuberculosis, which stayed in second place in the enumerations of 1986, 1992 and 1995, although for age-group 55+ in Java and Bali TB was in the fourth place while respiratory tract infections were ranked second. While cancers and accidents were important causes of death, for most older adults the real threats were related to the respiratory tract and the digestive tract, and included conditions and diseases which are difficult to diagnose using the 'verbal autopsy' techniques which are the foundation of the Household Health Surveys.

Maternal mortality rates

The actual magnitude of maternal mortality, defined as deaths among women who are or have been pregnant during the 42 days prior to death, is obscure. The sixth Five-Year Development Plan (Repelita VI) aims for a 50 per cent reduction of maternal mortality ratio (MMR) from 425 in 1992 to 225 per 100,000 live births by 1998 (GOI/UNICEF 1994: 33; Balitbangkes-DepKes/BPS 1994 : 41). Current trends suggest that this goal will be impossible to reach. In 1994, results of the Demographic and Health Survey 1994 disclosed an MMR estimated at 390 maternal deaths per 100,000 live births, which was a slight increase as compared to 360 per 100,000 live births estimated from the same survey but for the previous five years, 1984-88 (CBS *et al.* 1995: 210). Newspaper reports in July 1996 informed the public that WHO and UNICEF reported a much higher MMR, 650 per 100,000 live births in 1994 (*Republika*, 26 July 19961) than the levels officially estimated by the government. This rate was a recalculation of 1991 estimates using regression equations and United Nations projections for countries without accurate data, which gave an MMR of 647 per 100,000 live births for Indonesia (Stanton *et al.* 1995: 11). These estimates are meant to monitor changes on a decade by decade basis and are not meant to be used to monitor annual trends (WHO/UNICEF 1996: 7).

The existing health manpower capability to detect and refer 'at-risk' obstetric emergencies is still below expected standards, although the three leading causes of maternal mortality have been widely acknowledged: haemorrhage (antepartum and postpartum), sepsis and eclampsia. The actual cause of death is often the cumulative effect of several life-situation factors that include: poverty, early marriage, closely spaced births, heavy workloads, poor nutrition, poor sanitation, lack of access to clean childbirth practices, low education levels, and the overall disadvantaged social status of women. Most women with delivery-related problems reach hospital too late or not at all (Iskandar et al. 1996: 74-80).

Health care financing and utilisation

Health care financing

Expansion of government-run health facilities in the mid-1970s, and the increase of central government spending on health (up 172 per cent) during the Third Five-Year Plan (1979/80-1983/84) did not anticipate the chronic resource shortages which were to follow (World Bank 1994a: 3). In general, the Ministry of Health budget allocated as a proportion of the national development budget has shown no increase at all over the last 15 years. From 2.4 per cent of the total national development budget (APBN) in 1982/83, government's allocated health budget increased to 3.1 per cent in 1986/87, then began to decrease to 2.8 per cent in 1988/89, and went down as low as 1.4 per cent in 1989/90; it rose again to 1.9 per cent in 1991/92 and back to 2.2 per cent in 1992/93, which is still less than the percentage allocated in 1982/83 (DepKes-PusDaKes 1993: 104).

In terms of per-capita government annual health expenditure allocated to the 27 provinces, the provinces of East Timor and Irian Jaya rank highest, reaching Rp17,813 and Rp11,537 compared to the national average of Rp3,257 as of 1991/92. Six provinces received even less than Rp3,257 per-capita health expenditure (North Sumatra, Lampung, West Nusa Tenggara, Central Java, West Java, and East Java). East Java province received only Rp1,735 per capita annual health expenditure from the national budget (*ibid*.: 105-106, and Attachment V.B.2).[1]

The above figures illustrate insufficiency of financial support allocated for government health facilities. There is no doubt that resource constraints have a negative effect on general public health institution development, quality of care improvement, utilisation of services, and health personnel development. Lack of funding also hampers the efforts to attain a major goal in the development plan, to raise some or all of the country's 132 Class D hospitals, those classified as having no specialists, and an average of 62 beds, to Class C, a standard of seven specialists, and an average of 155 beds (World Bank 1994a: 24). The scarcity of resources will make it difficult for the government to increase the public sector health personnel, to put into place specialisation curricula, and to include training programs that can alleviate anticipated skill shortages in the government health delivery system at district level and below. Resource, facility and personnel constraints also mean that the average daily patient contacts in many hospitals and some health centres remain extremely low as potential users of the facilities are discouraged from seeking help by chronic inadequacy of services. A strategy to restructure and ex-

---

[1] Rp1,735 was approximately equal to A$1.

pand government expenditure patterns (make more efficient use of scarce public resources) must be implemented together with a policy to mobilise additional private and community resources to finance higher levels of spending.

Utilisation of government health facilities

At community level, the *puskesmas* or community health centre is the focus of basic primary health care (PHC) services in rural and urban service areas of roughly 30,000 people (*ibid.*: 2). Currently, there are over 6,600 health centres in operation, each employing 1-3 doctors depending on the number of people served (*ibid.*: 15). Two measures of utilisation are recorded routinely at this level: the average number of visitors per day; and the frequency of patient contacts. Official data collected from 22 provinces in 1991 recorded an average of 2.07 contacts per client, with a range from 0.5 to 3.1, and daily use of health centres ranging from 33 to 80 outpatient visitors a day in some districts of Java and Bali (DepKes-PusDaKes 1993: 83; World Bank 1994a: 90). About 21 per cent of existing *puskesmas* are equipped with 10 beds, with bed occupancy rates ranging from 0.39 per cent in West Java to 32.1 per cent in Irian Jaya (Rahardjo *et al.* 1996: 1, 78).

The hospital system is classified into Class A and B referral and teaching hospitals at province level and equipped with the full range of specialisations, and Class C and D serving as first-line referral at district level. On average Class C has 155 beds with 18 doctors on the staff, while Class D has 62 beds with 6 doctors on the staff (World Bank 1994a: 2,85). At this level, only one measure for outpatient services was recorded routinely: total of new visits per 100,000 people in the same year. The reported data indicated a decrease from 11,331 new visits in 1990 to 11,214 in 1991 (DepKes-PusDaKes 1993: 84). The bed occupancy rate is the utilisation indicator for hospitals' inpatient services. This indicator for all classes of public hospitals fell between 1984 and 1993; Class A fell almost 20 per cent (from 75 per cent to 60 per cent), Class B fell 23 per cent (79 per cent to 60 per cent), Class C fell 7 per cent (59 per cent to 55 per cent) and Class D fell 11 per cent (48 per cent to 43 per cent) during the last ten years (DepKes-PusDaKes 1993: 85; World Bank 1994a: 6). In the same period, occupancy rates of the Class D hospitals were never above 40 per cent, and over a quarter had utilisation rates of 30 per cent or less The hospitals with bed occupancy below 40 per cent were located in Sumatra, Kalimantan, and Sulawesi. The Eastern islands showed an average of 46 per cent Class D occupancy rates (*ibid*. 6).

The underutilisation of public services is contradictory to the increasing trend in morbidity rates observed in the population. The World Bank report of 1994 concluded that 'many government facilities and personnel are underutilised' (*ibid*.: 12). This problem seems to correlate with the availability of medical equipment and instruments, population density, and whether centres are located in Java-Bali or outside Java-Bali (*ibid*.: 90). In addition, utilisation of public health services is associated with the amount of land owned per household and the schooling level attained by women, especially among mothers aged 25-29 (*ibid*.: 91). The presence of a health centre or hospital alone will not change infant, child, maternal or general adult mortality rates, unless these health facilities are used (*ibid*.: 91). The problem of quality of care provided by the health system must be one of the factors associated with low utilisation. The fact that large numbers of doctors, nurses, midwives and paramedics were not fully occupied indicates inefficiency in the use of resources in the underutilised health centres or subcentres.

Socio-economic conditions

In the mid-1990s Indonesia completed its first Twenty-five Year Long-term Development Plan (PJP I 1969/70 - 1993/94). During these years, average economic growth was 6.8 per cent per annum. The inflation rate, which was as high as 650 per cent in 1966, was reduced to an average of 17.2 per cent in the 1970s, and further reduced to an average of 8.7 per cent per year in the 1980s (GOI/UNICEF 1994: 2). According to the same report, between 1969 and 1992, the industrial sector grew approximately 12 per cent per year. Economic growth and reduced population growth—from 2.32 per cent annually between 1971 and 1980 to approximately 1.66 per cent by the end of PJP I— have increased per-capita income from US$70 to approximately US$600-700 by 1994 (UNICEF 1994: 64). The number of people living below the official poverty line dropped drastically, from 70 million, or 60 per cent of the total population in 1970, to 25.9 million people by 1993, or approximately 13.7 per cent of the population (GOI/UNICEF 1994: 2). Improved economic conditions have also stimulated parallel improvements in the provision of social services, notably in the provision of universal primary education. Among adult women, illiteracy decreased from 53 per cent in 1971 to 21 per cent by 1990, whereas male illiteracy decreased from 28 per cent to 10 per cent in the same period. Net enrolment of the 7-12 year age group in primary education has risen from 41 per cent in 1968 to over 93 per cent in 1993 (*ibid.*: 3).

These socio-economic changes have brought rapid progress toward many of the child health goals. For instance: (1) 90 per cent of infants had received complete immunisation by 1993, and future focal points will be on polio eradication and the elimination of neonatal tetanus; (2) overall use of ORT is relatively high at 60 per cent although proper child feeding practices during illnesses are less likely to have been followed; and (3) child blindness due to vitamin A deficiency has been reduced through the distribution of high-potency vitamin A capsules. The percentage of children with xerophthalmia declined from 1.3 per cent in 1978 to 0.3 per cent in 1993 (*ibid.*: 4).

Access to clean drinking water has shown a relatively modest increase from 35 per cent in 1971 to 63 per cent in 1993 (84 per cent in urban, and 53 per cent in rural areas). UNICEF has also reported some persistent serious child problems: (1) acute respiratory infection (ARI) remains as the major cause of death for infants; (2) diarrhoea still occurs in 12 per cent of infants; and (3) low birth weight and child malnutrition are still common (*ibid.*: 3-4). Despite improved economic conditions, many of these problems are attributed more to poor behavioural practices (i.e., child care practices, personal hygiene and household sanitation) than to overall financial availability or household food security. An example is found in the rejection of the use of sanitary latrines, indicated by the trivial increase in the number of houses with latrines from 47 per cent in 1971 to 52 per cent in 1993 (GOI/UNICEF 1995a: 3-4).

Yet poverty remains a serious health problem demanding serious attention, for example: (1) the problem of urban densely settled slums; (2) the number of female-headed households (5.3 million in 1990) continues to increase, with strong evidence that such households are often poor; (3) legal protection of female labour and their occupational health and safety are inadequate, and average wages for women workers are lower than for male workers; and (4) the number of 'working children' continues to increase; it has been estimated that at least 2.1 million children below the age of 15 are working. Although many are still in school, it has to be admitted that some are working or surviving 'on the streets' in hazardous environments which expose them to infectious and parasitic diseases including HIV/AIDS (GOI/UNICEF 1994: 5).

Infections, accidents and violence: persistent challenges

HIV/AIDS

Between 1987 and 30 June 1996, 407 confirmed cases of HIV/AIDS were reported by the Ministry of Health(MOH). Of these, 303 were HIV positive and 104 were full-blown AIDS cases. By 1996, 63 AIDS deaths were reported. These cases were found in 15 out of the 27 provinces of Indonesia (Sujudi 1995; MOH 1996).

Among all HIV positive cases, 61 per cent were Indonesian citizens. Heterosexual contacts accounted for 68 per cent of HIV-positive cases, and 35 per cent of AIDS cases. Homosexual and bi-sexual contacts make up 11 per cent of HIV-positive cases and 47 per cent of AIDS cases. The sex ratio (M:F) is 7.5:1 for reported AIDS cases but 2:1 for HIV infection. This indicates that although in the early years of the epidemic the transmission route was homosexual contact, it has shifted quickly to heterosexual contacts in recent years (ibid.).

Most HIV-positive and AIDS cases have occurred among persons in the 15 to 49 year age-groups with a peak at between 20 and 29 years for HIV positive cases and between 30 and 39 years for AIDS cases (Dharmaputra, Ariawan and Iskandar 1996: 87-91). This ten-year lag between the peak of HIV-positive and AIDS is in line with the median time of progression for HIV-positive status to AIDS which is also around ten years. Until 30 June 1996, there were no paediatric cases formally reported to the MOH.

Although the numbers of reported HIV-positive and AIDS cases have been rapidly increasing, it is apparent that these greatly underestimate the real incidence and prevalence of the disease. Since a national surveillance system for HIV/AIDS has not been well implemented, WHO and USAID estimate a total of 40,000 to 50,000 infections by the end of 1993, while an official government estimate was around 20,000 seropositives. Underreporting of cases is very obvious, proved by the fact that almost all of the AIDS cases were detected during their late stages, while a well-established surveillance system should detect AIDS cases at their early clinical or even subclinical stages.

Other infectious and parasitic diseases (IPDs)

Indonesian morbidity data indicate that the incidence and prevalence of infectious and parasitic diseases such as: acute respiratory infections, diarrhoeal diseases, tuberculosis and vector-borne diseases, especially malaria, remain at high rates. Despite this condition, the community has the tendency to treat these diseases at home, by way of traditional medicine or modern medicines, including antibiotics, that are sold over the counter. As a result of this behaviour, Triatmodjo (1991: 951) found that in Jakarta, the level of resistance of *V. cholera* (in-vitro) towards Tetracycline has reached 2.9 per cent; towards Chloramphenicol 0.7 per cent; towards Ampicillin 4.3 per cent; and towards Sulphamethoxazole-Trimethoprim 2.1 per cent. In West Java, the resistance rates are even higher (5.5 per cent; 11.1 per cent; and 22.2 per cent respectively for the first three antibiotics mentioned above); but for Sulphamethoxazole-Trimethoprim, no resistance was found.

The same applies for TB resistance to drugs as reported by Kosasih, Soemantri, and Suwarno (1989: 247-251). The resistance level toward Rifampicin is 5.6 per cent, Kanamycin 48.2 per cent, Streptomycin 62.5 per cent, Isoniazid 37.5 per cent, Ethambutol 0.8 per cent, Pyrazinamide 0.43 per cent, and Para-Amino-Salicylic Acid 62.5 per cent. High levels of resistance to some drugs both limit the treatment options, and increase the cost of treatment for this very dangerous disease.

For the treatment of one of today's most common STDs, non-gonococcal urethritis (NGUs), Pohan (1990:431-433) has recommended Tetracycline derivatives such as Doxycycline and Minocycline instead of Tetracycline. But they are more expensive than Tetracycline phosphate which is available in every small trade store (*warung*) under the brand name of Super Tetra[R]. People often use doses of resistant antibiotics that are no longer useful for treatment, or they actually buy the effective antibiotics, but fail to comply with the recommended dosage for economic reasons. In addition to the already high incidence of cholera, malaria, TB, dengue, etc., future challenges will include the problems of more virulent disease outbreaks and the threat of food poisoning, similar to the recent outbreak in Japan caused by the O-157 colon bacillus infection which causes haemolytic uraemic syndrome resulting in death by kidney failure (*Jakarta Post* , 'Japanese Angered by Food-Poisoning Outbreak' 22 July 1996).

Accidents and violence

Accident statistics are very much underreported, and the Department of Manpower's data do not reflect the actual situation of industrial safety and health (ARPLA 1992: 17). In the early 1980s, reported accidents numbered 5,000-6,000 a year, but then increased rapidly from 1987 to 1989, reaching around 11,000 injuries in 1989. More than 50 per cent of these accidents were in the 21-30 year age-group (*ibid.*:17). The transport and communication industries had the highest reported fatal accident frequencies with 6.4 workers per 1,000 dying annually in 1989, whereas the average rate for all industries was 0.3 (*ibid.*: 18). The main type of fatal accidents in the transportation industry is presumed to be traffic accidents. In 1991, the MOH reported a ratio ranging from 3.4 deaths (in Maluku) to 14.1 deaths per 100,000 people (in South Kalimantan) related to traffic accidents (Dep-Kes-PusDaKes 1993: Attachment III.B.15). Unfortunately, there are no published data on occupational diseases or domestic violence. In the section on causes of deaths among children ages 1-4, accidental injuries was mentioned as one of the ten leading causes of deaths. Similarly, among young adults ages 15-34, accidents and injuries according to the HHS 1992 and 1995 were the principal causes of deaths. Personal attitude and behaviour such as lack of concern for personal safety (i.e., the neglect of safety devices used when driving automobiles or working in dangerous environments), lack of basic safety and health education, and lack of trainers and experts (besides employees' economic vulnerability) to promote safety and health programs, were identified by ILO as contributing factors to the high death and morbidity rates (ARPLA 1992: 19-20). Globalisation of information, technology, and modernisation have glamourised sex, alcohol and violence through mass media (magazines, video, laser-discs, films); however, their effects on the rise of adult mortality figures caused by injuries have not been analysed or recorded regularly.

Vital planning needs: more thorough analysis on age patterns of mortality

To improve the health of the people, information on the magnitude of risks and changes over the years, and the analysis of links between risk factors and diseases and causes of deaths are very important. Subsequently, increasingly detailed mortality data are needed in order to monitor the effect of health service interventions. Ideally, these data would be available through a continuous recording of deaths and their characteristics by civil or vital registration. But in a country like Indonesia, where fewer than approximately 60 per cent of the events are registered, the usefulness of registration data is severely limited, and unlikely to improve significantly without a major change in the organisational system for data collection, and an investment in training and monitoring the collection process. What are the alternatives to a full registration system? Crude death rates are certainly the easiest to calculate, but are not very useful for understanding mortality risks and processes. The infant mortality rates and related life expectancies are now quite easy to calculate, as long as the survey samples have reasonable size and quality. This was demonstrated by mortality analysis in the 1970s and 1980s, which concentrated heavily on the estimation of levels and trends of infant and child mortality, but provided little information on adult mortality because the relative rarity of adult deaths indicated a need for much larger samples than those being carried out at the time.

The calculation of death rates in different age-groups is essential to monitor trends in adult mortality. Especially with the emerging of more virulent infectious and parasitic diseases in the near future, it is strongly advisable to monitor changes in morbidity patterns and death rates per 1,000 people in adolescent and adult ages, as well as infants and children under five. Age specific death rate calculations require information on the population at risk, which are drawn from a different data collection system, usually from age and sex distributions of the population obtained from one or more census enumerations. This kind of analysis was not carried out in the mortality analyses of the HHS 1992 and 1995. Despite many clear limitations in survey design and sample size, the 1980 and 1986 HHS data published useful data on age-patterns of mortality in the form of age-specific death rate estimates, which, while clearly inadequate, at least gave some inspiration with regard to directions for policy analysis. By contrast, the more recent analysis from HHS 1992 and 1995 have merely presented the percentage-distribution of deaths over age-groups. The decision to do this may arise in part from fear that the surveys did not collect detailed information for the study of differentials, or simply from the fact that data have not been fully analysed.

Quality improvement to increase the accuracy of diagnosis is a continuing challenge to researchers (Ariawan, Miko, and Herdayati 1996: 31). Household interview techniques used by the Indonesian Household Health Survey inquiring about recent deaths of adult family members during the previous year must recognise the notable weakness of such approaches: a substantial underreporting of deaths (Ewbank 1984: 25). Errors can arise either because of differences in age groups covered or because of reference period error. In addition, Ewbank (*ibid.*: 18) warned that information on recent deaths is also affected by recent migration and by the frequent dissolution and regrouping of households following the death of the head of household. Literature gathered by the United Nations Secretariat (1984: 33) suggested that information on whether a respondent's mother is alive at the time of interview provides an indicator of adult female mortality, and similar information about fathers provides an indicator of adult male mortality. Information on survival of first spouse classified by sex and age of respondent, or years since first marriage, might provide another approach to the estimation of adult mortality. But as yet these are untried techniques in the context of Indonesian conditions.

Conclusion

The infant mortality rate is indeed an important statistical indicator, because it reflects not only health and nutritional status of newborns, but also the socio-economic level of the average household, and the general availability of health care delivery services. Trends in IMR clearly give important clues to comprehensive changes that are taking place in Indonesian society at large. Although some improvement was reported prior to 1950, the infant mortality level decreased steadily after 1950. By 1994, the government officially announced that IMR had reached 57 per 1,000 live births, under-five mortality rate was down to 75 per 1,000 live births, crude birth rate was 24 per 1,000 population, and crude death rate was 8 per 100,000 population. Unfortunately all these measures are derived from the same basic calculation of child survival, and cannot be verified through direct observation of the components of mortality: the deaths of people of various age groups and sex and over various regional and socio-economic categories. Thus while heralding these changes as great achievements, the government had to acknowledge that the only other mortality measure which has been estimated in a relatively independent fashion, the maternal mortality rate, remains high. However there is no consensus on what the actual level of maternal deaths might be. The most common estimate is the widely publicised 425 per 100,000 live births in 1993 (GOI/UNICEF 1995b: 1) but alternative estimates range from as low as 360 to as high as 650. All of these measures, though, are much higher than the rates found for other countries of Southeast Asia, and other countries of comparable levels of development. Thus, while the IMR is important, it is neither the only, nor even the most revealing measure of health and welfare status of the population.

The emergence of new and more virulent strains of infectious micro-organisms (TB, cholera, non-gonococcal urethritis and HIV) is associated with a different set of risk factors compared to the classical socio-demographic factors in the past, as it involves an increased importance of individual behavioural factors, which are importantly determined by sensitive issues such as sexual attitudes and compliance with medical treatment regimes. Unfortunately, the age-group with the highest level of morbidity and mortality from such infections is the productive age-group (15 years and above); hence the resultant deaths have immense economic effects, as well as psycho-social impact, on the nation. The negative effects on a family and society range from stigmatisation and isolation to ostracism. Indonesia has not given serious attention to directly monitoring mortality occurring in these age groups, instead giving exclusive priority to the reduction of mortality among infants and children and their mothers. Thus, if the morbidity and mortality of adults are to receive the attention warranted by the observed risks, a vigorous and innovative approach must be developed to collect more comprehensive and better-quality mortality data.

In the long run, it is the responsibility of the national government to upgrade the death registration system. If for no other reason there must be a realisation that reliance on surveys for mortality data implies the need for larger sample sizes, and thus more expensive surveys, to obtain valid estimates of adult morbidity and mortality. At some point the unit cost of developing accurate death records from an established registration system is considerably less than that needed to obtain reliable and valid data from regular retrospective surveys.

As this paper indicates, that point may have been passed years ago, but passed unnoticed because policy-makers and citizens did not realise just how totally inadequate were the data used for the design and monitoring of health systems.

12

Fertility and Family Planning: Prospects and Challenges for Sustainable Fertility Decline

Sri Moertiningsih Adioetomo

This paper examines whether current fertility levels and trends and family planning institutions provide the basis for continuing fertility decline into the 21st century.

Overview of the Indonesian fertility decline from 1965 to 1995

During the last 25 years Indonesia has experienced a remarkable fertility decline. Before the mid-1960s Indonesian women had on average six or more children; today they have only two or three children. Before the decline most parents enjoyed large families, both as status symbols if they were elite bureaucrats, or as human resources if they were peasants. In the present day, people are realising the benefits of having smaller numbers of children. The fertility decline has occurred across all ages of women's reproductive lives. The onset of the fertility transition was accomplished first when older women stopped bearing children, and later when younger women began to space their pregnancies.

Much of the fertility decline can be attributed to the Indonesian family planning program initiated in the early 1970s (Hull, Hull and Singarimbun 1977; Warwick 1986; Adioetomo, Kiting and Salman 1990). Efforts to legitimate the concept of fertility control, followed by the distribution of contraceptives and family planning services, and the promotion of a small family-size norm of two or three children, have made the Indonesian people family planning-literate. Nowadays, most women are able to name a number of modern contraceptive methods, as well as to indicate where they may be obtained. This is congruent with the increased rate of contraceptive use, from virtually zero before the 1960s to about half of married couples in 1994 (CBS *et al.* 1995). Values of small family size have developed. While in 1976 most women preferred to have between four and six children, in 1994 the distribution was more condensed at from two to four children, indicating that small family values are becoming more and more acceptable.

With a total fertility rate of 2.9 children per woman and contraceptive prevalence of 54 per cent in 1994 protecting 19,421 million acceptors in Indonesia, it seems very likely that the country will reach a replacement level of NRR equal to one and TFR of 2.1 in 2010 according to the World Bank Standard Projections (World Bank 1990a: 92, 93), or even in 2005 with TFR of 2.2 (Ananta and Adioetomo 1990). Especially important is the influx of large numbers of younger women entering the reproductive period in the coming years. These younger women tend to be more educated, more informed about modern life and opportunities, and more informed about fertility control. It is expected that these young women will continue the fertility transition to lower family sizes. However, there are also challenges which may hamper the further reduction in fertility. Because of the way current programs are designed and run, managers need enormous efforts and resources to maintain current contraceptive prevalence as well as cater for additional new acceptors each year. With the increasing number of acceptors, government is not likely to be able to provide fully subsidised services to family planning users. For this reason the family planning program is moving to privatise part or all of the service delivery costs according to the ability of consumers to meet these. Increasing attention is being directed toward motivating non-contracepting couples, many of whom are hard to reach or ambivalent about family planning because of concerns over the quality of care they might expect. The program is thus trying to improve the quality of service delivery. Obviously raising prices and raising standards of a complex mass coverage program present challenges to government in the effort to further reduce fertility.

Prospects of further fertility decline

The onset of Indonesian fertility transition is now seen as having occurred when the recorded fertility rate of 5.7 for the period of 1967-69 began to decline very rapidly reaching 2.9 in 1994. Many studies have attributed the decline in fertility to the efforts of the national family planning program. Backed up by strong political commitment, this program legitimised the idea of fertility control among government bureaucrats and community as well as religious leaders who were influenced by pro-natalist ideology and by the misperception that birth control was equivalent to abortion. The legitimation of contraceptive use among women was promoted through the rapidly improving administrative system, in which the provincial governors and their subordinates at lower administrative levels were made responsible for the implementation of the birth control initiative. The new idea of fertility control was introduced to the community through the practice of 'learning by doing' embedded in a paternalistic culture. This implies that family planning acceptance was determined by external motivation, and raises the question of whether members of the community had internalised the concept of family planning before accepting contraceptives.

What has very rarely been noted in the analysis of fertility decline is the fact that birth rates began to decline during the pronatalist era before the family planning program was initiated. Literature documents that latent demand for fertility control existed during the first two decades after independence. Educated middle-class women wanted to limit family size because of growing social and economic aspirations (Subandrio 1963; Hull 1975), and lower-class rural women wanted to stop childbearing because of the health and economic burden presented by frequent pregnancies. But, because means for fertility control were unavailable and the idea of birth control was not socially accepted, the adoption of effective means of contraception was limited. Nevertheless, during the 1950s and early 1960s, small groups of women and dedicated medical personnel started to provide family planning services oriented to improving mothers' and children's health (Hull, Hull and Singarimbun 1977). This provided the foundation for the implementation of a national family planning program to accommodate the growing demand for fertility control among women.

On the basis of the above trends and experiences, the shape of continued fertility transition depends on whether: (1) government will continue to support family planning activities; (2) the National Family Planning Coordinating Board (BKKBN) remains the key agency to promote mass acceptance; (3) small-family size norms of two or even fewer children are accepted, internalised and translated into appropriate birth control behaviour.

Judging from the political situation these days, strong support for the family planning program is likely to continue. The organisation of the family planning program is fairly securely fixed with the assignment of the head of the Family Planning Coordinating Board as the Minister of Population. Thus, the political commitment for efforts to achieve replacement level in 2005 with TFR 2.2 is likely to be maintained in the foreseeable future.

The issues of internalisation of small family size norms and the implementation of small ideal family size through the practice of contraception to limit fertility have to be carefully examined. It is often hypothesised that fertility decline will stall if desired family size fails to fall further and most women in need have been provided with contraceptives. The campaign of *dua anak cukup* (two are enough) changed the people's perception from 'family size is not a matter for choice' to 'numeracy' about preferred family size (Adioetomo 1993). The reported mean ideal family size dropped from 4.1 children in 1976 to 2.9 in 1994. However, the percentage of women wanting to have fewer than three children remained virtually constant in the 1990s, that is 56.1 per cent in 1987, 57.6 per cent in 1991, and 57.2 per cent in 1994 (CBS *et al.* 1995). In addition, 28.3 per cent and 17.3 per cent of women having three and four living children still want to go on bearing children or were undecided whether to stop or to go further.

There are still some women who have not internalised the small-family preference for two children but they increasingly see large families as a financial burden. Such women might be encouraged to translate their changed desired family size into contraceptive use to limit family size, which would effectively produce further fertility decline. On the other hand, educated women, or women who live in urban areas, or in Java and Bali are more likely to have already internalised the small family size of around two children (*ibid.*).

Latent demand for fertility control probably explains why contraceptive use increased dramatically in the first two decades of the program implementation. The slower rate of growth of contraceptive use in the late 1980s probably indicated that most of those with latent demand for fertility control had been satisfied by the program. But at that time others were accepting family planning because of strong peer pressure or pressure from government officials even though they might not have had a strong internalised desire for birth control. Thus, there are two kinds of women with different motivations, those who actually wanted to control fertility because of higher aspirations, and those who accepted family planning because of peer group or other external pressure. Both groups contributed large numbers of acceptors to increase prevalence rates during the first decade of the program implementation. But nowadays, those women have been replaced by younger generations, who are more educated and more exposed to mass media, and thus have higher aspirations for their lives and are therefore expected to have higher and more overt internalised demand for fertility control.

How big is this young generation? Infant mortality in the 1970s declined faster than fertility so larger proportions of babies born in the 1970s survived, resulting in a much larger number of women entering reproductive age in the nineties. With the new government commitment to nine years compulsory education it is expected that a lot more women will have higher education and will marry later. Surveys conducted after the mid-1970s have recorded that women with higher education, or who live in urban areas or in Java-Bali are much more likely to use contraception and have lower fertility than less educated women.

This is the argument sustaining confidence that further fertility declines are possible. But the course of the fertility transition will differ from that found in the last two decades. If during the last 25 years, the government played the key role in reducing fertility level through the supply-oriented approach, the future fertility decline needs to work with the women themselves. This advanced stage of fertility transition will be powered by forces of modernisation, urbanisation or globalisation of information and trade, more closely resembling the course of fertility transition as described by the powerful demographic transition theory developed from the European experience. At this stage, more than ever before, the national family planning program is committed to client needs and client preferences.

However, there remain a number of challenges faced by the family planning program in the continuing fertility transition, and to meet the goal of achieving replacement level fertility by 2005.

Challenges

The potential for the continuing fertility transition will have to face many challenges. Increasing efforts are being made to achieve replacement level in 2005, to meet the goal of a TFR of 2.0. But, this has to start with contraceptive prevalence of 58 per cent, implying 22,159 million users in 1994, and must grow at a rate of one million users annually. In the early days the Indonesian family planning (FP) program was characterised by high government subsidy for contraceptive services to clients. Increasingly new and continuing acceptors are paying for the supply and the provision of services since government alone cannot afford to provide free and subsidised contraception to all couples. Therefore, efforts to increase self-reliance in family planning are being encouraged.

The 1994 Indonesia Demographic and Health Surveys (IDHS) reported that 26 per cent of acceptors discontinued contraceptive use within one year of acceptance, either because of wanting more children or because of health and service quality concerns. Information and education, and better-quality services are being developed to meet these issues.

Another challenge is the issue of motivating current non-users to become acceptors. Among the 45 per cent of women not using contraception about 36 per cent have never shown any effort to control their fertility. It would be interesting to study in more detail the characteristics of these never-users to determine why they are not yet motivated to become acceptors, or whether they are still underserved by the program.

Privatisation

The Indonesian National Family Planning program was initiated with the public sector as its predominant funding source. For a quarter-century acceptors have obtained services free of charge from government hospitals, health centres (*puskesmas*), health posts (*posyandu*), family planning posts, family planning fieldworkers (PLKB), mobile family planning teams (TKBK/TMK), and family planning safaris.

But with increasing numbers of acceptors, government funding was insufficient to maintain 22 million users every year with an annual addition of one million new acceptors. Besides, funds from international donor agencies are declining. Privatisation of FP services offers the major avenue for program sustainability. A policy of *KB Mandiri* (self-reliant FP) was initiated and promoted first in 1989, with a focus on urban areas. The idea is to encourage those who have the capacity and willingness to pay for contraceptives to use private sources to obtain family planning services. The private sector in this case consists of the private hospitals, private clinics, private doctors, private midwives, pharmacies and drugstores, or voluntary community groups using their own resources to serve paying clients. To support the privatisation, Blue Circle contraceptives are distributed through private channels, such as pharmacists, private doctors and midwives' practices but at low costs within reach of many low income clients. The poor continue to have access to fully subsidised services.

When the KB Mandiri was launched, there was pessimism about whether the target of 50 per cent privatisation in 1994 could be achieved (World Bank 1990a). But findings from surveys have shown an increasing percentage of clients obtaining their services from private-sector sources. Surveys have recorded that the percentage of acceptors using subsidised government services decreased from 81 per cent in 1987 (CBS *et al.* 1989), to 75 per cent in 1991 (CBS *et al.* 1992), and further declined to only 49 per cent in 1994 (CBS *et al.* 1995). Conversely, the percentage of women using private sector sources increased from 12 per cent to 22 per cent and finally to 49 per cent in 1987, 1991 and 1994 respectively. Normally it is expected that government family planning services are free of charge and private sources provide services only on receipt of payment. But results from the 1994 IDHS show that about 31 out of the 48 per cent of acceptors obtaining family planning services from the public sector made some payment. On the other hand, a small portion of women (2.4 per cent) obtained free services from private-sector sources. A change in the categorisation of services provided by the *posyandu* and family planning posts (comprising 18 per cent of all users), which in 1991 were recorded as government sources but in 1994 were classed as private sources, gives the impression that contraceptive supplies from these sources were no longer given free to clients. Altogether, in 1994, three-quarters of acceptors have demonstrated self-reliance in fulfilling their fertility control needs.

A comparison of women who obtained family planning services free of charge with those who paid for the services found that rural women, having lower education and lower economic status and working in agriculture, are less likely to pay for services than urban women who have finished primary school and live in better houses. Younger women aged less than 30 years old having not more than two children showed very high self-reliance: they were twice as likely to pay for services. This pattern reinforces the better prospects for privatisation when the older generation are replaced by the younger, more urbane, more educated and more economically secure cohort of women (Adioetomo, Ganiarto and Hidayat 1996).

However, two questions remain to be answered: first, whether the price that the users paid constitutes full payment or continued subsidy by the government; second, the fact that a quarter of acceptors obtain family planning services without payment raises the question of whether they have no ability to pay, or whether they are not willing to pay.

A further study to distinguish whether payment for services consists of only registration fees or the amount being paid includes other components of contraceptive services, found results similar to the earlier study, except that once women pay more than the registration fee, they tend to seek out sources which give better quality of care, rather than just settling on a place nearby (*ibid.*). Again, this indicates that demand for better-quality care in family planning services is increasing. This is consistent with the 1994 IDHS findings that those who live in urban areas and are more educated are willing to pay for better services.

Prices that government providers charge clients usually are lower than those charged by private providers. It is expected, therefore, that acceptors from the lower socio-economic groups will choose government providers. However, about 40 per cent of acceptors from the second and the highest quartile of expenditure groups still obtain family planning services from government sources. But these women are willing to pay for maternal care services at the government-run *puskesmas* (Winfrey and Heaton 1996), showing among the middle-class women a lack of willingness to pay for private services.

This is consistent with other findings from the 1994 Indonesian Demographic and Health Survey, that better-educated and richer women who are members of groups of villagers receiving family planning activities obtain family planning services free even though they may clearly have the resources to pay fees (Adioetomo, Ganiarto and Hidayat 1996). There is a suspicion that free services are given to these well-to-do women as a 'privilege' which is regarded as a status symbol among government bureaucrats in villages. This suggests that efforts to increase privatisation in government family planning services is hampered by the government's own bureaucratic system. The existence of the subsidised services for all women means clients are not easily shifted from free to fee for service arrangements. Thus, it is suggested that the subsidy system should be restricted to poor women while those able to pay should bear the costs of the services they use.

Who are the people in need of assistance? Looking at the reasons for choosing particular sources for contraceptive services, it is found that proximity, low cost and availability of transport are the main reasons, especially for clients from rural areas and having lower education. For the urban and educated people, although there is still a preference for accessibility, privacy, competency and friendly staff proved to be the major considerations for choosing a particular service provider (CBS *et al.* 1995: Table 5.1.5.1). This indicates that quality of care in family planning is important, and therefore efforts to increase prevalence rates and to reduce discontinuation rate should include efforts to increase the quality of care.

The hard-to-reach

In considering the potential market for the family planning program it is important to consider married women of reproductive age who use contraception, those who used previously but have stopped using and those who have never used any contraception at all. As has been stated before, the 1994 IDHS found that 54 per cent of married women were currently using contraceptives, 16 per cent were previous users, and the rest (34 per cent) were women who had never tried to use any method at all. The reasons for not using contraception between former users and never-users are very different. The reasons given by never-users were mainly the desire to have children, but a substantial percentage of women stated that they were not using contraception because of disapproval, or religious reasons or lack of knowledge. This category of women can be considered as the hard-to-reach or hard-to-serve. They are mostly from rural areas, uneducated and poor, coming largely from the lowest expenditure quintile group

(Serrato and Melnik 1996). Thus, family planning managers have to improve their efforts to provide information, education and motivation, especially targeted to those currently opposing the idea of family planning, and those who reside in remote areas not well served by family planning services. It is quite likely that these poor women will also need full government subsidy for their contraceptive services.

Such women are very different from those who said they had used contraception in the past. Every year, about 26 per cent of current users discontinue contraceptive use. This is a very high percentage showing a source of high inefficiency in the family planning program. The reasons that former users are not using contraceptives are related to a desire to have children, but a substantial proportion cite health concerns, related to side effects. To meet the needs of these women requires a better quality of care and improvement in counselling, plus proper screening of women's health conditions prior to the services being given. Such a strategy may become a good solution to prevent women from discontinuing contraceptive use.

Quality of care

Beyond the question of serving women who have dropped out, concern over quality of care in family planning has increased in the last decade. There is a growing contention, especially after the 1994 International Conference on Population and Development (ICPD), Cairo, that family planning programs should be oriented more toward fulfilling clients' demands, rather than single-minded emphasis on demographic goals which can be seen as a more supply-oriented approach. It can be argued that the Indonesian family planning program was able to make couples realise that family size is a matter of choice and the program was instrumental in providing the means to achieve the newly defined desired family sizes. Therefore the task of the program is to help couples to meet their reproductive goals through the provision of good quality of care, which will eventually continue the fertility decline.

Quality of care however, is difficult to measure or even to define. From the clients' perspective, Bruce's (1990) selected indicators which may be used to measure quality of care include choice of method indicating accessibility of a mix of methods; provision of adequate information to clients which is related to the right of clients to obtain proper information about positive and negative aspects of contraception; technical competence of providers which protects clients' safety during the process of services; the interpersonal relationship between providers and clients which stresses the way clients are treated; mechanisms to encourage continuity of service; and appropriate constellation of services. However, not all of these indicators are easily applicable to the Indonesian setting (Iskandar and Dharmaputra 1996; Hull 1996; J. Fortney 1996, personal communication), because they may be considered too 'Western', putting too much attention on details in the process of contraceptive service delivery, while tending to underestimate the importance of factors such as the basic competence of the health care system and the social political context of a national family planning program in a developing society.

From an operational point of view, self-assessment of quality of care by providers to gauge correct operational procedures has been tried with unsatisfactory results. Providers tend to tick the 'yes' box, for most of the items in a checklist of questions about whether they actually follow correct procedure in their day-to-day operations. It is unclear whether they give these answers on the basis of experience or the knowledge they obtain from the training. A different approach was applied in the Indonesia Family Life Survey 1993 (IFLS), in which interviewers were given a checklist of procedures on intrauterine device (IUD) services and pills (two methods asked in the survey). In this survey respondent providers were asked to spontaneously explain the procedures followed in giving IUD or pill services, starting with the process of screening (anamnesis) and actions required before inserting the IUD. When a particular step was not mentioned by providers, the interviewers asked whether respondents normally take the particular step. The difference in the frequencies of spontaneous answers and spontaneous plus probed answers is remarkable. On the average only 40 to 60 per cent of respondent providers were able to spontaneously describe the correct procedure, but when they were probed, the spontaneous plus the probed answers added to almost 99 per cent (Adioetomo 1996). This implies that providers know correct procedure, but perhaps do not follow correct procedure regularly.

Another measure of quality from the 1993 IFLS is client satisfaction. This was measured from responses to questions on whether clients obtained the contraceptive methods they preferred, and their perception of their treatment during the process of service. It is often suspected that Indonesian family planning acceptors have less freedom than they should to choose contraceptive methods (Pariani 1994).

However, the IFLS 1993 found that 92-96 per cent of respondent current users stated that they obtained their preferred method. This raises the question of whether respondents really have a clearly defined method preference before they are given a service and if they do, how strong the preference might be (Adioetomo 1996). Many women probably accept whatever method is available and recommended at the service delivery point because of low cost and easy access, and report that this was their 'choice' in only a *post hoc* fashion (CBS *et al.* 1995).

Responses to survey questions about the way clients were treated are generally very positive (Adioetomo 1996; Hull 1996). Virtually all respondents of the IFLS reported that they were treated nicely and humanely (*ramah dan manusiawi*). Given the contrast of this to the reality of daily services observed in the community such patterns are unbelievable. These answers may indicate that clients have low expectations regarding quality of care, or that clients have little knowledge about their right to obtain good services. These two indicators reflect the difficulty in developing quality indicators, partly because of the low level of discernment among clients. It appears that questions on quality provoke the classic 'courtesy bias'.

As noted above, on the providers' side, the IFLS have found that there is a tendency for medical practitioners not to comply completely with the standard procedures in providing IUDs and pills. In the case of IUD services, not all topics required during the process of history-taking were spontaneously reported by respondent providers. Issues which were given high attention (reported by about 75 per cent of respondent providers), include questions on whether the woman had given birth, the number of children she had borne, the date of last menstruation, and explanations about possible side effects of using an IUD (Adioetomo 1996: Table 4.2.2.1.2). Issues about the woman's history of reproductive morbidity were given very low priority during the history-taking. Only 25 per cent of doctors working in government health centres stated spontaneously that they ask the woman about any history of pelvic infection, 42 per cent asked about irregular and heavy menstruation, 25 per cent asked about lower abdominal pain, 33 per cent asked about vaginal discharge. The percentages are somewhat similar for private midwives (26, 41, 28 and 30 per cent), and highest among private doctors (39, 54, 34 and 41 per cent). Actions taken before inserting IUDs were also asked in this survey. Sterilising IUD instruments, checking position and size of the uterus were given a lot of attention with around 70 per cent of respondents stating spontaneously that they do these before inserting an IUD. Internal checks for tumours or pregnancy were reported by about 60 per cent of practitioners. But the easiest steps, washing hands and wearing gloves before inserting IUD, were only mentioned spontaneously by about 60 per cent of respondents, meaning that another 40 per cent of providers either forgot to mention these important steps or do not conform to these requirements in day-to-day services. Even though private-sector providers are similarly unable to demonstrate spontaneous ability to report the required procedure of services, they appear to provide better services than those given in the health centres, if reports of direct observation by researchers are to be believed.

Surveys also show that facilities and equipment at the service delivery points are not well maintained (Raintung *et al.* 1995; Adioetomo 1996). The 1993 IFLS found that from interviewers' observations, most service delivery points in the sample were dirty, judging from spots on the wall and curtains, and from the conspicuous dirt and papers on the floor. It is interesting to find that only 40 per cent of doctors and midwives in private practice have a washbasin with running water. Of the others, about 50 per cent use basins with containers of clean water while the source of water for the rest was unknown. On the other hand, 75 per cent of health centres have running water. As for the safety of contraceptive services, this survey found that almost all private doctors, 80 per cent of private midwives and only 76 per cent of providers from the government health centres stated that they use disposable needles when dispensing injectable contraceptives. Those who use non-disposable needles stated that they sterilise the devices with sterilisers (38 per cent), or boil them in water (41 per cent), or use other procedures (10 per cent). However, the details of the process, particularly whether they sterilise needles after each use or at the end of the day, were not reported. Other surveys of health centres, focusing on injectable contraceptives, reported striking findings in which the disposable needles are not properly destroyed after use. Even in some areas in Java, used needles are collected by wandering traders and sold as toys. Repeated reuse of disposable needles, and use of non-disposable needles without proper sterilisation, are quite common practices in Raintung's sample of clinics in West Java and Central Java (Raintung *et al.* 1995).

In summary, studies on quality of care have found that quality of family planning services in Indonesia is far from satisfactory (Wibowo 1994; Raintung *et al.* 1995; Adioetomo 1996) in part because the quality of health services in general is so questionable. Standard operational procedures are not properly followed, commitment and responsibilities of providers are inadequate, and facilities and equipment are of such low standard that they preclude attainment of good quality of services. While these provider-perspective indicators are important, indicators of quality of care in family planning in terms of clients' satisfaction need to be developed to give more discerning indicators of quality of care.

Conclusion

This paper has argued that there is substantial potential for further fertility decline in Indonesia. Increasing education, urbanisation and globalisation of media and information will broaden and deepen demand for fertility control. Over time, fertility decline will be due to increasing demand (clients' demand) rather than because of supply-side pressure (targets) as happened during the 25 years since the national family planning program was initiated. But this increasing demand to be effective must be accommodated with increasing supply of appropriate services, increasing competence and responsibilities of providers as well as improving equipment and facilities supporting good-quality service.

Efforts to achieve replacement level in 2005 are only likely to bear fruit if government works to increase motivation of non-users, some of whom are hard to reach because of disapproval, lack of knowledge and geographic isolation. They are couples from rural areas who are likely to be poor and uneducated. Reaching and motivating them implies a special IEC strategy, and the continued availability of contraceptive subsidies targeted for those who are in need.

International pressure to increase reproductive health care in ways oriented towards clients' need, especially after the ICPD in Cairo in 1994, must be taken seriously. The Government of Indonesia is committed to this. The BKKBN has already made changes in strategy of implementation from supply oriented toward 'demand fulfilment'. But this change in strategy has to be widely disseminated among all family planning managers and providers at the lower administrative level to fully implement good quality of care.

13

Mortality and Fertility: The Challenges

Firman Lubis

Introduction

I have been asked by the conference organisers to discuss two contrasting topics at the same time: 'Mortality and Health'; and 'Fertility and Family Planning'. I have decided to focus my discussion on the area where the two of them strongly overlap which is maternal and child health. I think that this focus is particularly justified because reducing maternal and child mortality is the biggest challenge for Indonesia at this moment and will continue to be so for many years to come.

Mortality: more than just numbers

To speak about mortality takes me back to about 30 years ago when I did my internship for my final years at the medical school. I was an intern at the well known Cipto Mangunkusumo Hospital (RSCM) in Jakarta from 1965 until 1968. At that time, the hospital was known to the public as Rumah Sakit Umum Pusat (RSUP) or Central Public General Hospital. Many people still called it by its old Dutch acronym which was CBZ (pronounced as see-bee-set), the abbreviation of *Centrale Burgerlijke Ziekenhuis* (Central Civilian Hospital). This hospital was constructed by the Dutch colonial government in 1926 and since then has always been the biggest public hospital in the country.

During my internship, this hospital was famous because many people believed that if they were brought to this hospital, for sure they were going to die. This was not simply a joke, but a true and terrifying belief. Perhaps the notion was due to the fact that many of their parents, relatives and friends had died in the CBZ, so it was not strange if people thought that CBZ was only a death house rather than a healing house. I remember many experiences where this perception was shown to be common among the people. A good friend of mine had a motorcycle accident and was unconscious. He was taken to the only public hospital in Jakarta at that time where serious cases might be treated, which of course was the Cipto Hospital. I happened to be on duty when he was brought in. Since he was my friend, I immediately took his case and started to work on his injuries. As I helped him with his wounds, he slowly began to regain consciousness. His case was actually not so serious. He had a mild brain concussion and some superficial wounds. After a few minutes he recognised me. He asked me softly what was really happening to him. I said to him that he had had an accident but was in pretty good shape. He looked at me again blankly and began to look around very slowly. Suddenly he realised where he was. He grabbed my arm tightly and stared at me. He became hysterical and cried for mercy: 'I do not want to die!'. I calmed him down and said that he was not going to die, but it was very hard to convince him. I thought, if even a well educated person (he was a final year student at the School of Economics) had such an attitude toward the hospital, we could certainly understand the fear of the common people.

During those years, Indonesia was terribly poor. We were almost bankrupt. Income per capita was just about US$50 annually. You could imagine that life was really hard for most of the people. Our socio-political situation was also tense. Those of you who have read the book or seen the movie *Year of Living Dangerously* which took place in 1965, can imagine the situation. During the years of my internship, I was deeply concerned about the numerous deaths I witnessed, especially the deaths of mothers and children. For instance, every day I counted about five to ten women brought to the hospital because of septic abortions. These cases mostly ended with death. I kept asking myself: why do these mothers risk their lives by undertaking abortions? There must be strong reasons for attempting such terrible things, I thought. The answer actually was not so difficult. When you looked outside the treatment room, you could see the husband with five or six children waiting anxiously. Poverty and too many children were the main reasons pressing the women to get an abortion from a quack. Obstetrics complications were also common at that time when, owing to a late referral to the hospital, many of these mothers ended up sacrificing their lives too. In addition to the many maternal deaths I also saw many children die from incredibly simple causes which should have been easily preventable. All the sights and sounds of needless death were really painful for me and haunt me to the present day. Sometimes I relive these experiences as bad dreams.

Why do I start my discussion by mentioning these past experiences? Because all these personal observations mean that to me mortality is more than just numbers and figures. Needless death is the deepest tragedy and the saddest thing which could happen to a family. The numbers are not faceless but represent real people like us. The statistics are not only very good indicators for measuring the health status of a particular society but they also reflect the depth of their sadness, and in a very true sense, their welfare. This is especially true of maternal and child mortality. If a mother dies, it is not only a deep loss for her family, but most likely it will result in the break-up of the family. I remember very well from my experiences when I had to inform a husband and children of the death of their wife and mother. They were totally shocked and confused. Culture dictated that the widower remarry quickly, but in the process of forming a new family the children left by the deceased mother were often neglected and lost. This tragedy in the end placed a burden not only on the immediate individuals in the family, but on society as a whole.

Unacceptably high maternal and infant mortality

After this brief introduction, let us now look at the maternal and child mortality figures in Indonesia. At the moment, these two mortalities are still unacceptably high. If we look at the crude death rate (CDR), the figure in Indonesia now is about 8 per 1,000 population which is only slightly higher than the figure in the developed countries such as Australia (about 6 per 1000 population). But when we look at the infant mortality rate (IMR), the figure in Indonesia now is around 60 per 1000 live births, which is ten times higher than the rate of 6 per 1000 found in developed countries. The differential is even more striking if we look at the maternal mortality rate (MMR) where the figure in Indonesia, at 400 per 100,000 births, is about 100 times higher than the 4 per 100,000 births in the developed nations!

Data compiled from UNFPA estimates show the comparison of maternal and infant mortality between Indonesia and some other countries in the region as well as their GNP per capita (Table 13.1). Although Sri Lanka's and China's GNP per capita indicate greater poverty, their maternal and infant mortality are much lower than Indonesia's. This is of course shameful.

TABLE 13.1: Mortality indicators and GNP per capita, selected countries

	IMR	MMR	GNP/Capita US$
Indonesia	64	420	980
Sri Lanka	18	65	580
China	40	74	420
Malaysia	13	62	3,600

In terms of absolute numbers, there are about 320,000 infant deaths and 21,000 maternal deaths in Indonesia annually. The leading causes of maternal deaths are infection, bleeding and toxaemia; infants die from pneumonia, diarrhoea and neonatal tetanus. All these are actually easily prevented or treated. If Indonesia could lower its maternal and infant death rates to the level of Sri Lanka —which has about one-sixth to one-fourth of Indonesia's rates—there would be about 18,000 mothers and 250,000 infants saved from death annually. These numbers are substantial and I do not see any reason for Indonesia not to accomplish this if Sri Lanka and China could.

About ten to fifteen years ago, Prof. Emil Salim, then Minister of Population and Environment, was very concerned to save from extinction one or two Java tigers which many experts believed were still alive somewhere in the jungles of Java. Of course I shared his concern. I too was worried over the fate of this native animal of Java. But I thought at that moment, if we lack the compassion to save 18,000 of our mothers, how could we ever succeed in preserving these animals? We actually know and love and respect mothers. We have never seen the tigers.

Strengthening commitment to improve mothers' health

Programmatically and technically speaking, it is not very difficult for Indonesia to reduce its maternal and child mortality to Sri Lankan rates. What is needed is a stronger commitment to and investment in the Maternal and Child Health (MCH) program. If MCH could receive the same strong commitment as the family planning program, perhaps the unacceptable high maternal and child death rate could be reduced. This commitment implies a bigger budget allocation for the MCH program, but it also means an improved quality of care in both MCH and FP services and the social and economic empowerment of women.

Improving the health and welfare of mothers and children should actually be seen as a very valuable investment in national human resources. According to many human biology studies, the period from conception until three years of age is the most critical period in human development. What are considered to the most basic human qualities, such as physical potential and intelligence, are developed during the early years of human growth. Therefore, human resource development should start with healthy mothers who can have healthy pregnancies, births and infants.

One good example of how important a mother's health is to the quality of Indonesian human resources is the high prevalence of anaemia among pregnant women which, according to a number of studies, is over 60 per cent. This condition definitely affects fundamental brain development of the foetus and is irreversible. With weakened or limited brain capacity, the baby's developmental capabilities are limited. His or her chance to become a high quality human resource is then limited too.

Fertility and family planning in Indonesia

Indonesia's success in lowering fertility through its family planning program is well recognised. From the early 1970s the focus of the program was on reducing the total fertility rate (TFR) by 50 per cent before the year 2000. Over the subsequent two decades fertility fell in advance of targeted trends (Hull 1980; Hull and Hull 1984; Hull and Dasvarma 1988). The target was revised to aim for a halving of the TFR by 1995, but the 1994 Indonesian Demographic Health Survey made it clear that even this optimistic objective had been achieved ahead of schedule with a national rate of 2.86 recorded for the 1991-94 period, on a trend implying a rate of 2.6 or 2.7 at the end of 1994.

The decline in the total fertility rate by more than 50 per cent seems to indicate that the fertility transition is 'on course' in Indonesia. There have been several studies looking at components of Indonesia's fertility transition which acknowledge the supporting role played by changing marriage patterns (Jones 1984; Hull and Hull 1987); however, most agree that the family planning program has played the starring role in the transition to lower fertility (Adioetomo 1993; Adioetomo et al. 1990; Gertler and Molyneaux 1994; Hugo et al. 1987; Hull 1987; McNicoll and Singarimbun 1983; Warwick 1986). Even Gertler and Molyneaux's detailed quantitative model results, which stressed the dominance of socio-economic factors over program factors, acknowledged not only the program's important supply function but its complex political incentive system as crucial contributors to the transition.

Despite the remarkable achievement of lowering fertility rates, the Indonesian family planning program is not free from criticism. These critics come mostly from international sources, but some are also domestic. Most of these critics focus on the way the program has been implemented which, according to them, was heavily driven by the government, using a target-driven approach, and an 'authoritarian' style which ignored questions of quality in the provision of services. These criticisms to some extent have been taken seriously by the BKKBN. Recently, important changes to their policies have been made in response to the critics. Over a decade ago, the KB Mandiri program was launched, which aimed at handing the Family Planning program over to the private sector. In 1993, the target system was replaced by demand fulfilment or *Pemenuhan Permintaan Masyarakat* (PPM) approach. Efforts to improve the quality of care in the family planning services are also being made by the BKKBN.

Current discussions about fertility and family planning performance have tended to focus quite specifically on the achievement of replacement-level fertility. In this regard, some interesting basic questions have emerged. Can Indonesia's fertility rate continue to decline as it has been doing over in the last 25 years? What changes need to be made to secure a more sustainable fertility decline? What are the implications of the broader reproductive health goals adopted in the 1994 International Conference on Population and Development (ICPD) for the Family Planning program? Finally, what will be the nature and role of the Family Planning program in the context of socio-cultural and political change in Indonesia in the coming years?

These basic questions can actually serve as starting points for consideration of the major issues and challenges faced by the Family Planning program in the near future.

Issues and challenges of the FP program

Increasing contraceptive prevalence rate

Despite Indonesia's success in reducing its TFR by half in the past quarter century and economic and social developments pointing to even lower rates in future, the contraceptive prevalence rate (CPR) appears to have reached a plateau over the last few years at just over 50 per cent, well below the level of three-quarters needed to reach replacement-level fertility of 2.1.

Innovative approaches are needed to achieve a higher CPR by responding to the unmet need for contraception, shown by surveys to affect approximately 12 per cent of married couples. This level of unmet need will not remain constant over time but is likely to increase as the desire for smaller families becomes increasingly established in the population. Thus, there appears to be a potential for further lowering fertility rates simply based on the fulfilment of spontaneous demand for contraception and further increases in the age at first marriage. The answer to the question of how to increase the CPR relies heavily on how the program can improve the quality and the expansion of services.

Improving the quality of service delivery

The two main foci of family planning service delivery are improving the quality of care and expanding family planning services. Indonesia has one of the more successful FP programs built on strong government commitment and community participation. Given the level of success and the maturity of the family planning movement, it is now important to look at specific ways to improve the quality of care. Through rising levels of education and increased awareness of issues, owing largely to improved communications, there will be increasing pressure from the public for quality issues to be addressed. This changing environment provides both a challenge and an opportunity. Indonesia's success in providing a far-flung population with family planning services and enlisting strong community involvement, resulting in increased contraceptive prevalence and lower fertility, is world renowned. The challenge now is to demonstrate the feasibility of achieving further declines in fertility through a strong emphasis on quality of care in its Family Planning program. The key point is that there will be many forces contributing to further fertility declines if family planning services emphasise the client's choice of method, counselling on side effects, improved interpersonal relations, technical skills on the part of health providers, client satisfaction with services, and other changes reflecting an emphasis on client needs and preferences.

Expansion of services

Contraceptive prevalence appears to have remained at approximately 50 per cent since the late 1980s. It is interesting to note that according to the last Demographic and Health Survey, 12 per cent of married women of reproductive age say they want either to space their births or to limit their family size, yet they are not using contraception. It is important at this point to identify and analyse why they are not using contraception. An in-depth study on these couples should be conducted to facilitate development of innovative strategies to reach them.

The expansion of services would also widen the range of methods couples use. At this moment the acceptance of voluntary sterilisation is relatively low (less than 5 per cent). Those younger couples who want to stop their fertility and people in older age groups in general (i.e. those over 35 years old) should be offered permanent methods. Not only it is safer, cheaper and easier for them, but it can help reduce the maternal mortality rate among women over 35 years of age. No developing country, except Mauritius, has attained contraceptive prevalence of 65 per cent or more, without 13 to 28 per cent, or more, of couples using voluntary sterilisation. Also, when contraceptive prevalence rests heavily on temporary methods which have significant pregnancy rates due to either method or couple failure, the backstop of safe abortion is needed for women who refuse to accept such failures as inevitable risks of using some methods of contraception.

Another important area in the expansion of services is the challenge of increasing male involvement. About 95 per cent of family planning users are female. Increasing active male participation in family planning will not only balance responsibility for reproductive health care more evenly between men and women but it can also increase the overall level of active family planning use. Effective family planning services for men should be designed to suit their needs, meaning services that men find attractive, convenient, high-quality, comfortable and accessible.

Strengthening FP institutionalisation

Since the Indonesian Family Planning program started BKKBN has developed its long-term program in three phases: expansion, maintenance and institutionalisation. With fertility rates being what they are now, many consider the program to have already reached the institutionalisation phase. This means that FP has been already perceived as a need by the majority of families in Indonesia. In this phase, the strong role of government in promoting FP should be phased out and services should be transferred to the hands of the private sector. As part of this program's evolution, BKKBN developed what is called self-reliant FP or KB Mandiri in the mid-1980s. The essence of KB Mandiri is privatisation of the program. Also, some years ago, BKKBN changed the word 'program' into 'movement'. The difference is that as a movement, FP activities are no longer government-centred but people-centred. According to the Chairman of BKKBN, it is not simply for the people but by the people.

The shift toward privatisation and client-centred policy should be further strengthened by involving more NGOs and other private institutions as leading actors in the program, and should create more openness of the program.

Expanding FP to include broader reproductive health aspects adopted by ICPD Cairo.

Indonesia is considered a leader for the Third World countries in family planning. It serves as a centre for international training and a founding member of the South to South Partners Initiative to foster co-operation in family planning training and development.

As an active participant of the ICPD in Cairo, Indonesia has to implement the adopted results of ICPD which stress the importance of quality of care, client satisfaction, women's health, and the inclusion of youth as part of the broader reproductive health mandate.

14

Health and Mortality, Fertility and Family Planning: The Current Situation

Gouranga Lal Dasvarma

The papers on Health and Mortality by Meiwita Iskandar (Chapter 11) and on Fertility and Family Planning by Sri Moertiningsih Adioetomo (Chapter 12) provide comprehensive pictures of the recent situation in these aspects of the population of Indonesia. I will attempt to add selected information in respect of maternal and child health and fertility and family planning based on recent research carried out at the Flinders University.

Health and mortality

First, I present a summary of the findings of research on maternal health care utilisation (more specifically, pregnancy care) and child health (more specifically, infant feeding and diarrhoea).

Maternal health care

Adequate maternal health care during pregnancy (antenatal care) should consist of four visits to an antenatal clinic, with at least one visit in every trimester of the pregnancy. These visits are necessary to provide advice on nutrition, to give the needed doses of tetanus toxoid injection and to check for and treat any abnormality in pregnancy or identify possible complications for referral (Pachauri 1995: 30).

Romdiati (1996) analysed data from the 1991 Indonesian Demographic and Health Survey to examine the patterns and determinants of maternal health care in Indonesia, with special reference to West Java. The information on maternal health care utilisation available from the IDHS 1991 pertained only to health care during pregnancy (antenatal care) and during childbirth (intra-natal care). Her analysis revealed that although a high proportion (about 80 per cent) of pregnant women in West Java received antenatal care, a third or more of them were either late in visiting a health facility or did not make the recommended number of at least four visits to the health facility. Age of the women was associated with the timing and adequacy of antenatal care in a curvilinear fashion, the youngest women (aged 15-19) and the oldest women (aged 40-49) receiving less care than women of other age-groups. In terms of intra-natal care, more than 85 per cent of births were at home and 79 per cent attended by traditional birth attendants (TBAs). A multiple logistic regression analysis carried out by Romdiati showed that women's education and their household economic status were two of the strongest predictors of maternal health care utilisation in terms of both antenatal and intra-natal care in West Java.

The study has brought out implications for future data collection in this important aspect of women's health care utilisation, some of which are as follows. An unexpected finding of the study was that women in agricultural occupations and those living in rural areas were more likely to use adequate modern maternal health care facilities. Future surveys should have samples large enough to allow satisfactory quantitative comparisons of the effect of rural versus urban residence on the utilisation of maternal health care. To get better data on household economic status it is suggested that information be collected on land ownership (for rural households) and household income (for rural and urban areas). Probably the IDHS 1991 was not the survey for including detailed follow-up questions regarding the use or non-use of maternal health care, but there should be some attempt at collecting such explanatory information. For example, the curvilinear relationship between age of women and the use of adequate, modern antenatal care may be due to differences in attitude of these women toward antenatal care, therefore information on their attitude, or reasons for not seeking such care should be collected. This study could not provide a complete picture of maternal health care in that it excluded post-partum health care utilisation, because there was no information on that aspect of maternal health care. Future surveys should include some items of information on post-partum health care utilisation. The study is particularly relevant in the context of renewed emphasis on maternal and women's reproductive health in Indonesia.

Child feeding and diarrhoea

The association of feeding practices and the incidence of diarrhoea among children under two years has been investigated by Purnama (1995) using data from the 1991 Indonesian Demographic and Health Survey (CBS *et al.* 1992). More than 95 per cent of children aged 0-3 months are breastfed in Indonesia. The average duration of breastfeeding of all children varied between 24 months in rural areas and 18.8 months in urban areas. On average, about 80 per cent of all children under two years were being currently breastfed in Java-Bali, the highest percentage (91 per cent) being for children under 5 months and lowest for children aged 18-23 months. Among the provinces in Java-Bali, Yogyakarta had the highest proportion of children under two being currently breastfed (88 per cent), and the longest duration of breastfeeding (20 months). Colostrum, the first milk produced after birth, which is rich in anti-infective properties and protein, but discarded in many instances for its yellow colour and thick consistency, was given in varying proportions among the provinces, viz., 71 per cent in Jakarta and 46 per cent in East Java. An interesting finding from the IDHS 1991 data was that there was a negative association between duration of breastfeeding and the proportion of mothers who gave colostrum to their newborn.

By classifying feeding type into four categories, (1) 'no breastfeeding', (2) 'exclusive breastfeeding', (3) 'breastfeeding and bottle feeding', and (4) 'breastfeeding and bottle feeding and supplementary foods', the study demonstrated that for all children under two years feeding type was significantly associated with the occurrence of diarrhoea, the exclusive breastfeeding category exhibiting the lowest prevalence of diarrhoea. The influence of exclusive breastfeeding on diarrhoea was the strongest for children under four months. The timing of the initiation of supplementary feeding was an important factor in the incidence of diarrhoea. Two separate analyses of socio-economic determinants of breastfeeding and of diarrhoea indicated that rural residence of mothers, use of contraception, and mothers' education and working status were significant predictors of breastfeeding, while feeding mode, mothers' education and use of contraception were significant predictors of diarrhoea. Purnama (1995) could not explain the exact mechanism by which the above factors influenced breastfeeding or the incidence of diarrhoea, but there are several policy implications of this study. Since current use of contraception emerged as a strong predictor of both breastfeeding and of diarrhoea, the role of family planning field workers (who are directly involved in providing contraceptive services in Indonesia) is seen as being very important in helping mothers improve their child feeding and diarrhoea management skills.

Fertility and family planning

Fertility

The continuation of the downward trend in fertility in Indonesia is confirmed by results from the two latest Indonesian Demographic and Health Surveys of 1991 and 1994 (CBS 1992, 1995) with total fertility rates (TFRs) of 3.02 and 2.85 in 1988-91 and 1991-94 respectively. However, the TFRs in two provinces, East Java and North Sulawesi, which had achieved near-replacement level fertility in 1988-91 with TFRs of 2.13 and 2.25 respectively, have apparently increased in 1991-94 to 2.22 and 2.62 respectively. This means an increase of 4 per cent in East Java and 16 per cent in North Sulawesi. Given the small absolute increase and the short interval between the two surveys, it is difficult to conclude whether these figures indicate a true increase in fertility or a stalling of fertility decline in these two provinces, or simply reflect sampling and other possible data problems. Whatever the conclusion, these recent trends pose a number of important questions and it would be interesting to investigate the reasons for this trend. Two postgraduate students in Population Studies at Flinders University are examining fertility trends in East Java and North Sulawesi and will attempt to explain these figures.

Teenage fertility

Teenage fertility has important social, economic and health implications. Children born to teenage mothers are also susceptible to increased risks of morbidity and mortality. The question of teenage fertility has been touched on in the general report of the 1994 Indonesian Demographic and Health Survey (CBS *et al.* 1995).

Hamid (1996) examined data from Indonesian population censuses of 1971, 1980 and 1990 and IDHS 1994 to study the levels and

patterns of teenage fertility[1] in Java-Bali. The level of teenage fertility
(i.e. the average number of children ever born to women aged 15-19)
has fluctuated during the 24 years 1971-94, with small increases between 1971 and 1980 and between 1990 and 1994. The proportion of
ever-married teenage women with three or more children has declined
over time. The decline in teenage fertility in Java-Bali from 1971 to
1990 was associated with the teenagers' increased educational attainment and increased labour force participation. A somewhat unexpected finding was that teenage fertility in urban areas was higher
than that in rural areas of Java-Bali from 1971 to 1990, but the differential appeared to disappear in 1994.

Analysis of the IDHS 1994 data (*ibid.*) shows the expected negative relationship between age at marriage and teenage fertility. There
was still a substantial proportion of women in 1994 (27 per cent in
urban and 38 per cent in rural areas of Java-Bali) who got married at
15 years or less, below the minimum legal age at marriage. Teenagers
who were ever or current users of contraceptives exhibited higher
fertility than never users, but this has been explained by the suggestion
that owing to cultural and societal expectations, teenagers do not
delay their first child birth and start using contraceptives only after
the first child is born. Fifty four per cent of the teenagers ever using a
contraceptive had at least one living child. The relationship between
educational attainment and the number of children ever born followed
an inverted U-shaped pattern. In the rural areas working teenagers
had lower fertility than non-working teenagers, but the opposite was
true in urban areas. Household economic status showed a U-shaped
relationship with teenage fertility. The study by Hamid (*ibid.*) has
shown some interesting findings, but for a better understanding of
teenage fertility and its determinants, a properly designed study with
a sufficiently large sample is required.

---

[1] Teenage fertility is defined as the number of children ever born to women
aged 15-19, the number of births to women aged 13 and 14 being negligible
(Hamid 1996: 9-10).

The demand for family planning

Total demand for family planning is the sum of contraceptive prevalence (current use) and unmet need for family planning (Westoff and Ochao 1991), i.e. the sum of actual demand and potential demand. Sinaga (1996) used this concept to analyse the factors affecting demand for family planning in the provinces of Kalimantan based on data from the 1994 Indonesian Demographic and Health Survey (CBS 1995). Contraceptive prevalence in Kalimantan was 50 per cent in 1994. The level of unmet need was estimated to be 11 per cent implying an estimated 61 per cent demand for family planning. Among the various factors associated with demand for family planning in Kalimantan, it was interesting to find that while experience of child loss had no significant association with the overall demand for family planning, it displayed opposite associations with the two components of demand, i.e. a significantly negative association with current use of contraceptives, and a significantly positive association with unmet need.

Results of a multivariate analysis show that demand for family planning was significantly influenced by geographic factors (place and province of residence), household factors (availability of electricity in the household), demographic factors (current age of the woman, number of living children and particularly that of sons), fertility preference factors (desire for future children and discussion of family planning with the husband), and program factors (visit by family planning field workers). Among these factors, visits by family planning field workers was found to be the most significant in generating demand for family planning, followed by husband's agreement in contraceptive use. The findings have some important policy implications regarding the program factors (visits by family planning field workers) and husband-wife communication in family planning.

Contraceptive social marketing

Adioetomo (Chapter 12) mentioned that in the wake of the International Conference on Population and Development in Cairo the Indonesian Family Planning Coordinating Board has changed its strategy from a supply oriented program to a demand fulfilment oriented program.

In this context it is perhaps relevant to present a summary of the study by Adhisuria (1995) who examined the role of the contraceptive social marketing (CSM) program in increasing the demand for private sector family planning in four selected provinces, viz., North Sumatra, DKI Jakarta, West Java and East Java in which are situated the major urban centres of Medan, Jakarta, Bandung and Surabaya respectively. Using data from the 1987 Indonesian National Contraceptive Prevalence Survey and the 1991 Indonesian Demographic and Health Survey, she analysed the trends in private sector family planning use and showed that, on a conservative estimate, about 40 per cent of family planning users in the year 2000 will use a private source. One of the policy recommendations of the study is to increase public demand for contraception by combining the CSM program with improvements in the quality of family planning services. Another important policy recommendation is to direct the fully privatised family planning services like the *Gold Circle* to the highest socio-economic groups and the *Blue Circle* to the medium socio-economic groups and continue with the government subsidised programs for the low socio-economic groups.

The above summary of findings of studies on wide-ranging topics, together with the contents of the chapters by Iskandar and Adioetomo, show that the mortality-health and fertility-family planning sectors of the population situation in Indonesia are very dynamic and undergoing rapid transitions in the respective fields.

Looking to the Future

15

Indonesia's Population Growth and Distribution in the 21st Century: Projections and Speculations

Geoffrey McNicoll

In 1962, a year after the country's first modern census, Indonesia's population reached 100 million. During 1997, according to Biro Pusat Statistik (BPS) (Central Bureau of Statistics) estimates, it will pass 200 million. The period of this doubling has seen large declines in birth and death rates, as the socio-economic transformation of the country has got under way. Nevertheless, Indonesia still faces a further massive absolute increase in population. This potential increase, with its likely accompaniments and possible consequences, is my subject.

My time frame is the next 50 or so years: to 2050. Demographers have some advantage in looking ahead that far, since age-structure dynamics constrain the possibilities. For example, nearly all of the population that will be aged 50 plus in 2050 (perhaps 30 or 40 per cent of the total population at that time) is already with us. In contrast, virtually none of the capital stock and little of the technology that will then be in use is around today. The United Nations' (UN) first attempt at a long-range population projection, published in 1958, foresaw a world population in 2000 of 6.27 billion; the actual figure, by current estimates, is likely to be 6.16 billion, within 2 per cent of the projection (UN 1958, 1994c; both are medium variants). The Indonesian component of the 1958 projection was 217 million; the current UN figure for Indonesia's population in 2000 is 213 million: again a difference of about 2 per cent. (The BPS figure is 210 million—BPS 1993.)

The confidence generated by this apparent predictive accuracy over four decades is lessened by recognising that a large dose of good luck was involved—an accident of offsetting rather than compounding errors. In truth, demographers have no crystal ball.[1] In the 1940s, the best guess at the world population of 2000 was 3.3 billion. In the 1970s, BPS expected Indonesia's year-2000 population to be more than 225 million. It is comforting that economists' errors in forecasting can be even more striking: around 1950 Japan was seen as a candidate for basket-case status, with Malthusian pressures closing in; ten years later, expert observers were putting Indonesia in the same category, while the South East Asian economy seen as nearest to 'take-off' was Burma (Thompson 1949; Morawetz 1977).

Mainline population projections: surprise-free futures

With that caveat, what does Indonesia's demographic future now look like? Probably the most plausible aggregate trajectory is one of the 'surprise-free' projection series constructed by the United Nations or the World Bank. The most recent available are the 1994 UN series and the World Bank's 1994-95 series (UN 1994a, 1994c; Vu, Massiah and Bulatao 1994). The initial (1990-95) parameters of both agree well with the findings of the 1994 Indonesian Demographic and Health Survey.

Indonesia's current total fertility rate (roughly, the average lifetime number of children born per woman) is about 2.9 and the annual population growth rate about 1.5 per cent. In the UN medium-variant projection, fertility drops to replacement level by 2010 and remains there (for the World Bank, the equivalent year is 2005). The population growth rate is sustained by the still large proportions of the population at childbearing ages (the so-called momentum effect), but nevertheless drops steadily, falling below 1 per cent per year by 2015

---

[1] Looking at how past population projections in general have fared as predictions, rather than picking out a single apparent success case, gives a sobering result. Standard errors of medium estimates stay reasonably constant for some 30 years, then mount rapidly. For the current UN medium global population forecast for 2100, 11 billion, the results of experience suggest there is a one-in-three chance of the actual population being less than 7 billion or more than 16 billion. See Lee (1991); the standard-error studies are Keyfitz (1981) and Stoto (1983).

This is the track of the later phase of a fairly rapid demographic transition. What always surprises people who are not familiar with population dynamics is the amount of puff in the final gasp of the transition. By 2050, in this scenario, the population will have expanded by more than 50 per cent—adding another 100 million people. Indeed, growth would continue even longer: the ultimate stationary population implied by the World Bank's projection is 355 million, almost exactly double Indonesia's 1990 population.

This outcome can be compared with that projected for other populous countries. The World Bank's figures for the ten largest countries as of 1995 are shown in Table 15.1. (The comparable UN figures depict slightly larger populations in the later years.) The last column of the table gives the expected percentage increase to 2050: the increase for Indonesia, though substantial, is appreciably less than projected for India and Bangladesh, and much less than for Pakistan and Nigeria. (In this dubious league table, by 2050 Pakistan has moved ahead of Indonesia to become the fourth largest country, Japan has dropped out of the ten, and Ethiopia has moved into eighth place.)

The last three rows of the table show the corresponding figures for the other populous ASEAN countries. Indonesia's expected growth is similar to Thailand's, and is well below the increase projected for the Philippines and Vietnam.

Much can happen to alter these population futures, and almost certainly will. In particular, there is no obvious reason why fertility should flatten out exactly at the replacement level of 2.1 children. For Indonesia, the UN's 'high' and 'low' projection variants in the 1994 series bracket that assumption with two other possibilities: one having fertility converge to 2.6, the other to 1.6—i.e., a 2-3 child average family and a 1-2 child average. The differences in the resulting population trajectories are dramatic (totals, in millions):

	2000	2010	2020	2030	2040	2050
Low	210	229	242	251	253	247
Medium	213	240	264	287	305	319
High	215	250	286	324	363	402

**TABLE 15.1: World Bank population projections (in millions)
and projected population increase (per cent), Indonesia and
selected other countries, 1995-2050**

	1995	2000	2025	2050	% incr. 1995-2050
Ten most populous countries in 1995					
China	1,199	1,255	1,471	1,556	30
India	934	1,016	1,370	1,623	74
United States	263	276	323	335	27
Indonesia	**193**	**206**	**265**	**304**	**58**
Brazil	161	172	224	254	57
Russia	149	150	153	152	2
Pakistan	130	148	243	316	144
Japan	125	127	124	115	-8
Bangladesh	121	132	182	218	80
Nigeria	111	128	217	288	159
Other populous ASEAN countries					
Vietnam	74	82	117	142	92
Philippines	69	77	115	143	107
Thailand	61	65	81	91	51

Source: Vu *et al.* 1994: 270-1.

In a nutshell, according to these projections, the 2050 population of Indonesia could be close to 250 million and beginning to fall; 320 million and still just growing (by a million or so per year); or 400 million and adding 4 million a year. Given this range, the difference between the medium-variant UN's 319 million for 2050 and the World Bank's 304 million is inconsequential.

The accumulating experience of low-fertility populations around the world would suggest that long-run average fertility is more likely to lie below than above 2.1. Average fertility in Europe in the early 1990s was 1.6, in the US 1.9, in Japan 1.5, in South Korea 1.7, and in Taiwan 1.7. (Of course, any such average could accommodate substantial swings in the birth rate. Family size is governed not only by secular changes in society and economy but also by business-cycle effects and by apparently arbitrary shifts in cultural attitudes towards the family.[2]) On balance, then, we can guess that Indonesia's population will top out at less than 300 million—conceivably, much less. A fairly conservative surprise-free forecast would be for an additional population in the range 50-100 million.

The smooth transition scenarios I have been discussing are instances of what Ronald Lee (1991) terms 'forecasting without feedback'. There is no systems model extending beyond the strictly demographic domain that supports the trajectories generated. There is no negative feedback on mortality or fertility resulting from sheer numbers of people. Yet, at least in the early decades, the scenarios are not simple extrapolations. The assumptions of secular mortality and fertility decline embody a large chunk of theory about the systematic connections between demographic trends and socio-economic development (albeit—oddly—theory that many demographers are at pains to reject[3]).

---

[2] The relative frequencies of childlessness and of one-, two-, and three-child families (this seems to be virtually the full extent of childbearing options under modern economic conditions) and the timing of births, will be a consequence of radically decentralised decisions, but decisions that reflect society-wide economic and social pressures and inherently unpredictable 'bandwagon' or 'cascade' effects. Societies may therefore have to live with potentially large fluctuations in annual numbers of births.

[3] Perhaps because demographers do reject it, the projections are sometimes used as a stimulus for action rather than as a statement of expectation. The contraceptive-supply requirements that would be needed if the medium-variant trajectory is to be attained are computed, and the trajectory in effect is set up as a target.

Regional population distribution and settlement patterns

Discussions of Indonesian population trends usually highlight the density contrasts between the major regions of the country: Java, we are told, is so dense; the rest (in the main) so sparse. The large differentials seem to be of endless fascination: and a kind of affront that calls for policy action, as if they violated some ideal norm of uniformity. That, surely, has been one motivating factor behind the transmigration program. Of course no such norm exists. Uniformity might sometimes be approached in a purely agrarian economy, but a major dimension of development everywhere is economic *concentration, of* human resources as well as capital. In this process, as a necessary statistical fact, regional densities lose most of their information content.

Java's share of the total population has been falling slowly, from about two-thirds at the time of independence to just below 60 per cent today, driven both by fertility differences and by net outmigration. The combined population of the regions outside Java currently increases yearly by about 1.7 million; Java, by 1.4 million. In an Indonesia of, say, 250 million, Java's share may well still be above one-half. But predictions here are treacherous. Regional fertility differentials may narrow in the future with agricultural frontiers closed and urbanisation well advanced, but age-structure and migration effects may become more important in influencing regional population growth. Interregional migration, however, will increasingly be part of rural-urban or urban-urban movements: the major rural-rural flows that have contributed significantly to rural settlement outside Java are unlikely to be sustained much longer.

The broad outlines of Indonesia's future economic geography, and hence settlement patterns, are probably already set. In Java, non-agricultural employment will be centred in the large urban industrial areas extending out from the main cities of Java—especially Jakarta and Surabaya and their adjacent coastal strips and their corridors to Bandung and Malang; but also Semarang, Yogyakarta and Surakarta. The combined labour market that will be able to be tapped by these current and emerging urban-industrial areas potentially encompasses much of Java's population. Outside Java, other concentrations of industrial development in parts of Sumatra, Kalimantan, and Sulawesi will be associated with major export industries or established trade and migration links with neighbouring countries; in enclaves associated with service support for agribusiness and extractive industries; and in regions advantaged by certain other locationally distinct industries such as tourism. There will be corresponding 'backward' regions—perennially, Eastern Indonesia—where the global economy is much less felt and subsistence agriculture remains dominant. To some extent, governments can deliberately influence these patterns by investment allocation and other development policies, for example by improving surface transport and by designating free-trade zones. More important influences, however, lie deep in the past, in accidents of history (Batavia, for instance), given substance by the network and other externalities that make for increasing returns and given continuing relevance by the path-dependency of social and economic change (see Arthur 1988; Krugman 1991).

There are forces here that governments have little purchase over—and that those with free-market inclinations often prefer not to interfere with, even though the outcome may be to accentuate interregional inequality. China's strenuous efforts in the Maoist era to favour development of its interior provinces came to nought once the Dengist reforms freed up the entrepreneurial energies of Shanghai and Guangzhou. In Indonesia, starting with some of the same imperatives towards centralised economic management, an analogous retreat in (or loss of) economic control over dynamic regions distant from Jakarta is not implausible as growth continues. A half-century offers ample time for a possibility such as northern Sumatra emerging as a major economic player in sectors beyond its existing resource industries—rivalling if not eclipsing Java's industrial centres, in the manner of sunbelt-rustbelt shifts in the United States, with corresponding population flows.

For the most part, however, changes in Indonesia's broad regional demographic balance are likely to be glacial. The same cannot be said of the rural-urban balance. Indonesia is urbanising apace and will continue to do so. From a very low base at independence, the proportion urban increased slowly until about 1970 and rapidly thereafter. UN estimates and projections show the percentage in urban areas increasing as follows (UN 1995b):

1950	12	1995	35
1960	15	2000	40
1970	17	2010	50
1980	22	2020	57
1990	31	2025	61

This series does not extend beyond 2025. A plausible expectation would be for Indonesia in 2050 to have the proportion urban currently found in the forerunner economies of the region, South Korea, for example, which is now about 77 per cent urban. (The fraction is still increasing but very slowly.) With continued 4 per cent annual growth in per capita income, Indonesia would reach Korea's present economic level by mid-century (Hill 1996:241). At these high proportions urban, however, urban and rural residence become increasingly comparable in incomes, occupations, and access to government services and tend to lose whatever behavioural significance they once had. And as long-distance commuting becomes feasible, many rural communities are gradually transformed into *de facto* bedroom suburbs, whatever their formal designation. Urbanisation is effectively complete.

Equally important in describing the process of urbanisation are the changing growth rates of urban and rural populations. Indonesia's urban growth rate reached about 5 per cent per year in the 1970s and 1980s, but began diminishing in the 1990s and, in these projections, will have dropped to 2 per cent by 2025. The growth rate of the rural population has been virtually zero through the present decade. BPS estimates show a rural population of 124 million in 1990 and again in 1998, with a 'peak' of 125 million reached in 1994 (BPS 1994a). This stationary plateau, however, is made up of a rural population in Java that has been declining since the 1980s and one that in many other regions will still be increasing beyond 2000. Even if the urban-rural division fully coincided with a division between economic sectors, there is no sharp economy-wide 'turning point' such as that assumed in labour-surplus growth theory.

The demography of generations

Much of demography is to do with behaviour keyed to age. The changing age distribution of a population over time tells us much about the social and economic problems it is facing. And the array of age groups at a given time is the residue of the society's demographic history: each age group is a 'birth cohort' that has experienced a unique sequence of formative and deformative pressures. The behavioural identification of cohorts has been a significant categorisation in Indonesia's modern political history. It is also a mainstay of popular sociology.

The rate of change of particular age-groups in a population can differ markedly from the overall population growth rate. An important finding of the 1961 Indonesian census was the magnitude of the post-independence baby boom in the country. (That census was the first time the age distribution of the country had been recorded.) A paper written by Nathan Keyfitz and Widjojo Nitisastro in 1964, 'Age Distribution as a Challenge to Development', drew attention to the dramatic increase then taking place in the size of Indonesia's youth cohort: the annual number of people turning 15, in their definition.[4] If the census age data were accurate, this size was in the process of doubling over the 1960s. These youths were seen as claimants on the society and economy, demanding education and jobs. They were also, of course, as became evident in 1966 and 1967, contributors to political change, as members of KAMI for instance.

The baby boom contrasted with the earlier 'hollow' years of depression and war in the 1930s and 1940s, when birth rates (or, more strictly, birth-cum-child survival rates) were unusually low. And it was followed by the steady fall in fertility (and improvement in mortality) that gathered pace in the 1970s, as the economy grew and an energetic birth control program was mounted. Imprinted on the age distribution, these events have long-run implications. As a simple way of capturing these implications, we might divide the population into 20-year age groups (0-19, 20-39, 40-59, 60+) and compute the time-trends in growth rates for each category. This is done in Table 15.2.

---

[4] This was published as a chapter in the second edition of Keyfitz and Widjojo's book *Soal Penduduk dan Pembangunan Ekonomi* (1964).

TABLE 15.2: Population growth rates of 20-year age groups, Indonesia, decade averages 1950-2050, according to UN medium-variant projections (per cent per year)

	0-19	20-39	40-59	60+
1950-60	1.9	2.2	1.8	0.1
1960-70	2.6	1.6	2.1	2.1
1970-80	2.1	2.2	2.7	2.5
1980-90	1.0	3.1	2.0	3.7
1990-00	0.1	2.3	2.9	3.1
2000-10	-0.1	1.2	3.3	2.6
2010-20	0.0	0.3	2.6	3.5
2020-30	0.0	0.0	1.3	3.6
2030-40	0.0	0.0	0.5	3.1
2040-50	0.0	-0.1	0.1	1.8

Source: United Nations 1994c: 442-3.

- Under the assumption of replacement-level fertility soon achieved and maintained, and with the 1970s' fertility decline now showing up in a smaller reproductive-age population, the population below aged 20 ceases growing in the 1990s. With the numbers pressure easing, educational resources, it can be hoped, will increasingly be directed towards raising the comparatively low secondary school enrolment rates and towards quality improvements.
- The 20-40 population—those at peak labour force ages—is still expanding rapidly: 57 million in 1990, 72 million in 2000, 81 million in 2010. But the slackening is apparent after 2000, and there is little further growth after 2010. We can be more precise about labour force entrants, or at least entry to labour force ages: measuring this by one-fifth of the age group 15-20, the annual numbers of entrants

have been growing fast in recent decades (from 1.9 million in 1960 to 4.3 million in 1995), but from now on will be virtually constant—the pay-off from the fertility decline. (Under the low-variant projection the number starts decreasing after about 2010.) Continued strong economic growth combined with this demographic supply constraint should be felt in upward pressures on base-level wages, though the supply may also be affected by changes in labour force participation rates, especially of women.

- The numbers at older labour force ages—the 40-60 year range— follow the same pattern of declining growth but two decades later.
- Finally, the 60+ population, its numbers reflecting the birth and child-survival trends of long ago and current and expected improvements in adult mortality, grows faster than Indonesia's population as a whole ever has. The absolute numbers make a striking progression (in millions, with percentage of population in brackets):

1950	5	(6)
1970	6	(5)
1990	12	(6)
2010	21	(9)
2030	42	(15)
2050	69	(22)

Ultimately, if life expectancy rises as predicted, nearly one-third of the population would be in this age group.

There is nothing unusual about Indonesia in these trends. They mirror those of any population that has undergone fairly rapid fertility decline and steady mortality improvement. The absolute numbers are of course impressive: the 4 million-plus youths seeking entry jobs for the first time this year in Indonesia is close to the number for the rest of ASEAN together; it compares to 3.5 million in the United States. (The figure for China, however, is 20 million; for India, 18 million.)

Family futures: Asian exceptionalism?

In Western low-fertility societies, families are widely seen as in trouble. One-fifth or more of women may remain childless. For women generally, low fertility makes for increased commitment to the workforce; greater economic autonomy makes for lower rates of marriage and readier divorce; high geographic mobility weakens inter-generational ties. Family values remain important in political rhetoric but much less so in hard policy: public finance increasingly comes to treat citizens as individuals rather than as members of a family unit. Consensual unions and childbearing out of marriage become commonplace. Lower adult mortality makes for higher and more prolonged durations of old-age dependency, with strong pressures for the state to manage part of the necessary transfer payments—yielding the familiar imminent budgetary crisis as those payments balloon under population ageing, and familiar stop-gap measures to repair publicly financed pay-as-you-go pension schemes.

How much of this is in Indonesia's future? Historically, family systems have proved to be a peculiarly resilient feature of societies, with cultural distinctiveness in them maintained for long periods. While this historical constancy would probably not be sustained under modern urban-industrial conditions, the changes need not result in convergence to a single Western-style pattern. The Japanese family, for instance, remains distinctive in many respects. Certainly the rhetoric of some Asian governments suggest the expectation that in their bailiwick the social cohesion of the family unit, and in particular its socialisation and welfare functions, will not decay. Their critiques of Western society routinely include, along with general disapproval of social indiscipline, a disparaging comment on family dissolution, implying a determination not to follow suit.[5]

---

[5] Cf. the comment by a Roman Catholic cardinal in reference to the feminist-influenced draft Programme of Action for the 1994 Cairo population conference: 'the failed social policies of many developed countries should not be foisted on the world's poor' (*New York Times*, 15 June 1994).

Or is that more hope than expectation? In the long run, I believe there is little reason not to expect the strong pressures of urban life and high-consumption lifestyles to work their ways on families everywhere. Thus in Indonesia, patriarchal attitudes and behaviour, never as strong as in many other parts of Asia, will retreat further; individualism will increase (arranged marriages are already rare). Even if voluntary childlessness never approaches Western rates, one-child families may well become increasingly popular and the ready supply of close kin then necessarily diminishes. Attempts elsewhere to mandate the support of elderly parents by their children (or child)—for example, as in China's 1980 marriage law—seem to concede the trend towards a breakdown of voluntary intra-family transfers. But the attempt to coerce such transfers is probably in vain, amounting to an effort to finance a welfare state, so to speak, off the books.

The remarkable accomplishments of past development efforts in reducing poverty levels in Indonesia, working through broad rural and agricultural development programs and through expansion of schools and health services, cannot be relied upon to serve as a safety net for those with fragile claims on the social product. The comparatively low budgetary provisions for social insurance may be contingent on assumptions about private transfers that are reaching the end of their shelf life. Major policy deliberations concerning the scale and design of welfare-state institutions in Indonesia cannot be postponed for much longer—if they are not to be made by default, an option that would have the state continuing to take a minimalist welfare role, balanced no doubt by a continued stringent stance against social unrest.

Population and environment: issues and non-issues

First, the non-issues. It is likely that most kinds of environmental change, while important in some respects for productivity and in many respects for the quality of life, have no influence on the course of population growth. This goes against the views of a vociferous group that has retained the alarmist perspective of the early Malthus, whether influenced, like Malthus, by a view of human fallibility or, like modern ecologists, by distress at environmental degradation and awareness of the boom and bust cycles of animal populations. For the most part, demographers, in this respect like economists and sociologists, retain a fundamental belief in human resourcefulness and adaptability, whether through individual agency or through institutional design.

But there are exceptions. Degradation can be so drastic that public health is seriously damaged and death rates rise, or the economic base is destroyed and people must seek livelihoods elsewhere. Within a country such effects are usually associated with incompetent or corrupt government: the destruction of the Aral Sea basin, caused by misconceived Soviet agricultural policy, is a frequently cited case. Kasperson et al. (1995), who have studied endangered environments around the world (that is, environments endangered for human use— theirs is 'shallow' or 'light green' ecology), believe that the Aral region is beyond repair. In the same study, they have included Kalimantan among a group of regions where degradation, though well short of that stage, was nevertheless quite advanced. Avoidance of irretrievable degradation for such situations is a matter of scientific knowledge, political will, financial resources, good institutional design, and organisational capacity.

Environmental change may be inherently beyond the capacity of government to influence before the event. Natural disasters would often lie here, but so too do some anthropogenic changes. Increases in 'greenhouse' gases in the atmosphere may lead to thermal expansion of the oceans and rising sea-levels, and to other changes that will affect agricultural productivity and lowland coastal settlement. Although most likely to be gradual, giving ample response time for adjustment, there may be non-linear effects on a quite short time scale. See Soemarwoto (1991: 233) for a map of affected coastal regions in Indonesia.

Environmental change as a consequence rather than determinant of population change should also be mentioned. Java already has a population density above that of Bangladesh and more than twice that of the Netherlands, or, a nearer comparison, of Honshu. In prospect, as we have seen, is an additional 25-50 million people, living in urban or suburban communities and with much higher levels of per capita income than at present. Higher disposable incomes are transformed not only into consumer durables but also into the 'consumption' of space: in recreational activities and through private vehicle ownership and discretionary travel. This is hardly a pleasing prospect to persons who value the natural environment. It need not be incon-

sistent with retention or re-creation of considerable amenity value in
nature (though wilderness may be too much to ask for). Achieving
such a future for Java, however, will be a very large task.

A different but complementary kind of amenity must be sought
locally for the residents of Jakarta. The population within the administrative boundaries of the Daerah Khusus passed 9 million in 1994 and
is expected to reach 10 million in 2000 (Biro Pusat Statistik 1994). The
UN's more vaguely delimited Jakarta 'urban agglomeration' is estimated to have encompassed 11.5 million persons in 1995, making it
the world's eleventh largest city, and to reach 21 million in 2015,
making it fifth (after Tokyo, Bombay, Lagos, and Shanghai, and almost equal with São Paulo and Karachi; see UN 1995b). Population
growth has been slowing, but not the income-linked congestion effects
of automobile numbers that are increasing annually by 12 per cent
(*Jakarta dalam Angka 1994*) or the water supply, flooding, waste disposal, and air pollution problems that planners will be confronting for
many years to come. Such problems tend to be disguised to the
outsider by the identification of the city with its modern core of high-
rise housing, shopping malls, hotels, and business offices: what McGee
and Yeung (c1993) call the 'city of consumption and spectacle'. Jakarta
along with Bangkok, Shanghai, and quite a few other megalopolises,
combine such cores with surrounding low-income housing, squatter
settlement, open markets, and small-scale commerce, producing 'a
kind of layering of the built environment in which the modern city is
high rise connected by "flyover" for automobile transport that passes
over the "lower order" city, reminding one of the architectural fanta-
sies of the Buck Rogers science fiction cities of the future'—and promising 'continuing battle for urban space between the two classes that
inhabit the city' (*ibid.* 64-65).

'Surprise' scenarios

So much for routine expectations; what about the non-routine? True
surprises, genuinely new and consequential happenings, are impossible to discuss in any systematic fashion and by definition cannot be
assigned subjective probabilities. I prefer to take a more expansive
definition, allowing for events that fall under familiar categories but
that are unanticipated when and where they occur or in many of their
details. Here are the usual suspects.

Economic reversals:

Rates of growth that double the size of national economies in less than a decade have become routine in East and South East Asia. The detailed patterns are described in the breathless anecdotes of John Naisbett's *Megatrends Asia* (1996). In the more measured tones of the ANU's Asia Pacific Economics Group (in *Asia Pacific Profiles 1996*), the strong South East Asian economies, Indonesia included, 'are firmly on a path to high incomes and deep integration into an advanced international economy' (p.24). Halloran (1996), citing World Bank and CIA sources, gives a rank order of world economies in 2020 as follows (with ppp GNP estimates in trillion 1995 US dollars): China (20), US (13), Japan (5), India (4.8), Indonesia (4). If taken as prediction rather than mere extrapolation these would be remarkable figures—though hazardous: ten years earlier, the CIA would probably have put the Soviet Union in the middle of the list.

But the received picture of thriving miracle economies in South East Asia, moving along the track first beaten by Japan and subsequently negotiated by South Korea and Taiwan, is not the only future that can be visualised. Paul Krugman, that notable disbeliever in the Asian miracle, slyly remarks of the hypergrowth economies that 'there may be one or two Brazils out there' (*Economist*, 9 December 1995: 33-34). Or Mexicos: Indonesia, along with Thailand and China, are seen by some as potential candidates for a Mexico-style economic crisis. (Australia, far from a hypergrowth performer, is too.)

A severe economic reversal has major adverse effects on welfare; its demographic effects, on the other hand, may be quite muted. Fertility decline, to the extent it is driven by the gap between economic aspirations and realities, may be largely unaffected. (Brazil's fertility trended downward regardless of its economic course.) Mortality is perhaps less insulated, although mortality levels are to a significant degree a function of education and individual 'health-seeking' practices, matters not subject to short-run fluctuations: the reversal in Russian mortality would be the main counter-example, but that has been largely attributed to life-style factors. Migration is the most common demographic response to economic crisis, mainly comparatively short-range movement to the larger cities where subsistence claims against the government can be more effectively exercised.

A more general, 1930s-type, economic depression affecting trading economies worldwide would be a different matter. Indonesia in the early 1930s experienced a collapse of exports and substantial reversion to a subsistence economy; the demographic consequences on births and child deaths were severe—evident through careful analysis of later age distributions (see US National Research Council 1987: 25-8). The vastly more complex economy of today is likely to be no less vulnerable, though capacities for public response are of course much greater.

Political turmoil

Scenarios in which Indonesia's demographic future would be significantly influenced by domestic political conditions seem comfortably remote. To those who knew Indonesia in the 1950s and 1960s this is a remarkable state of affairs. We might contrast Indonesia's course in this respect with that of Pakistan, a country that could once have seemed similarly placed. Pakistan's health services are in shambles, fertility transition has barely begun, and government administrative capacities—including any purchase it might have over demographic trends—seem to be diminishing rather than expanding.[6] Indonesia's political and administrative conditions could hardly be more different. In Indonesia, the next decades will plausibly see a steady move away from authoritarian government, following patterns of political development familiar in some other parts of the region, together with the institutionalisation of succession arrangements. The certainty of cautiousness in the management of this process should preclude potential faultlines in the society (religious, ethnic, regional, and class) opening too wide, though experience elsewhere shows the many possibilities for miscalculation.[7] As before, however, even substantial glitches along the way may be of limited demographic significance.

---

[6] Robert Kaplan (1996:329), admittedly a somewhat jaundiced observer, describes Pakistan as 'a decomposing polity based more on criminal activities than on effective government'.

[7] In looking to Indonesia's future, Hal Hill (1996, chap. 12) remarks on the 'continuing ethnic schism' between Chinese and *pribumi* as a source of concern, and, under the heading 'holding the country together,' he points to 'the divides between "inner" and "outer" Indonesia, between East and West, and between the four major mineral exporting provinces (Aceh, East Kalimantan, Riau, and Irian Jaya) and the rest of the country'.

At the international level, long-range political predictions are particularly foolhardy, especially for a period and region in which there will be major shifts in economic (and military) as well as population relativities. Indonesia somehow entirely avoids being mentioned in Samuel P. Huntington's (1993) apocalyptic vision of 'the clash of civilizations' in the post-Cold War world: it just does not seem to fit, certainly not in the oddly-described grouping of 'Islamic-Confucian states', the putative China-Middle East axis that Huntington sees emerging. Futurists less inclined to relinquish nation-states as salient actors find plenty of potential action in Pacific Asia, notwithstanding the mesh of overlapping pacts in economic and security affairs that increasingly cover it.

Natural disasters

For surer demographic impact there is a now familiar list of calamities originating in the natural environment or in its overstressing by human activity. By and large these are not country-specific. Consider, for instance, whether Indonesia could ever experience a serious food shortage. The price responsiveness of food production, both domestically and in the major grain-exporting countries, make this highly unlikely for a country that is now well above subsistence levels of consumption. Average cereal yields in Indonesia are still a third less than in Japan, giving appreciable further scope for expansion (Dyson 1996:189). Shortages are thus not likely to creep up on the country.[8] Increased grain imports, if needed to make up for partial crop failure, would be readily afforded, though displacing less creditworthy customers (food availability problems in many poor countries are still very much with us). Almost the only scenario that might defeat these responses is one that entailed massive simultaneous crop failures in some of the major producing regions; from new crop diseases, or from atmospheric aerosols and particulates (as in the great 1815 eruption of Gunung Tambora on Sumbawa, that caused the northern hemi-

---

[8] Economic mismanagement and political folly can turn 'routine' crop failure into major disaster, as happened in the great Chinese famine of 1959-61 in which excess deaths were over 20 million. A preventative strategy would rely on effective markets and information systems on the one hand and policies to avoid 'entitlement' collapses on the other.

sphere's 'year without a summer'), or from discontinuous climate change. Such eventualities have low but non-zero probability.[9]

Simulation studies do not support a large role for famine in past population growth (see Watkins and Menken 1985). Disease is another matter. The 'great mortalities' of human history have been chiefly attributable to disease. Effects of new or newly virulent pathogens appearing in an unprotected population were seen in the bubonic plague in medieval Europe and the Euro-Asian diseases in the post-Columbian New World. Density of settlement and intensity of contact across human societies have today virtually eliminated population isolates. But humanity as a whole is a kind of isolate with respect to some animal pathogens—HIV being only the most recent example, according to the prevailing theory about its origin. AIDS is not—and with care will not become—a significant cause of death in Indonesia, unlike Thailand and Thailand's northern neighbours (Chin 1995). But the AIDS epidemic reveals the fragility of the assumption that a unilinear mortality decline is all but inevitable. The current resurgence of a raft of other infectious diseases, aided by the growing resistance of bacterial pathogens to available antibiotics, reinforces the point.

Concluding remarks

Discussing the world of 2050 would be a fool's game if one waited around to see what happened. Since I will not, it is a safe enterprise. But my conclusions are also uncontroversial. Demographically, Indonesia is moving in and into familiar territory. Its population trajectory resembles that of many other countries of the region, indeed of the world, a similarity that extends also to its projected course in the

---

[9] Tambora-scale events are given an average frequency of once per 100-200 years. (The 1963 Gunung Agung eruption was two orders of magnitude smaller.) The so-called nuclear winter scenario would be a human-caused analogue. Discontinuity in climate change—a sudden regime shift—or in ecosystem response are increasingly recognised possibilities that lie largely outside the scope of current modelling (see Darmstadter and Toman 1993).

future.[10] There are large uncertainties about the size of the ultimate peak population, but proportionately no more than there are for most other countries. The implied age-structure changes, population ageing in particular, are necessary consequences of the emerging low-fertility regime. The regional distribution of the population is largely set by existing patterns. Family changes are less predictable but experience elsewhere suggests the possibilities.

Absorption of these increases and adjustment to the changes are nevertheless a major task, coinciding as it does with the country's economic transformation, with its urbanisation, and with a sustained rise in per capita consumption. Indonesia's society and physical environment have somehow accommodated an increase of 100 million to the population in the last 35 years, though with evident strains on both institutions and ecosystems. As many as another 100 million people may be waiting in the wings. The proportionate increases are not unusual; the absolute magnitudes, significant for many issues of governance, have few parallels.

There are things to go wrong. (Outlooks for Indonesia have become so sanguine that most risks are downside.) A smooth advance to economic prosperity, a fully tranquil development of civil society with accompanying retreat of state roles, and the absence of any environmental crises along the way, are hardly to be expected, though I have suggested that demographic change may be comparatively insensitive to a range of economic, political, and environmental disturbances. Larger changes in international conditions may be a more important source of demographically-relevant surprise.

I should comment, finally, on a subject that is perhaps pointedly omitted in the above discussion: the government's family planning program. In the usual interpretation, a jump-started fertility decline has been one of the New Order's notable programmatic successes. Viewed in a longer time frame, however, we could say that the political

---

[10] I have tended to choose East and South East Asian countries for comparison. Other choices (India? Iran?) would also be instructive in some respects. I note, however, the recent story Ben Barker (1995:245) recounts of resident diplomats in Nigeria warning a visiting foreign expert 'not to compare the country to Indonesia because "it infuriates the Nigerians"'.

turbulence and economic mismanagement of the 1960s delayed the onset of a fertility decline that would otherwise have been the predictable accompaniment of orderly economic and social development (as in Taiwan and Thailand, where the declines date from the 1950s and 1960s respectively). The Indonesian program's vigour and occasional strong-arm methods were needed to catch up. China's course was quite parallel: Maoist pronatalism and the disorder of the Cultural Revolution gave way to a high-pressure birth control effort in the 1970s, the famous 'later-longer-fewer' campaign, that halved fertility over the decade.

Does the current level of Indonesian fertility and its pace of decline depend on continued government propagation and subsidy of modern contraception? The World Bank, always more statist in this sphere than in others, seems to believe so; for example, expressing scepticism of the feasibility of more than nominal user fees for family planning services (World Bank 1990). The Family Planning Board has an institutional interest in concurring—or finding other work to do. The alternative position, more plausible *a priori* though of course untested in this case, is that fertility patterns are roughly on a track dictated by the exigencies of family life and a competitive labour market under rapid social and economic change, with fertility headed to a level somewhat below replacement. We should hope that this position is correct. Since government interference in family size decisions can hardly be long sustained over the course of political development, a desired and achieved total fertility rate that stalled at a level significantly above two could quite quickly saddle Indonesia with an additional 50 or (in the UN's high-variant case) 100 million people.

16

Defining a Future for Population Data

Terence H. Hull

This note poses, and partially addresses, three issues inspired by the papers presented to the 1996 Indonesia Update. These are:

1. Can Indonesian demography thrive in the twenty-first century if it continues to be dependent on dysfunctional bureaucratic systems of data collection?
2. Is the apparent accuracy of the published indirect measures of demographic analysis real? Do the published numbers reflect the truth about the demographic patterns, and is the implied precision of calculations showing quite specific numbers to decimal places justified?
3. Does the focus on urban-rural, provincial, and educational differentials in fertility and mortality studies provide a sufficient basis for the study of the socio-economic setting of demographic trends?

It seems that in the foreseeable future the answers to these questions will be no. In part this is because of a lack of awareness of the nature and seriousness of the population data problems in Indonesia, but there is also a degree to which bureaucrats and political leaders might simply wish not to know (*tidak mau tahu*). At times political leaders press for numbers which achieve political goals, with little regard whether the statistics can be believed. There is also an illusion of accuracy created by the prevailing practices of official publication which give rise to serious misinterpretations of underlying demographic realities.

Dysfunctional bureaucratic systems of data collection

To speak of the bureaucratic systems of data collection as being dysfunctional is to point to a more important issue than simple coverage and regularity of data collection. The Central Bureau of Statistics (BPS), often in collaboration with other government agencies, has done an excellent job of designing and implementing surveys and censuses from which it is possible to estimate some simple measures of fertility and mortality. However experts are quick to point out a wide range of chronic shortcomings which should be rectified, and in the absence of correction, must be kept in mind when interpreting the results of analyses. Among the most serious are the lack of routine calculation and publication of standard errors of estimates which underlie all measures based on sample surveys. Rather than quoting total fertility rates to two decimal places, the expression should be a figure plus or minus the error in estimation inherent in small sample sizes. In some cases the standard errors would be large enough to throw into question the significance of the apparent difference between two rates, and this is important information for any policymaker attempting to monitor demographic trends.

Another common shortcoming is the failure of many researchers to consider the deeper issues of validity and the potential for confusion in the translation of questions and responses between a number of languages. Indonesia's rich cultural heritage is reflected in the large number of quite distinct languages used by its people, yet most researchers fail to address the problems of translating Indonesian-language questions accurately into Javanese, Batak, Balinese, or the hundreds of other languages used in daily conversation in the Archipelago. If interviewers handle these translations on an *ad hoc* basis, and fail to follow guidelines for interpretation set out by the Central Bureau of Statistics, we have no way of determining whether the respondents truly shared an understanding of the concepts underlying the questions. In most cases the distortions are probably minor, but when it comes to preferences, attitudes and feelings ('how many children would you like to have') the nuances can be subtle, and when it comes to culturally based institutions ('are you married?') the range of interpretations of behavioural facts can be very wide, and encompass quite contrasting conditions. At the very least there would seem to be a case for the development of standard lexicons for the interpretation of common survey and census concepts across the many languages of

Indonesia. Better still would be the development of data collection designs which have budgets to carry out local analyses of the impact of translation on the meaning of the results.

From another viewpoint Indonesia's increasing integration in global economic and intellectual systems means that translation of standard questionnaires from English is increasingly the norm, as evidenced in the Demographic and Health Surveys which receive technical assistance from a US-based organisation, and parts of the decennial population censuses which look to the family of United Nations organisations for suggestions of effective instruments of data collection. International collaboration maintains a dialogue between Indonesian and English through many stages of the activity, right up to the construction of tables, and the preparation of final reports. Again, it is difficult to attain close matches of meaning between Indonesian and English in the tables and the interpretations of patterns of response, particularly when the subject relates to expressions of feelings or reports of the operation of unique cultural institutions. Foreigners seeking to understand the 'private' health sector in Indonesia can be seriously misled if they do not understand that virtually all government health practitioners have evening practices which are 'private' but which may utilise the facilities and supplies of the public sector. Conversely the public clinics may tell patients to buy medicines and supplies from private pharmacies before they can obtain the 'free' government services. In such cases translation is not merely a matter of searching for words in a dictionary; it requires explanations of the meaning of a wide variety of complex social institutions.

Two of the most effective tools for dealing with these issues are not widely used. First is the systematic and open testing of question design and implementation through carefully constructed pre-tests of survey instruments. The Central Bureau of Statistics regularly carries out such tests, but does not publish the results. As a result the efforts are neither studied by professionals for their own edification nor criticised by professionals who might have specialist knowledge of the languages or concepts in use.

Second is the routine implementation and publication of post-enumeration surveys. These are checks by highly trained supervisors of the interviews carried out by regular field staff. In the revisits the supervisors ask a subset of the questions from the original interview to see the extent to which the answers are the same. Any difference may be due to several factors—a difference in wording, a real change in the behaviour or opinions of the respondent, or even a difference in respondents. Post-enumeration surveys also serve to check on the honesty of the interviewers. Sadly, they are seldom carried out in Indonesia, and when implemented almost never fully analysed or published. They offer the opportunity to estimate the degree of non-sampling error inherent in particular questions but this is regarded as embarrassing to the data collector. They also provide a foundation for correcting the results, either formally through a correction factor, or informally through the placement of emphasis in the analytical report.

Other important types of dysfunctional bureaucratic systems which inhibit the collection of useful demographic data are the systems which are too complex and vexed by conflicts of authority to produce routine data on events or activities. For instance, the lack of routine national and regional data on births, deaths, illness, and medical treatments seems to be more a problem of organisation and commitment in the Ministry of Health than a problem of difficulty of data recording. Similarly, the constant complaint over lack of birth and death registration figures is more a problem of sorting out the political authority to run the system than it is a difficulty of encouraging citizens to register and report. When vital registration began in the early part of the century it was designed as part of the responsibility of the Ministry of Health. The notion was that doctors would be the key people responsible for recording births and deaths since they were most likely to be aware of the events. Later the responsibility shifted to the civil bureaucracy under the Ministry of Internal Affairs and the assumption was that the hamlet or neighbourhood heads would be most likely to learn of vital events in their region, and report them to higher authorities. Over the years the Central Bureau of Statistics, the State Ministry of Population and the National Family Planning Program have all expressed some interest and claimed some authority for the registration of births and deaths, but the registration system remains marginalised as a source of demographic data. The discussion among different government agencies is not always happy or productive, as demonstrated in the Ministry of Internal Affairs' frosty rejection of the idea of a national population registration number (*Nomor Induk Penduduk*) proposed by the Minister for Population.

Though politicians sometimes comment that the citizens lack the skills, motivation or education to participate in registration systems, the evidence seems to weigh more heavily on the shortcomings of the

Government to provide the organisation, co-ordination and budgets to make the system work. Demographers may speak out on the short-comings of the data system, though many are too intimidated by the frowns of the powerful to make much of the problems, and they may put forward suggestions for improvements, but recent history sug-gests that their voices fall on deaf ears. Thus it is difficult to imagine how Indonesian demography will thrive in future, if the politicians and policy-makers refuse to acknowledge the need for change.

Illusions of accuracy

More subtle problems arise in the interpretation of what the BPS produces, and the understanding of the limits of the information they publish. On this score bureaucrats from the highest to the lowest levels make innumerable mistakes. Sometimes they are simply naive, as in the famous controversy in the 1980s when the rate of population growth was both miscalculated and misinterpreted. A published growth rate of 2.34 captured the public imagination because the numbers 2-3-4 were the name of a popular brand of kretek cigarette. Quickly the population count became known as the 2-3-4 Census and public discussion focused on the seemingly magic number given as the growth rate. Unfortunately the calculation was incorrect because it failed to adjust for the inclusion of areas in the 1980 Census which had not been part of the 1971 count. Most seriously the analysts included the over 500,000 population of East Timor with no adjust-ment for the fact that it had been a Portuguese colony in 1971. Rather than 2-3-4 the true number was variously estimated as 2.33 or 2.32, but in any case might have simply been expressed as around 2.3. Then the incorrect estimate was taken to be a sign that the family planning program had 'failed' because the growth rate had not fallen dramati-cally. In fact the rate of population growth has only a tenuous link with current fertility rates, and fertility rates themselves give only part of the picture of the effect of a program dedicated to provision of contraception to the population. Rather than a failure, the correct analysis of the 1980 Census showed that the fertility rate had fallen substantially, and this was claimed as a success for the BKKBN. It took the BPS and the BKKBN the remainder of the decade to educate policy-makers and journalists on the intricacies of these relationships, and to focus their attention on total fertility rates rather than popula-tion growth rates in evaluating family planning programs.

Yet even today the effort to create an informed audience for demographic statistics is hampered by the persistence of illusory accuracy in the calculations. Sometimes this is related to the publication of over-specific figures: rates to three or four decimal places, or huge, complex tables based on elaborate assumptions and relying on theoretical models while hiding the limitations of the actual measurements carried out in the field. In fact, we often have very little basis for confidence in estimates of such important statistics as the Maternal Mortality Ratio, the expectation of life at birth or the current use of contraception. The samples are small, the questions on surveys are often confusing and the techniques of data manipulation are crude. This does not mean that the figures are useless. They can be very useful, but must be interpreted with caution and a full understanding of the assumptions and technical procedures on which they are based.

Expanding dimensions of the socio-economic

Demographic and other statistics provide descriptions of the structure and function of societies. Birth rates, death rates and migration rates are descriptions of behaviour, and indicators of social function and social change. In conjunction with other social measures, like the possession of education, participation in the formal work force and place of residence, close examination of the levels and trends of demographic measures gives insights into the workings of society and suggests areas in which beneficial policies might be directed. Thus it is not surprising to find so many Indonesian surveys and censuses analysed in terms of these social measures. In particular women's education, husband's occupation, and urban-rural residence frequently appear as social measures which shape demographic changes. Yet to the average Indonesian the more critical factors in life are income and wealth. Often residence and occupation are only rough indicators of economic status, and education is a product rather than a determinant of economic standing; the well-to-do are best able to send their children to secondary and higher levels of education, which form the basis of future occupations. With some notable exceptions, though, few researchers examine measures of economic status in their analyses of demographic trends. The reasons why this should be so are complex and contentious, but at base there seems to be a degree of disquiet in discussions of economic differences because of the fear that this might open on to Marxian-style class analysis of social issues, a taboo in a society haunted by the ghosts of the communist-related conflicts of the 1950s and 1960s. Nonetheless, when analyses of income and wealth differentials of fertility and mortality have been carried out they have always been very fruitful of insights into social problems, and suggestions for policy improvements. In an age when much public discussion centres on issues of privatisation, fees for services, and community participation, it is imperative to understand how such changes would affect people of different income and wealth groups. To accomplish this requires both better and more regular measurement of economic status, the linking of economic measures to demographic statistics, and the development of a socially acceptable vocabulary for the discussion of economic analyses of demographic trends.

In short, Indonesian population studies in future face some difficult challenges. The weakness of current data systems and measures is something few policy-makers fully appreciate, and this makes suggestions for improvement fall on deaf ears. The appearance of accuracy produced by many demographic techniques discourages analysts from pointing out the margins of error, and warning politicians of the fragility of the estimates. Among some researchers the fear of addressing questions of economic status squarely blocks off one of the most important and potentially fruitful avenues of analysis. These are the types of challenge which could be ignored, but the costs, in terms of misunderstandings, political conflict, and inappropriate governmental plans, would probably be greater than the benefits of complacency.

17

From Fertility Control to Quality-Oriented Population and Human Resource Development Policies

Agus Dwiyanto

Introduction

Following the success in controlling its population growth in the last two decades, Indonesia is now faced with a new challenge of population and the development of human resources, as it prepares to enter the new century. Owing to changes in age structure, the country has witnessed a tremendous increase in its young and productive population. However, it is unfortunate that this development has been accompanied by a population characterised by low levels of education attainment, hence, having access to low quality jobs, and a high rate of unemployment. This raises concerns about the readiness of Indonesia to face the challenges of the new century, particularly in preparing its human resources to accommodate demands of a more open and competitive global economy.

This chapter describes the population profile of Indonesia (see Table 17.1) and highlights some population and human resource development (HRD) issues facing Indonesia as it prepares to enter the 21st century. It argues that Indonesia is now facing different population and HRD problems that require a major shift in policy from fertility-control policies to quality-oriented HRD policies. Thus, Indonesia needs a new vision to direct its HRD programs and activities. Moreover, variabilities in population and HRD issues among regions require the government to decentralise its population and HRD policy making, to be more responsive to their local problems. To support the implementation of the new vision in population policy, a re-engineering of public bureaucracies is desirable to make them committed to the new direction of population and HRD activities.

TABLE 17.1: Demographic indicators of Indonesia, 1993-2013

	1993	1998	2003	2008	2013
Total population ('000)	189,136	204,423	219,380	233,571	246,520
Males	94,317	101,953	109,419	116,493	122,939
Females	94,818	102,470	109,961	117,078	123 571
Growth rate (%)	1.66	1.51	1.37	1.20	1.01
Total fertility rate	2.87	2.60	2.38	2.21	2.06
Crude birth rate	24.5	22.5	20.9	19.0	17.2
Crude mortality rate	7.9	7.5	7.2	7.1	7.1
Infant mortality rate	58	50	43	37	31
Life expectancy	62.7	64.6	63.3	67.9	69.3

Source: BPS (1993) in Wilopo (1996).

The population profile of Indonesia in the 21st century

After a long and hard struggle to enforce systematic population and health policies, the government of Indonesia has successfully achieved significant population changes. The total fertility rate (TFR) has declined during the first stage of development from 5.3 in 1969 to 2.8 in 1994. It is projected that by the year 2000, the TFR will be close to 2.6. The same success story has been registered in reducing the infant mortality rate. During the same period, the government has successfully reduced the infant mortality rate from 153 to 55 per 1,000 live births. By the year 2003, it is projected that the infant mortality rate will have dropped to about 43. With all these successes, Indonesia has significantly slowed its population growth and changed its population structure. By now, some provinces like Yogyakarta, East Java, Bali, Jakarta, and North Sulawesi have reached replacement levels (Kasto 1996). However, because Indonesia already has a large population, it is projected that by the close of the century, its population will increase to more than 210 million (BPS 1993).

In addition, the success of Indonesia in reducing these fertility and mortality rates has fundamentally changed the age structure of its population. By the year 2000, there will be a decrease in the proportion of population aged 0-14 from 36.7 per cent in 1990 to 30.6 per cent, while the proportion of those aged 15-64 will increase from 59.5 per cent to 64.8 per cent during the same period. Simultaneously, the proportion of those aged above 65 years old will increase from 4.6 per cent to 6 per cent. These changes in the age structure might, however create new population problems.

One of the challenges facing the government, resulting from changes in the age structure, is the growing size of the population in the productive age, which will certainly increase the size of the work force. It is estimated that by the year 2000, the growing size of the workforce might create serious problems for the government if the labour market does not respond to this increase. Given the rate of job creation in the last decade, it is estimated that during the next five years the increase in the workforce will be much greater than that of available job opportunities. Thus, by the year 2000, it is estimated that problems associated with unemployment will be much more critical for the government than ever before.

The problem will be even more pressing among the more educated workforce, whose unemployment rate is higher than is the case for the less educated. Moreover, if the labour market becomes more open and competitive as the ASEAN free market takes shape in the year 2003, the unemployment rate of the educated workforce will be still higher owing to the migration of professional workers from other ASEAN countries. This might raise some political problems because people with high education qualifications tend to be more critical and powerful in agitating for their needs. If this issue is not carefully addressed, it might create serious problems for the government.

Another interesting feature of population issues facing Indonesia in the 21st century is the growing number and proportion of the elderly. This raises some policy issues, as social values and norms shift toward nuclear families. As indicated by the average number of family members, which has continuously declined in the last decades and will achieve 4.1 in the year 2000 (Effendi 1996), the norm of the nuclear family has been institutionalised in the community. This has implications for the lives of the elderly since most of them live separately from their children. The fact that public services and facilities for this age group are seriously lacking and the few available are mostly of low quality, has inevitably increased public concern. Thus, the socio-economic welfare of the elderly will be an important issue facing the government in the 21st century.

Looking at the population profile of Indonesia raises a number of questions. What are the population, social, and economic problems that will face Indonesia in the 21st century as a result of these population changes? How do these population indicators work in the different provinces, areas, and social economic status groups? What policies should be formulated to respond to these problems?

Population problems facing the government of Indonesia in the 21st century

From observation of the population profile of Indonesia in the 21st century, it is apparent that the government has successfully controlled population growth. This success in reducing fertility and infant mortality rates certainly creates new challenges and problems, such as the growing number of elderly people, the bigger proportion of the work force, and shift in the values toward nuclear families. These new phenomena will of course be more apparent in the immediate future and have to be properly addressed by the government.

Although it seems that the success in controlling population growth has not been matched by the same degree of success in improving the quality of population and human resources, it is clear that using some standard indicators to measure the quality of HRD such as school participation rate, infant mortality rate, and nutrition status, significant progress in improving the quality of human resources has been made. But there is still a long way to go.

Observing the educational attainment of the population 10 years and above provides an illustration of problems facing the government in improving the quality of human resources. Results of the 1993 Susenas (National Socio-Economic Survey) indicated that more than 76 per cent of the population 10 years and above has completed primary school or less, and about 11.3 per cent and 10.7 per cent respectively, completed junior and senior high school. Looking at the characteristics of the young population, i.e. those aged 15-29, as reported by the 1990 Census, indicates that 62 per cent have a very low level of education (primary school or less), their unemployment rate is about 6.5 per cent, 53 per cent work in the agricultural sector, and about 96 per cent of them have low-paying jobs (Kasto 1996). Although changes will certainly occur in future, it is expected that the characteristics of the population will not be much different in the year 2000, implying that there will still be serious deficiencies in the quality of human resources.

Another important issue facing the government of Indonesia in the 21st century is the gaps in population and human resource indicators between provinces, rural-urban areas, and among the poor and the rich people. As reported by CBS, the gaps in performance among provinces in various demographic and human resource indicators such as infant mortality rate, total fertility rate, education attainment, nutrition, and health are quite wide. Some provinces particularly in Java, such as Yogyakarta, East Java, Jakarta, and Bali have performed best in reducing their fertility and mortality rate during the last decades, while other provinces of the outer islands such as NTB, Central Sulawesi, Central Kalimantan, and some other provinces still have relatively high fertility and mortality rates. The same conclusion can be reached for human resource indicators such as education and health. This gap certainly contributes to the differences in demographic and human resource profiles between provinces of Indonesia, which might require different policies.

Variations in performance exist between groups, particularly between the poor and the rich, between the urban and rural locations, and between males and females, not only in demographic indicators but also other human resource indicators, such as health status, schooling, and access to social services (World Bank 1990b). The poor and rural people performed worse in both demographic and human resource indicators than the urban and rich. The gap in demographic and human resource performance is very much related to people's economic well-being, which is indicated by their average expenditures (*ibid.*). Since these tend to be very unevenly distributed, it is expected that these gaps in human resource performance will continue and even tend to widen in future.

In view of these problems, the close of the century is probably not going to be very easy for the government. Indonesia is facing more and bigger challenges, particularly in improving the quality of its population and human resources. Failure to respond to these problems will create difficulties for the government and the people in facing the open economy and global market in future years. As the labour market becomes more open, failure to improve the quality and competitiveness of human resources will worsen the already saturated labour market in Indonesia, with the migration of professionals and skilled workers from other countries and the unemployment of low-skilled Indonesians. Thus, the quality of human resources will be a key factor determining the sustainability of Indonesia's development and the cohesiveness of society.

Policy shifts

In regard to the problems facing Indonesia in the 21st century, a number of questions arise here: what next? What policy choices should be taken by the government to respond to these problems? What policies and programs are needed to make population and human resources a positive element in sustaining the development processes of Indonesia?

To address these questions, we should first look at the 1993 Basic State Policies (GBHN) which explicitly regard human resource development as equally as important as economic development. This indicates that the government perceives HRD as a strategic point to make the development process in Indonesia sustainable. The problem that arises here however, is that there is no national vision and policy which can give clear directions to human resource development activities. The situation is made worse by the fact that population and HRD in Indonesia involve highly fragmented bureaucracies which often develop their own visions biased toward their bureaucratic interests and norms. This is a potential obstacle to the effective implementation of HRD policies in Indonesia.

Judging from the population profile and problems facing Indonesia in the 21st century, a major policy shift is essential. After more than two decades, the government has been engaged in implementing very strong anti-natalist policies and successfully controlling population growth; it is about time, therefore, for the government to reconsider future challenges facing the Indonesian population and human resource development. The declines in fertility during the last decades have provided a chance for the government to pay more attention to other aspects of population problems: the quality of population and human resources. This does not mean that the government should abandon its fertility-control policies, but a more quality-oriented population and human resource policy should be formulated to meet challenges in the new century.

To facilitate a shift in orientation of these population policies from quantity-control to quality-improvement, a strong vision of future population and human resource development which emphasises quality has to be rebuilt and socialised into the bureaucratic and the public networks. This vision has to be clear and provide directions to relevant departments and ministries in formulating their policies and programs to improve the quality of the population and human resources.

It is apparent that the shift in policy from fertility-control to quality-improvement policies is not going to be an easy task. After decades of institutionalising bureaucratic norms and cultures to support fertility-reduction oriented policies through 'targetism' and other means, it is now time for the government to create new norms, values, and culture to sensitise the bureaucracies and policy makers with new challenges and issues facing them in the 21st century. Thus, a strong vision which emphasises population quality is necessary but is still not enough. It has to be followed by a strong commitment from the central government to transform this vision into reality.

As controlling fertility has been an obsessive ideology during the first stage of development, it is not surprising that the implementation of population and HRD policies has so far been biased toward fertility reduction. Family planning programs and activities, for example, have been merely directed at achieving demographic objectives, while their potential to contribute to the empowerment of women through their education and reproductive health has been disregarded. Under the old vision, any policy and program which threatened to disrupt the achievement of demographic targets tended to be abandoned. Since biases toward fertility-control objectives have lasted for so long and have been institutionalised in all levels of public bureaucracies, the implementation of the new vision will be difficult unless government transforms the new vision into more concrete population policies and programs.

In addition, the government of Indonesia should also re-engineer its public bureaucracy at all levels to support and sustain the achievement of the vision. This can be done by developing new measures of successful performance of bureaucrats. As widely understood, one key success of the implementation of fertility-control policies in

Indonesia is the use of target achievement for the use of contraceptives as an important criterion for the success of a *Bupati* and the head of a subdistrict (*Camat*). This has been an effective means for the government to drive the *Bupati* and the *Camat* to support family planning activities. Thus, because of much pressure and the desire to achieve the user target, *Bupatis* and *Camats*, with the use of their own creativity, have often used all the measures available to them, including coercion, to lure their reproductive couples to use contraceptives. As Indonesia is now facing a new era and challenge, government should change its tools to measure or evaluate the success of a *Bupati* and a *Camat* with an entirely new set of procedures which are relevant to the new challenges.

Another important policy shift which should be carried out by the government is to decentralise its population and HRD policies. The fact that there are big variations among provinces in population and HRD indicators reminds us that a national and uniform policy is probably not the best choice. More decentralised policies would be more able to address the problems and challenges facing provinces and local governments. Thus, the government should provide more autonomous power to the local governments to formulate their own population and HRD programs. In this way, local governments will be able to develop population and HRD policies and programs which are more responsive to their local needs and challenges. Under decentralised policy making, such provinces as Yogyakarta which have achieved a replacement-level fertility and have a growing proportion of elderly population may focus their efforts on enabling the elderly to make their lives healthy and productive, and reduce emphasis on family planning activities in favour of other programs. Other provinces which are facing different problems may formulate different population and HRD programs and policies which are suitable for their respective needs.

Both central and local governments should also pay more attention to the disadvantaged groups, such as women, the poor and the rural people. As noted earlier, these groups have performed worse than other groups in population and HRD indicators. Thus, specifically designed policies are needed to improve their access to HRD programs and activities. Otherwise, gaps in HRD performance may endanger the sustainability of the Indonesian development process.

The implementation of quality-oriented population and HRD policies as suggested here will only be successful if followed by a strong commitment by the government at both the central and the local government level. The implementation of these policies is also very costly and thus the government needs to allocate more funds to population and HRD programs and activities. But that is the price that Indonesia has to pay if it is to survive and thrive in the next century.

18

Implications of Indonesia's Future Population

Aris Ananta, Evi Nurvidya Anwar and Diah Suzenti

What is a projection?

A projection is not a prediction. A projection can be wrong and it must be able to be wrong. A projection is useless if it cannot be wrong.

Previous experience in Indonesia shows that the projections are indeed always wrong but the exercise is not wrong. In this case, it is even good to be wrong. Nitisastro (1970) and Iskandar (1976) are two examples of wrong and very useful projections.

Table 18.1 shows that even Nitisastro's Projection A (the most optimistic scenario) produces a population of 198 million in 1991, which is much above the 179 million according to the 1990 Population Census. The crude birth rate was projected to be 31.8 per 1,000 in 1986-91, which is above the realised 27.9 per 1,000 in 1986-89. It is interesting, however, that the projection of mortality rate is very close to what was realised. It was projected that life expectancy at birth would be around 62.5 years in 1991. Indeed, the life expectancy at birth was about 61.2 for males and about 65.0 for females in 1991-94.[1]

Thus, is the Nitisastro projection useless? No. Note that this projection was prepared using only data from the 1961 Population Census. It was prepared around the political, economic and social

---

[1] The data for 1991-94 is derived from information on infant mortality rate in the Indonesian Demographic and Health Survey (IDHS) 1994, which is, then converted into e_0 with the Regional Model Life Table of Coale and Demeny.

Aris Ananta, Evi Nurvidya Anwar and Diah Suzenti

TABLE 18.1: Nitisastro's population projections for Indonesia, 1961-2001

	Projection A		Projection B		Projection C		Projection D	
	Total population ('000)	Annual rate of increase (per 1,000)	Total population ('000)	Annual rate of increase (per 1,000)	Total population ('000)	Annual rate of increase (per 1,000)	Total population ('000)	Annual rate of increase (per 1,000)
1961	97,019		97,019		97,019		97,019	
		21.6		23.8		23.8		23.8
1966	108,058		109,166		109,166		109,166	
		19.8		22.0		23.2		21.8
1971	119,346		121,717		122,520		121,663	
		20.1		22.3		25.2		22.3
1976	132,062		136,022		138,787		136,012	
		23.5		25.7		29.8		24.9
1981	149,413		154,486		160,916		153,956	
		27.4		29.1		33.8		26.4
1986	171,393		178,454		190,217		175,702	
		28.6		30.1		35.6		26.0
1991	197,843		207,266		226,978		200,057	

Source: Nitisastro 1970: 206, Table 74.

conditions in the period of 1960-70. However, this projection contributed by influencing the government of Indonesia (and the society) to start being concerned about the potential negative effect of high population growth in Indonesia. The lesson from this projection was that Indonesia ought to make the effort to curtail the population growth rate—that reduction in the population growth rate will help speed up the economic performance. (The prevailing thought before the start of the New Order was that it was not necessary to talk about population growth. Indeed, a high rate of population growth was considered to be beneficial to the economy.)

Later on, using 1971 Population Census data, Iskandar (*ibid.*) revised Nitisastro's projection. He produced four scenarios, among which the most optimistic one was the fourth, which produced an NRR equal to one in the year 2001. Iskandar mentioned that this scenario was very optimistic, and the scenario would be observed only if the family planning program was highly successful. Indeed, he believed that the third scenario, where fertility decline is not as fast as in the fourth scenario, was more likely to happen.

In scenario 3, the number of population in 1991 was 197 million (Table 18.2), and it was still as big as 194 million in the most optimistic (fourth) scenario. TFR was projected to be still as high as 4.1 in scenario 3, and 3.6 in the most optimistic scenario. The result from the 1991 and

TABLE 18.2: Iskandar's population projections for Indonesia, 1971-2001(thousands)

	Scenario I	Scenario II	Scenario III	Scenario IV
1976	139,877	139,877	139,877	139,877
1981	159,837	158,761	157,639	157,131
1986	183,980	180,507	176,846	175,160
1991	213,072	205,480	197,412	193,634
1996	248,160	234,011	218,986	211,893
2001	290,500	266,191	240,676	228,667

Source: Iskandar 1976: 64-67.

1994 Indonesian DHS show that the TFR was already about 3.3 in the 1988-91 period and about 2.9 in the 1991-94 period. Thus even the most optimistic scenario of Iskandar's projection is still overestimating the size of population and fertility rate.

Indeed, the chosen scenario of the LD (Lembaga Demografi— Demographic Institute, Faculty of Economics, University of Indonesia) projection (Ananta and Adioetomo 1990) had shown that the most optimistic scenario of Iskandar's projection is very likely to happen in Indonesia. This results in TFR = 2.4 which produces NRR = 1, in 2001. LD's chosen projection shows that TFR will be 2.237 and expectancy of life at birth about 67.5 for females and 65.0 for males, which also produce NRR = 1, in the period of 2000-2005.

Therefore, Iskandar's projection is also wrong. Yet, it had been very useful since, at that time, the projection was widely used to show some possible scenarios of Indonesian population. When the planners (and the society) do not like the scenario, they have to make some interventions.

And this is what has been observed so far. Indonesia has carried out interventions so that the projections are always wrong, in the direction of better than projected. This should be called a desirable mistake.

In this spirit, this paper attempts to present some scenarios of Indonesian population up to the year 2025. It also illustrates some possible socio-economic implications of the population projection.

Projections of Indonesian population have been carried out by many different institutions. A number of such projections, all of them incorporating, at least, the results of the 1990 Indonesian Population Census, are presented in Table 18.3. It is clear that whoever produces the projection, there are general similarities across different projections. With this general similarity, the following sections discuss some socio-economic implications of the future Indonesian population. For convenience, however, the projection by LD will be used for exposition. See Table 18.4 for four scenarios of population projection according to LD.

TABLE 18.3: Indonesia's population according to various population projections, 2005 and 2020

	LD	GMU	WB	UN
2005				
Population ('000)	222,841	230,280	218,877	-
Net reproduction rate	1.001	1.000	1.026	1.030
Total fertility rate	2.237	2.600	2.324	2.230
E_0 (female)	67.50	71.00	63.45	70.30
E_0 (male)	65.00	68.00	63.45	66.10
Annual rate of increase	1.23	1.35	1.19	1.19
Percentage 60+	7.97	7.74	7.80	-
Percentage <15	28.11	30.30	28.59	-
2020				
Population ('000)	254,215	270,980	254,627	264,103
Net reproduction rate	0.828	-	1.000	0.990
Total fertility rate	1.800	2.100	2.190	2.100
E_0 (female)	70.56	75.9	67.42	-
E_0 (male)	66.4	72.0	67.42	-
Annual rate of increase	0.68	1.06	0.91	0.97
Percentage 60+	11.34	10.16	10.66	11.10
Percentage <15	22.09	24.17	24.59	23.60

E_0 = Life expectancy at birth.

LD = Lembaga Demografi (Demographic Institute, Faculty of Economics, University of Indonesia).

GMU = Population Studies Center, Gadjah Mada University.

WB = World Bank.

UN = United Nations.

Sources: Ananta and Anwar 1995a; BPS 1993; Sucipto and Tukiran 1995; Bos *et al.* 1995.

**TABLE 18.4: Four projections by Lembaga Demografi[a] for
population growth in Indonesia, 1995-2025**

	Chosen Scenario	Scenario 1	Scenario 2	Scenario 3
Population growth ('000)				
1995	194,800	196,155	194,540	192,918
2000	209,535	212,744	209,029	205,307
2005	222,841	228,380	222,088	215,852
2010	235,071	242,218	233,078	224,003
2015	245,699	254,014	241,605	229,349
2020	254,215	263,553	247,387	231,629
2025	261,441	270,628	250,326	230,892
Population growth (%)				
1990-95	1.66	1.80	1.64	1.47
1995-2000	1.46	1.62	1.44	1.24
2000-2005	1.23	1.42	1.21	1.00
2005-2010	1.07	1.18	0.97	0.74
2010-2015	0.88	0.95	0.72	0.47
2015-2020	0.68	0.74	0.47	0.20
2020-2025	0.56	0.53	0.24	-0.06

[a]Lembaga Demografi = Demographic Institute, Faculty of Economics, University of Indonesia.

Source: Ananta and Anwar 1995a.

When will zero growth occur?

Though the growth rate of population keeps declining, the total number of population will keep rising. It could reach 254 million in the year 2020. As shown in Figure 18.1, the most optimistic scenario will produce a number of 231 million, and the most pessimistic one will produce 263 million in 2020. If after 2020 the fertility rate fluctuates around the rate in 2015-2020 but the mortality rate continues to decline with the previous trend, the Indonesian population will reach its maximum at 278.1 million in 2045. After 2045 Indonesia will experience a negative population growth rate. The absolute number of population will decline.

FIGURE 18.1: Rate of population growth: Indonesia, 1995–2025

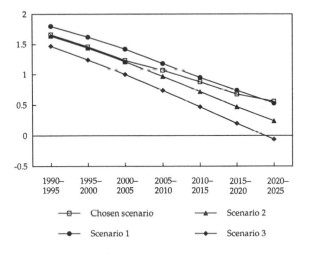

Source: Demographic Institute, FEUI (1995)

Yet, the declining number of population is not a cause for worry. Suppose that the population declines by 1 per cent annually. After 25 years, the year 2070, the Indonesian population will be 216.6 million, which is still larger than 194.8 million, the current (1995) Indonesian population. In the year 2100, after experiencing negative population growth rate for 55 years, the population will be 160.4 million, which is still larger than the population in 1971 (146.8 million). Thus, there is no need to worry about a declining number of total population for at least another 100 years.[2]

---

[2] It should be noted, however, that a negative rate growth can be achieved as soon as in the period of 2020-2025 if the future path of Indonesian population follows the third scenario. The third scenario assumes a continuous fast decline in fertility, even after NRR reaches 1.0. It also assumes that the population growth rate had been as low as 1.5 per cent annually in the period of 1990-95. Nevertheless, the authors believe that this third scenario is highly unlikely.

Whatever the future path of the Indonesian population, what policy makers should be concerned about is not merely the number, but the composition (and quality) of population. The provision of contraceptives to ensure that they are widely and cheaply available for the majority of the population still needs to be continued despite the already declining growth rate of population. A population with a negative growth rate, but with a labour force which is better educated and healthier, is a much better population than one with a positive growth rate but which is less educated and in poorer health.

However, the rising number of population, at least until 2020, will still have many implications for many different aspects of development planning. With the rising income per capita, for example, the still rising number of population also means a rising market.

Declining growth rate of population and employment

Though the number of population will keep rising, the rate of growth will keep declining. As shown in Figure 18.1, the chosen scenario results in the highest growth rate of population by the year 2025. This is because the chosen scenario assumes a smaller decline in fertility after NRR is equal to one.

Yet, whatever the scenario, the growth rate will keep declining. It will affect the growth rate and number of working age population, labour force and employment. As shown in Table 18.5, the rate of growth of working-age population, labour force and employment will keep declining. Those who read Indonesian literature on employment may be disturbed because of the projected rate of growth of employment.

In Indonesian literature on employment, 'employment' is often translated into *kesempatan kerja*, which literally means 'employment opportunity'. This assumes that every employment opportunity is translated into one working person; that an increase (decrease) in employment opportunities implies an increase (decrease) in the number of working persons. It should be noted, however, that one person may have several jobs. A decline (a rise) in economic performance may reduce (increase) the number of jobs one held and, at the same time, still maintain the same number of persons working.

The fact is that whenever the society is poor, everybody is forced to work, everybody is employed. Thus, the employment growth rate is usually influenced only by the growth rate of labour force and the population growth rate. Therefore, the projected decline in employment growth rate has nothing to do with the performance of economy in the future, it is simply a reflection of a declining population growth in Indonesia.[3]

Further, economic policies to improve labour conditions should not be measured by the growth rate of employment. The growth rate of employment tends to decline, simply because of the fast decline in fertility rate since the 1970s, and thus, in population growth rate.

Reduction in unemployment and underemployment?

Indonesia has no unemployment benefits. Those who are unemployed do not get anything from the government. The poor cannot afford to be unemployed because there is nobody who can support them while they are not working at all. The poor, instead, are forced to work at whatever can help them earn income. It is not surprising, therefore, that unemployment is always low in Indonesia. The rate was about 1.7 in 1980 (BPS 1983) and rose to about 3.2 per cent in 1990 (BPS 1992a). Ananta, Anwar and Wongkaren (1994) projected that the rate will rise to 5 per cent in the year 2005 and 8 per cent in the year 2020.[4] The unemployment rate will keep rising because of the rising income and education. Thus, reduction in (open) unemployment rate should not be used as a policy target. Open unemployment will decline only when the economic performance is poor and more people are forced

---

[3] Without this understanding, the projected decline of employment growth rate may be interpreted as a projected decline in employment opportunities, especially because in Indonesia employment is translated into *kesempatan kerja* which literally means employment opportunities, instead of employment.

[4] It should be noted that the measurement of unemployment is based on census data, not survey data. The unemployment rate is already as high as 4 per cent according to the latest survey (Sakernas 1994).

**TABLE 18.5: Rate of growth of working-age population,
labour force and employment: Indonesia, 1990-2020**

	Working-age Population[a]	Labour Force[a]	Employment[b]
1990-1995	2.43	3.05	2.90
1995-2000	1.81	2.78	2.70
2000-2005	1.69	2.40	2.25
2005-2010	1.44	2.05	1.88
2010-2015	1.19	1.75	1.54
2015-2020	1.00	1.41	1.15

[a]Ananta and Anwar 1995a.
[b]Ananta, Anwar and Wongkaren 1994.

to accept whatever work they can find. Declining unemployment rate is a bad, rather than good, indicator of economic success in Indonesia.

There is now a tendency in Indonesian literature on labour markets not to focus on (open) unemployment, but to use underemployment. Often, underemployment is measured by number of hours worked in a week. Persons who are working less than the standard number of hours are called underemployed. Unfortunately, as with open unemployment, this measure also has some flaws. Who can be underemployed? Who can afford to work less than the standard number of hours in a week? Are part-timers worse off than full-timers or even than those working 'more' than full time who often still have difficulty in earning a decent living?[5] How about those who are working 60 hours, for instance, and still get very low earnings? Does the measurement of underemployment, using percentage of working persons working less than a certain number of hours in a week, really reflect poverty and/or economic performance?

---

[5] Full-timers are those who are working exactly at the standard number of hours in a week and more than full-timers are those who are working more than the standard number of hours in a week.

Therefore, emphasis should be diverted from both unemployment and underemployment. Efforts might be better spent on direct measurement of economic performance and poverty conditions. Earnings distribution and earnings differentials are some alternatives.

It is suggested here that the government of Indonesia attempt to replace the indicator of unemployment (or underemployment) with other indicators, which are more relevant for policy and planning purposes. Macro-economic textbooks used by Indonesian students both in Indonesian and foreign universities may have contributed to this misunderstanding of unemployment issues in Indonesia.

Rising education

Education, as measured by formal education, will keep rising. Table 18.6 shows the projected educational attainment in Indonesia. This also implies that the same level of job will require workers with higher educational attainment. This can be interpreted as progress, because the same job is and will be done by people with higher education than before.

Ananta (1995) also speculated that wage differentials according to education will narrow. Recent data show that the tendency has already been observed. That means the rate of return of gaining more education will be relatively smaller and smaller. It seems that performance in the real work market will be a better indicator of wage differential, rather than formal educational attainment (see Table 18.7).

Rising education, coupled with rising income, will also produce a high rate of open unemployment. People have higher income and so they have more opportunities to be unemployed. Their higher aspirations make them more 'choosy' in determining the jobs they want to take, especially because their 'choosy' behaviour is supported by higher income. It will not be surprising if open unemployment, especially for the well educated, rises in the future.

However, it does not necessarily mean priority should be focused on the highly educated people. Those who have low education are not unemployed because they cannot afford to be unemployed. They are too poor to be unemployed. They are forced to accept whatever work they can have, in order to survive. Therefore, the concern on highly educated unemployed should not be at the expense of concern about the employed with low education.

TABLE 18.6: Projection of educational attainment, 1990-2020 (per cent)

	1990	1995	2000	2005	2010	2015	2020
Less than primary school	74.3	68.2	61.4	55.0	49.7	44.4	40.0
Junior high school	12.4	14.7	17.9	21.3	22.9	24.1	24.5
Senior high school	11.5	14.7	17.6	19.6	22.0	24.5	26.5
University	1.8	2.3	3.1	4.1	5.4	7.1	9.0
Total	100.0	100.0	100.0	100.0	100.0	100.0	100.0

Source: Calculated from Oey-Gardiner and Gardiner (Chapter 19, this volume).

TABLE 18.7: Index of wage differentials by schooling and gender, 1977-90 (< Primary = 100)

	Male				Female			
	1977	1982	1987	1990	1977	1982	1987	1990
< Primary	100	100	100	100	100	100	100	100
Primary	151	142	128	122	149	151	128	126
Junior secondary	275	203	170	158	396	290	225	203
Gen. senior secondary	245	249	212	214	380	368	304	287
Voc. senior secondary	328	262	214	209	483	375	348	319
Tertiary	1,033	410	372	366	1,428	582	551	508

Source: Tzannatos and Sayed 1995.

Will people be healthier?

Indonesian life expectancy at birth will keep rising, from about 61.3 for males and about 64.4 for females in 1990-95 to about 68.4 for males and 70.6 for females in 2015-2020. This means that Indonesians will live longer and longer, and the mortality rate will keep declining.

However, if the past experience in many developed countries applies to Indonesia, there will be also more and more 'frail' people.[6] People will not die because of sickness, but they will be sick longer and more frequently. Thus, in the absence of effective interventions, the future Indonesia population will be filled with an increasingly frail population, prone to get sick and getting sick for longer periods.

The direct expenditure for health will rise. More importantly, the reduction in productivity may become a much bigger loss because of the rising morbidity and rising potential earning power of the Indonesian population.

A policy on promotive and preventive health must soon be adopted, in order to prevent an excessive cost of treating sickness, which is good for business in medicine in curative health care but bad

---

[6] Riley mentioned, using data from the history of European countries, that there is a negative correlation between mortality and morbidity. There are four explanations for this negative correlation. First, the declining mortality occurs almost at the same time as improvement of statistical data collection of morbidity. Thus, it is not surprising that the decline in mortality is accompanied by an apparent rise in morbidity. The second reason is that the decline in mortality also goes hand in hand with the rising awareness of people on the meaning of sickness. A condition which was not called sick previously may later be considered as sick. The third reason is that as mortality declines, the number of surviving, relatively frailer, persons will rise. Thus, this is the application of the 'survival of fittest' rule. When mortality is high, only the fittest will survive. When mortality declines, those who are not very fit will also survive. Medical technology can now save the life of many who would previously have died, but may not guarantee the quality of life of those who are surviving. Thus, it raises the percentage of those who get sick. The fourth reason is behavioural. The decline in mortality is also accompanied by worsening life style. Therefore, declining mortality may also mean rising morbidity. Readers are referred to Crimmins and Ingegneri (1993) for an excellent discussion on this issue of the negative correlation between morbidity and mortality rates.

for the people and the economy as whole. The rising demand for medicine and curative health care will reduce productivity and hence the capacity of the economy to produce. Rising prices and inflation may result . Thus, promotive and preventive health policy will also help keep inflation low.

Fortunately, Indonesia is currently thinking of encouraging these promotive and preventive policies. According to the concept of JPKM (Jaminan Pemeliharaan Kesehatan Masyarakat), society pays for activities which prevent people from being sick. JPKM is often called the 'Managed Health Care System.' Insurance companies may also be encouraged not to campaign for health insurance, which pays people when they are sick. Health insurance companies should change their products toward encouraging people not to get sick and producing products which encourage buyers to implement promotive and preventive activities.

It is encouraging that the Minister of Health, Sujudi, stresses that JPKM is one of the main programs to prevent the potential rising health cost in Indonesia.[7] This program can be carried out by either the government or the private sector. The private sector has attempted to apply the JPKM concept.[8] If this kind of concept can be widely implemented, the Indonesian population will be healthier and may avoid rising health cost in the future.

A particular implication for old people is discussed separately in Chapter 10.

---

[7] He mentioned this in a seminar conducted by IDI (Ikatan Dokter Indonesia—Indonesian Medical Doctor Association), quoted from *Warta Ekonomi*, 15 July 1996, p. 9.

[8] A recent example is PT International Health Benefits Indonesia, a collaboration between Health Benefits Pty Ltd Australia and PT Asuransi Jiwa Tugu Mandiri(*Warta Ekonomi*, 15 July 1996, p. 9.

Rising population mobility

The declining number of children per family, rising income, rising education, rising information, and better transportation and communication facilities will be accompanied by rising mobility, both permanent and non-permanent, of the Indonesian population.[9] Table 18.8 reveals that there are some groups of provinces which experienced a rising index of outmigration, there are those which experienced a declining index, and there are also some which experienced almost no change in the index. Yet Table 18.8 also reveals that the majority of provinces experienced a declining index, meaning that their populations are increasingly less likely to move out their provinces permanently. Six provinces remain stable, and five provinces experienced a rising tendency for their population to move out.

It is also obvious, from Table 18.8, that no index is greater than 1.0. The rates for provinces in Canada, for example, were mostly greater than 1.0 in the period 1966-71 (Termote 1980). However, despite the initially relatively lower index, the majority of the provinces in Indonesia have shown a declining tendency of outmigration. It is interesting to note that one of the provinces with a rising index is Jakarta, which is often believed to be a magnet for people from outside Jakarta. Yet people in Jakarta have become more likely to leave Jakarta than before. The Jakarta phenomenon may hint at the trend of suburbanisation. This pattern may indicate that Indonesia has been and will be moving through the mobility transition faster than Canada.[10]

---

[9] Permanent mobility, which is often termed migration, is a movement with an intention to stay in a different region. Non-permanent mobility is a movement without the intention of changing the place of residence. Operationally, in Indonesia, someone is said to move permanently if he or she has stayed in a new residence for more than six months.

[10] Further discussion on mobility transition in Indonesia is referred to Ananta (1995).

TABLE 18.8: Gross out-migraproduction rate by province, 1975-80 and 1985-90[a]

	Provinces	Sex	Gross out-migration rate	
			1975-80	1985-90
Declining	Jambi	male	0.52	0.48
		female	0.43	0.35
	South Sumatra	male	0.49	0.46
		female	0.40	0.35
	Bengkulu	male	0.37	0.34
		female	0.35	0.27
	North Sulawesi	male	0.29	0.26
		female	0.28	0.25
	Central Sulawesi	male	0.25	0.23
		female	0.23	0.17
	West Sumatra	male	0.78	0.62
		female	0.67	0.49
	West Java	male	0.38	0.18
		female	0.34	0.16
	Central Java	male	0.58	0.50
		female	0.51	0.48
	East Java	male	0.33	0.26
		female	0.27	0.22
	Bali	male	0.36	0.28
		female	0.26	0.20
	West Nusa Tenggara	male	0.29	0.17
		female	0.25	0.10
	Maluku	male	0.39	0.31
		female	0.26	0.21
	South Sulawesi	male	0.48	0.35
		female	0.31	0.24
	South-east Sulawesi	male	0.65	0.38
		female	0.48	0.30
	East Nusa Tenggara	male	0.26	0.20
		female	0.21	0.12
Rising	East Kalimantan	male	0.29	0.52
		female	0.27	0.39
	DI Yogyakarta	male	0.41	0.53
		female	0.38	0.50
	Irian Jaya	male	0.33	0.38
		female	0.33	0.22
	Lampung	male	0.17	0.31

TABLE 18.8 (cont.): Gross out-migraproduction rate by province, 1975-80 and 1985-90[a]

Provinces	Sex	Gross out-migration rate	
		1975-80	1985-90
	female	0.15	0.24
DKI Jakarta	male	1.06	1.52
	female	0.91	1.41
Stable DI Aceh	male	0.20	0.21
	female	0.16	0.16
North Sumatra	male	0.38	0.38
	female	0.30	0.29
West Kalimantan	male	0.21	0.21
	female	0.20	0.16
Central Kalimantan	male	0.32	0.40
	female	0.27	0.30
South Kalimantan	male	0.41	0.41
	female	0.34	0.32
Riau	male	0.41	0.42
	female	0.35	0.32
East Timor	male	na	0.39
	female	na	0.11

[a] This index, called the 'gross outmigra-production rate', is a summation of age-specific outmigration rates. The gross outmigra-production rate shows the average number of outmigrations a person would make in a lifetime if following the age-specific outmigration rates of contemporaries, and is an improvement on conventional crude migration measures. The index is an age-adjusted measurement of migration.

na = not available.

Sources: Ananta and Anwar 1995b.

The declining index of outmigration may be disguising the fact that non-permanent mobility is on the rise. It is unfortunate that, until now, there is no satisfactory measurement of non-permanent mobility at the province level. Yet many small-scale studies have shown rising non-permanent mobility in Indonesia.

The Indonesian population will no longer be limited to the labour market in their current place of residence, but they will increasingly see the whole of Indonesia as their prospective labour market. They will go to wherever there are promises of better living.

Further, the Indonesian labour force will increasingly consider foreign countries as their potential labour market as well. Cheap and unskilled labour will go to the more advanced countries unless these countries restructure their economies such that they do not demand such labour. The rising minimum wage and labour benefits in the formal sector in Indonesia will enhance the need for the surplus of unskilled and cheap labour in the informal sector to find work abroad. As long as there is demand from foreign countries, the potential for migration of cheap unskilled labour from Indonesia will continue. Efforts to prevent this potential will only result in a black market for this kind of labour and will be very costly to control.

Movement of skilled labour to foreign labour markets will also rise as a result of the relatively more rapid rise in the number of skilled workers in Indonesia, and the lack of sufficiently attractive jobs for them in Indonesia.

On the other hand, foreign labour will also see Indonesia as a prosperous labour market. Not only will highly skilled labour flow into the Indonesian labour market, but more and more less highly skilled labour will come to Indonesia. The impact of rising minimum wages and other accompanying labour benefits in raising labour costs in the formal sector will induce firms, both domestic and international, to move away from unskilled labour-intensive industries to skill-intensive and capital-intensive industries. Unreadiness of the Indonesian labour force to respond to this rapid shift will provide attractive opportunities for foreign workers.

The loss of Indonesian workers overseas may be seen as brain drain, but it may also be seen as brain gain. If the Indonesian government makes policies such that their experiences working abroad are a means to enhance their human capital, then, later on, they may be lured back to work in Indonesia. But the movement overseas of skilled workers who do not return is a brain drain, which is harmful for the economy.

The increasing mobility of the Indonesian population may also contribute to the rising potential for conflict as many different cultures and religions which did not meet before now meet more frequently. The government should not curb this increasing population mobility, but policies should be created to overcome or to prevent the emergence of conflict as a result (Tirtosudarmo 1996).

The potential for rising conflict may also come from the rising inflow of foreign workers to Indonesia, not necessarily of the highly skilled variety. Yet it is not wise to stop the inflow of foreign workers since Indonesia is a part of the contiuing globalisation process, which implies an integration of all markets in the world.

Rising urbanisation

Not only will the percentage of rural population decline, but the absolute number of rural population will also decline. The percentage of rural population was still about 69 per cent in 1990, but it is projected to decline to 58 per cent in 2000, 45 per cent in 2020 and 43 per cent in 2025. The absolute number of rural population was about 123.8 million in 1990, but will fall to 122.0 million in 2000, 113.9 million in 2020 and 111.4 million in 2025. It is more usual, however, to talk about the rate of urbanisation, the percentage of urban population, rather than the percentage of rural population. Table 18.9 shows that the urbanisation rate in Indonesia will rise from about 30.9 in 1990 to 41.8 in 2000, 55.2 in 2020 and 57.4 in 2025.

The decline in the percentage and absolute number of rural population is because of the migration of rural population from rural areas to urban areas and the reclassification of rural areas into urban areas due to rural development. Presidential decree No. 27 has stated that in 2020 the urbanisation rate in Indonesia must be as high as 70 per cent. This aim should be achieved by implementing the policy of Bangga Suka Desa (Pembangunan Keluarga dengan Suasana Perkotaan di Pedesaan—Family Development with Urban Context in the Rural Area).

The Bangga Suka Desa policy is actually a nice repackaging of an old theory of rural development. This policy is to accelerate rural development such that the people who live in rural areas can soon live surrounded with urban facilities. If this policy can be well implemented during the next 25 years, the projected urbanisation rate shown in Table 18.9 will be underestimated. The table shows that the

**TABLE 18.9: Projected urban and rural populations
and rate of urbanisation, 1990-2025**

	Urban ('000)	Rural ('000)	Rate of Urbanisation (%)
1990	55,433	123,811	30.9
1995	71,657	123,143	36.8
2000	87,577	121,958	41.8
2005	102,534	120,307	46.1
2010	116,481	118,590	49.6
2015	129,245	116,454	52.6
2020	140,310	113,905	55.2
2025	150,052	111,389	57.4

Source: Ananta and Anwar 1995a: Table No. 2.11.

urbanisation rate will be only about 57 per cent in the year 2020, that is about 13 percentage points below the targeted rate.

Yet a different picture may appear when the scenario is based on the past experience of 'error' in projecting the urbanisation rate. Without information from the 1990 Population Census, Ananta and Arifin (1991) projected that the rate of urbanisation will be about 52 per cent in the year 2020. With the availability of information from the 1990 Population Census, Ananta and Anwar (1995a), revised the earlier projection. They projected that the urbanisation rate will be about 57 per cent in the year 2020. Thus, there is a 5 percentage point error.

If there will be another 5 percentage point error with the availability of the 2000 Population Census, and again with the 2010 Census, and with the 2020 Census, then the rate of urbanisation in the year 2020 will be about 72 per cent, a little higher than the targeted rate. Hence, is the target as mentioned in the presidential decree reasonable? We already mentioned in the introduction to this chapter that our earlier projections were all wrong but had been very useful and they were always on the more pessimistic side. Therefore, if past experience can be used as a relevant guide, it is not unlikely that the target of 70 per cent in the year 2020 can be achieved. Of course, this supposes that Indonesia will work hard for the success of rapid rural development (the so-called Bangga Suka Desa policy).

The next question is: 'Is it necessarily desirable to achieve an urbanisation rate of 70 per cent in the year 2020?' It all depends on what goes along with the urbanisation process. If the urbanisation process follows the 'correct' urban life style, then the achievement of the 70 per cent urbanisation rate in the year 2020 will become something very desirable. The policy of rural development, the Bangga Suka Desa policy, should therefore also pay close attention to creation of the 'correct' urban life style—as Indonesia has been successful in the process of creating the norm of small, happy and prosperous family.

Feminisation of the labour market

The labour force participation rate is projected to keep rising, as shown in Table 18.10, especially the rate of the female labour force. The overall rate will rise from 54.7 in 1990 to about 66.5 in 2020; while the rate for the female labour force will rise from about 38.1 in 1990 to about 54.2 in 2020. The annual rate of growth of total labour force will decline from 3.0 per cent in 1990-95 to 1.4 per cent in 2015-2020; while the annual rate of growth of the female labour force will decline from 3.8 per cent in 1990-95 to 1.7 per cent in 2015-2020.

In short there will be more and more female workers in the market. The decline in fertility, the rise in education, the rising economic opportunities and the advance in technology will have been responsible for this rising feminisation of the labour market. Yet the rising feminisation should also be anticipated with great care. Reproduction-related morbidity of the female labour force should receive appropriate attention. The rising tendency of feminisation may go hand in hand with the rising problems of health related to their reproductive organs. These problems may be costly, not only in terms of the direct expenditure to cure this disease, but also, in particular, in terms of the opportunity cost of the female labour force. As their potential earning power rises, the opportunity cost of being sick will rise as well!

TABLE 18.10: Labour force participation rate
(per cent)

	Female	Male	Total
1990	38.1	71.1	54.7
1995	41.7	71.5	56.5
2000	44.9	73.9	59.3
2005	47.5	75.6	61.5
2010	49.9	76.9	63.4
2015	52.3	78.1	65.2
2020	54.2	78.8	66.5
2025	55.8	79.4	67.6

Source: Ananta and Anwar 1995a: Table No. 2.16.

What else?

This has been a very short paper attempting to foresee some possible future scenarios of population change and the resulting implications. There are still many other interesting points to be discussed.

    With the limitation of space, the above mentioned topics are considered the most important. Further detailed discussion on each subtopic is also needed. Readers are referred to Ananta, Wongkaren and Cicih (1995) for a discussion of the impact of future demographic changes in Indonesia.

19

The Education Explosion

Mayling Oey-Gardiner and Peter Gardiner

Background

The purpose of this presentation is to provide estimates on how well
educated the Indonesian population will be over the course of the
next PJPT II or Second Long-term Planning period of 1995-2020. While
the Indonesian government continues to attract potential investors in
export-oriented and labour-intensive industries with Indonesia's
cheap labour, the results of these projections show that it is time to
change this view. The future will be characterised not only by a large
population but also by one which is increasingly more educated and
sophisticated, as both consumers and producers.

To estimate the future education qualifications of the population
we start with a standard cohort population projection. The following
fertility and mortality assumptions are taken from Biro Pusat Statistik
(BPS) in *Proyeksi Penduduk Indonesia Menurut Propinsi 1990-2020.*[1]

- TFR is to decline from 3.326 during 1985-90 to 2.009 children per
  woman between 2020 and 2025.
- Life expectancy is to improve from around 60 in 1990-95 to just over
  70 by the year 2020.

---

[1] Owing to different smoothing procedures our results differ slightly from
those produced by BPS.

Population projections

Overall the total population is projected to rise from 179 million in 1990 to 262 million in 2020, implying a rather low average growth of only 1.27 per cent per annum. Such growth is much lower than the peak of 2.34 per cent reached during the 1970s.

Slow effect of fertility decline on population growth

The slowdown in the growth of the overall population is of course a function of Indonesia's successful national family planning program. A woman of childbearing age gave birth to about 5.6 children during the early 1970s, but today to only about 2.9 children. Some of the highlights of the projected population are as follows (see Figure 19.1):

- The dynamics of population growth have a long-lasting effect. Considering the internationally acclaimed successes in Indonesia's family planning program, one would have expected substantial declines in the youth to the end of PJPT II ending in 2020. Our projections show, however, that the population less than 25 years will remain fairly stable throughout this period.
- The number of children under five is expected to decline from 22 to 20 million children, or only 10 per cent less over the projection period of 30 years.
- Even the number of school-age children aged 5 to 14 is expected to be reduced by only around 5 per cent, from 44 to 42 million.
- The decline in the above two age groups will be compensated by rising numbers of those aged 15 to 24 years, usually referred to as first-time job seekers. This age group is expected to expand from 35 million in 1990, reaching a peak in 2005 when there will be about 44 million, thereafter slowly declining to 43 million by the end of the second long-term planning period. It should be emphasised that most of the rise projected for the 1990-2005 period has already taken place, and the growth between 1995 and 2005 is expected to be quite modest.

FIGURE 19.1: Indonesia's projected population, 1990-2020

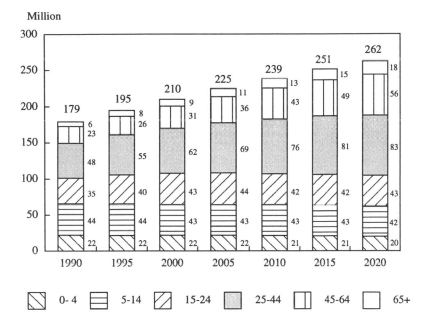

Long-lasting effect of past fertility behaviour will be on those aged 25+

- The 'baby boom' effect of the 1950s will remain with us until well beyond 2020. All age groups beyond 25 years will continue to expand from 77 million in 1990 to 157 in 2020, slightly more than double in 30 years.
- We divide those aged 25 and over into three groups: the career development ages of 25-44 years; the career stabilising ages of 45-64 years; and the retired aged 65 and over.

- The career development ages constitute the largest group, which can be expected to grow from 48 million to 83 million. These numbers imply an average annual growth of 1.8 per cent per annum, much higher than the overall population growth rate of 1.27 per cent.
- Those stabilising their careers are expected to grow from 23 million to 56 million or doubling in 30 years which implies an average annual growth of 2.97 per cent.
- The fastest growing age group will be the retired, about whom other demographers have written. This group is expected to treble from 6 to 18 million in 30 years, implying an average growth of 3.66 per cent per annum. In other words, by the end of PJPT II we can expect as many retirees in Indonesia as Australia's current population, a staggering thought.

Education projections

While Indonesia built its recent economic success on export-oriented industrialisation by selling masses of cheap labour, the future should see a turnaround. For all the success in raising primary enrolment ratios, the majority of the population is still poorly educated. Among the working age population, here defined as 15 years and over, three-quarters have at most completed their primary schooling only; only 26 per cent had completed at least their lower secondary education.

If the current education policy is successfully implemented and the people respond similarly as to the primary school program then we can expect an *education explosion*, characterised by the following highlights:

- At the end of PJPT II two-thirds of Indonesia's working-age population will have completed at least their lower secondary education (see Figure 19.2). This represents a fourfold increase from 29 to 120 million people or rising from 26 per cent to 60 per cent of the population 15 years and over.
    - At the beginning of the projection period in 1990 among the first-time job seekers aged 15-24 years, 15 million or 43 per cent had completed at least their lower secondary schooling; by the year 2020 this group will have expanded to 35 million or 81 per cent.

**FIGURE 19.2: Population aged 15+ with lower secondary
education or above[a]**

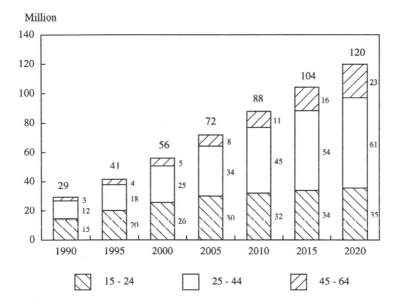

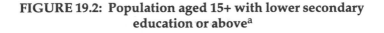

[a] Assumes that the proportion of those aged 20-24 with lower secondary
education rises from 45 per cent in 1990 to 85 per cent in 2020.

- Larger numerical and relative growth in numbers with lower secondary schooling will be recorded for those in their career development ages of 25-44 years: a fivefold increase from 12 to 61 million.
- Even faster growth will be recorded by those aged 45-64 years, among whom the numbers with lower secondary schooling will rise sevenfold, from 3 to 23 million people.

• The upper secondary educated will increase fivefold, from 15 to 71 million people (see Figure 19.3).

**FIGURE 19.3: Population aged 15+ with upper secondary
education or above**[a]

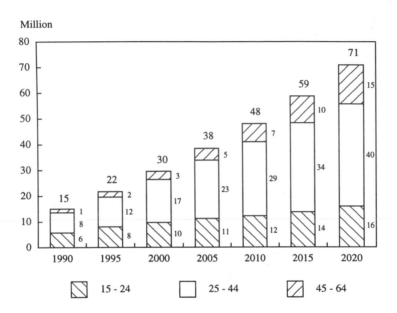

Million

| | 15 - 24 | | 25 - 44 | | 45 - 64 |

[a] Assumes that the proportion of those aged 20-24 with lower secondary
education rises from 30 per cent in 1990 to 67 per cent in 2020.

This expansion is consistent with the current basic education policy
to reach universal lower secondary enrolment by 2005. Available
information suggests that to date the break is at the primary level,
the main reason being the cost of education. Once children continue
to lower secondary schooling, the probability of continuing to upper secondary school is rather high. At present, lower secondary
school fees are three times those of primary schooling. While most
of the poor can afford primary school fees, lower secondary school
fees often become prohibitive for the poor, especially in large families.

Assuming similar successes at raising lower secondary enrolment (and this is admittedly a rather brave assumption) there will be a major flow-on effect in expanding significantly the number attending and completing their upper secondary education. As a result we can expect that if today only one out of every seven persons of working age has completed upper secondary schooling, by the end of PJPT II the ratio will become one out of every three persons.

- Among first-time job seekers the number of upper secondary school graduates will rise almost threefold, from 6 to 16 million persons;
- Among those in the career development ages of 25-44 years, the estimates show a fivefold increase from 8 to 40 million persons.
- Among those stabilising their careers, aged 45-64 years, the explosion is almost unimaginable, increasing from 1 to 15 million persons.

• The tertiary or post-secondary educated working age population becomes nine times as large (see Figure 19.4).

Given today's conditions, when less than 1 per cent or only 2 million people have completed any post-secondary education, consisting of diploma and university programs, in 30 years time we can expect a ninefold increase to 18 million people, roughly equivalent to Australia's current population.

- The majority of those with post-secondary education will be aged 25-44 years, but their proportion will decline from three-quarters in 1990 to 70 per cent in 2020.
- Even so, the number of tertiary-educated first-time job seekers aged 15-24 years can be expected to increase from 200,000 to 2.3 million persons.
- Similarly, those in their career stabilising years (45-64) who have completed any post-secondary education will also grow more than 10-fold, from 300,000 to 3.2 million people.

FIGURE 19.4: Population aged 15+ with tertiary education or above[a]

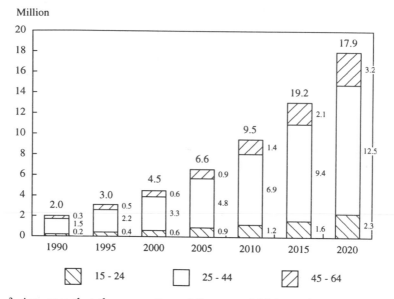

[a] Assumes that the proportion of those aged 25-29 with tertiary education rises from 4 per cent in 1990 to 19 per cent in 2020.

Concluding notes

We have given a quantitative picture of what is in store: an unprecedented education explosion. Today one often hears about how poorly Indonesians are educated as still seven out of every ten persons have at the most completed their primary education, but this is often related to low productivity among Indonesian workers. As the people's education rises, their productivity should also rise. The question is whether not only Indonesian but also our neighbours' policy makers are aware of this impending eruption.

APPENDIX

Assumptions on educational achievement

- Simple cohort population projections constitute the basis for the projections on the education of the population.
- The base education composition was derived from the 1990 Population Census.
- Following the current education policy, we assume accelerated enrolments at the lower secondary level.
- Projections were made for cumulative education categories, e.g. primary or more, lower secondary or more, upper secondary or more, and tertiary.
- Factors were determined and applied to the proportion with a particular level of education or more for the age group where no substantial increases will occur. These are shown below:

Education	Age Group
Some primary	10-14
Primary	15-19
Lower secondary school	20-24
Upper secondary school	20-24
Tertiary	25-29

TABLE A19.1: Factors for the education projections: females

	Age	1995	2000	2005	2010	2015	2020
Primary or less	10-14	1.005	1.005	1.000	1.000	1.000	1.000
	15-19	1.000	1.000	1.000	1.000	1.000	1.000
Primary	10-14	1.040	1.040	1.040	1.040	1.040	1.040
	15-19	1.040	1.020	1.020	1.020	1.010	1.010
	20-24	1.000	1.000	1.000	1.000	1.000	1.000
Lower secondary	10-14	1.050	1.050	1.050	1.050	1.050	1.050
	15-19	1.200	1.200	1.100	1.100	1.050	1.050
	20-24	1.300	1.300	1.200	1.200	1.100	1.100
Upper secondary	15-19	1.200	1.200	1.200	1.200	1.100	1.100
	20-24	1.200	1.200	1.150	1.150	1.100	1.000
Tertiary	15-19	1.000	1.000	1.000	1.000	1.000	1.000
	20-24	1.400	1.400	1.400	1.400	1.400	1.400
	25-29	1.300	1.300	1.300	1.300	1.300	1.300
	30-34	1.200	1.200	1.200	1.200	1.200	1.200

TABLE A19.2: Factors for the education projections: males

Education	Age	1995	2000	2005	2010	2015	2020
Priimary or less	10-14	1.005	1.005	1.000	1.000	1.000	1.000
	15-19	1.000	1.000	1.000	1.000	1.000	1.000
Primary	10-14	1.040	1.040	1.040	1.040	1.040	1.040
	15-19	1.040	1.040	1.020	1.020	1.010	1.000
	20-24	1.000	1.000	1.000	1.000	1.000	1.050
Lower secondary	10-14	1.050	1.050	1.050	1.050	1.050	1.050
	15-19	1.200	1.200	1.100	1.100	1.050	1.050
	20-24	1.300	1.300	1.200	1.200	1.100	1.100
Upper secondary	15-19	1.200	1.200	1.200	1.200	1.100	1.100
	20-24	1.200	1.150	1.150	1.000	1.100	1.050
Tertiary	15-19	1.000	1.000	1.000	1.000	1.000	1.000
	20-24	1.400	1.400	1.400	1.400	1.400	1.400
	25-29	1.300	1.300	1.300	1.300	1.300	1.300
	30-34	1.200	1.200	1.200	1.200	1.200	1.200

20

Letter from the Year 2020

Aris Ananta

Before coming to this session I found a letter on my doorstep. I want to read it to you.

Canberra, 24 August 2020, 2.00 p.m.

Dear Aris,

I have just attended the Indonesian Update 2020. The last session was so interesting. It focused on what Indonesian demographers were talking about in the 1990s. Well, 24 years ago, also in Canberra, they discussed the future direction of Indonesian population.

However, we now understand that what they said in 1996 was all wrong! I am very sad and depressed to reach this conclusion.
Do you think that the projections made in 1996 were all wrong and useless? Or do you agree with the conclusions reached in the Indonesian Update 2020?

Sincerely,

Your 2020 friend

Here is my reply to my future friend:

Dear Friend,

I can really sympathise with your depression. However, let us go further back. Not only to 1996, but to the 1960s and the 1970s.

Do you know Pak Widjojo Nitisastro? He was the first Indonesian demographer. He produced the first Indonesian population projections in the 1960s. It turns out that even his most optimistic scenario was still not as good as what we have observed. His projection was wrong.

Do you know Pak Nathanael Iskandar? He was the first director of the first demographic institute in Indonesia. He revised Pak Widjojo's projection in the 1970s. Also, my dear friend, his most optimistic scenario was still not as good as what we have experienced. His projection was also wrong.

Dear friend, everybody seems to forget about these old projections. Why don't we realise that their projections were wrong?

Well, it is obvious today that their projections were wrong. But, although they were wrong, they have been very useful for development planning in Indonesia. Pak Widjojo's projection was instrumental in changing the Indonesian policy from pro-natalist to anti-natalist. Pak Iskandar's projection was instrumental in pushing the effort to reduce fertility.

We are indeed very happy that they are wrong. Otherwise, if they had not been wrong, our present condition would not be as good as it is now. So, projection can be wrong and it should be able to be wrong. Otherwise, it was useless. The projections of Pak Widjojo and Pak Iskandar were both wrong and very useful.

My dear friend, let us now turn our time machine back to 24 August 1996 in the Australian National University, when they had the Indonesian Update 1996. Look! One of the demographers said:

Because of time constraint, I cannot describe in detail my projection of the Indonesian population. You can see all my assumptions in my full paper, which I have given to the organisers. *Bapak-bapak dan Ibu-ibu yang terhormat* ... Let us pray that all projections we have made will be both wrong and very useful ...

My friend, I hope you are happy with my reply and I am looking forward to seeing you again in 2020.

Sincerely,

Aris Ananta

REFERENCES

Abimanyu, Anggito, 1996. 'Indonesia: Distribution System Study', research report submitted to the Energy-Industry Division, Country Department III East Asia and Pacific Region, World Bank, Washington DC, PAU-Economic Studies, Gadjah Mada University, Yogyakarta.

_____, and Guozhong Xie, 1995. *Indonesia: Industrial Competitiveness Study*, Washington DC: World Bank.

Adhisuria, Audry, 1995. 'Family Planning Sustainability and Contraceptive Social Marketing in Indonesia', unpublished course work for MA thesis, Graduate Program in Population and Human Resources, Faculty of Social Science, Flinders University of South Australia, Adelaide.

Adioetomo, Sri Moertiningsih, 1993. 'The Construction of a Small-Family Size Norm in Java', PhD thesis, Australian National University, Canberra.

_____, 1996. 'The Quality of Care in Family Planning Services. Indonesia Family Life Survey 1993. A Summary Report'. Demographic Institute, Faculty of Economics, University of Indonesia, Jakarta.

_____, Eko Ganiarto and Zainul Hidayat, 1996. *Faktor Faktor Yang Mempengaruhi tingkat Kemandirian KB* [Factors Influencing Self-reliance in Contraceptive Use]. Jakarta: Demographic Institute, Faculty of Economics, University of Indonesia.

_____, Ayke S. Kiting and Salman Taufik, 1990. 'Fertility Transition in Indonesia. Trends in Proximate Determinants of Fertility', in Population Studies in Sri Lanka and Indonesia Based on the 1987 Sri Lanka Demographic and Health Survey and the 1987 National Indonesia Contraceptive Prevalence Survey, New York: Population Council and DHS/IRD.

Adji, Arti, 1995. 'Industrial Concentration and Price Adjustment, Indonesian Case Study: 1975-1992'. Yogyakarta: Magister Manajemen Program, Gadjah Mada University.

_____,'1996. Industrial Concentration and Price Adjustment: Indonesian Selected 5-Digit Industries'. Yogyakarta: Magister Manajemen Program, Gadjah Mada University.

Ananta, Aris, 1995, 'Transisi Mobilitas Penduduk Indonesia', in *Transisi Demografi, Transisi Pendidikan dan Transisi Kesehatan di Indonesia*, Aris Ananta (chief compiler). Jakarta: Kantor Menteri Negara Kependudukan/BKKBN.

_____, and Sri Moertiningsih Adioetomo, 1990. Perkembangan Penduduk Indonesia menuju tahun 2005 [The Growth of the Indonesian Population toward the Year 2005]. Jakarta.: Demographic Institute, Faculty of Economics, University of Indonesia.

_____, and Evi Nurvidya Anwar, 1995a. Projection of Indonesian Population and Labor Force: 1995-2025. Jakarta: Demographic Institute, Faculty of Economics, University of Indonesia.

_____, and Evi Nurvidya Anwar, 1995b. 'Perubahan Pola dan Besaran Migrasi Propinsi: Indonesia, 1975-1980 dan 1985-1990' [Changes in Pattern and Magnitude of Provincial Migration: Indonesia, 1975-1980 and 1985-1990], in Secha Alatas (ed.), *Migrasi dan Distribusi Penduduk di Indonesia [Migration & Population Distribution in Indonesia]*. Jakarta: State Ministry of Population/National Family Planning Coordinating Board.

_____, and Evi Nurvidya Arifin, 1991. *Projection of Indonesian Population: 1990-2020.* Jakarta: Demographic Institute, Faculty of Economics, University of Indonesia.

_____, Evi Nurvidya Anwar and Turro S. Wongkaren, 1994. 'The Future of Indonesian Population', Prisma, 53: 3-17.

_____, Chotib and M.U. Ira Setiati, 1995. *Population Projection 1995-2025: Bali.* Jakarta: Demographic Institute, Faculty of Economics, University of Indonesia.

_____, Sugihardjo and Dewi Prihastuti, 1995. *Population Projection 1995-2025: Yogyakarta.* Jakarta: Demographic Institute, Faculty of Economics, University of Indonesia.

_____, Sugihardjo and Dodi Setiadi, 1995. *Population Projection 1995-2025: East Java.* Jakarta: Demographic Institute, Faculty of Economics, University of Indonesia.

_____, Sugihardjo and Diah Widyawati, 1995. *Population Projection 1995-2025: South Sumatra.* Jakarta: Demographic Institute, Faculty of Economics, University of Indonesia.

_____, Turro S. Wongkaren and Lilis Heri Mis Cicih, 1995. *Beberapa Implikasi Perkembangan Penduduk Indonesia dalam PJP II* [Some Implications of the Development of Indonesian Population in PJP II]. Jakarta: Kantor Menteri Negara Kependudukan/BKKBN.

Anwar, Evi Nurvidya, Chotib and Dewi Prihastuti, 1995. *Population Projection 1995-2025: East Nusa Tenggara.* Jakarta: Demographic Institute, Faculty of Economics, University of Indonesia.

Ariawan, Iwan, T.Y. Miko and Milla Herdayati, 1996. 'Laporan Penelitian Studi Validasi Teknik Autopsi Verbal pada SKRT 1995', PusLitKes LP-UI and Balitbangkes-DepKes RI, Depok, unpublished document.

ARPLA, 1992. *Profile on Occupational Safety and Health in Indonesia.* Bangkok: ILO and Pacific Regional Center for Labor Administration (ARPLA).

Arthur, W.B., 1988. 'Urban Systems and Historical Path-Dependence', in Jesse H. Ausubel and Robert Herman (eds), *Cities and Their Vital Systems.* Washington DC: National Academy Press.

Asia Pacific Profiles 1996., Canberra: Asia Pacific Economics Group.

Balitbangkes-DepKes. RI and BPS, 1994. *Survai Kesehatan Rumah Tangga (SKRT) 1992.*, Jakarta: BPS.

Bandiyono, S. , 1987. *Migrasi Permanen: Penduduk Jawa Timur.* Jakarta: PPT-LIPI.

_____, 1993. *Migrasi Permanen: Penduduk Bali.* Jakarta: PPT-LIPI.

Barker, Ben, 1995. 'South East Asian Economic Experience and Prospects: A Summary', in Young C. Kim (ed.), *The South East Asian Economic Miracle.* New Brunswick, NJ: Transaction Publishers.

Bird, Kelly, 1996. 'Survey of Recent Developments', *Bulletin of Indonesian Economic Studies*, 32 (1): 3-32.

Biro Pusat Statistik (BPS), 1974. *1971 Population Census, Population of Indonesia,* Series D. Jakarta: BPS.

_____, 1983. *Population of Indonesia, Results of the 1980 Population Census,* Series S2. Jakarta: BPS.

_____, 1982. 'Tingkat kelohiran dan Kematian di Indonesia yang Dihitung Berdasarkan Hasil Sensus Penduduk 1971, SUPAS dan Sensus Penduduk 1980' [Levels of Fertility and Mortality in Indonesia Based on the 1971 Census, 1976 SUPAS and the 1980 Census], Jakarta.

_____, 1987. *Population of Indonesia, Results of the 1985 Intercensal Population Survey*, Series SUPAS No. 5. Jakarta: BPS.

_____, 1988. 'Klasifikasi Urban-Rural Berdasarkan PODES-SE 1986', Jakarta.

_____, 1991a. Penduduk Indonesia: Tabel Pendahulian Hasil Sub Sampel Sensus Penduduk 1990. Jakarta: BPS.

_____, 1991b. *Population of Indonesia 1990*, Series L1, Jakarta: BPS.

_____, 1992a. *Population of Indonesia: Results of the 1990 Population Census.*, Series S2. Jakarta: BPS.

_____, 1992b. *Population of DI Yogyakarta: Results of the 1990 Population Census*, Series S2.12. Jakarta: BPS.

_____, 1992c *Population of East Nusa Tenggara: Results of the 1990 Population Census*. Series S2.16. Jakarta: BPS.

_____, 1992d. *Population of South Sumatra: Results of the 1990 Population Census*, Series S2.06. Jakarta: BPS.

_____, 1992e. *Statistik Pendidikan Survei Sosial Ekonomi Nasional*. Jakarta: BPS.

_____, 1993. *Proyeksi Penduduk Indonesia Per Propinsi (1990-2020)* [Projection of Indonesian Population by Province 1990-2020]. Jakarta: BPS.

_____, 1994a. *Proyeksi Penduduk Indonesia per Kabupaten/Kotamadya 1990-2000*. Jakarta: BPS.

_____, 1994b. *Statistik Pendidikan Survei Sosial Ekonomi Nasional 1992.*. Jakarta: BPS.

_____, 1994c. *Proyeksi Penduduk per Propinisi 1990-2020*. Jakarta: BPS.

_____, 1995a. *Profit Statistik Wanita, Ibn dan Anak di Indonesia*. Jakarta: BPS.

_____, 1995a. *Pedoman Pencacah—Survei Penduduk Antar Sensus 1995*. Jakarta: BPS.

_____, 1995b. 'National Socio-Economic Survey: Welfare Statistics 1994', Jakarta.

Booth, Anne, 1994. 'Repelita VI and the Second Long-Term Development Plan', *Bulletin of Indonesian Economic Studies*, 30(3): 3-40.

Bos, Eduard, My T. Vu, Ernest Massiah and Rodolfo A. Bulatao, 1995.*World Population Projections, 1994-95 edition: Estimates and Projections with Related Demographic Statistics*. Baltimore: Johns Hopkins University Press.

Browder, J., J. Bohland and J. Scarpaci, 1995. 'Patterns of Development on the Metropolitan Fringes: Urban Fringe Expansion in Bangkok, Jakarta, and Santiago', *Journal of the American Planning Association*, 61 (3): 310-27.

Bruce, Judith, 1990. 'A Fundamental Element of the Quality of Care: A Simple Framework', *Studies in Family Planning*, 21(2:March/April):61–90.

Budiarso, L. Ratna, 1987, 1981. *Laporan Survei Kesehatan Rumah Tangga 1980*. Jakarta: Balitbankes-DepKes RI.

Budiarso, L. Ratna, 1987. 'Pola Kematian', in L.R. Budiarso, S.S. Soesanto, Z. Bakri et al. (eds), *Prosiding Seminar Survai Kesehatan Rumah Tangga 1986. Jakarta, 14-15 Desember 1987*. Jakarta: Balitbangkes-PusLit Ekologi.

_____, Z. Bakri, S.S. Soesanto, *et al.*, 1986. *Survai Kesehatan Rumah Tangga 1986*. Jakarta: Balitbangkes-PusLit Ekologi.

_____, Putrali and Muchtaruddin, 1980. *Survei Kesehatan Rumah Tangga 1980*. Jakarta: DepKes-Balitbangkes.

Campbell, Oona M.R. and Wendy J. Graham, 1991. 'Measuring the Determinants of Maternal Morbidity and Mortality: Defining and Selecting Outcomes and Determinants, and Demonstrating Associations', Maternal and Child Epidemiology Unit Publication No. 4, London School of Hygiene and Tropical Medicine, London.

CBS, NFPCB and DHS/IRD Westinghouse, 1989. *Indonesia. National Contraceptive Prevalence Survey 1987*. Columbia, MD: DHS/IRD Westinghouse.

CBS, NFPCB, MOH and DHS/Macro International, 1992. *Indonesia. Demographic and Health Survey. 1991*. Columbia, MD: DHS, Macro International.

CBS, NFPCB, MOH and Macro Int. Inc., 1995. *Demographic and Health Survey 1994*. Jakarta: CBS.

CBS/UNICEF. 1984. *An Analysis of the Situation of Children and Women in Indonesia.*. Jakarta: CBS.

Chin, James, 1995. 'Scenarios for the AIDS Epidemic in Asia', *Asia-Pacific Population Research Reports* (East-West Center), No. 2. Honolulu: East-West Center.

Clark, David H. and Mayling Oey-Gardiner, 1991. 'How Indonesian Lecturers Have Adjusted to Civil Service Compensation', *Bulletin of Indonesian Economic Studies*, 27 (3): 129-41.

Collier, W.L., K. Santoso, Soentoro and R. Wibowo (n.d.), 'New Approach to Rural Development in Java: Twenty-five Years of Village Studies in Java', mimeo.

Crimmins, Eileen M. and Dominique Ingegneri, 1993. 'Trends in Health among the American Population', in Anna M. Rappaport and Sylvesteer J. Schieber (eds), *Demography and Retirement: The Twenty-First Century*. London: Praeger.

_____, Mark D. Hayward and Yasuhiko Saito, 1994. 'Changing Mortality and Morbidity Rates and the Health Status and Life Expectancy of the Old Population', *Demography*, February: 159-75.

Darmstadter, Joel, and Michael A. Toman (eds), 1993. *Assessing Surprises and Nonlinearities in Greenhouse Warming*. Washington, DC: Resources for the Future.

Dasvarma, G.L., 1986. 'Infant Mortality in Indonesia: A Review of Recent Evidence', *Demography India*, 15(1): 61-75.

Demographic and Health Surveys (DHS), 1995. *Demographic and Health Survey 1994*. Jakarta: DHS.

Departemen Pendidikan dan Kebudayaan (DPK), 1994a. *Pembangunan Pendidikan dan Kebudayaan Menjelang Era Tinggal Landas* [Developments in Education and Culture towards Take-Off. Jakarta: DPK.

_____, 1994b. *Statistik Pendidikan Wanita di Indonesia* [Educational Statistics of Women in Indonesia. Jakarta: DPK.

DepKes-PusDaKes, 1993. *Profil Kesehatan Indonesia 1992.* Jakarta: DepKes-PusDaKes.

_____, 1995. *Profil Kesehatan Indonesia 1995,* Jakarta: Ministry of Health.

Dharmaputra, Nick G., Iwan Ariawan and Meiwita B. Iskandar, 1996. *Situation Analysis on HIV/AIDS and Its Impact on Children, Women and Families in Indonesia.* Depok: Center for Health Research University of Indonesia and UNICEF.

Djaja, Sarimawar, S. Soemantri and K.N. Siregar, 1996.'Pola Penyakit Sebab Kematian di Jawa-Bali Survei Kesehatan Rumah Tangga 1995', Working Paper in Seminar Sehari Kelompok Terbatas Hasil Awal Survei Kesehatan Rumah Tangga 1995, Ministry of Health, Jakarta.

Douglass, M., 1995. 'Global Interdependence and Urbanization Planning for the Bangkok Mega-Urban Region', in T. McGee and I. Robinson (eds), *The Mega-Urban Regions of Southeast Asia.* Vancouver: University of British Columbia Press, pp. 45-77.

Dyson, Tim, 1996. *Population and Food: Global Trends and Future Prospects.* London: Routledge.

Edmundson, W. and S. Edmundson, 1983. 'A Decade of Village Development in East Java', *Bulletin of Indonesian Economic Studies,* 19 (2): 46-59.

Effendi, Sofian, 1996. 'Perubahan Struktur Keluarga Dalam Perspektif Pencapaian Keluarga Sejahtera' in Agus Dwiyanto *et al.* (eds), *Penduduk dan Pembangunan.* Yogyakarta: Aditya Media, pp.69-81.

ESCAP , 1994. *ESCAP Population Data Sheet.* Bangkok: ESCAP.

_____, 1995. *Population Data Sheet,.* Bangkok: ESCAP.

ESCAP-UN, 1993. 'State of Urbanization in Asia and the Pacific, 1993', New York.

Ewbank, Douglas C., 1984. 'Uses of Mortality Data for Evaluating the Success of Specific Health and Development Programmes', in *Data Bases for Mortality Measurement. Papers of the Meeting of the United Nations/WHO Working Group on Data Bases for Measurement of Levels, Trends and Differentials in Mortality,* Bangkok 20-23 October 1981. New York: United Nations , pp. 18-30.

Firman, T., 1989. 'Pembangunan Kota-Kota Baru di Wilayah Metropolitan Jabotabek' [Development of New Cities in the Jabotabek Metropolitan Region], *Prisma*, 18 (6): 49-60.

_____, 1991. 'Rural Households, Labour Flows and the Housing Construction Industry in Bandung', *Tijdschrift voor Economische en Sociale Geografie*, 82 (2): 94-105.

_____, 1992. 'The Spatial Pattern of Urban Population Growth in Java, 1980-1990', *Bulletin of Indonesian Economic Studies*, 28 (2): 95-109.

_____, 1994. 'Migrasi Antarprovinsi dan Pengembangan Wilayah di Indonesia', *Prisma*, 7: 3-15.

_____, 1995. 'Urban Restructuring in Jakarta Metropolitan Region: An Integration into a System of "Global Cities"', in Proceedings of the Conference on Cities and the New Global Economy, Government of Australia and OECD, Melbourne, 20-23 November, 1994.

_____, 1996a. *Pola Urbanisasi di Indonesia: Kajian Data Sensus 1980 dan 1990*. Jakarta: Lembaga Demografi Universitas Indonesia dan Kantor Menteri Negara Kependudukan.

_____, 1996b. 'Urban Development in Bandung Metropolitan Region: A Transformation to Desa-Kota Region', *Third World Planning Review*, 18 (1): 1-22.

_____, and I.A.I. Dharmapatni, 1995. 'The Emergence of Extended Metropolitan Regions in Indonesia: Jabotabek and Bandung Metropolitan Area', *Review of Urban and Regional Development Studies*, 7: 167-88.

Fraser, Arvonne, 1987. *The UN Decade For Women: Documents and Dialogue*. Boulder, CO: Westview Press.

Fujita, K., 1991. 'A World City and Flexible Specialization: Restructuring of the Tokyo Metropolis', *International Journal of Urban and Regional Research*, 15 (2): 69-284.

Furuya, K., 1995. 'Labour Migration and Skill Development: Japan's Trainee Program', *Asian Migrant*, 8 (1): 4-13.

Gardiner, P. and M. Oey-Gardiner, 1990. 'Indonesia', in W.J. Serow, C.B. Nam and D.F. Sly (eds), *Handbook on International Migration*. New York: Greenwood Press , pp. 207-24.

_____, and M. Oey-Gardiner, 1991. 'Pertumbatian dan Perluasan Kota di Indonesia' [Growth and Lateral Expansion of Cities in Indonesia], *Kompas*, 7 May.

Gertler, Paul J and John W Molyneaux, 1994. 'How Economic Development and Family Planning Programs Combined to Reduce Indonesian Fertility', Demography, 31 (1): 33-63.

GOI/UNICEF, 1994. *1995-2000 Programme of Cooperation, Government of Indonesia and UNICEF: Master Plan of Operations*. Jakarta: UNICEF.

_____, 1995a. 'Maternal and Child Survival, Development and Protection 1995-2000', *Master Plan of Operations and Plan of Operations*. Jakarta: UNICEF.

_____, 1995b. *The Situation Analysis of Children and Women in Indonesia 1995*, Jakarta: UNICEF.

Goodal, B., 1987. *Dictionary of Human Geography*. Harmondsworth: Penguin.

Gunawan, M. and Erwidodo, 1993. 'Urbanisasi dan Pengurangan Kemiskinan', *Prisma*, 3 (12): 44-56.

Habir, Ahmad D., 1991. 'The Development of Business Education in Indonesia', in Hal Hill (ed.), *Indonesia Assessment 1991*, Political and Social Change Monograph 13. Canberra: Australian National University, pp.120-34.

Halloran, Richard, 1996. 'The Rising East', *Foreign Policy*, 102(Spring): 3-21.

Hamid, Abdul, 1996. 'Teenage Fertility in Java-Bali', 1994, unpublished course work for MA thesis, Graduate Program in Population and Human Resources, Faculty of Social Sciences, Flinders University of South Australia, Adelaide.

Hatmadji, Sri Harijati, Diah Widyawati and Tri Retno Herdiana, 1993. 'Status of the Education of Women in Indonesia', report prepared as part of the Asian Development Bank, Regional T.A. No. 5513, Education of Women in Asia Project. Jakarta:ADB.

Hennessy, Patrick, 1994. 'Who Looks after the Elderly?', *OECD Observer*, June/July: 15-18.

Hetler, C.B., 1990. 'Survival Strategies, Migration and Household Headship', in L. Dube and R. Palriwala (eds), *Structures and Strategies— Women, Work and Family*. New Delhi: Sage Publications, pp. 175-99.

Hidayat, M., 1995. 'Mekanisme Pengadaan Tanah Bagi Pembangunan Perumahan: Tantangan dan Harapan di Masa Depan', Makalah disampaikan pada Lokakarya Penataan Ruang Dalam Perspektif Pertumbuhan dan Pemerataan Pembangunan, diselenggarakan oleh CIDES, Bappenas, dan Kantor Menteri Negara Agraria/ BPN, Bandung, 10 October.

Hiebert, M., 1995. 'Give and Take', *Far Eastern Economic Review*, May, pp. 54-59.

Hill, H., 1991. *Indonesia Assessment 1991*, Political and Social Change Monograph 13. Canberra: Australian National University.

_____, 1992. 'Survey of Recent Developments', *Bulletin of Indonesian Economic Studies*, 28 (2): 3-41.

_____, 1994. 'The Economy', in H. Hill (ed.), *Indonesia's New Order: the Dynamics of Socioeconomic Transformation*. Sydney: Allen & Unwin Pty Ltd.

_____, 1996. *The Indonesian Economy Since 1966: South East Asia's Emerging Giant*. Cambridge: Cambridge University Press.

Hugo, G.J., 1975. 'Population Mobility in West Java, Indonesia', unpublished Ph.D. thesis, Department of Demography, Australian National University, Canberra.

_____, 1978. *Population Mobility in West Java*. Yogyakarta: Gadjah Mada University Press.

_____, 1979. 'Indonesia: Patterns of Population Movement to 1971', in R.J. Pryor (ed.), *Migration and Development in South-East Asia—A Demographic Perspective*. Kuala Lumpur: Oxford University Press, pp. 177-91.

_____, 1981. 'Road Transport, Population Mobility and Development in Indonesia', in G.W. Jones and H.V. Richter (eds), *Population Mobility and Development: Southeast Asia and the Pacific*, Monograph No. 27. Canberra: Development Studies Centre, Australian National University, pp. 355-86.

_____, 1982a. 'Sources of Internal Migration Data in Indonesia: Their Potential and Limitations', *Majalah Demografi Indonesia*, 17 (9): 23-52.

_____, 1982b. 'Circular Migration in Indonesia', *Population and Development Review*: 59-83.

_____, 1985. 'Structural Change and Labour Mobility in Rural Java', in G. Standing (ed.), *Labour Circulation and the Labour Process*. London: Croom Helm, pp. 46-88.

_____, 1988. 'Population Movement in Indonesia Since 1971', *Tijdschrift voor Economische en Sociale Geografie*, 79 (4): 242-56.

_____, 1992. 'Women on the Move: Changing Patterns of Population Movement of Women in Indonesia', in S. Chant (ed.), *Gender and Migration in Developing Countries*. London: Belhaven Press, pp. 174-96.

_____, 1993a. 'Indonesian Labour Migration to Malaysia: Trends and Policy Implications', *Southeast Asian Journal of Social Sciences*, 21 (1): 36-70.

_____, 1993b. *Manpower and Employment Situation in Indonesia 1993*. Jakarta: Indonesian Department of Labour.

_____, 1995. 'Indonesia's Migration Transition', *Journal für Entwicklungspolitik*, 11 (3): 285-309.

_____, 1996a. 'Labour Export from Indonesia: An Overview', *Asean Economic Bulletin*, 12(2): 275-98.

_____, 1996b. 'Urbanisation in Indonesia: City and Countryside Linked', in J. Gugler (ed.), *The Urban Transformation of the Developing World*. New York: Oxford University Press, pp. 133-83.

_____, forthcoming. 'Urbanization in Indonesia: City and Countryside Linked', in Gugler (ed.), *Pattern of Third World Urbanization*, Oxford University Press.

_____, Terence H. Hull, Valerie J. Hull and Gavin W. Jones, 1987. *The Demographic Dimension in Indonesian Development*. Singapore: Oxford University Press.

Hull, Terence H., 1980. 'Fertility Decline in Indonesia: A Review of Recent Evidence', *Bulletin of Indonesian Economic Studies*, 20 (3): 95-119.

_____, 1987. 'Fertility Decline in Indonesia: An Institutionalist Interpretation', *International Family Planning Perspectives*, 13 (3): 90-95.

_____, and G.L. Dasvarma, 1988. 'Fertility Trends in Indonesia, 1967-1985', *Bulletin of Indonesian Economic Studies*, 24 (1):115-21.

_____, and Valerie J Hull. 1987. 'Changing Marriage Behaviour in Java: The Role of Timing of Consummation', *Southeast Asian Journal of Social Sciences*, 15 (1): 104-19.

_____, and John E. Rohde (1978), 'Prospects for Rapid Decline of Mortality Rates in Java', *Working Papers* No 16, Population Institute-UGM, Yogyakarta.

_____, Valerie J. Hull and Masri Singarimbun, 1977. 'Indonesia's Family Planning Story. Success and Challenge', *Population Bulletin*, 32(6):4-51.

Hull, Valerie J., 1975. 'Fertility, Socio-economic Status, and the Position of Women in a Javanese Village', PhD thesis, Australian National University, Canberra.

_____, 1996. 'Improving Quality of Care in Family Planning: How Far Have We Come?', *South-East Asia Regional Working Papers*, Population Council, Jakarta.

Huntington, Samuel P., 1993. 'The Clash of Civilizations', *Foreign Affairs*, Summer: 72(3):22-49.

Indonesia, Department of Labour, 1995. *Profil Sumber Daya Manusia Indonesia* [The Human Resource Profile of Indonesia], Jakarta.

IPPF, 1988. *Medical Bulletin*.

Iskandar, Meiwita B. and Nick G. Dharmaputra, 1996. *Quality of Care in Family Planning. An Analytical Review for Future Policy Oriented Research in Indonesia*. Depok: Center for Health Research, Research Institute University of Indonesia.

_____, Budi Utomo, Terence Hull, Nick G. Dharmaputra and Yuswardi Azwar, 1996. *Unraveling the Mysteries of Maternal Death in West Java. Reexamining the Witnesses*. Depok: Center for Health Research, Research Institute of University of Indonesia.

Iskandar, N., 1976. *Beberapa Proyeksi Penduduk untuk Indonesia menurut Pulau-Pulau Utama 1971-2001* [Some Population Projections for Indonesia by Main Islands 1971-2001]. Jakarta: Lembaga Demografi, Fakultas Ekonomi, Universitas Indonesia.

Jabotabek Metropolitan Development Plan Review (JMDPR), 1992. *Preliminary Planning Report*. Jakarta: Culpin Planning Ltd. PT Lenggogeni,

Huszar Brammah and Associate Ltd., Lembaga Penelitian Perencanaan Wilayah dan Kota (LPP), Institut Teknologi, Bandung.

Jakarta dalam Angka, 1994. Jakarta: Special Capital of Jakarta.

James, William, 1996. 'Sustaining Growth of Exports of Manufactured Goods and Industrialization in Indonesia: Competition and Technology issues', paper presented at 20th ACAES Conference on Asian Economies, organised by ACAES (American Committee on Asian Economic Studies), Malaysian Economic Association (MEA) and University of Malaya (UM), Kuala Lumpur, May.

Jones, Gavin W., 1988. 'Urbanization Trends in Southeast Asia: Some Issues for Policy', *Journal of Southeast Asian Studies*, 19 (1): 137-54.

_____, and S.G.M. Mamas, 1996. 'The Changing Employment Structure of the Extended Jakarta Metropolitan Region', *Bulletin of Indonesian Economic Studies*, 32(1):51-70.

Kaplan, Robert D., 1996. *The Ends of the Earth: A Journey at the Dawn of the 21st Century.* New York: Random House.

Kartasasmita, G., 1995. 'Penataan Ruang Dalam Perspektif Pertumbuhan dan Pemerataan Pembangunan', Makalah Disampaikan pada Lokakarya Penataan Ruang Dalam Perspektif Pertumbuhan dan Pemerataan Pembangunan, Diselenggarakan oleh CIDES, Bappenas, dan Kantor Menteri Negara Agraria/BPN, Bandung, 10 October.

Kasai, S., 1988. 'Remittances of Out-Migrants to their Original Families: Evidence from two Indonesian Villages', *Journal of Population Studies*, 11: 15-29.

Kasperson, Jeanne X., Roger E. Kasperson and B.L. Turner II (eds), 1995. *Regions at Risk: Comparisons of Threatened Environments.* Tokyo: United Nations University Press.

Kasto, 1996. 'Proyeksi Penduduk dan Rumah Tangga Indonesia', in Agus Dwiyanto et al. (eds), *Penduduk dan Pembagunan.* Yogyakarta: Aditya Media, pp.31-52.

Kasto and Henry Sembiring, 1995. *Profil Kependudukan Indonesia Selama PJP I dan Awal PJP II.* Yogyakarta: Pusat Penelitian Kependudukan UGM.

Keban, Y.T., 1994. 'Studi Niat Bermigrasi di Tiga Kota', *Prisma*, 7: 17-47.

Kelabora, Lambert and Kenneth Orr, 1977. 'Stimulating the Appetite and Coping with the Consequences in Indonesia', in Kenneth Orr (ed.), *Appetite for Education in Contemporary Asia*, Development Studies Centre Monograph No. 10. Canberra: Australian National University.

Keyfitz, Nathan, 1981. 'The Limits of Population Forecasting', *Population and Development Review*, 7(4): 579-93.

_____, 1985. 'Development in an East Javanese Village, 1953 and 1985', *Population and Development Review*, 11(4):695-719.

_____, and Widjojo Nitisastro, 1964. *Soal Penduduk dan Pembangunan Indonesia* (2nd edition). Jakarta: Pembangunan.

_____, Mayling Oey-Gardiner and Donald R. Snodgrass, 1988a. 'Higher Education in Indonesia: Draft of a Briefing Book, Volume II: Autonomy, Layering, and Honors', Center for Policy and Implementation Studies, Jakarta.

_____, Mayling Oey-Gardiner, David Clark and Dewi Ratna Sjari Manof, 1988b.. 'Higher Education in Indonesia: Draft of a Briefing Book', Volume III, Center for Policy and Administration Studies, Jakarta.

Knock, P., 1994. 'Economic Crisis and Urban Restructuring (1972-1983)', in *Urbanization: Introduction to Urban Geography*. Englewood Cliffs, NJ: Prentice Hall.

Knodel, John and Gavin W. Jones, 1996. 'Post-Cairo Population Policy: Does Promoting Girls' Schooling Miss the Mark?', *Population and Development Review*, 22(4): 683-702.

Kosasih, Ottoh, E.S. Soemantri and W. Suwarno, 1989. 'Resistensi Kuman Tuberkulosa Terhadap Beberapa Jenis Obat Anti-tuberkulosis', *Medika*, 15 (3): 247-51.

Krugman, Paul, 1991. *Geography and Trade*. Cambridge, MA: MIT Press.

Kuncoro, Mudradjat, 1993. 'The Political Economy of Decentralization in Indonesia: Toward Cultivating the Grass-Roots?' *Indonesian Quarterly*, 3 (21).

Lee, Ronald D., 1991. 'Long-run Global Population Forecasts: A Critical Appraisal', in Kingsley Davis and Mikhail S. Bernstam (eds), *Resources,*

Environment, and Population: Present Knowledge, Future Options (Supplement to *Population and Development Review*, 16:.44-71).

Leinbach, T.R. and A. Smith, 1994. 'Off-Farm Employment, Land and Life Cycle: Transmigrant Households in South Sumatra, Indonesia', *Economic Geography*, 70(3):273-96.

Lin, G.C.-S., 1994. 'Changing Theoretical Perspectives on Urbanization in Asian Developing Countries', *Third World Planning Review*, 16 (1): 1-23.

LPK, 1994. *Lampiran Pidato Kenegaraan Presiden Republik Indonesia di depan Dewan Perwakilan Rakyat, 15 Auguast 1994: Pelaksanaan Repelita V.* Jakarta: Department of Information.

Manning, C.G., 1986. 'The Green Revolution, Labour Displacement, Incomes and Wealth in Rural Java', mimeo, Flinders University, Adelaide.

Manning, Chris and Sisira Jayasuriya, 1996. 'Survey of Recent Developments', *Bulletin of Indonesian Economic Studies*, 32 (2):3-43.

Mantra, I. B. and S. Kasai, 1987. *Population Mobility and Link Between Migrants and Family Back Home: A Case Study of Two Villages in Yogyakarta Special Region, Indonesia.* Yogyakarta: Gadjah Mada University.

_____, and M. Molo, 1985. Studi Mobilitas Sirkuler Penduduk ke Enam Kota Besar di Indonesia. Kerjasama Kantor Menteri Negara Kependudukan den Lingkungan Hidup dengan Pusat Penelitian Kependudukan UGM, Laporan akhir Yogyakarta, Pusat Penelitian Kependudukan.

_____, T.M. Kasnawi and Sukamandi, 1986. *Mobilitas Angkatan Kerja Indonesia Ke Timor Tengah. Final Report Book 1.* Yogyakarta: Gadjah Mada University.

McDonald, Peter F., Mohamad Yasin and Gavin Jones, 1976. 'Levels and Trends in Fertility and Childhood Mortality in Indonesia', *Indonesian Fertility-Mortality Survey*, Monograph No. 1. Jakarta: LD-FEUI.

McGee, T.G., 1991a. 'The Emergence of Desa Kota Regions in Asia: Expanding an Hypothesis', in N. Ginsburg, B. Koppel and T.G. McGee (eds), *The Extended Metropolis: Settlement Transition in Asia.* Honolulu: University of Hawaii Press, pp. 3-26.

_____, 1991b. 'Southeast Asian Urbanization: Three Decades of Change'. *Prisma*, 51: 3-16.

_____, 1992. *Indonesia: Towards a New Spatial Order.* Jakarta: IUIDP Implementation Support Project INS/89/014 .

_____, 1995. 'Retrofitting the Emerging Mega-Urban Regions of ASEAN: an Overview', in T. McGee and I. Robinson (eds.), *The Mega-Urban Regions of Southeast Asia,* University of British Columbia Press, Vancouver, pp. 3-26.

_____, and I. Robinson, 1995. *The Mega-Urban Regions of Southeast Asia, National Report for Habitat II (1996), Annex I, National Committee for Habitat II, Jakarta, Indonesia.* Vancouver: University of British Columbia Press.

_____, . and Yue-man Yeung, c1993. 'Urban Futures for Pacific Asia: Towards the 21st Century', in Yue-man Yeung (ed.), *Pacific Asia in the 21st Century: Geographical and Development Perspectives.* Hong Kong: Chinese University Press, pp.47-67.

McNicoll, Geoffrey and Masri Singarimbun, 1983. *Fertility Decline in Indonesia: Analysis and Interpretation.* Washington, DC: National Academy Press.

MOH-Subdirectorate of STD and Yaws Control, 1996. 'Cumulative AIDS/ HIV(+) in Indonesia by Year up to June 30, 1996', unpublished data, Jakarta.

Morawetz, David, 1977. *Twenty-five Years of Economic Development.* Washington, DC: World Bank.

Naisbett, John, 1996. Megatrends Asia: *Eight Asian Megatrends that Are Reshaping Our World.* New York: Simon & Schuster.

Naylor, R., 1992. 'Labour Saving Technologies in the Javanese Rice Economy: Recent Developments and a Look into the 1990s', *Bulletin of Indonesian Economic Studies,* 28(3):71–91.

Nitisastro, Widjojo, 1970. *Population Trends in Indonesia.* Ithaca: Cornell University Press.

NUDS, 1985. Final Report of NUDS (National Urban Development Strategy), Ministry of Public Works and United Nations Development Programme, Jakarta.

Oey-Gardiner, Mayling, 1988. 'Sipenmaru: Suatu Telaah' [System to Select New Students: An Analysis], in N. Keyfitz, M. Oey-Gardiner and D. R. Snodgrass, 'Higher Education in Indonesia: Draft of a

Briefing Book', Center for Policy and Implementation Studies, Jakarta.

_____, 1989. 'Female School Attendance in Indonesia', paper prepared for the World Bank.

_____, 1991. 'Gender Differences in Schooling in Indonesia', *Bulletin of Indonesian Economic Studies*, 27 (1), pp. 57-80.

Ogawa, Naohiro and Noriko Tsuya, 1993. 'Demographic Change and Human Resource Development in the Asia-Pacific Region: Trends of the 1960s to 1980s and Future Prospects', in Naohiro Ogawa, Gavin W. Jones and Jeffrey G. Williamson (eds), *Human Resources Din evelopment Along the Asia-Pacific Rim*. Singapore: Oxford University Press, pp.21–65.

Ogawa, Naohiro, Gavin W. Jones and Jeffrey G. Williamson (eds), 1993. *Human Resources in Development Along the Asia-Pacific Rim*. Singapore: Oxford University Press.

Pachauri, Saroj, 1995. 'Defining a Reproductive Health Package for India: A Proposed Framework, South and East Asia', Regional Working Paper No. 4, New Delhi, Population Council.

Palmore, James A. and Robert W. Gardner, 1994. *Measuring Mortality, Fertility, and Natural Increase*. Fifth EditionHonolulu: East-West Center.

Pariani, Siti, 1994. 'Kelangsungan Pemakaian Kontrasepsi di Jawa Timur, Pengalaman Lapangan 1987-1988' [Continuation Rate of Contraceptive Use in East Java. Field Experience in 1987-1988], *Jurnal Jaringan Epidemiologi Nasional*, 1994(1): 21-29.

Pernia, Ernesto M., 1991. 'Higher Education in Asia: Indonesia in Comparative Perspective', in Hal Hill (ed.), *Indonesia Assessment 1991*, Political and Social Change Monograph 13. Canberra: Department of Political and Social Change, Research School of Pacific Studies, Australian National University, pp.135–50.

Pohan, Saut Sahat, 1990. 'Pengobatan Urethritis Non-gonore dengan Doksisiklin', *Medika*, 16 (6): 431-33.

Population Reference Bureau (PBR), 1995. *World Population Data Sheet 1995*. Washington, DC: PBR.

Presidential Speech, 1996. 'Pidato Kenegaraan Presiden Republik Indonesia didepan Dewan Perwakilan Rakyat', Jakarta, 16 August.

Purnama, Halip, 1995. 'Feeding Practice and Diarrhoea in Children Under Two in Java and Bali, 1991', unpublished course work for MA thesis, Graduate Program in Population and Human Resources, Faculty of Social Sciences, Flinders University of South Australia, Adelaide.

Purwaningsih, Sri Sunarti, forthcoming. 'Female International Labour Migration, Migration and Child Survival', Phd thesis, Demography Program, Research School of Social Sciences, Australian National University, Canberra.

Rahardjo, Tribudi W., Agus Suwandono, Budi Haryanto *et al.*, 1996. 'Penilaian terhadap peranan Puskesmas Tempat Tidur terutama untuk Kesehatan dan Kelangsungan Hidup Ibu dan Anak', unpublished research report , PusLitKes LP-UI dan DepKes R.I., Depok.

Raintung, Agustini E., Siti Fatimah Muis, Tuti Harbandinah, Tonny Sadjimin, Tri Yunis Miko and Gus Permana, 1995. *Masalah Keamanan Pelayanan Kontrasepsi Suntik Indonesia* [Issues on Safety of Injectable Contraception Services, Indonesia. Jakarta: Population Council.

Republic of Indonesia, 1993. *Indonesia: A Quarter Century of Progress (1968-1993)* Tables and Graphs, Jakarta.

Rietveld, P., 1988. 'Urban Development Patterns in Indonesia', *Bulletin of Indonesian Economic Studies*, 24 (1): 73-95.

_____, Sadyadharma and Sudarno, 1988. 'Rural Mobility in Java: The Village Economy and the Rest of the World', *Singapore Journal of Tropical Geography*, 9(2):112-24.

Rimmer, P., 1995. 'Moving Goods, People and Information: Putting the ASEAN Mega-Urban Regions in Context', in T. McGee and I. Robinson (eds), *The Mega-Urban Regions of Southeast Asia*. Vancouver: University of British Columbia Press, pp. 3-26.

Rogers, Andrei, Luis J. Castro, Nathan Keyfitz, Jacques Ledent, Dimiter Philipov, Frans Willekens, Jeffrey G. Williamson, 1984. *Migration, Urbanization and Spatial Population Dynmaics*. Boulder, CO: Westview Press.

Rohde, John E., Terence H. Hull, and Lukas Hendrata, 1978. 'Pola Kematian di Jawa dan Implikasinya pada Kebijaksanaan Kesehatan Rakyat dalam Pelita III', *Prisma* 7(3):64-76.

Romdiati, Haning, 1996. 'Patterns and Determinants of Maternal Health Care Utilisation in Three Provinces of Java, 1991 with Special Reference to West Java', unpublished course work for MA thesis, Graduate Program in Population and Human Resources, Faculty of Social Sciences, Flinders University of South Australia, Adelaide.

Rondinelli, D.A. and H. Evans, 1983. 'Integrated Regional Development Planning; Linking Urban Centers and Rural Areas in Bolivia', *World Development*, 11 (1): 31-53.

Sassen, S., 1991. *The Global City: New York, London, Tokyo*. Princeton: Princeton University Press.

_____, 1994. *Cities in a World Economy*. London: Pine Forge Press.

Serrato, Carl A. and Glenn Melnick, 1995. 'The Indonesian Family Life Survey: Overview and Descriptive Analysis', RAND research working paper, DRU-1191-AID, submitted to USAID Jakarta.

Sinaga, Jalonsen, 1996. 'Factors Affecting the Demand for Family Planning in Kalimantan, 1994', unpublished course work for MA thesis, Graduate Program in Population and Human Resources, Faculty of Social Sciences, Flinders University of South Australia, Adelaide.

Singarimbun, M., 1986. 'Sriharjo Revisited', *Bulletin of Indonesian Economic Studies*, 12(2):117-25.

Sjahrir, K., 1989. 'Migrasi Tukang Bangunan: Beberapa Faktor Pendorong', *Prisma*, 5: 47-60.

_____, 1993. 'The Indonesian Economy: A Case of Macro Success and Micro Challenge', in C. Manning and J. Hardjono (eds), *Indonesia Assessment 1993*, Political and Social Change Monograph 20. Canberra : Australian National University, pp.240–258.

Soegijoko, B.T. and I. Bulkin, 1994. 'Arahan Kebijaksanaan Tata Ruang Nasional', *Prisma*, 23 (2): 21-40.

Soemarwoto, Otto, 1991. 'Human Ecology in Indonesia: The Search for Sustainability in Development', in Joan Hardjono (ed.), *Indonesia: Resources, Ecology and Environment*. Singapore: Oxford University Press, pp.212-35.

Stanton, Cynthia, Kenneth Hill, Carla AbouZahr and Tessa Wardlaw, 1995. 'Modelling Maternal Mortality in the Developing World', paper presented at the National Seminar on Maternal, Infant, and

Underfive Mortality in Indonesia, CBS and UNICEF, Jakarta, December.

Stoto, Michael, 1983. 'The Accuracy of Population Projections', *Journal of the American Statistical Association*, 78 (381): 13-20.

Subandrio, Hurustiati, 1963. 'The Perspective Role of Men and Women in Indonesia', in Barbara Ward (ed.), *Women in the New Asia: The Changing Social Roles of Men and Women in South and South-East Asia*. Paris: UNESCO. pp. 230-242.

Sucipto, Tri and Tukiran, 1995. *Proyeksi Penduduk Indonesia tahun 1990-2050* [Projection of Indonesian Population 1990-2050]. Yogyakarta: Pusat Penelitian Kependudukan, Universitas Gadjah Mada.

Sugihardjo, Chotib and Dodi Setiadi, 1995. *Population Projection 1995-2025: Central Java*. Jakarta: Demographic Institute, Faculty of Economics, University of Indonesia,

Sujudi, 1995. 'Epidemiologi AIDS dan Permasalahannya di Indonesia', paper presented at Semiloka Evaluasi Pelaksanaan Program Penanggulangan AIDS, Jakarta, 10-11 October.

Suleeman, Evelyn, 1993. 'Women's Education in Indonesia', unpublished paper prepared for ESCAP.

Thompson, Warren S., 1949. 'Future Adjustments of Population to Resources in Japan', in *Modernization Programs in Relation to Human Resources and Population Problems*. New York: Milbank Memorial Fund, pp.142-53.

Tirtosudarmo, Riwanto, 1996. 'Mobilitas Penduduk dan Konflik: Analisis dan Prospek Menjelang Abad ke-21', in Aris Ananta and Chotib (chief compilers)., *Mobilitas Penduduk di Indonesia*, Jakarta: Kantor Menteri Negara Kependudukan/BKKBN and Lembaga Demografi, Fakultas Ekonomi, Universitas Indonesia.

_____, and P. Meyer, 1993. 'Migration', in H. Dick, J.J. Fox and J. Mackie (eds), *Balanced Development: East Java in the New Order*. New York: Oxford University Press, pp. 101-19.

Titus, M., 1993. 'Small Town Production Relation and Regional Functions in Central Java, Indonesia', *Indonesian Journal of Geography*, 23-25 (64-66): 1-28.

Tomich, T.P., 1992. 'Survey of Recent Developments', *Bulletin of Indonesia Economic Studies*, 28 (3: 3-39.

Torres, Amaryllis T. and Fernandez, Lyodelia O., 1985. *Mobilizing Women for Development: Case Experiences in the Integration of Family Planning in Livelihood Projects.* Manila: Population Centre Foundation.

Triatmodjo, Pudjarwoto, 1991. 'Distribusi Geografis Pola Resistensi Vibrio Cholera Terhadap Beberapa Jenis Antibiotik', *Medika*, 17 (12): 951-55.

Tzannatos, Zafiris and Haneen Sayed, 1995. 'Training and Labor Market in Indonesia: Policies for Productivity Gains and Employment Growth', paper presented in the International Seminar on Training Restructuring and the Labor Market in Indonesia, held by the Ministry of Manpower and the World Bank, Jakarta.

U.S. National Research Council, 1987. *Recent Trends in Fertility and Mortality in Indonesia.* Honolulu: East-West Center.

UNDP (United Nations Development Program), 1995. *Human Development Report 1995.* New York: Oxford University Press.

UNICEF, 1991, 1994, 1995. *The State of the World's Children .* New York: Oxford University Press.

United Nations, 1958. *Future Growth of World Population,* (Population Studies, No. 28). New York: UN.

_____, 1994a. *The Sex and Age Distribution of the World Population: The 1994 Revision.* New York: UN.

_____, 1994b. *World Contraceptive Use 1994.* New York: United Nations.

_____, 1994c. *World Population Prospects: The 1994 Revision.* New York: UN, Population Division.

_____, 1995. *The World's Women 1995: Trends and Statistics, Social Statistics and Indicators,* Series K No. 12. New York: UN.

_____, 1995. *World Urbanization Prospects: The 1994 Revision,* New York: UN.

_____, 1995. *World Population Prospects: The 1994 Revision.* New York: United Nations.

United Nations Development Programme (UNDP), 1991, 1993, 1994, 1995, 1996. *Human Development Report*. New York: Oxford University Press.

United Nations Secretariat, 1984. 'Approaches to the Collection of Mortality Data in the Context of Data Needs', in *Data Bases for Mortality Measurement. Papers of the Meeting of the United Nations/WHO Working Group on Data Bases for Measurement of Levels, Trends and Differentials in Mortality, Bangkok 20-23 October 1981*. New York: UN, pp. 33-44.

Utomo, Budi, 1982. 'Mortality Trends and Differentials in Indonesia 1950-1975', in Lado Ruzicka and Harold Hansluwka (eds), *Mortality in South and East Asia: A Review of Changing Trends and Patterns 1950 - 1975*. Geneva: WHO.

_____, and Meiwita B. Iskandar, 1986. 'Mortality Transition in Indonesia 1950-1980', *Asian Population Studies Series*, No. 74,. Bangkok: ESCAP.

Vatikiotis, M., 1991. 'Neglected Renewal Brings Anxiety', *Far Eastern Economic Review*, 18 April: 35-36.

Vu, My T., Ernest Massiah and Rodolfo A. Bulatao, 1994. *World Population Projections, 1994-95 Edition*. Baltimore: Johns Hopkins University Press for the World Bank.

Wahyuni, E.S., 1991. 'Migrasi di Jawa Barat Berdasarkan Supas 1985', *Project Working Paper Series* No. A-16. Jakart: Pusat Studi Pembangunan, Lembaga Penelitian, Institut Partanian Bogor.

Ward, Barbara (ed.), 1963.*Women in the New Asia: The Changing Social Roles of Men and Women in South and South-East Asia*. Paris: UNESCO.

Warwick, Donald, 1986. 'The Indonesian Family Planning Program: Government Influence and Client's Choice', *Population and Development Review*, 12 (3):453-490.

Watkins, Susan Cotts and Jane Menken, 1985. 'Famines in Historical Perspective', *Population and Development Review*, 11(4): 647-75.

Westoff, C.F., A.K. Blanc and L. Nyblade, 1994. 'Marriage and Entry into Parenthood', *Demographic and Health Surveys Comparative Studies*, No. 10. Calverton, MD: Macro International.

_____, and Luis H. Ochao, 1991. 'Unmet Need and the Demand for Family Planning', *Demographic and Health Surveys Comparative Studies*, No. 5, Calverton, MD: Columbia Institute for Resource Development.

WHO and UNICEF, 1996. 'Revised 1990 Estimates of Maternal Mortality: A New Approach by WHO and UNICEF', official document, WHO/FRH/MSM/96.11 and UNICEF/PLN/96.1, Geneva.

White, B., 1979. 'Political Aspects of Poverty, Income Distribution and Their Measurement: Some Examples from Rural Java', *Development and Change*, 10: 91-114.

Wibowo Adik, 1994. *Analisis Lanjut dari Studi Analisis Pelaksanaan dan Pelayanan Keluarga Berencana pada 'Service Delivery Points' Pemerintah Indonesia* [Further Analysis on the Implementation and Family Planning Services at Public Service Delivery Points]. Jakarta: Population Council.

Wilopo, Siswanto Agus, 1996. 'Kebijaksanaan Kependudukan Selama Repelita VI', in Agus Dwiyanto *et al.* (eds), *Penduduk dan Pembangunan.* Yogyakarta: Aditya Media, pp. 367-98.

Winfrey, William and Laura Heaton (1996), *Market Segmentation Analysis of the Indonesian Family Planning Market: Consumer, Provider and Product Market Segments*. Washington: The Futures Group International, OPTIONS II Project.

World Bank, 1984. 'Economic and Social Development: An Overview of Regional Differentials and Related Processes', main report from *Indonesia: Selected Aspects of Spatial Development*, Report No. 4776-IND. Washington, DC: Country Programs Department, East Asia and Pacific Regional Office, World Bank.

_____, 1989. 'Indonesia: Issues in Health Planning and Budgeting', Report No. 7291-IND, (restricted distribution only), Jakarta.

_____, 1990a. *Indonesia: Family Planning Perspectives in the 1990s.* Washington DC: World Bank.

_____, 1990b. Indonesia: *Strategy for a Sustained Reduction in Poverty.* Washington, DC: World Bank.

_____, 1993a. *Economic Growth and Public Policy*. Oxford: Oxford University Press.

_____, 1993b. *World Development Report*. New York: Oxford University Press.

_____, 1994. 'Indonesia's Health Work Force: Issues and Options', Report No. 12835-IND. Jakarta.

_____, 1994a. 'Indonesia Public Expenditures, Prices and the Poor', Report No. 11293-IND, Washington D.C.

_____, 1994b. *World Development Report*. New York: Oxford University Press.

_____, 1995. 'Staff Appraisal Report, Indonesia Fourth Health Project: Improving Equity and Quality of Care', Report No. 13991-IND, Jakarta.

_____, 1996. 'Indonesia: Dimensions of Growth', Report No. 15383-IND, Washington, D.C.

_____, 1996. 'Indonesia: Dimensions of Growth', Washington, DC.

Xie, Guozhong and Oscar De Bruynkop, 1995. 'Indonesia: Clogged Distribution Channels', paper presented to the conference Building on Success: Maximizing the Gains from Deregulation, Jakarta.

Index